MASTER VISUALLY®

by James Pyles

Visual™

D1073581

Windows® Server 2003

Wiley Publishing, Inc.

Master VISUALLY® Windows® Server 2003

Published by
Wiley Publishing, Inc.
111 River Street
Hoboken, NJ 07030-5774

Published simultaneously in Canada

Library of Congress Control Number: 2004116453

ISBN: 0-7645-7922-3

Manufactured in the United States of America

10 9 8 7 6 5 4 3 2 1

1K/QX/QR/QV/IN

Trademark Acknowledgments

Contact Us

For general information on our other products and services please contact our Customer Care Department within the U.S. at 800-762-2974, outside the U.S. at 317-572-3993 or fax 317-572-4002.

For technical support please visit www.wiley.com/techsupport.

WILEY

U.S. Sales

Contact Wiley
at (800) 762-2974 or
fax (317) 572-4002.

Praise for Visual Books...

"If you have to see it to believe it, this is the book for you!"
—PC World

"A master tutorial/reference — from the leaders in visual learning!"
—Infoworld

"A publishing concept whose time has come!"
—The Globe and Mail

"Just wanted to say THANK YOU to your company for providing books which make learning fast, easy, and exciting! I learn visually so your books have helped me greatly – from Windows instruction to Web development. Best wishes for continued success."
—Angela J. Barker (Springfield, MO)

"I have over the last 10-15 years purchased thousands of dollars worth of computer books but find your books the most easily read, best set out, and most helpful and easily understood books on software and computers I have ever read. Please keep up the good work."
—John Gatt (Adamstown Heights, Australia)

"You're marvelous! I am greatly in your debt."
—Patrick Baird (Lacey, WA)

"I am an avid fan of your Visual books. If I need to learn anything, I just buy one of your books and learn the topic it in no time. Wonders! I have even trained my friends to give me Visual books as gifts."
—Illona Bergstrom (Aventura, FL)

"I have quite a few of your Visual books and have been very pleased with all of them. I love the way the lessons are presented!"
—Mary Jane Newman (Yorba Linda, CA)

"Like a lot of other people, I understand things best when I see them visually. Your books really make learning easy and life more fun."
—John T. Frey (Cadillac, MI)

"Your Visual books have been a great help to me. I now have a number of your books and they are all great. My friends always ask to borrow my Visual books - trouble is, I always have to ask for them back!"
—John Robson
(Brampton, Ontario, Canada)

"I write to extend my thanks and appreciation for your books. They are clear, easy to follow, and straight to the point. Keep up the good work! I bought several of your books and they are just right! No regrets! I will always buy your books because they are the best."
—Seward Kollie (Dakar, Senegal)

"What fantastic teaching books you have produced! Congratulations to you and your staff."
—Bruno Tonon (Melbourne, Australia)

"Thank you for the wonderful books you produce. It wasn't until I was an adult that I discovered how I learn—visually. Although a few publishers claim to present the material visually, nothing compares to Visual books. I love the simple layout. Everything is easy to follow. I can just grab a book and use it at my computer, lesson by lesson. And I understand the material! You really know the way I think and learn. Thanks so much!"
—Stacey Han (Avondale, AZ)

"The Greatest. This whole series is the best computer-learning tool of any kind I've ever seen."
—Joe Orr (Brooklyn, NY)

Credits

Project Editor
Maureen Spears

Acquisitions Editor
Michael Roney

Product Development Manager
Lindsay Sandman

Copy Editor
Kim Heusel
Marylouise Wiack

Technical Editor
Steve Wright

Editorial Manager
Robyn Siesky

Manufacturing
Allan Conley
Linda Cook
Paul Gilchrist
Jennifer Guynn

Screen Artist
Jill A. Proll

Illustrator
Ronda David-Burroughs

Book Design
Kathie S. Rickard

Project Coordinator
Nancee Reeves

Layout
Amanda Carter
Jennifer Heleine
Heather Pope

Proofreaders
Cindy Ballew

Quality Control
Laura Albert
Amanda Briggs
Charles Spencer
Brian Walls

Indexer
Joan Griffitts

Vice President and Executive Group Publisher
Richard Swadley

Vice President and Publisher
Barry Pruett

Composition Director
Debbie Stailey

About the Author

James Pyles, A+, Network+, and CCNA, is a technical writer and freelance consultant who has participated in numerous Ethernet rollouts, workstation upgrades and installations, operating system upgrades, network equipment installations and upgrades, and help desk support functions. He has also supported a usability lab for a major hardware manufacturer as well as worked as a consultant for a wireless network provider in his community. He has written online courses and contributed to several books on Windows XP, Windows Server 2003, and networking hardware, protocols, and security. James currently is on staff as a technical writer for EmergeCore Networks in Boise, Idaho. James has a bachelor's degree in Psychology and Computer Network Support, and a Masters in Counseling.

If you have feedback for the author, or questions about the content in *Master VISUALLY Windows Server 2003*, you can contact the author at the Mtech Services Web site Discussion Board. You can access the Discussion Board at www.mtechservices.ca/General/, where you will find the forum title *Master Visually Windows Server 2003 by James Pyles*.

Author's Acknowledgments

I appreciate the opportunity the great folks at Wiley have given me to participate as the author of this book. I particularly want to thank Mike Roney for having faith in my abilities, Maureen Spears for her patience, wisdom, and invaluable guidance, and Steven Wright for making sure that every technical detail in this book is completely current and accurate. I also am grateful to Kim Heusel and Marylouise Wiack at Wiley for all of their efforts and the long hours they have put into reviewing the text. I would also like to thank Clara Czegeny for all the time she has spent helping me organize the resources I needed to write his book, Marie Perry for all the hours she has spent supporting me during this project, my friend Ian McLean for encouraging me to become an author in the first place, my agent Carole McClendon who has an uncanny knack for finding just the right projects for me, and as always, my lovely wife Lin who has been faithfully supportive of me as I have been writing this book.

PART I
Active Directory Operations

1) Active Directory Domains and Trusts

2) Functional Levels

3) Flexible Operations Masters

4) Active Directory Sites and Services

5) Active Directory Users and Computers

6) Active Directory Command Line Tools

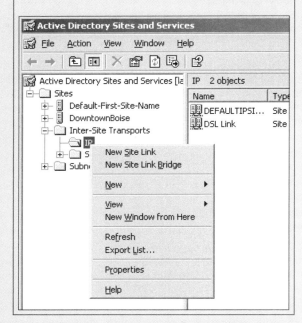

PART III
Managing Storage and Hardware

9) Data Storage Disk Systems

10) Shared and Redirected Folders

11) NTFS Share Permissions

12) Manage Devices and Device Drivers

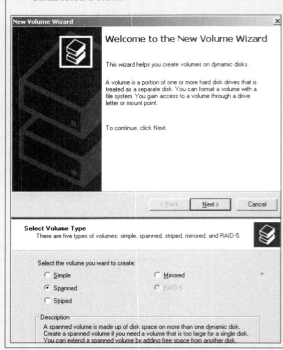

PART II
Managing Your Server Roles

7) Server Management

8) Printing

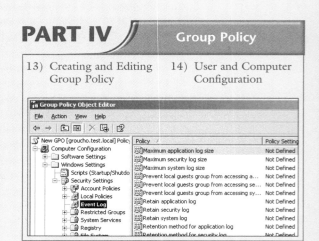

PART IV
Group Policy

13) Creating and Editing Group Policy

14) User and Computer Configuration

WHAT'S INSIDE

PART V — Server Security

15) Windows Settings and Security Settings in Group Policy

16) Server Security Configurations

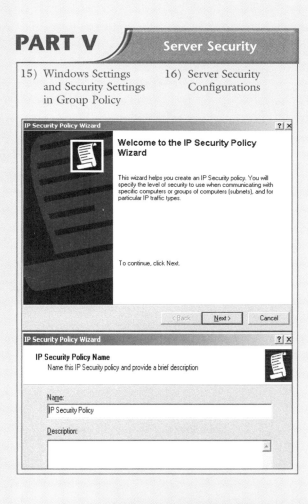

PART VI — Network Your Server

17) Internet Connections

18) Remote Connections

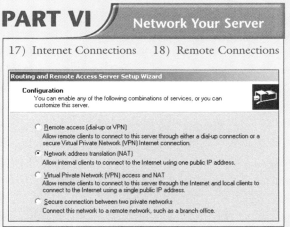

PART VII — SharePoint Services

19) Install SharePoint

20) The Intranet as a Work Area

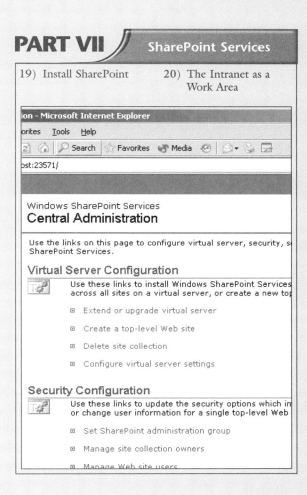

PART VIII — Server Maintenance

21) Backup and Recovery

22) Active Directory Maintenance

23) Monitoring the Server

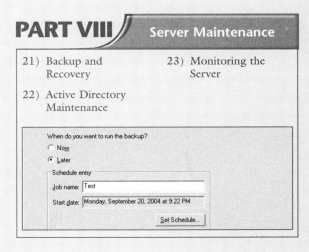

PART I

Active Directory Operations

① Active Directory Domains and Trusts

Understanding Active Directory Domains
and Trusts 4
Create a Forest Trust 6
Create a Shortcut Trust 12
Validate a Trust 16
Change Authentication Scope of a Trust 18

② Functional Levels

Understanding Functional Levels 20
Raise Domain Functional Levels 22
Raise Forest Functional Levels 24

③ Flexible Operations Masters

Understanding Flexible Operations Masters 26
Designate a Global Catalog Server 28
Register and Install a Schema Snap-In 30
Create a Schema Attribute 34
Create a Schema Class 36
Deactivate a Schema Object 38
Transfer a Domain Naming Master 40
Transfer a PDC Emulator 42
Find FSMO Roles with the ntdsutil
Command Line Tool....................................44
Transfer an Infrastructure Master Using
ntdsutil 48

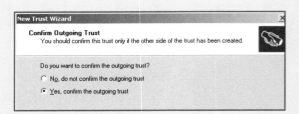

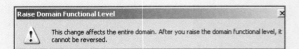

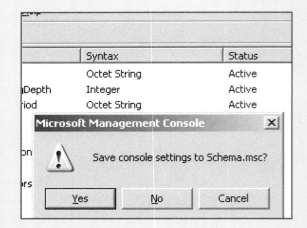

TABLE OF CONTENTS

4 Active Directory Sites and Services

Understanding Active Directory Sites
    and Services...52
Create a New Site 54
Add a Domain Controller to a New Site 56
Choose a Licensing Server for a Site 58
Assign a Subnet to a Site 60
Configure Site Links 62
Configure a Site Link Bridge 64
Designate a Preferred Bridgehead Server 66
Configure Intersite Replication 68

5 Active Directory Users and Computers

Understanding Active Directory Users
    and Computers 70
Create a User..72
Create a Group and Add a User.......................74
Add a Group to Another Group 78
Create an Organizational Unit and
    Add a Group 80
Delegate Control of an Organizational Unit.....82

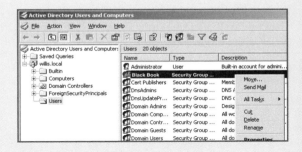

6 Active Directory Command Line Tools

Understanding Active Directory
    Command Line Tools 86
Using dsadd.exe..88
Using dsget.exe 90
Using dsquery.exe 92
Using dsmod.exe 94

PART II — Managing Your Server Roles

⑦ Server Management

Manage Your Server Roles 98
Open the Manage Your Server Wizard 100
Configure a DNS Server 102
Configure a DHCP Server..............................106
Configure a File Server 110
Configure a Print Server 112
Configure a Mail Server................................116
Configure a WINS Server 118

⑧ Printing

Understanding Printing 120
Configure Point and Print Services 122
Enable Web-Based Printer Management 124
Change the Location of the Print
      Spooler Folder..128
Set Printer Priority and Availability Levels 132
Working with Print Queues 134

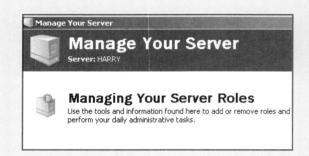

PART III — Managing Storage and Hardware

⑨ Data Storage Disk Systems

Understanding Data Storage Disk
      Systems 138
Convert a Basic Disk to a Dynamic Disk
      Manually 140
Convert a Basic Disk to a Dynamic Disk
      on the Command Line 142
Increase Disk Performance on a
      Dynamic Disk 144

TABLE OF CONTENTS

Reactivate a Missing or Off-Line Disk 146
Create a Partition or Logical Drive 148
Create a Simple Volume.................................152
Add a New Hard Drive and Initialize
    the Drive...156
Create a Spanned Volume 158
Extend Simple and Spanned Volumes 162
Create a Striped Volume 164
Create a Mirrored Volume............................168
Create a RAID 5 Array 172

10 Shared and Redirected Folders

Understanding Shared and
    Redirected Folders 176
Create a Shared Folder with Windows
    Explorer 178
Create Shared Web Folders 180
Create Shares with the Shared Folders
    Snap-In..182
Enable Windows File Protection with
    Group Policy..186
Restrict Offline File Usage with
    Group Policy..188
Enable a Computer to Use Offline Files..........190

11 NTFS Share Permissions

Understanding NTFS Share Permissions 192
Set Basic Share Permissions 194
Set NTFS Disk Quotas 196
Set NTFS File Compression............................198
Set NTFS Data Encryption 200
Set Up Shadow Copies 202
Assign NTFS Permissions to Users
    and Groups 204
Determine NTFS Effective Permissions 206
Change Ownership of Files and Folders..........210

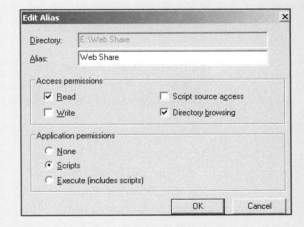

⑫ Manage Devices and Device Drivers

Understanding Manage Devices and
Device Drivers 214
Install PnP Devices 216
Troubleshoot Installed Devices 218
Troubleshoot with Device Manager 220
Configure Automatic Updates 222
Manually Update Device Drivers 224
Roll Back Device Drivers 226
Identify Unsigned Device Drivers
with sigverif.exe 228
Set Driver Signing with System Properties 230
View USB Hub Power Allocations 232

PART IV — Group Policy

⑬ Creating and Editing Group Policy

Understanding How to Create and
Edit Group Policy 236
Create a Standalone GPO Editor 238
Create an Unlinked GPO...............................240
Open the Group Policy Object Editor 242
Link a GPO to an Organizational Unit 244
Create a New GPO in an
Organizational Unit 246
Edit a GPO in an Organizational Unit...........248

⑭ User and Computer Configuration

Understanding User and Computer
Configuration 250
Deploy a Software Package 252
Configure Web Browser Proxy Settings
with Windows Settings 254

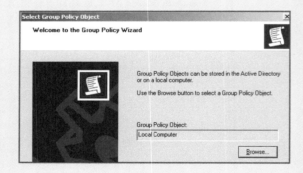

TABLE OF CONTENTS

Configure Windows Automatic Updates
with Administrative Templates..................256
Add Administrative Templates in
the GPO Editor 258
Configure Loopback Policy Mode 260
Configure Block Policy Inheritance 262
Configure No Override Option 264
Modify the GPO Policy Application
Sequence..266
Configure Filtering on a GPO 268
Disable a GPO Node....................................270
Disable a GPO..272

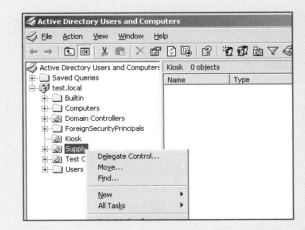

PART V — Server Security

15 Windows Settings and Security Settings in Group Policy

Understanding Windows Settings and
Security Settings in Group Policy 276
Set Password Policies 278
Set Account Lockout 280
Set Audit Policy for Event Viewer 282
Set User Rights Assignment...........................284
Set Security Options 286
Set Event Log Security 288
Configure Restricted Groups 290
Configure System Services 292
Configure Registry Security 294
Configure File System Security 296
Configure Wireless Network Security.............298
Set Software Restriction Policies 302
Set IP Security Policies 304

⑯ Server Security Configurations

Understanding Server Security
    Configurations 308
Create a REG File 310
Create a Reserve File 312
Enable Monitoring for Anonymous
    Active Directory Access 314
Rename the Default Administrator
    Account 316
Create a Decoy Administrator Account 318
Deny Logon Access to the Domain 320
Install Certificate Services 322
Lock Down Your Server with
    Trust-No-Exe 326

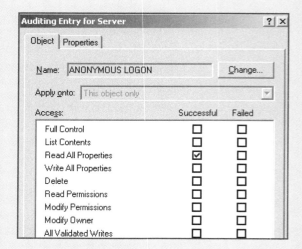

PART VI
Network Your Server

⑰ Internet Connections

Understanding Internet Connections..............330
Set Up an Internet Connection 332
Set Up a Demand-Dial Internet
    Connection 334
Set Up Routing and Remote Services
    for NAT 338

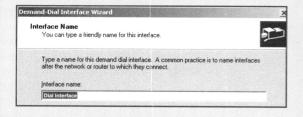

TABLE OF CONTENTS

⑱ Remote Connections

Understanding Remote Connections 342
Set Up VPN Services 344
Set Up VPN Client 348
Enable Terminal Services for Remote
    Desktop 352
Enable Remote Assistance 354
Install Terminal Services with Configure
    Your Server Wizard 356
Install Terminal Services License Server 358
Manage Terminal Services Users 360
Install IPv6 Protocol 362

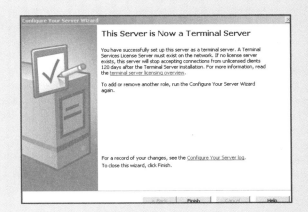

PART VII   SharePoint Services

⑲ Install SharePoint

Understanding SharePoint Installation............366
Install IIS v6 and ASP.NET 368
Install SharePoint Services 370

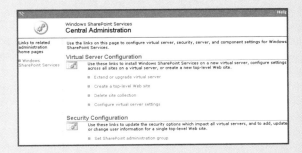

⑳ The Intranet as a Work Area

Understanding the Intranet as
    a Work Area 372
Configure a Virtual Server 374
Extend a Virtual Server 378
Create a Top-level Web Site 380
Configure Self-service Site Creation................382
Access Default Site from IIS and Create
    New Site 384

PART VIII Server Maintenance

㉑ Backup and Recovery

Understanding Server Disasters 388
Understanding Backup and Recovery..............389
Back Up the System State with
    Backup Utility..390
Back Up the Registry with ASR and
    Create System Recovery Disk 394
Schedule Data Backups 398

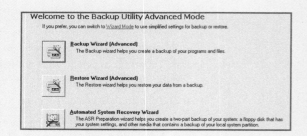

㉒ Active Directory Maintenance

Understanding Active Directory
    Maintenance 404
Move the Active Directory Database 406
Perform Offline Defragmentation of
    Active Directory 410
Using replmon..416
Using repadmin 418

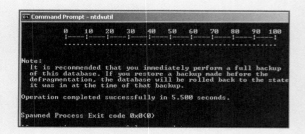

㉓ Monitoring the Server

Tools to Monitor your Server 420
Using chkdsk and chkntfs 422
Customize the Event Viewer 424
Configure Detail Level in Event Viewer..........426
Filter Event Viewer Logs 428
Add a Counter to the System Monitor............430
Create Counter Logs 432

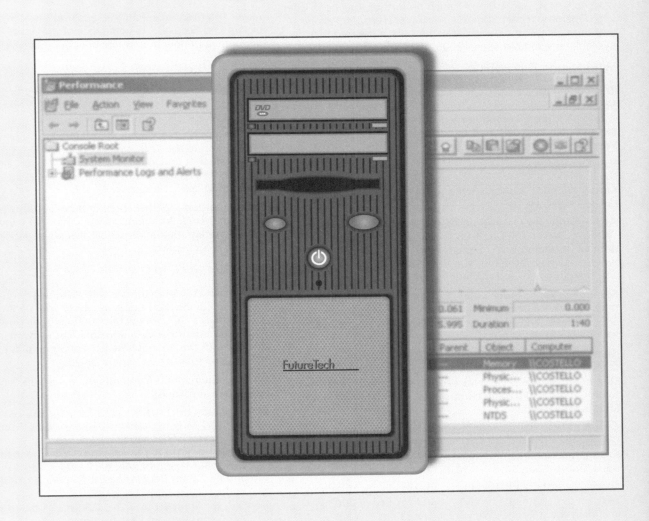

How to Use this Master VISUALLY Book

Do you look at the pictures in a book or newspaper before anything else on a page? Would you rather see an image than read how to do something? Search no further. This book is for you. Opening *Master VISUALLY Windows Server 2003* allows you to read less and learn more about the numerous features available in Windows Server 2003.

Who Needs This Book

This book is for a reader who is unfamiliar with the various features and abilities in Windows Server 2003 but is IT literate. It is also for more computer literate individuals who want to expand their knowledge of the different features that Windows Server 2003 has to offer.

Book Organization

Master VISUALLY Windows Server 2003 has 23 chapters and is divided into 8 parts.

Active Directory Operations, Part I, describes the role of Windows Server 2003 domain controllers in a Windows domain, including how to create trusts between different types of domains, the function of Flexible Operations Masters, and how to create and manage Active Directory objects.

Managing Your Server Roles, Part II of this book, shows you how to create different server roles including DNS servers, DHCP servers, and file servers, as well as how to manage various print related tasks.

Managing Storage and Hardware, Part III, focuses on managing hard disk storage, including how to convert a Basic Disk to a Dynamic Dick, working with shared and redirected folders, using NTFS share permissions, and managing devices and device drivers.

Group Policy, Part IV, describes how to create and work with Group Policy Objects (GPOs), link a GPO to a container such as an Organizational Unit, and deploy software packages using Group Policy.

Server Security, Part V, addresses a wide variety of security settings and techniques used on Windows Server 2003 including using Group Policy security settings.

Network Your Server, Part VI, teaches you how to configure your server to connect to the Internet and how to set up remote connections, such as VPN and Terminal Server connections.

SharePoint Services, Part VII, covers how to install the necessary programs and how to use this service to create a virtual conference and shared task environment in your network.

Server Maintenance, Part VIII, explores tasks involving server Backup and Recovery, maintenance of the Active Directory database, and how to monitor Windows Server 2003.

Chapter Organization

This book consists of sections, all listed in the book's table of contents. A *section* is a set of steps that show you how to complete a specific computer task.

Each section, usually contained on two facing pages, has an introduction to the task at hand, a set of full-color screen shots and steps that walk you through the task, and a set of tips. This format allows you to quickly look at a topic of interest and learn it instantly.

Chapters group together three or more sections with a common theme. A chapter may also contain pages that give you the background information needed to understand the sections in a chapter.

What You Need to Use This Book

This book was written for use with Windows Server 2003 Enterprise Edition. You can order a free trial Windows Server 2003 software CD at www.Microsoft.com/windowsserver 2003/evaluation/trial/default.mspx. This software allows you to work with the Windows Server 2003 operating system for 180 days to evaluate its performance.

System Requirements for Windows Server 2003 Enterprise Edition are as follows:

- Minimum CPU speed is 133 MHz for x86-based systems and 733 MHz for Itanium-based systems. Recommended CPU speed is 733 MHz.
- Minimum RAM is 128 MB and Recommended RAM is 256 MB. Maximum RAN is 32 GB for x86-based systems and 64 GB for Itanium-based systems.
- Multiprocessor support is up to 8 CPUs.
- Disk space for set up is 1.5 GB for x86-based systems and 2.0 GB for Itanium-based systems.

HOW TO USE THIS BOOK

Using the Mouse

This book uses the following conventions to describe the actions you perform when using the mouse:

Click

Press your left mouse button once. You generally click your mouse on something to select something on the screen.

Double-click

Press your left mouse button twice. Double-clicking something on the computer screen generally opens whatever item you have double-clicked.

Right-click

Press your right mouse button. When you right-click anything on the computer screen, the program displays a shortcut menu containing commands specific to the selected item.

Click and Drag, and Release the Mouse

Move your mouse pointer and hover it over an item on the screen. Press and hold down the left mouse button. Now, move the mouse to where you want to place the item and then release the button. You use this method to move an item from one area of the computer screen to another.

The Conventions in This Book

A number of typographic and layout styles have been used throughout *Master VISUALLY Windows Server 2003* to distinguish different types of information.

Bold

Bold type represents the names of commands and options that you interact with. Bold type also indicates text and numbers that you must type into a dialog box or window.

Italics

Italic words introduce a new term and are followed by a definition.

Numbered Steps

You must perform the instructions in numbered steps in order to successfully complete a section and achieve the final results.

Bulleted Steps

These steps point out various optional features. You do not have to perform these steps; they simply give additional information about a feature.

Indented Text

Indented text tells you what the program does in response to you following a numbered step. For example, if you click a certain menu command, a dialog box may appear, or a window may open. Indented text may also tell you what the final result is when you follow a set of numbered steps.

Notes

Notes give additional information. They may describe special conditions that may occur during an operation. They may warn you of a situation that you want to avoid, for example the loss of data. A note may also cross reference a related area of the book. A cross reference may guide you to another chapter, or another section with the current chapter.

Icons and Buttons

 Icons and buttons are graphical representations within the text. They show you exactly what you need to click to perform a step.

You can easily identify the tips in any section by looking for the Master It icon. Master It offer additional information, including tips, hints, and tricks. You can use the Master It information to go beyond what you have learn learned in the steps.

Operating System Difference

This book assumes you are using Windows Server 2003 Enterprise Edition. You will receive different results if you follow the instructions in this book using another version of Windows Server.

On September 2, 2004, Microsoft released Windows SharePoint Services Service Pack 1. This service pack provides significant enhancements to SharePoint Services. It also improves ability and performance of the software. To download this service pack, go to www.microsoft.com/downloads/details.aspx?FamilyID=875da47e-89d5-4621-a319-a1f5bfedf497&displaylang=en. You can find detailed information about SharePoint Services in Chapters 19 and 20.

1

Active Directory Domains and Trusts

Understanding Active Directory
Domains and Trusts....................................4
Create a Forest Trust....................................6
Create a Shortcut Trust..............................12
Validate a Trust...16
Change Authentication Scope of a Trust 18

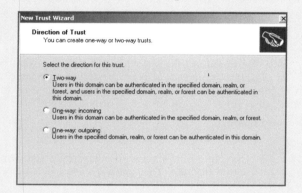

2

Functional Levels

Understanding Functional Levels..................20
Raise Domain Functional Levels 22
Raise Forest Functional Levels....................24

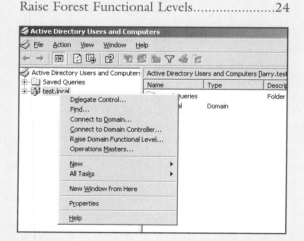

3

Flexible Operations Masters

Understanding Flexible Operations
Masters 26
Designate a Global Catalog Server...............28
Register and Install a Schema Snap-In..........30
Create a Schema Attribute...........................34
Create a Schema Class................................36
Deactivate a Schema Object 38
Transfer a Domain Naming Master 40
Transfer a PDC Emulator 42
Find FSMO Roles with the ntdsutil
Command Line Tool 44
Transfer an Infrastructure Master
Using ntdsutil 48

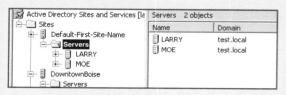

4

Active Directory Sites and Services

Understanding Active Directory Sites and
Services 52
Create a New Site 54
Add a Domain Controller to a New Site 56
Choose a Licensing Server for a Site 58
Assign a Subnet to a Site 60
Configure Site Links 62
Configure a Site Link Bridge.......................64
Designate a Preferred Bridgehead Server......66
Configure Intersite Replication 68

5 — Active Directory Users and Computers

Understanding Active Directory
Users and Computers...................................70
Create a User 72
Create a Group and Add a User 74
Add a Group to Another Group 78
Create an Organizational Unit and
Add a Group 80
Delegate Control of an Organizational
Unit..82

6 — Active Directory Command Line Tools

Understanding Active Directory
Command Line Tools 86
Using dsadd.exe 88
Using dsget.exe...90
Using dsquery.exe 92
Using dsmod.exe...94

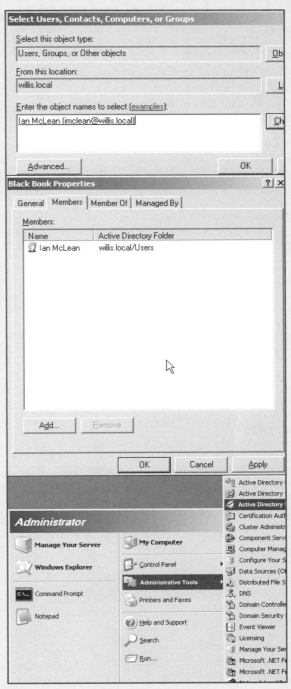

Understanding Active Directory Domains and Trusts

With Windows Server 2003 Active Directory Domains and Trusts structure, you can control the information flow, access to resources, security, and the type of relationship among different domains, domain trees, and domain forests throughout your enterprise network environment. This can ease your administrative burden of large domains and multi-domain infrastructures, saving time, effort, and expense. When you create a trust relationship between two domains, you can make a link between them that lets authentication passwords through either from one domain to another or both ways between domains. That way, you can be a user in one domain and still authenticate to and access resources on another domain. You can also create an Active Directory replication environment that treats multiple domains as if they were one container.

Active Directory

Active Directory is the Microsoft implementation of directory services that allows you to store and search for any object in your domain or in multiple domains. Active Directory Services categorizes everything in a domain as objects. Objects can include users, computers, printers, servers, file shares, application data, and more. Active Directory objects can be physical or logical objects. All objects are stored in a single file in Active Directory that includes all objects and schema information called ntds.dit. Every Domain Controller in the domain has an exact copy of the ntds.dit database as well as a special shared folder called SYSVOL. The SYSVOL folder inhabits an NTDS partition and contains information regarding Group Policy Objects and login information.

Domains

You can create a domain as a container for all Active Directory objects and isolate them from other parts of your Enterprise network infrastructure. A *domain* is a security container, an Active Directory database replication boundary, and is the basic container for defining DNS and Internet namespace. With Windows NT, you have to use a domain to define any type of control and administrative container and you have to create numerous domains for each part of your business network that have differences in security and administration. Starting with Windows 2000 Server domains and continuing with Windows Server 2003, you can create a single domain and still preserve all the security and trust functions that required multiple domains using Windows NT. You can still create multiple domains for security reasons with Windows Server 2003. Other types of container objects serve the same purpose as the numerous domains required under Windows NT.

domain.com

Domain Controllers

A *domain controller* is a specialized role for a Windows Server 2003 server. You can promote your server to a domain controller so that it can construct, receive and replicate a copy of the Active Directory database. Your domain controller has information about every object in the domain, and network users can search it to find people, computers, and resources on the domain at all times. The domain controller also constantly updates its database so that users have the most recent information. Finally, the domain controller passes along or replicates its most recent database to other domain controllers as changes occur. With Windows NT domains, not all domain controllers were equal. In each domain, you had to create a Primary Domain Controller or PDC, which held the master copy of the Active Directory database. All other domain controllers were Backup Domain Controllers, or BDCs, and each BDC held a copy of the database.

DOMAIN CONTROLLER

Trees and Forests

You can create a single domain to make it a complete Active Directory container capable of providing all the resources you need for your business to function with no limitations. You can also create subdomains called *child domains*. The first domain you create is called the root or *parent domain*. A root or parent domain can have a namespace such as microsoft.com. A child domain shares the parent domain namespace contiguously and has a name such as sales.microsoft.com. A parent domain with one or more child domains is called a *domain tree*. One root domain that has a relationship with another root domain is called a *domain forest*. The two root domains do not have a contiguous namespace and sometimes do not share the same Windows Server operating system Active Directory type. For example, you can make the namespace of two root domains in a domain forest microsoft.com and wiley.com.

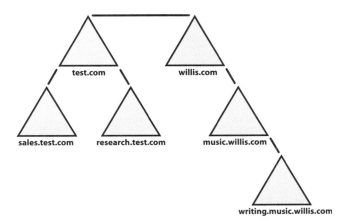

Domain Tree Trusts

You can create a *trust* between one domain and another, which means that users can share resources back and forth between two or more domains as if the resources were all part of one domain container. When you use Windows NT domain trusts, you can only configure a one-way,

nontransitive trust between two NT domains. This means you can only create a trust where one domain is trusted and the other domain is trusting. You have to create a separate trust relationship in the other direction between the two domains so they can mutually trust each other.

When creating trust, remember that interrelationship does not guarantee trust. For example, you can create a trust relationship between Domain A and Domain B, and another trust between Domain B and Domain C; however, Domain A and Domain C do not automatically trust each other. You must create another, separate trust between A and C before they trust each other. With the introduction of Windows 2000 Server and Windows Server 2003 Active Directory, you can now create two-way transitive trusts automatically between different domains in the same domain tree so that a trust between A and B is automatically two-way. Further, you have a trust where if B and C trust each other, A and C automatically trust each other.

Domain Forest Trusts

You can create trust relationships between two unrelated domain trees, but you cannot automatically create two-way transitive trust relationships. You must create forest trust relationships the same way you create domain trust relationships with Windows NT. Because this is a relationship between two unrelated domains, you must carefully create trust relationships with a greater element of security. You can own both domains, maintain separate namespaces, and allow one domain to access resources on a second domain and limit how the second domain accesses resources on the first. Users on any domain with two-way transitive trusts can access any other domain in the forest transparently. A transitive trust is one where two or more parent domains and their child domains all trust each other. The trust at the parent level transverses down to the child domains based on the parent trust. A transparent trust is one where the user is not aware of how the trust relationships transverse numerous domains and domain trees. From their point of view, they can access a child domain in a different tree as if the resource existed in their own domain. For more on forest trusts, see the section "Create a Forest Trust."

Create a Forest Trust

Y ou can use Windows Server 2003 Active Directory to create a forest trust relationship between two separate domains. This allows the two domains to have the same relationship with each other as they do with subdomains within the same domain tree. You can share resources between the two root domains and between subdomains in each of the separate domain trees. For more on forest trusts, see the section "Understanding Active Directory Domains and Trust" earlier in this chapter.

You can only create a forest trust relationship between two domains running Windows Server 2003 Active Directory.

You can create the forest trust only if you raise the forest functional level of both domain trees to Windows Server 2003 Mode. The Windows Server operating systems you use on your domain controllers defines the domain tree and forest functional levels or modes and the Active Directory features you can use. For more on domain and forest functional levels, see Chapter 2.

If you want your Windows Server 2003 domain tree to form a trust relationship with a domain using Windows 2000 Server domains or Windows NT Server domains, you can only create an external trust relationship and cannot create a true domain forest.

Create a Forest Trust

1 Click Start.

2 Click Administrative Tools.

3 Click Active Directory Domains and Trusts.

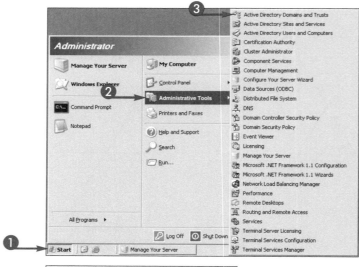

The Active Directory Domains and Trusts snap-in appears.

4 Right-click the domain.

5 Click Properties.

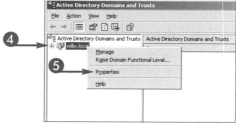

The Domain Properties dialog box appears.

⑥ Click the Trusts tab.

⑦ Click New Trust

The New Trust Wizard appears.

⑧ Click Next.

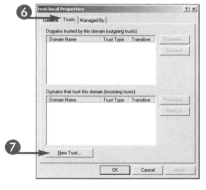

The Trust Type page of the Wizard appears.

⑨ Click the Forest trust option (☐ changes to ☉).

⑩ Click Next.

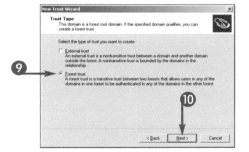

On the Domain Properties box Trusts tab, how many different trusts can I create there?

▼ You can create as many trust relationships as you want to serve the needs of your domain. For example, you can create independent trust relationships from your domain to serveral other domains. You can also create different types of trusts from the Trusts tab in the Domain Properties box. You can also limit the number of trusts you create so that you can track which domain trees trust other domain trees. If you lose track of the number and type of trusts you create, you may find it difficult to troubleshoot trust problems.

When do I select the This domain only option on the Sides of Trust page of the New Trust Wizard?

▼ When you click this option (☐ changes to ☉), it only creates one side of a trust relationship. You can create only one side of the trust, but you cannot complete the trust relationship until you create the other side of the trust. You use this kind of relationship in situations where you are in partnership with another domain and the other domain does not want to release domain administrator credentials. You and the other domain administrator must separately create the sides of the trust and the trust relationship becomes active.

continued

Create a Forest Trust
(Continued)

You can custom make a forest trust to meet the specific needs of your domain and another, noncontiguous domain. Doing this tightly controls security access to your domain resources. The trust relationship between your domain and the other domain is actually an authentication relationship. You authenticate onto your domain from a computer by typing your username and password on the logon screen of the computer. The nearest domain controller verifies your credentials and you are then allowed access.

When you create a trust relationship with another domain, you actually create automatic authentication for your users from your domain to the other domain and all the resources it contains. Because you create a trust that is transparent, your users never notice that they are accessing resources outside their domain.

You can create trust relationships that are two-way, one-way incoming, or one-way outgoing. Specific configuration controls allow you to control the level of access security you want between the two domains. When you create a two-way trust, you must have administrator credentials for the other domain to complete trust creation.

For more on authentication relationships and transparent trusts, see the section "Understanding Active Directory Domains and Trusts."

Create a Forest Trust (continued)

The Direction of Trust page of the Wizard appears.

⑪ Click the Two-way option (○ changes to ◉).

● You can also select a One-way direction.

Note: For more on creating a one-way trust, see the section "Create a Shortcut Trust."

⑫ Click Next.

The Sides of Trust page of the Wizard appears.

⑬ Click the "Both this domain and the specified domain" option (○ changes to ◉).

⑭ Click Next.

The User Name and Password page appears.

⑮ Type the administrator name for the other domain.

⑯ Type the administrative password for the other domain.

⑰ Click Next.

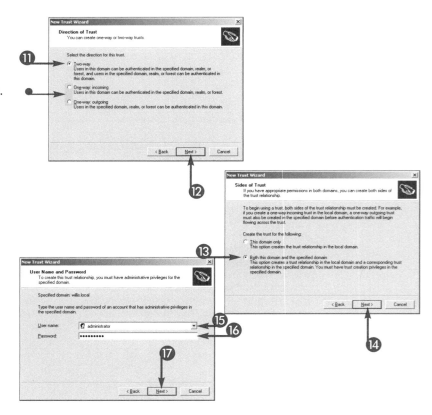

The Ongoing Trust Authentication Level –
Local Forest page of the Wizard appears.

⑱ Click the Forest-wide authentication option
(○ changes to ⦿).

⑲ Click Next.

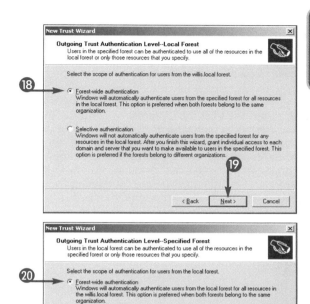

The Ongoing Trust Authentication Level –
Specified Forest page of the Wizard appears.

⑳ Click the Forest-wide authentication option
(○ changes to ⦿).

㉑ Click Next.

Are all trusts with nonrelated domain trees such as External and Realm trusts considered nontransitive trusts?

▼ No. You can create a forest trust between two domains and you can make your forest trust transitive, but only if you specify this as you step through the Create a New Trust Wizard. This means that the child domains can share the trust relationship as long as you create the trust that way. You can also create an external trust that is not transitive. Instead, the external trust you create is bound between just the two domains and does not invole any of the child domains.

Why do I have to create the authentication level for both the local forest and the specified forest?

▼ If you choose to create both sides of the trust at the same time and have access to the administrator username and password for the other domain, you must approve authentication in both your domain and the other domain as well. This means that you must get the administrative authentication information for the other domain. Otherwise, you can create only one side of the trust and need to have the administrator in the other domain provide authentication for the two-way trust to be implemented.

continued

Create a Forest Trust

(Continued)

You can create and verify both the trust selections and the trust itself in order to construct the elements that allow the trust to operate. You can test that trust relationship while you are still using the Create a New Trust Wizard. You can go back and correct any problems you may have introduced to the trust in the Wizard and retest the trust before completing the Wizard and activating the trust relationship.

You can also choose to wait until later to verify the trust, or not verify the trust at all. You can let your users verify the

trust in actual use. Using best practice procedures, you should test both sides of the trust inside the Wizard to avoid potential problems. You can also use the information you present in the Wizard to confirm how the trust is configured. You can verify the name of the domains you have set to establish a trust, the direction of the trust, and the trust type. You can verify that you have correctly created the trust authentication levels for both local and specified domains.

Create a Forest Trust (continued)

The Trust Selection Complete page of the Wizard appears.

㉒ Click Next.

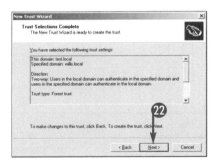

The Trust Creation Complete page of the Wizard appears.

㉓ Click Next.

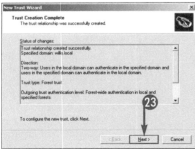

The Confirm Outgoing Trust page of the Wizard appears.

㉔ Click the Yes, confirm the outgoing trust option (◯ changes to ⦿).

● You can click No (◯ changes to ⦿) when you want to delay confirming trusts until after you create a complex trust structure.

㉕ Click Next.

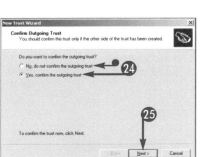

The Confirm Incoming Trust page of the Wizard appears.

㉖ Click the Yes, confirm the incoming trust option (☐ changes to ◉).

● You can click No, do not confirm the outgoing trust option (☐ changes to ◉).

Note: For more on clicking these options, see the section, "Create a Shortcut Trust."

㉗ Click Next.

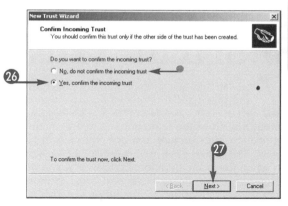

The Completing the New Trust Wizard appears.

㉘ Click Finish.

Your trust relationship is not complete until authentication changes are replicated to all domain controllers in the forest.

Why would I choose to verify only one side of the trust but not the other?

▼ You can verify only one side of the trust when the other domain administer wants to verify the other side. You can also choose to verify only one side of the trust if you elect to create only one side of a trust in an External Trust. The New Trust Wizard offers you selections that you use when you create different kinds of trusts. The Confirm Outgoing Trust and Confirm Incoming Trust pages of the New Trust Wizard are where you can verify one, the other, or both sides of the trust.

On the Completing the New Trust Wizard page, why do astericks appear before the domain names listed.

▼ You have created an authentication situation where anyone in one domain may authenticate to any resource in another domain. In Windows Server 2003, one format used to authenticate to a domain is username@domain.com. The asterick (*) is a wildcard symbol that means any username that appears before the domain name is considered valid. In other words, jpyles@test.com can authenticate as well as maldridge@test.com. This permits any of your users, computers, or processes on the test.com domain to automatically access the trust without a separate logon process to the other domain.

Create a Shortcut Trust

You can create a shortcut trust that enables users and processes in one child domain to directly access users and resources in a child domain in a different branch of the same domain tree without using the trust relationship structure that goes through the parent domain. This allows your users to access processes faster than when using the traditional two-way transitive trust relationship. This is because the traditional relationship processes users' resource queries up one branch of the domain tree, through the root, and down the other branch.

When you create a trust, even in the same tree, you are really creating an authentication process between the

parent domain and each of the individual child domains. You are not aware of it because you created a trust that is automatically transitive and transparent. For example, the domain called engineers.research.microsoft.com needs to access the domain called programmers.development. microsoft.com. Each part of the namespace represents part of the authentication process that your users must traverse. You can create a path that allows engineers and programmers to trust each other as if they were the only two domains in the tree.

For more on transitive and transparent trusts, see the section "Understanding Active Directory Domains and Trust.

Create a Shortcut Trust

① Click Start.

② Click Administrative Tools.

③ Click Active Directory Domains and Trusts.

The Active Directory Domains and Trust snap-in appears.

④ Right-click the domain name.

⑤ Click Properties.

The Domain Properties dialog box opens.

⑥ Click New Trust.

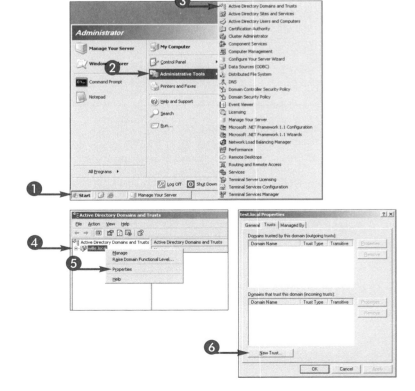

The New Trust Wizard appears.

⑦ Click Next.

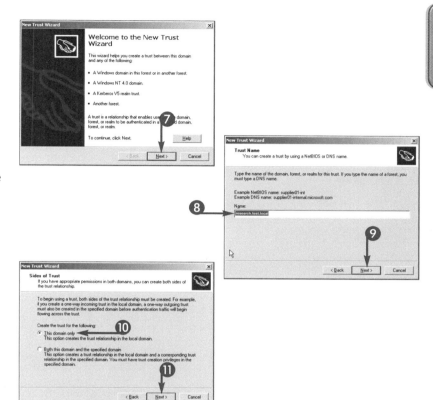

The Trust Name page of the Wizard appears.

⑧ In the Name field, type the name of the other domain.

⑨ Click Next.

The Sides of Trust page of the Wizard appears.

⑩ Click the This domain only option (◯ changes to ◉).

⑪ Click Next.

How does the Create a New Trust Wizard know what kind of trust to create?

▼ The Wizard uses your selections to determine which types of trusts to offer you. When you type the name of a child domain in the Wizard, you indicate the type of trust you want to create. The Wizard accesses the Active Directory domain tree topology, identifies the domain you have indicated is a child domain and determines that the only type of trust you can create is a shortcut trust. If you are not offered the expected type of trust when you run the Wizard, you must go back and determine if you met all the required conditions for this type of trust.

On the Trust Name page of the New Trust Wizard, why must I type the DNS name of the forest rather than the NetBIOS name?

▼ You can use NetBIOS name resolution inside of a single domain or domain tree. The Windows Internet Name Server (WINS) can provide hostname to address resolution within the domain. You can use WINS servers in a single Windows domain to let hosts locate each other without the use of Domain Name Services (DNS) servers. Two or more forests are connected by WAN links including the Internet and any traffic routed across Wide Area Networks require DNS hostname to address resolution. If you do not use the DNS name of a forest for a forest trust, your domain will not be able to find the other domain.

continued

Create a Shortcut Trust

(Continued)

When you create a shortcut trust, you can verify your selections. Verifying the selections you make allows you to construct a correctly working shortcut trust the first time. By using the built-in checking features in the New Trust Wizard, you ensure that your users can use the trust and have it behave reliably as soon as you create it.

Although the two domains in the shortcut trust share a contiguous namespace, you create a shortcut trust with the Wizard in the same way you create any external trust. The

shortcut trust is nontransitive and not automatically two-way because you bypasss the two-way transitive features of the standard domain tree trust. While it might seem as if you can restrict access of one domain to the other by creating a one-way trust, both child domains are still part of the two-way transitive trust created when the domain tree was made. You must configure a password for the trust with this type of trust. The password is independent of the administrative password that accesses the parent or any of the child domains. The shortcut trust password is unique to the specific trust you create.

Create a Shortcut Trust *(continued)*

The Trust Password page of the Wizard appears.

⑫ Type the trust password.

⑬ Type the trust password again in the Confirm trust password field.

⑭ Click Next.

The Trust Selections Complete page of the Wizard appears.

⑮ Review the information.

⑯ Click Next.

The Trust Creation Complete page appears.

⑰ Review the information.

⑱ Click Next.

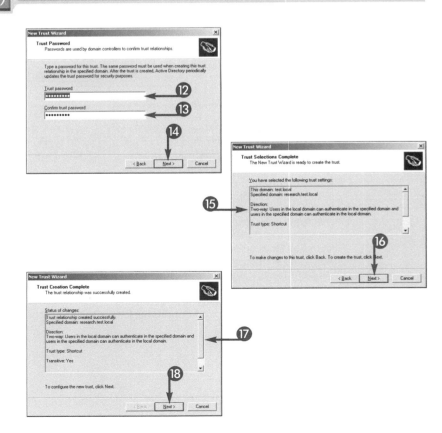

The Confirm Outgoing Trust page appears.

⓭ Click the No, do not confirm the outgoing trust option (○ changes to ●).

● You can also click the "Yes, confirm the outgoing trust" option (○ changes to ●).

Note: For more on this option, see the section "Create a Forest Trust."

⓴ Click Next.

The Confirm Incoming Trust page appears.

㉑ Click the No, do not confirm the incoming trust option (○ changes to ●).

㉒ Click Next.

Completing the New Trust Wizard page appears.

㉓ Click Finish.

Windows Server 2003 creates the shortcut trust.

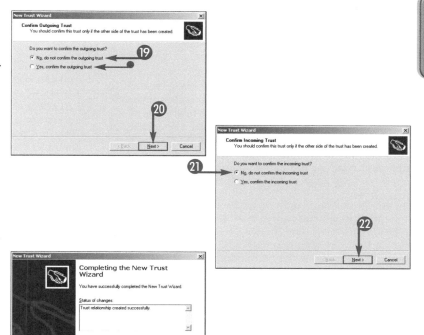

When I create a shortcut trust between two child domains in the same domain tree, why do I have issues with security?

▼ You do not create a shortcut trust to increase the level of security between two child domains in the same tree. While it is true that you do not have to create a two-way trust automatically between the two child domains using the shortcut trust, the primary purpose of the trust is to create a direct authentication link between two child domains that frequently access resources between their two domains. Even if you created a one-way shortcut trust, they still have a two-way transitive trust relationship because they belong to the same tree.

Why does Active Directory periodically change the shortcut trust password for me?

▼ You can manage trust security manually by periodically changing the shortcut trust password, but Active Directory offers to do this task for you to ease your burden of administration. Active Directory has a similar feature where you specify the password account features for domain users. You can configure password accounts to automatically force users to change passwords at certain periods, enforce a high level of complexity in passwords and prevent users from using the same password too often. For more on configuring password accounts for domain users, and creating a user, see Chapter 5.

Validate a Trust

You can validate a trust after you initially create it to verify that the trust relationship functions properly or to diagnose a potential problem with the trust. You can use this simple method to establish the usability of a trust relationship between domains within the same tree or domains in two separate forests. Trusts are very complicated relationships and if you do not construct them carefully, you can have a nonworking trust.

There are times when you may create a trust between two domain trees in a forest or two separate domain forests and you decide not to validate the trust relationship. When you validate a trust between two domains, you are verifying the authentication set up between the domains.

You can also determine if a trust relationship, which was previously working, is no longer functioning properly. You first check the network connections between network subnets and separate network infrastructures to make sure that your domain controllers are all communicating. You then can investigate the trust relationship. Please note that you can use the validate a trust feature as the first step in solving a trust problem, but that function cannot repair any problem you find. Although the cause of a trust relationship problem can be widely varied, you can go back and verify that all of the prerequisite conditions for creating the trust have been met.

Validate a Trust

① Click Start.

② Click Administrative Tools.

③ Click Active Directory Domains and Trusts.

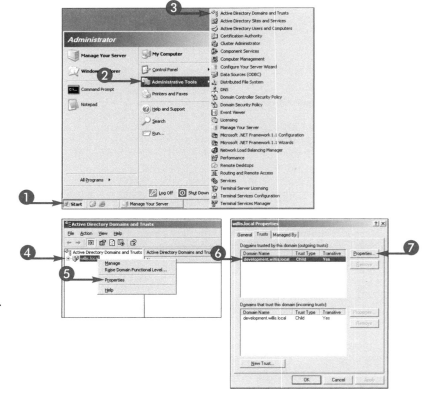

The Active Directory Domains and Trusts snap-in appears.

④ Right-click the domain name.

⑤ Click Properties.

The Domain Properties dialog box appears.

⑥ Click the trust you want to validate.

⑦ Click Properties.

The Trust Properties dialog box appears.

8 Click Validate.

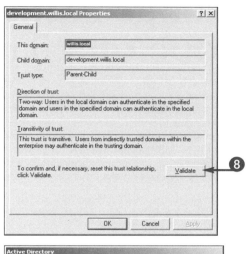

The Active Directory authentication dialog box appears.

9 Click the Yes, validate the incoming trust option (⊙ changes to ⊙).

10 In the User name field, type the administrator logon name.

11 In the Password field, type the administrative password.

12 Click OK.

A trust validation message appears.

13 Click OK.

The trust relationship is verified.

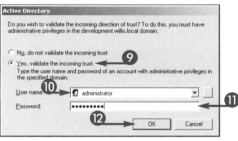

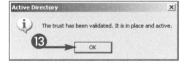

Can I verify both sides of a trust relationship at the same time?

▼ No. You can use the Domain Properties dialog box to choose either the incoming or the outgoing trust and then verify that trust. You cannot select both trust relationships at the same time. You can verify one trust direction and the other trust direction, one after the other, while the Active Directory Domains and Trusts snap-in is open. You can also verify different sides of a trust at different times. For example, if you create a trust that users primarily access in one direction and not the other, you can verify only that one direction. If you want to later use the other direction, you can verify it then.

Do I have to have administrative privileges for the other domain in the trust to verify my outgoing trust?

▼ No. You can verify the outgoing trust from your domain because you already are authenticated. You only need the credentials of other domain administrators to access their domains and to verify the incoming trusts from them to you. When you verify your outgoing trust, a message appears asking if you also want to verify the incoming trust. You can verify the incoming trust, but you have to verify the outgoing trust in a separate request.

Change Authentication Scope of a Trust

You can construct or change a trust relationship between your domain and another domain entity so that the relationship is no longer domain-wide. Doing so restricts access to secure resources to the other domain. You can designate a few users, or just one group or department, the authority to authenticate with the other domain through the trust relationship so that most users on your domain cannot access resources on the other domain forest.

You can only choose two different forest trust authentication types. You can choose Forest-wide authentication, which is the preference for situations where both domain forests belong to the same organization. For example, Cisco owns Linksys, although both organizations maintain their own domain namespace. Cisco and Linksys benefit from having a forest trust.

You can choose Selective authentication when you want to create a forest trust between two completely separate and independently owned organizations. With this option, you can preserve the security of each organization. You can have control of exactly which types of resources on your domain you allow the other domain to access.

Change Authentication Scope of a Trust

1 Click Start.

2 Click Administrative Tools.

3 Click Active Directory Domains and Trusts.

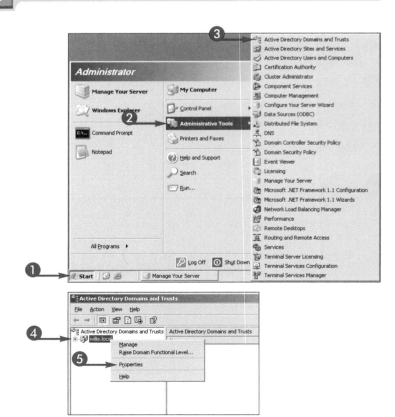

The Active Directory Domains and Trusts snap-in appears.

4 Right-click the domain name.

5 Click Properties.

The Domain Properties dialog box appears.

6 Click the trust you want to change.

7 Click Properties.

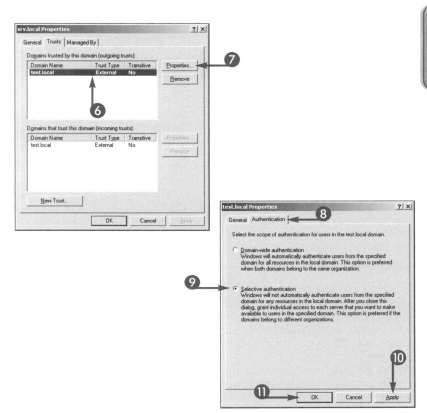

The Trust Properties dialog box appears.

8 Click the Authentication tab.

9 Click the Selective authentication option (○ changes to ⊙).

10 Click Apply.

11 Click OK.

The Authentication Scope is now changed.

How do I ensure that the specific users or groups designated to access the other domain forest can authenticate that forest?

▼ You can provide the specific authentication logon name and password only to those groups you want to have access. In order to do this, you must add the users or groups to the Access Control Lists (ACLs) of the services or resources you want them to access. When any of your domain users attempt to access the shares in the other domain forest, instead of automatically being authenticated, they see a logon screen. Users without access do not know the proper username and password to log on to the other domain forest through the Selective Authentication.

What if I want two different groups in my domain to only have access to separate resources in the other domain forest.

▼ You can give both groups access to the selective authentication username and password credentials for the other forest domain shares. In the Properties box for the resources you want a particular user or group to access, you must add that user or group to the Access Control List and set the permission level you want them to have. You can then set the access control lists for the separate shares so that only one selected group from your domain has any access to that share using the access control lists for each share in the other forest. For more on access permissions, see Chapter 11.

Understanding Functional Levels

You can raise the functional level of your domain to allow Windows Server 2003 domain controllers to interact with other types of domain controllers in your single domain or domain tree. This means you can use only the features that all the different domain controllers have in common. Functional levels were first introduced with Windows 2000 and have been expanded in Windows Server 2003. Windows 2000 Server uses two functional modes — *mixed mode*, which provides for backward compatibility with Windows NT 4.0 primary domain controllers, and *native mode*, which provides for the new Active Directory features in a pure Windows 2000 Server environment. With Windows 2000 modes or functional levels, you can only operate on the level of the domain. This lets you install a Windows Server 2003 DC on a domain when you cannot upgrade all of your DCs to 2003 all at once and need 2003 to interoperate with older Windows operating systems.

You can allow your Windows Server 2003 to operate on several different domain functional levels. At each functional level, your Windows Server 2003 domain controllers can only utilize the features that the other domain controllers use on the domain. In other words, your domain is limited to the *lowest common denominator* of domain controller features.

Domain Functional Levels

There are four domain functional levels available in Windows Server 2003 Active Directory: Windows 2000, Windows 2000 native, Windows Server 2003 Interim, and Windows 2003.

- **Windows 2000 level:** You can use this level to allow for backward compatibility with Windows NT 4.0 domain controllers. This limits the functionality and security of your domain tree to what is normally provided on Windows NT domains.

- **Windows 2000 native level:** Like native mode in Windows 2000, this level supports only features available on Windows 2000 Active Directory domains. When your domain controllers are at this functional level, you cannot use any Windows NT 4.0 domain controllers on the domain. You can use this functional level only with Windows 2000 and Windows Server 2003 domain controllers. You can operate your domain in this mode for an indefinite period of time. You can also use this mode to gradually upgrade your Windows 2000 domain controllers to Windows Server 2003.

- **Windows Server 2003 Interim level:** This level is a special functional level specifically for situations where you are actively upgrading Windows NT 4.0 domain controllers to Windows Server 2003 domain controllers. You only use this level to support NT security and features and you cannot support Windows 2000 domain controllers.

- **Windows Server 2003:** This is the highest functional level you can use with Windows Server 2003 domain controllers and it only supports Windows Server 2003 domains and cannot support downlevel Windows operating system domain controllers. All domain controllers you place in the domain must be at this level in order for you to raise the forest functional level to Windows Server 2003.

Forest Functional Levels

You can use forest functional levels, a brand-new Windows Server 2003 feature, to configure all your Active Directory domain forest trusts. This allows you to operate with different combinations of Windows Server operating system sets. There are three forest functional level; Windows 2000 Native Mode is used to install Windows Server 2003 in a Windows 2000 forest with no Windows NT DCs. Windows Server Interim Mode is used only to upgrade a Windows NT forest to Windows Server 2003. Windows Server 2003 Mode is used for a forest with only Windows Server 2003 DCs. The advantage of having a variety of Domain Controller types not only in the domain tree, but also in multiple forests is that you can create trusts with other forests and avoid upgrading all the domain controllers in all the domains in the forest to Windows Server 2003. In this case, you can take this new Windows Server 2003 feature and make it backwardly compatible with downlevel Windows Server operating systems.

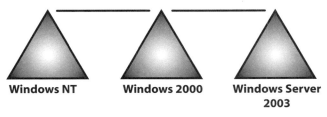

Windows NT   **Windows 2000**   **Windows Server 2003**

You can use the Windows 2000 forest functional level, leave your forest functional level at this default setting, and let your forest support domains using any of the Windows operating system domain controllers, including Windows NT, Windows 2000 Server, and Windows Server 2003. You can use this forest functional level when you create a forest domain trust relationship with another domain forest operating with a minimum of one Windows Server 2003 domain controller. All of the other domain controllers can be of any other type.

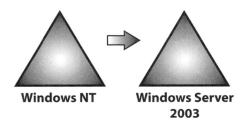

Windows NT   **Windows Server 2003**

You use the Windows Server 2003 interim forest functional level only when you are upgrading Windows NT 4.0 domain controllers to Windows Server 2003 domain controllers. This forest level only supports your trust when you use Windows NT and Windows 2003 domain controller functions. This forest functional level functions similarly to the domain functional level that has the same name. You cannot use this forest functional level as a long-term trust solution between domain forests.

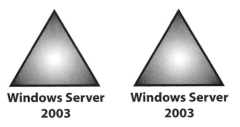

Windows Server 2003   **Windows Server 2003**

You can use the Windows Server 2003 forest functional level only to support Windows Server 2003 domain controllers in your domain trees and forests. You cannot raise your domain forest trust functional level to Windows Server 2003 until you have first raised all of the domains and domain trees in your forests to the Windows Server 2003 domain functional level.

Raise Domain Functional Levels

You can raise the domain functional level of your domain tree to gain access to additional features offered at higher levels when you upgrade to more recent Windows Server domain controller operating systems. You must make sure that all of the domain controllers in your domain or domain tree are upgraded to the operating systems required by that level. You first convert your domain tree to the Windows Server 2003 functional level, and then you rename domain controllers, update logon time stamps, and use Kerberos Key Distribution Center version numbers and the User Password on the InetOrgPerson object. These are all features you can use once you have raised your domain functional level.

You promote a Windows Server 2003 member server to a domain controller using the dcpromo command. When you set the configuration of your new domain controller, you can select the security settings for that server. When you choose the more secure option, you are only offered the last two domain functional levels — Windows 2000 native and Windows Server 2003. The more secure selection enables your domain controller to use only the two highest domain functional levels. With the lesser setting, your domain controller uses all four domain functional options.

Raise Domain Functional Levels

① Click Start.

② Click Administrative Tools.

③ Click Active Directory Users and Computers.

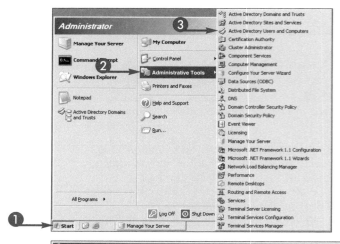

The Active Directory Users and Computers snap-in appears.

④ Right-click the domain you want to raise.

⑤ Click Raise Domain Functional Level.

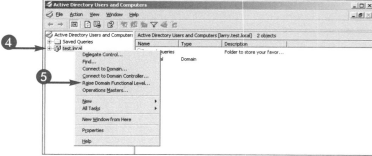

The Raise Domain Functional Level dialog box opens.

6 Click here and click the Windows Server 2003 option.

7 Click Raise.

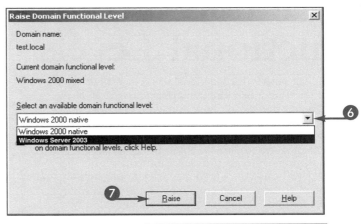

A box appears warning you that you cannot reverse the functional level upgrade.

8 Click OK.

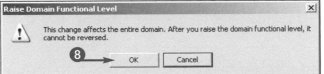

A confirmation dialog box appears confirming your changes.

9 Click OK.

The functional level is raised.

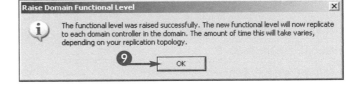

MASTER IT

Once I raise my Domain Functional level, can I go back to a lower level if I need to add a downlevel Windows Server Domain Controller?

▼ No. You can raise your Domain Functional level from a lower to higher level, but you cannot reverse the process. Once you raise a functional level, you can never go back. This means that once your domain is at Windows Server 2003, you cannot introduce other domain controllers running Windows NT or Windows 2000. Before raising your domain functional level to a higher mode, you must make sure that all of your domain controller operating systems have been upgraded to the system appropriate for the level.

Do I have to raise my domain to a higher domain functional level or can I leave it at Windows 2000?

▼ No. You do not have to raise the functional level but by not doing so, you are not taking full advantage of all the features, listed in the introduction to this section, that operate at the Windows Server 2003 functional level. You can also have member servers running any Windows Server operating system. You only need to upgrade the operating systems of domain controllers when you raise the domain functional level of your domain.

Raise Forest Functional Levels

You can raise forest functional levels in a similar way to raising domain functional levels so that all of the different domains in your domain forest trust relationships can operate a variety of different Windows Server domain controller operating systems. You can then continue to use a mixed domain controller environment in your multiple domain forest trust environment. Alternatively, you can plan a rollout process to upgrade selective or all of the domain controllers in the forest to more recent versions of Windows Server operating systems.

You can use this never-before-available function of Windows Server 2003 domain controllers to create an enterprise-level

upgrade and infrastructure design plan for your forest relationships. You can take dozens of Windows NT domains operated by several companies, establish a basic trust relationship, and gradually collapse the large number of Windows NT domains into as few as one domain per forest by upgrading the domain controller operating systems. Then, you cannot only use more advanced domain controller features, you can also ease the burden of administration for you and the other domain managers in the other forests. For more about how Windows NT requires a larger number of domains and domain administration, see Chapter 1.

Raise Forest Functional Levels

① Click Start.

② Click Administrative Tools.

③ Click Active Directory Domains and Trusts.

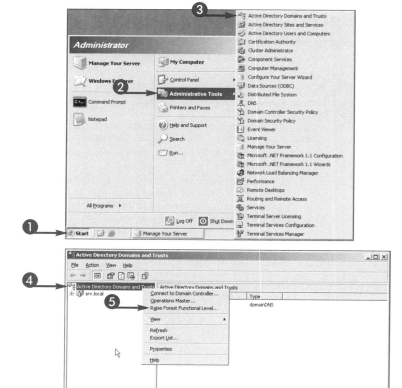

The Active Directory Domains and Trusts snap-in appears.

④ Right-click Active Directory Domains and Trusts.

⑤ Click Raise Forest Functional Level.

The Raise Forest Functional Level dialog box appears.

⑥ Click here and click the Windows Server 2003 functional level option.

⑦ Click Raise.

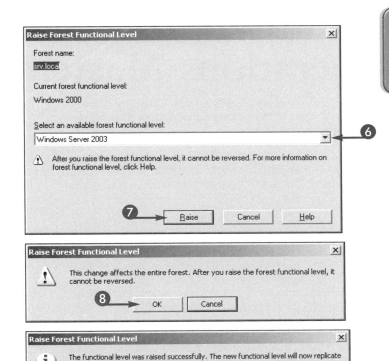

A box appears warning you that you cannot reverse the functional level upgrade.

⑧ Click OK.

A confirmation dialog box appears confirming your changes.

⑨ Click OK.

The forest functional level is raised.

Do I also raise the domain functional level in Active Directory Domains and Trusts the way I raise the forest functional level?

▼ You cannot use the same Active Directory snap-in for managing both domain and forest functional levels. You must use the Users and Computers snap-in for domain functional levels because you are administering a feature limited to domain controllers on a single domain. All domain controller Active Directory objects are stored in a special container in this snap-in. You can use the Domains and Trusts snap-in to administer a wider scope of domains. For more on raising the domain functional level, see the section "Raise Domain Functional Levels."

What if I raise all the domains in the forest to Windows Server 2003 and later want to add a trust with a domain forest using Windows NT or Windows 2000 domain controllers?

▼ You cannot add a new domain forest to your forest trusts unless all the domain controllers are upgraded to Windows Server 2003. You can create an external trust relationship with the new domain set, but your level of operation with the domain forest in an external trust is limited to the lowest common denominator of the domain controller operating system.

Understanding Flexible Operations Masters

You can select which of the Active Directory domain controllers in your domain tree and forests assumes certain specialized roles. This ensures that roles are equally balanced on your domains and that the special services that the domain controllers roles provide remain available when required. A domain controller is a server role that provides authentication, security and resource access to users and services in a domain. All domain controllers in a domain tree and forest are considered peers because they contain identical copies of the Active Directory database.

This section discusses the basic differences between Windows NT, Windows 2000, and Windows Server 2003 domain controllers and the different Flexible Operations Master roles. A *Flexible Operations Master* can be any one of five roles required of a Windows Server 2003 domain controller to allow required domain-related functions to be performed.

Windows NT

When you administer Windows NT domain controllers, you must use only one master domain controller, called a *primary domain controller* (PDC), in the domain. The PDC is the only domain controller in the Windows NT domain that contains a writable copy of the directory database. You must assign all other domain controllers in your Windows NT domain to be backup domain controllers (BDCs). BDCs contain read-only copies of the directory database. You must make any changes to the directory database on the PDC. Only the BDCs are peers to each other. *Peer domain* controllers are those that have an equal function or capacity in a domain or DCs that contain identical copies of the Active Directory database.

Writable Copy — PDC

Read-only Copy — BDC

Windows 2000 and Windows Server 2003

You can use domain controllers that are truly considered peer DCs on your domain when you use either Windows 2000 Server or Windows Server 2003 domain controllers. When you use those server operating systems on domain controllers, you can make changes to the Active Directory database from any domain controller in the domain tree or forest. Each of your domain controllers is considered a peer to all the others, and all the Active Directory database information changes are continually replicated to all the other DCs.

Domain-Wide Operations Masters

You can assign two different classes of flexible operations masters to a domain controller depending on the scope of the role. The first scope you can use is a domain-wide scope. Flexible operations masters that operate within this scope are necessary in each domain in a domain tree or forest. You must make sure that each of these domain-wide operations masters is placed in all domains including each parent and child domain. There are three domain-wide operations master roles. The three domain-wide operations masters are the PDC emulator, the Infrastructure master and the Relative identifier (RID) master.

Forest-Wide Operations Masters

You must assign a forest-wide operations master role to at least one domain controller in each Active Directory domain forest. You can assign more than one domain controller to a forest-wide role, but a minimum of at least one per forest is required. All domain controllers in the different domains in the forest look to the forest-wide operation master for forest-wide services. There are two forest-wide operations master roles; the Schema master and the Domain naming master.

The First Domain Controller

You create a domain tree and forest automatically when you create the first domain controller. By default, the first domain controller is created with all five flexible single operations master roles. You must create other domain controllers in the parent or in a child domain, to perform any domain-wide FSMO roles. You can assign any other domain controllers you create as operation master roles based on where you place then and where the operation master roles are needed.

Infrastructure Master

You can use the infrastructure master to keep and update references of objects in other domains so that your domain has a record of changes made in Active Directory objects in different domains in the domain tree. For example, say Domains 1, 2, and 3 all have trust relationships with each other. A user in Domain 1 often accesses resources in Domain 2 but never contacts Domain 3. If you make any change to this user in Domain 1, the infrastructure master keeps the change in Domains 2 and 3. This enables other domains to record and, if necessary, access changes concerning the Domain 1 user. There must be an infrastructure master in each domain in a forest.

RID Master

You can use a *relative identifier* (RID) master to assign security identifiers to any object created in a domain. This allows the object to be considered unique on the domain.

The security identifier is what you use to make it possible to create an object unique in a domain. If an AD object does not have a unique identifier, AD cannot distinguish it and a user cannot locate it. You allow the RID master to assign blocks of security identifiers to all domain controllers in your domain. Each of your domain controllers then uses these numbers to create new objects. When a domain controller runs out of security identifiers, it contacts the RID master to acquire another block. If, at this time, the RID master is offline, you cannot create any new objects in the domain. There must be one or more RID masters in a domain.

PDC Emulator

You use a PDC emulator when you have Windows NT backup domain controllers still operating in your domain. For more about PDC emulators and the specific functions of this domain-wide flexible operations master role, see the section "Transfer a PDC Emulator." There must be one or more PDC masters in a domain. You may need to add PDC emulators depending on the load required in your domain.

Schema and Domain Naming Masters

You can use these two flexible operations masters in their forest-wide roles to provide their special services to each domain controller in the domain forest. For more on these forest-wide operations masters, see the sections "Transfer a Domain Naming Master" and "Register and Install a Schema Snap-In."

Designate a Global Catalog Server

You must create at least one global catalog server in your Active Directory domain forest to have a domain controller containing a catalog list of resources in different domain trees in the forest. While the global catalog server is not always included in the list of flexible operations masters; it provides a specialized domain controller role. The global catalog server keeps track of objects within the domain forest involving each domain. The global catalog server cannot hold a complete copy of

each and every object in every domain. Instead, it keeps a copy of the global catalog, which it uses to point to the location of domain tree objects in the forest.

The global catalog server uses a partial copy of the domain directory, and it replicates its catalog to all global catalog servers in the forest. Your global catalog server uses only a subset of information about the contents of all the domains in the forest. If a user in Domain A attempted to locate a resource in Domain D in another part of the forest, the global catalog server helps locate the resource.

Designate a Global Catalog Server

① Click Start.

② Click Administrative Tools.

③ Click Active Directory Sites and Services.

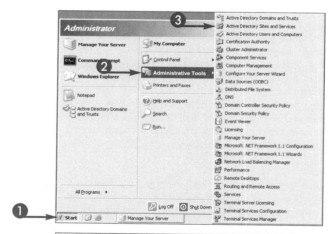

The Active Directory Sites and Services snap-in appears.

④ Expand Sites.

⑤ Expand Default-First-Site-Name.

⑥ Expand Servers.

⑦ Expand an individual server.

⑧ Right-click NTDS Settings.

⑨ Click Properties.

The NTDS Settings Properties dialog box appears.

⑩ Click the General tab.

⑪ Click the Global Catalog option (☐ changes to ☑).

⑫ Click OK.

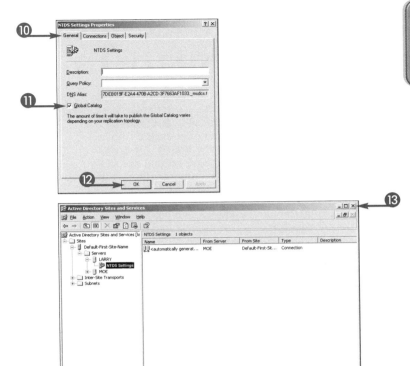

The changes are applied and the Global Catalog Server role is assigned.

⑬ Close the Active Directory Sites and Services snap-in.

Is the global catalog server automatically created on the first domain controller in the first domain along with the rest of the flexible operations masters?

▼ Yes. When you create the first domain tree, you also create the first forest, even if you create no other domains. You can refer to the global catalog server as another forest-wide operations master although it functions outside the official lists of those speciality types. While you can have any number of Global Catalog servers in a domain, Operation Masters are unique. When you create the first domain controller, the forest-wide roles do not play a significant role in managing resources until you create another domain tree.

If the global catalog server is automatically created on the first domain controller in a domain tree and domain forest, why is there a procedure to create more?

▼ You can use only one global catalog server in an Active Directory domain forest and have it work effectively, but you also have advantages when you create others. Your users must access a global catalog server in a separate forest to find resources in that domain forest. The Global Catalog servers in your own forest can only locate objects in your forest. You can create additional global catalog servers and place them closer to users who access other forests more often.

Register and Install a Schema Snap-In

Y ou can create a schema master in your Active Directory domain forest so that your schema master can create and manage all of the types of Active Directory objects and the attributes of each of those objects. Your schema master controls the specific types and descriptions of each Active Directory object so that every domain controller in the forest uses the same descriptors to identify the same objects.

The Active Directory schema master you create comes with a built-in set of schemas for all of the objects that you can use in an Active Directory environment. Types of Active

Directory objects the schema master knows are users, computers, groups, organizational units, printers, and so on. Your schema master uses attributes for users to describe their qualities. Examples of user attributes that the schema master uses include real name, logon name, address, telephone number, and e-mail address.

You can create a schema master through a different process than you create most other flexible operations masters and you cannot access the Schema Manager snap-in until the registration process is complete.

For more on Schema and Domain Naming Masters, see the section "Understanding Flexible Operations Masters."

Register and Install a Schema Snap-In

① Click Start.

② Click Command Prompt.

The Command Prompt shell appears.

③ Type **regsvr32 schmmgmt.dll** at the end of the command prompt line.

④ Press Enter.

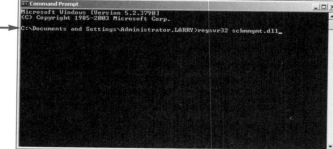

The RegSvr32 success window opens.

5 Click OK.

The DllRegister Server is registered.

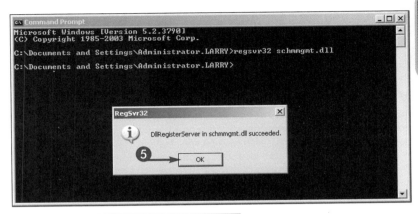

6 Click Start.

7 Click Run.

The Run dialog box appears.

8 Type **mmc**.

9 Click OK.

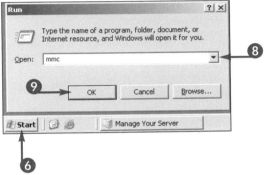

What does typing the command regsvr32 schmmgmt.dll at the command line do?

▼ You can only access the Active Directory schema records directly at the domain controller holding the schema master role. You can access the schema from other domain controllers if you register the schmmgmt.dll (dynamic link library) at the domain controller first. Once your domain controller has registered the DLL file, you can use it to manage the schema from a different location.

What does opening the MMC stand-alone console do as far as accessing the schema master.

▼ You can create an independent schema master snap-in at the Microsoft Management Console (MMC). This is added to the Administrative Tools menu, which you can access by clicking Start and then clicking All Programs. You can create a custom-made snap-in console file to manage the Active Directory schema rather than using any of the built-in snap-ins that Microsoft includes in the operating system interface. You can then create your own particular tool sets to accomplish specific tasks.

continued

Register and Install
a Schema Snap-In *(Continued)*

You can use the Microsoft Management Console (MMC) to add a wide variety of snap-ins to a console. This lets you construct a single console where you can access different types of snap-in tools and manage a number of different Active Directory features from a single location. You can also save a custom-made snap-in so you can use it repeatedly. You can access the snap-in in the Administrative Tools menu and you can delete the snap-in when you are through with it.

You can access a wide variety of Active Directory snap-ins in the Administrative Tools menu in every domain controller in the domain tree or forest. Although the schema master is

created automatically, you can only access the schema through the snap-in, even from directly on the schema master. You can view the schema by accessing the snap-in but you can only make modifications if you are a member of the Schema Admins group.

You can use the schema built in to a Windows 2000 Server domain controller when you upgrade it to Windows Server 2003 only if you use a command shell utility called `adprep`. See Chapter 6 for more on the use of the command shell.

The mmc stand-alone console appears.

⑩ Click File.

⑪ Click Add/Remove Snap-in.

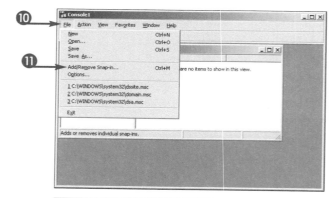

The Add/Remove Snap-in dialog box appears.

⑫ Click Add.

The Add Standalone Snap-in appears.

⑬ Click Active Directory Schema.

⑭ Click Add.

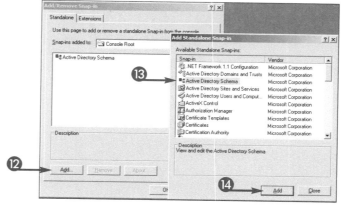

The Schema Snap-in appears in the Add/Remove snap-in.

⑮ Click File.

⑯ Click Save As.

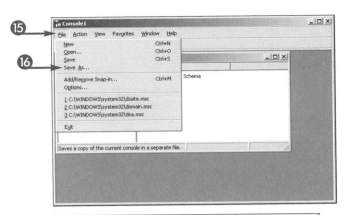

The Save As window appears.

⑰ Type a name for the Schema snap-in.

Note: *Although you can name the Schema snap-in anything, the default is schema.msc. See the second tip in this section for details.*

⑱ Click Save.

The schema snap-in is saved with the name that you typed.

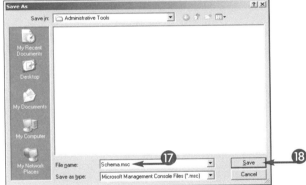

Can I add another stand-alone snap-in to the Schema snap-in console?

▼ You can add any number of stand-alone snap-ins to the console snap-in, but only if you want to accomplish a particular task. For example, when you open the Add Standalone Snap-in box, you can select from a wide variety and combination of different services. You can use them to create different consoles depending on the type of specific tasks you want to accomplish. If you only want to manage Active Directory Schema, you add the Schema snap-in to the stand-alone console.

How should I name the Schema snap-in console?

▼ The example for this section saved the Schema snap-in console as Schema.msc because it is a logical name for this function. However, you can name your console file anything you want as long as it is something you can remember. You can name the Schema snap-in George.msc, but using that name serves little purpose. Of course, your Schema snap-in must have the .msc extension. Even if you do not type it in the filename field, the extention is added if *.msc is in the filename field.

Create a Schema Attribute

You can create a schema attribute to add a specific quality to an Active Directory object in the schema, thereby customizing one or more descriptors of the object to fit organizational needs. For example, your company may use a nonstandard category to identify domain users, and locating important user-based resources is impossible without adding that category as a schema attribute. You can adjust the attributes of any preexisting schema object to meet business requirements.

You can create unique schema attributes for custom-made applications your company uses. You must prevent any schema attribute you make from conflicting with standard schema attributes for the same objects. You can plan your

schema creation in advance and test your changes to the schema attribute in a test lab to verify that it works properly before making the change in your production environment. Creating a schema object is a permanent action. Once a schema object is created it can only be deactivated, not deleted.

Although beyond the scope of this section, some of the things you can do with a schema attribute includes preventing some schema attributes from replicating in Active Directory to reduce replication traffic and free network bandwidth for more important traffic; or deciding that the last logon time of a user is not a critical piece of information and does not need to be replicated.

Create a Schema Attribute

① Click Start.

② Click All Programs.

③ Click Administrative Tools.

④ Click Schema.msc.

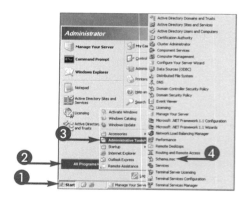

The Active Directory Schema snap-in appears.

⑤ Expand the Active Directory Schema.

⑥ Click Attributes.

The Attribute list appears.

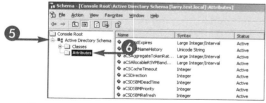

⑦ Click Action.

⑧ Click New.

⑨ Click Attribute.

A dialog box appears warning you that creating schema objects is a permanent operation.

⑩ Click Continue.

The Create New Attribute dialog box opens.

⑪ Type a name for the object.

⑫ Type a name for the LDAP display.

⑬ Type a unique X500 Object ID.

⑭ Type an optional description.

Note: *For more information concerning the code in steps 11 to 13, visit the Microsoft Web site at http://msdn. microsoft.com/library/default.asp? url=/library/en-us/netdir/ad/ characteristics_of_attributes.asp.*

⑮ Click here and select Access Point.

⑯ Click OK.

⑰ Click the Close button (☒).

The Microsoft Management Console appears.

⑱ Click Yes.

Your schema attribute is created.

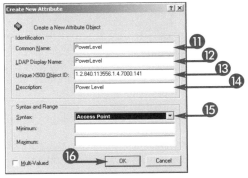

What is the relationship between the Common Name and the LDAP Display Name of a schema attribute?

▼ You can use the Common Name as the name the attribute will be most commonly called. The Common Name must be unique but it is closely tied to the LDAP Display Name. Programmers and system Administors use the LDAP Name when they create schema attributes at the program level. LDAP is an industry-standard protocol that allows users to query and update information in a directory service such as Active Directory. AD does not use the Common Name to locate information.

What is the Unique X500 Object ID?

▼ You use the X500 Object ID (OID) as a unique numerial identifier assigned to each schema attribute or class. The X500 standard was created by the International Standards Organization (ISO) to define a distributed directory service. The type of values you can use for the Object ID is defined by this set of standards. You can or cannot input the description or minimum and maximum string length values because they are optional. You must input the OID because it is a required field. You can input a value for the Object ID, but if there is a duplicate value in use in the schema, you cannot create the attribute.

Create a
Schema Class

You can create a schema class in order to create a brand-new Active Directory object. If your company needs an object or objects that are not included in the schema, you can create new objects instead of taking a preexisting schema object and inserting new attributes. You can create a new schema object, for example, if your company programmer develops a unique proprietary application used only by your business.

You can create a schema class just like you create a schema attribute. For more information on creating a schema attribute, see the previous section. A schema class is a collection of attributes that make up the whole, single

Active Directory object type. A user is considered a schema class. You can create many different attributes for a class object, but you must create the class before creating any attributes. See the section "Create a Schema Attribute" for more information.

Examples of schema class objects include users, computers, printers, servers, and applications. You can create a schema class object, but you still must create class attributes to define the object qualities. Otherwise, Active Directory cannot locate the new class object and users cannot search for and access the new object. Creating a schema object is a permanent action and cannot be reversed. You can deactivate a schema object but you cannot delete it.

Create a Schema Class

1 Click Start.

2 Click All Programs.

3 Click Administrative Tools.

4 Click Schema.msc.

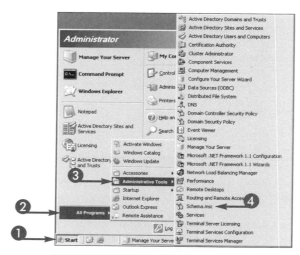

The Active Directory Schema snap-in appears.

5 Right-click the Classes folder.

6 Click New.

7 Click Class.

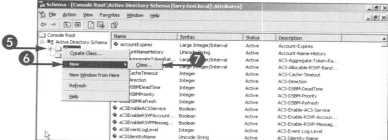

A dialog box appears warning you that creating schema objects is a permanent operation.

8 Click Continue.

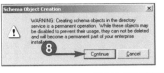

The Create New Schema Class dialog box appears.

9 Type a common name for the schema class.

10 Type an LDAP Display Name.

11 Type a unique X500 Object ID.

Note: For more on the code in steps 9 to 11, visit the Microsoft Web site at http://msdn.microsoft.com/ library/default.asp?url=/library/en-us/netdir/ad/ characteristics_or_object_classes.asp.

12 Type an optional description.

13 Click here and select Auxiliary.

14 Click Next.

The Create New Schema Class Mandatory/Optional dialog box appears.

15 Click Finish.

The new Schema class is created.

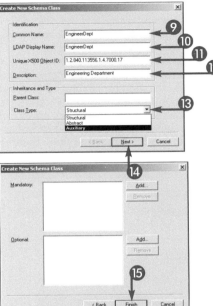

How do I obtain a Unique X500 Object ID to assign newly created Classes and Attributes?

▼ You do not receive a Unique X500 Object ID from your domain controller or schema master. The schema master does not randomly generate the Unique Object ID numbers. You request the OID numbers from the particular standards organization responsible for that particular class or attribute category. For example, the International Standards Organization (ISO) is responsible for issuing Unique X500 Object ID numbers. You can contact other similar organizations such as the International Telecommunications Union for id numbers that they provide that are used by schema objects.

Why do I receive a warning message when I try to create a schema class in the Active Directory Schema Snap-in?

▼ You cannot destroy or delete a schema class or attribute. Once you create a schema object, you can never delete the object. Doing so causes the schema and the schema master to become unstable and even inoperable. You must plan how you create a new schema class and determine if it causes any conflicts in Active Directory and is detrimental rather than beneficial to your domain. Creating and modifying the schema or schema object is an extremely complex task and should only be attempted by a member of the Schema Admins group. For more information you can download a white paper on schema modification by going to www.microsoft.com/downloads/details.aspx ?familyid=d1de764c-8e26-455f-bee5-34fb1ca9f2c4 &displylang=en.

Deactivate a Schema Object

You can deactivate a schema object if you generate errors while creating the object. Errors that result in a problem in Active Directory may require that you undo your mistake, but you can only do this to a degree. You cannot delete a schema object from the schema master without causing Active Directory to become unstable and unreliable. You can only deactivate the schema object. You cannot deactivate schema objects on schema masters that utilize any other operating system except Windows Server 2003. You can only reinstall the server operating system and domain controller where the schema master resided.

When you deactivate a schema object, the object becomes inert, having no impact on the system, but is still present in the schema. You can create or change a simple schema object in the schema snap-in and make more complicated changes involving the schema with scripts using Microsoft Visual Basic. You can create an object such as a particular proprietary application program, but if that program becomes outdated or obsolete, you can only modify it or deactivate it.

Deactivate a Schema Object

1. Click Start.
2. Click All Programs.
3. Click Administrative Tools.
4. Click Schema.msc.

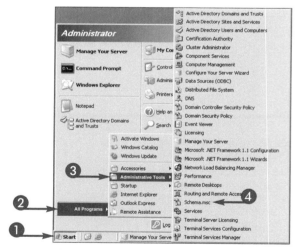

The Active Directory Schema snap-in opens.

5. Expand Classes.
6. Scroll to the specific class.

⑦ Right-click the class.

⑧ Click Properties.

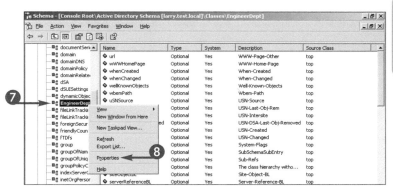

The class you want appears.

⑨ Click the General tab.

⑩ Click the Class is active option to deselect it
(☑ changes to ☐).

A dialog box appears warning you that you
will not be able to make any further
changes to the schema object if you make
it defunct.

⑪ Click Yes.

⑫ Click OK.

The schema object becomes deactivated.

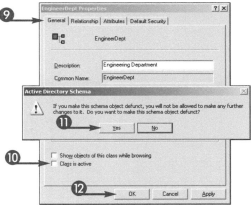

Can I deactivate a class and later reactivate it?

▼ No. You cannot reactivate a class once you have
deactivated it. You receive a warning just before you
apply the change to deactivate the class or make it
defunct that the change is irreversible. You should
only deactivate a schema object if you are sure you
will never need that object in your Active Directory
structure again. Another reason to deactiveate a
schema class is if the object is causing instability to
your Active Directory domain tree or forest and you
cannot correct it any other way.

Is there any way at all to delete a schema object?

▼ You can only delete a schema object in an Active
Directory domain tree or forest by completely
reinstalling Active Directory. At the very least, you
must demote the domain controller using the
FSMO schema master role to a member server using
the dcpromo command. Then you can either
reinstall Active Directory on that server by using
dcpromo again to promote it to a domain controller
or assign the schema master FSMO role to another
operational domain controller.

Transfer a Domain Naming Master

You can transfer the domain naming master to another Windows Server 2003 domain controller. You generally do this to assign the role to a more powerful server and to make sure this role is on the same domain controller as the global catalog server. Microsoft recommends that you install the domain naming master role on or transfer it to the same domain controller where the global catalog server resides. When you place both the Domain Naming Master and the Global Catalog server on the same domain controller, they both have immediate

access to the database necessary for them to locate objects in other domains in the forest. For more on global catalog servers, see the section "Designate a Global Catalog Server."

When you make the first domain controller in a new domain, you create all of the FSMO roles on the first domain controller. When you create a larger domain tree and forest, you can move the flexible operations master roles to domains and networks where you are more likely to access them. In addition, you can place the roles on or near other domain controllers that need access to the other roles.

Transfer a Domain Naming Master

① Click Start.

② Click Administrative Tools.

③ Click Active Directory Domains and Trusts.

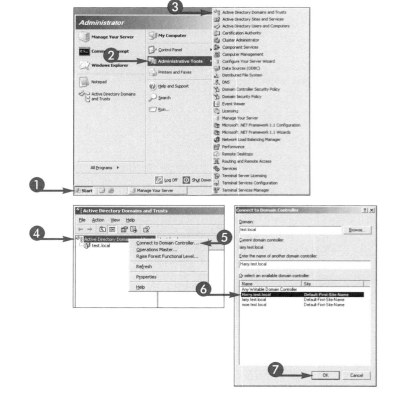

The Active Directory Domains and Trust snap-in appears.

④ Right-click the Active Directory Domains and Trusts folder.

⑤ Click Connect to Domain Controller.

The Connect to Domain Controller dialog box appears.

⑥ Click the domain controller name that you want to make the domain naming master.

⑦ Click OK.

The Connect to Domain Controller dialog box closes.

⑧ Right-click the Active Directory Domains and Trusts folder.

⑨ Click Operations Master.

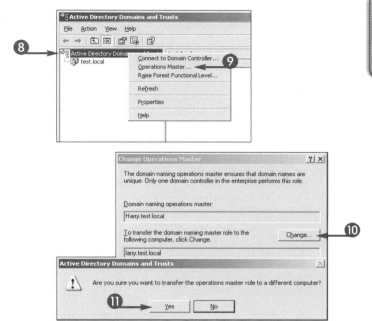

The Change Operations Master dialog box appears.

⑩ Click Change.

A warning box appears asking if you are sure you want to transfer the role to a different computer.

⑪ Click Yes.

A box appears confirming a successful transfer.

⑫ Click OK.

The domain naming master role now resides on another domain controller.

What happens if I do not place the domain naming master on the same domain controller as the global catalog server?

▼ You can avoid noticable delays on your network when you create a new domain in the Active Directory forest if you place these two FSMO roles on the same domain controller. If your network connection breaks down and the domain naming master and the global catalog server cannot communicate with each other, you cannot create any new domains. In this event, you either need to move both roles to the same domain controller or repair the network connection.

Why does a warning box appear when I am about to transfer the domain naming master from one domain controller in the forest to another?

▼ Although you can place your flexible operations master domain controllers anywhere in your domain forest, where you place them has a tremendous impact on whether the Active Directory operates correctly. You can use the opportunity the warning gives you to verify that the domain controller you chose to receive the domain naming master role is the correct one for your domain forest. You can also transfer this role when you are at another domain controller; right-click AD Domains and Trusts and select Connect to Domain Controller. Then browse to the DC where you want to transfer the role.

Transfer a PDC Emulator

You can transfer the PDC emulator operations master to place this particularly important FSMO role near any Windows NT PDC servers in your Active Directory domain tree. Doing so enables any Windows NT client computers to log on to the domain. You cannot have any Windows NT PDC servers on your Windows Server 2003 domain, so the PDC emulator provides the same service in a mixed NT and 2003 domain environment. Your NT Workstation clients cannot log on to the domain or change their passwords without access to NT BDC and an NT PDC server.

You must also place one PDC emulator in the domain so that it is equally accessible to all the other domain controllers in the domain tree. The PDC emulator provides timekeeping services for all domain controllers; your server loses time synchronization necessary for numerous Active Directory tasks if the PDC emulator is offline or out of reach. You can place several PDC emulators in key locations in your domain for load balancing and failover protection.

You transfer the PDC emulator role using the same process as you do when you transfer the infrastructure master and the RID master roles.

Transfer a PDC Emulator

① Click Start.

② Click Administrative Tools.

③ Click Active Directory Users and Computers.

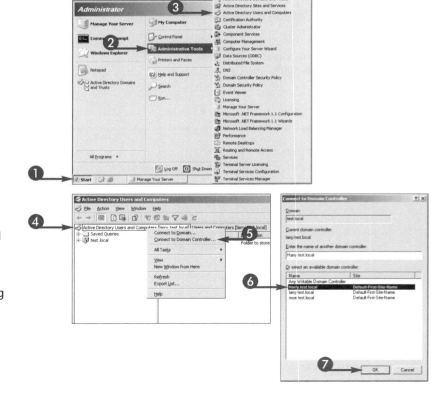

The Active Directory Users and Computers snap-in appears.

④ Right-click the Active Directory Users and Computers folder.

⑤ Click Connect to Domain Controller.

The Connect to Domain Controller dialog box appears.

⑥ Click the domain controller name to which you want to transfer the role.

⑦ Click OK.

The Connect to Domain Controller dialog box closes.

⑧ Right-click the domain name.

⑨ Click Operations Masters.

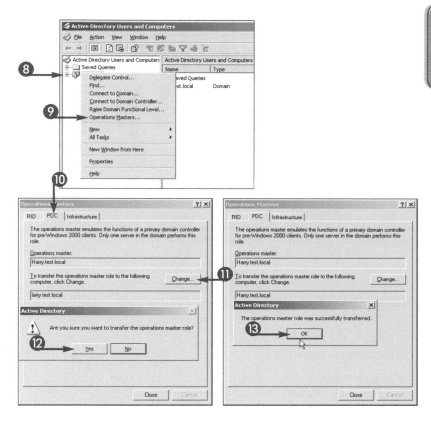

The Operations Masters Properties box appears.

⑩ Click the PDC tab.

⑪ Click Change.

A warning box appears asking if you want to transfer the operations master role.

⑫ Click Yes.

An Active Directory box opens verifying that the role transfer was successful.

⑬ Click OK.

You have successfully transferred the PDC emulator role to another domain controller.

Why do I use Active Directory Domains and Trusts to transfer the domain naming master and use Active Directory Users and Computers to transfer the PDC emulator?

▼ You transfer domain naming master with Active Directory Domains and Trusts because this flexible operations master role serves all the domain trees in the forest. The PDC emulator is a domain-wide role. The configuration settings for all domain-wide operations masters are controlled by the Active Directory Users and Computers snap-in, so while the process you use in the transfer seems the same, the scope is different.

When I transfer a domain-wide flexible operations master role, is the only difference in transferring a particular role just the tab I choose in the Operations Masters properties box?

▼ Yes. You can transfer all three of the domain-wide roles — PDC emulator, relative ID master, and infrastructure master — in the same properties box. Each of the domain-wide FSMO roles is very different from each other, but the transfer process is the same because the scope of services they provide is the same. By contrast, the two forest-wide flexible operations masters are transferred by two different processes.

Find FSMO Roles with the ntdsutil Command Line Tool

You can use the `ntdsutil` command-line tool to find which domain controllers contain which FSMO roles. This allows you to properly place your special domain controller roles in your domain tree and forest. In addition, you must know exactly which domain controllers hold which particular roles. You can only determine which domain controllers hold which roles using the `ntdsutil` command line interface tool.

The `ntdsutil` command-line tool performs a wide variety of functions, as you can see in other sections of this chapter. You can use it as a management tool in Active

Directory to perform several maintenance operations including information analysis, database integrity checks, and soft recovery of the Active Directory database. Although the example in this section finds FSMO roles, you can determine where your FSMO domain controllers are in the domain, as shown in the section "Transfer a Domain Naming Master." You can also use the `ntdsutil` utility to locate all the FSMO roles when you have an existing domain tree that you have created but never documented.

Find FSMO Roles with the ntdsutil Command-Line Tool

① Click Start.

② Click Command Prompt.

The Command Prompt shell appears.

③ At the end of the prompt command line, type **ntdsutil**.

④ Press Enter.

The ntdsutil prompt appears.

⑤ Type **roles**.

⑥ Press Enter.

The fsmo maintenance prompt appears.

7 Type **connection**.

8 Press Enter.

```
Command Prompt - ntdsutil
Microsoft Windows [Version 5.2.3790]
(C) Copyright 1985-2003 Microsoft Corp.

C:\Documents and Settings\Administrator.TEST>ntdsutil
ntdsutil: roles
fsmo maintenance: connection        7
```

The server connections prompt appears.

9 Type **connect to server**, and then type the name of the server you are on.

10 Press Enter.

```
Command Prompt - ntdsutil
Microsoft Windows [Version 5.2.3790]
(C) Copyright 1985-2003 Microsoft Corp.

C:\Documents and Settings\Administrator.TEST>ntdsutil
ntdsutil: roles
fsmo maintenance: connection
server connections: connect to server harry       9
```

A message appears stating that you are binding to the named server.

11 Type **quit.**

Note: Once you connect with the target server, you must type quit to return to the fsmo maintenance prompt where you will continue the task.

12 Press Enter.

```
Command Prompt - ntdsutil
Microsoft Windows [Version 5.2.3790]
(C) Copyright 1985-2003 Microsoft Corp.

C:\Documents and Settings\Administrator.TEST>ntdsutil
ntdsutil: roles
fsmo maintenance: connection
server connections: connect to server harry
Binding to harry ...
Connected to harry using cred 11 ials of locally logged on user.
server connections: quit       11
```

Do I have to go to each domain controller in the domain tree or forest and issue the ntdsutil command on each physical machine to find out the FSMO roles they hold?

▼ No. You can use the connections command prompt and type **connect to server** and use the server name of whatever server in the domain tree or domain forest you want to query about FSMO roles. You can bind with domain controllers in your root domain, any child domain, and any other domain in the forest as long as you have trust relationships established. For more on trust relationships, see Chapter 1.

Can I use ntdsutil to perform any other type of FSMO role change or transfer?

▼ Yes. You can seize a flexible operations master role as well as transfer it. You can use ntdsutil to seize a role when the domain controller using the particular role suffers a catastrophic failure and does not recover. The server is not online so you cannot contact it to transfer the role. You can seize the role and enable another domain controller to take over the original role, but the first FSMO must never come online and try to resume the role.

continued

Find FSMO Roles with the ntdsutil Command Line Tool *(Continued)*

When you use the `ntdsutil` command-line utility, you can also use a number of other subcommands that allow you to perform detailed configuration tasks in Active Directory from the command shell. You can use the connections subcommand under FSMO maintenance to connect to any other specific domain controller from your current location. You can use the select operation target subcommand to choose a site, server, domain, or role on which to focus and to which you can apply other commands. You can also use FSMO maintenance to either transfer or seize an FSMO role.

You can use these subcommands like different branches off of the main command path. You must type **quit** after you finish with a particular command path so that you can begin to use another path. This is why you must quit the connections command path after connecting to a particular server, for example, before you can select an operation target or use any of the other subcommands.

You can type a wide variety of other commands besides roles under `ntdsutil` to achieve a number of other tasks and each of the commands under `ntdsutil` lets you manage different aspects of Active Directory.

Find FSMO Roles with the ntdsutil Command-Line Tool *(continued)*

The fsmo maintenance prompt appears.

⑬ Type **select operation target**.

⑭ Press Enter.

The select operation target prompt appears.

⑮ Type **list roles for connected server**.

⑯ Press Enter.

A list of all the fsmo roles held by this server appears.

```
Command Prompt - ntdsutil                                              _ | □ | ×
Microsoft Windows [Version 5.2.3790]
(C) Copyright 1985-2003 Microsoft Corp.

C:\Documents and Settings\Administrator.TEST>ntdsutil
ntdsutil: roles
fsmo maintenance: connection
server connections: connect to server harry
Binding to harry ...
Connected to harry using credentials of locally logged on user.
server connections: quit
fsmo maintenance: select operation target
select operation target: list roles for connected server
Server "harry" knows about 5 roles
Schema - CN=NTDS Settings,CN=LARRY,CN=Servers,CN=Default-First-Site-Name,CN=Site
s,CN=Configuration,DC=test,DC=local
Domain - CN=NTDS Settings,CN=LARRY,CN=Servers,CN=Default-First-Site-Name,CN=Site
s,CN=Configuration,DC=test,DC=local
PDC - CN=NTDS Settings,CN=HARRY,CN=Servers,CN=Default-First-Site-Name,CN=Sites,C
N=Configuration,DC=test,DC=local
RID - CN=NTDS Settings,CN=HARRY,CN=Servers,CN=Default-First-Site-Name,CN=Sites,C
N=Configuration,DC=test,DC=local
Infrastructure - CN=NTDS Settings,CN=LARRY,CN=Servers,CN=Default-First-Site-Name
,CN=Sites,CN=Configuration,DC=test,DC=local
select operation target: _
```

⑰ Type **quit** at the select operation prompt.

⑱ Type **quit** at the fsmo maintenance prompt.

⑲ Type **quit** at the ntdsutil prompt.

A message appears saying that you are disconnecting from the server.

⑳ Type **exit**.

㉑ Press Enter to close the command emulator.

```
Command Prompt                                                        _ | □ | ×
ntdsutil: roles
fsmo maintenance: connection
server connections: connect to server harry
Binding to harry ...
Connected to harry using credentials of locally logged on user.
server connections: quit
fsmo maintenance: select operation target
select operation target: list roles for connected server
Server "harry" knows about 5 roles
Schema - CN=NTDS Settings,CN=LARRY,CN=Servers,CN=Default-First-Site-Name,CN=Site
s,CN=Configuration,DC=test,DC=local
Domain - CN=NTDS Settings,CN=LARRY,CN=Servers,CN=Default-First-Site-Name,CN=Site
s,CN=Configuration,DC=test,DC=local
PDC - CN=NTDS Settings,CN=HARRY,CN=Servers,CN=Default-First-Site-Name,CN=Sites,C
N=Configuration,DC=test,DC=local
RID - CN=NTDS Settings,CN=HARRY,CN=Servers,CN=Default-First-Site-Name,CN=Sites,C
N=Configuration,DC=test,DC=local
Infrastructure - CN=NTDS Settings,CN=LARRY,CN=Servers,CN=Default-First-Site-Name
,CN=Sites,CN=Configuration,DC=test,DC=local
select operation target: quit         ⑱
fsmo maintenance: quit
ntdsutil: quit
Disconnecting from harry...
                                              ⑳
C:\Documents and Settings\Administrator.TEST>
```

⑰ ⑲

After I connect to the server I am on, why do I type quit **rather than stay connected and continue to query the server about the fsmo roles it holds?**

▼ You must type **quit** to exit the connection prompt and return to the fsmo maintenance prompt. You remain connected to the server, but must access another prompt so you can continue your task. You use the quit command only to quit that particular command prompt. You can issue subsequent commands to discover the FSMO roles the server holds; however, you can only issue them from that particular command prompt.

When I completed the FSMO query, why must I type quit **at each of the three command prompts before exiting the command-line emulator?**

▼ You must back out of each of the levels of the command path because you are still connected to the remote server. If you abruptly close the command-line window, the connection does not automatically terminate and the remote server is still in a hold state waiting for the next command query until it times out and severs the connection. If you abruptly close out of the command window, the connection will eventually time out.

Transfer an Infrastructure Master Using ntdsutil

You can use the command-line to transfer Flexible Single-Master Operations roles when the graphical user interface (GUI) is not available. This is particularly useful when you have no other method of creating an interface with the domain controller and Active Directory. Although you can use most of the Windows Server 2003 domain controller configuration wizards or other graphical tools most of the time, a malfunction of your domain controller can make it impossible to boot into the operating system and desktop. You can still access the operating system through a command-line interface, and you can still issue commands such as transferring an operations master or many other types of commands.

You can take advantage of the command line if you prefer to work with your domain controllers at the command shell. While working at the command line, you must remember more specific commands, but you also can work faster and you can progress through the necessary steps more quickly than following a wizard.

You also have the advantage of transferring all five FSMO roles using the same command set. Because you can transfer all five FSMO roles in the same set, the example in this section only uses the infrastructure master transfer.

transfer an infrastructure master using ntdsutil

① Click Start.

② Click Command Prompt.

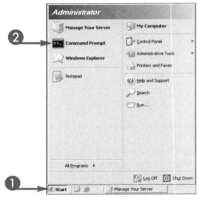

A command-line emulator appears.

③ Type **ntdsutil**.

④ Press Enter.

The ntdsutil prompt appears.

⑤ Type **roles**.

⑥ Press Enter.

The fsmo maintenance prompt appears.

7 Type **connection**.

8 Press Enter.

The server connections prompt appears.

9 Type **connect to server** and then type a server name.

10 Press Enter.

ntdsutil seems like a very powerful tool. How can I get a list of what each of the command prompts that ntdsutil performs?

▼ You can open a command-line interface on a domain controller and type **ntdsutil** to get the ntdsutil prompt. You can then type **help** or **"?"**. A list of the commands available under that utility appears. To find out options available under subcommands, at the ntdsutil prompt type a subcommand, for example **fsmo maintenance** to get to that particular prompt. Then type **help** or **"?"** again.

Using the connections command, can I connect to any other domain entities besides a specific domain controller?

▼ At the server connections prompt you can type **connect to domain**, then type the domain name, and press Enter. You will receive a message stating that you are binding to a domain controller at that domain. Instead of just the name of the domain controller appearing, you see the following syntax:\\server.domain.com. You then connect to whatever server or computer you specified in your syntax string. You may be asked for a username and password if you are not already logged on with sufficient credentials to access that device.

continued

Transfer an Infrastructure Master Using ntdsutil *(Continued)*

Yஅou can transfer a forest-wide flexible operations master role from the command line as easily as you can transfer a domain-wide FSMO role. You can use the same command sets because at the command shell, the interface is exactly the same. Regardless of the scope at which you are operating — as long as you have a trust relationship with the other domain forest to which you connect — you can connect to the forest the way you can contact a domain controller in a child domain in your tree or a domain controller in the same domain.

You can work at the command-line interface and neither be aware of the different systems to which you can connect nor know the level of the command structure in which you are working. The command prompts change so you know in which command window you are operating. You can work in the GUI, and because you access each snap-in differently, you know where you are in the command structure.

You will see one difference in transferring a domain-wide and a forest-wide role in that a warning window appears asking you if you really want to transfer the infrastructure master.

Transfer an Infrastructure Master Using ntdsutil *(continued)*

The server connections prompt appears.

⑪ Type **quit**.

⑫ Press Enter.

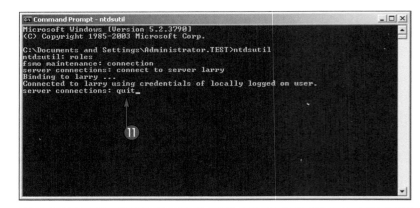

The fsmo maintenance prompt appears.

⑬ Type **transfer infrastructure master**.

⑭ Press Enter.

The Role Transfer Confirmation Dialog box appears asking if you want to complete the transfer.

⑮ Click Yes.

A list of fsmo roles known by the server appears showing the transfer.

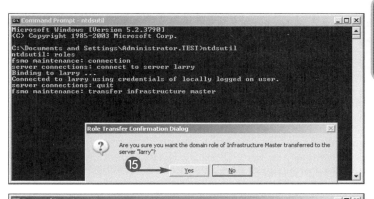

⑯ Type **quit** at the fsmo maintenance prompt.

⑰ Press Enter.

⑱ Type **quit** at the ntdsutil prompt.

⑲ Press Enter.

⑳ Type **exit**.

㉑ Press Enter.

The command-line emulator closes.

How can I be sure that I have really transferred the infrastructure master role or any other role from the command line?

▼ You can check the infrastructure master transfer only by using ntdsutil, as you can see in the section "Transfer a PDC Emulator." You can transfer the infrastructure master at the command line or in the GUI. You can check the GUI to verify the transfer of the infrastructure master by opening the Domains and Trusts snap-in, right-clicking Domains and Trusts, and clicking Operations Master.

Can I place the infrastructure master on a domain controller that holds another FSMO role?

▼ You can physically transfer more than one FSMO role onto a single domain controller, but Microsoft recommends that you do not place the infrastructure master on the same domain controller as the global catalog server. You may receive numerous errors in Event Viewer if you place both of these roles together. When you add a new domain, the infrastructure master writes that information to its database differently than the global catalog server does. If both roles are on the same server, errors can occur to their database records.

Understanding Active Directory Sites and Services

You use sites to provide a single, physical location for frequent replication of the Active Directory database within the site and to promote quicker logons and faster access to resources without slowing down throughput on the network. A *site*, which is the basic physical container in Active Directory, is a location containing a grouping of domain controllers, member servers, client computers, and other well-connected networked devices. You must have at least one site in your domain structure for your Active Directory domain to function. Each of the sections in this chapter describes an important step in the new site configuration process; Active Directory manages replication of site information.

When you create the first domain controller in the first domain tree and forest, the first default site is also automatically created. You can construct three types of relationships, or models between sites and domains: single site/single domain, multiple sites/single domain, and multiple sites/multiple domains.

A well-connected *network* consists of one or more subnets connected on a fast, reliable network. This means that networked devices within a site are all connected on a local area network (LAN). By comparison, wide area networks (WANs) are slower, less reliable, and cannot connect to different parts of a site by a WAN link. For this reason, a site is usually a single location such as an office building, factory complex, or campus.

Physical Networking of a Site

A site consists of a single or multiple subnets. A *subnet* is a division or subdivision of a network IP addressing scheme using default or custom-made subnet masks. Each subnet comprises an individual network, and traffic between networks can only be exchanged through a router. You can create any number of individual networks connected by routers and still have them make up a single site. To take full advantage of a site topology, you place a variety of Flexible Single-Master Operations (FSMO) roles in your site. You can read more about FSMO server roles in Chapter 3. Although, the first domain controller in a domain is a global catalog server by default, you can place one in your site to speed up user requests for information about other domain objects in the forest.

Single Site and Single Domain

A single site/single domain is a situation in which both the domain and the site are contained in a single location. A single domain can encompass offices in an entire nation or even multinational offices around the globe. You can use the single site/single domain option when first building an Active Directory business domain in a single location. You can use this model when your domain encompasses a single physical location, which also functions as a single site.

Multiple Sites and Single Domain

You use the multiple sites/single domain scenario, which is the most popular site/domain topology, when you run a single Active Directory business domain in a company operating in multiple locations. Each location exists as a site, and WAN links connect the multiple sites. An example of this is Microsoft.com, which is a single domain entity operating multiple sites around the globe.

Multiple Sites and Multiple Domains

You use the multiple sites/multiple domains model when operating two or more business entities. These business entities should each require its own Active Directory domain namespace and utilize multiple physical sites in your business infrastructure. You commonly use this scenario when one company has acquired other companies and you have determined it is in your best interest to allow each acquired company to use its own domain namespace. An example of this model is cisco.com and linksys.com; owned by Cisco, both share physical and domain resources while operating separate domain namespaces.

SITE 1
domain.com
willis.local

SITE 2
domain.com

SITE 3
willis.local

Replication and Network Bandwidth

Domain controllers within a single site replicate more frequently at high rates of speed and replicate less frequently at slower speeds between different sites. *Replication* is the process used in Active Directory to distribute any changes in the AD database to all Domain Controllers so that they all have identical copies of the database. Replication allows you to contact any DC in your domain and have identical access to domain resources. For this reason, you configure the replication frequency and length differently between sites than within sites.

Within a site, you can have domain controllers replicate often and regularly during a 24-hour cycle because modern LAN links operate at least at 100 mbp/sec. You do not notice a slowdown on your local network during Intrasite Active Directory replication between sites. You configure Active Directory replication between sites less frequently and only during hours when business is not being conducted. You have a latency period in updating Active Directory records from other sites in the domain but this is a trade-off because frequent replication over a slow WAN link significantly impairs Active Directory queries to other sites during normal operating hours. Active Directory replication between sites is also compressed to conserve WAN bandwidth and improve data transfer throughput.

SITE 1

SITE 2

Intersite Replication Cost

You can assign a cost to a WAN link between two or more sites based on the speed and reliability of the link. This is not a monetary cost, but rather your assessment of how dependable the link is. You assign a lower cost value to a WAN link if it is faster and more reliable. Domain Controllers use more reliable links first when replicating the AD database. For example, you expect a lower cost for a highly reliable T3 link, and a higher cost for an unreliable link using a 56k modem over standard phone lines. For more on changing the replication cost of a WAN link, see the section "Configure a Site Link."

Create a New Site

The advantage of creating a new site is that you can ensure quick access to Active Directory resources and services to users at a new physical location in your business. When you create the first domain controller in the first domain tree and forest, the first default site is called Default-First-Site-Name and the first domain controller is placed in it. You can rename your first default site to identify the site more accurately, for example Indianapolis or Downtown, but you do not have to change the name.

All domain controllers created either in the root domain or in child domains are automatically placed in Default-First-Site-Domain, regardless of where they are physically located. Although Active Directory automatically created your first default site, you must create any additional sites manually.

Any site you create is considered just an object in the Active Directory database. Once you create a site, resources at the new site are not available to other sites in the domain tree or forest until you configure the information about the creation of the new site and it is replicated to domain controllers throughout the domain infrastructure. Each of the sections in this chapter describes an important step in the new site configuration process; Active Directory manages replication of site information.

Create a New Site

1. Click Start.
2. Click Administrative Tools.
3. Click Active Directory Sites and Services.

The Active Directory Sites and Services snap-in appears.

4. Right-click the Sites folder.
5. Click New.
6. Click Site.

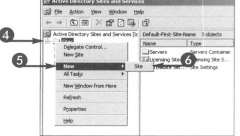

The New Object – Site dialog box appears.

⑦ Click DEFAULTIPSITELINK.

⑧ Type the site name in the Name field.

⑨ Click OK.

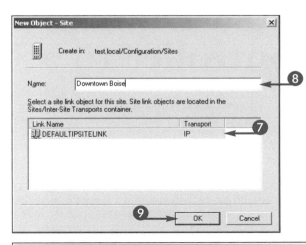

An Active Directory notification appears.

⑩ Click OK.

You have created a new site.

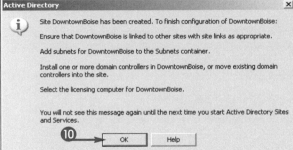

Are site names always one word long?

▼ Yes. Unlike a filename in a Word document, for example, you cannot create a long site name using spaces between words. A site name cannot contain spaces or special characters such as { | } ~ [ ] ' : ; < = > ? @ ! " # $ % ^ & ` ( ) + \ / , * . For sites requiring names of more than one word, type the two words without spaces.

Do I have to select the DEFAULTSITELINK for IP transport between sites when I create a new site?

▼ No, but you must select a site link before you can create a new site. DEFAULTSITELINK is created automatically when the first domain tree is created and all sites are connected by this default link. You can create new site links manually.

How do I move a computer from one Active Directory Site to another?

▼ You must physically move the computer to the new site. Then you move the computer in Active Directory from one site to another inside the Move Server box in the Active Directory Sites and Services snap-in. In the snap-in, expand the site where the computer is currently. Right-click the computer name and click Move Server. In the Move Server box, click the site name where you want to put the computer then click OK.

Add a Domain Controller to a New Site

When you add a domain controller to a new site, you enable your users at the site to log on to the domain much faster. In addition, users can more quickly locate and access resources within the site and at other sites in the Active Directory domain tree and forest. You do not have to add a domain controller to a site — you can create a site that functions without a domain controller or even without a member server. However, your users may experience much slower access to most resources because users will always be making Active Directory queries over a slow WAN link to domain controllers and member servers at other locations.

You can add at least one domain controller to a site and probably more depending on the size of the site and how many users and resources your site contains. Also, if you run a multiple-domain Active Directory infrastructure, you can make one domain controller in the site a global catalog server or enable universal group caching so your users do not have to connect to a global catalog server to authenticate to the domain.

Add a Domain Controller to a New Site

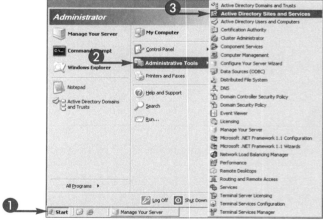

1 Click Start.

2 Click Administrative Tools.

3 Click Active Directory Sites and Services.

The Active Directory Sites and Services snap-in appears.

4 Expand Sites.

5 Expand Default-First-Site-Name.

6 Expand Servers.

7 Right-click the server you want to move.

8 Click Move.

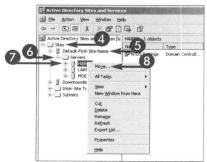

The Move Server dialog box appears.

9 Click the site where you want to place your server.

10 Click OK.

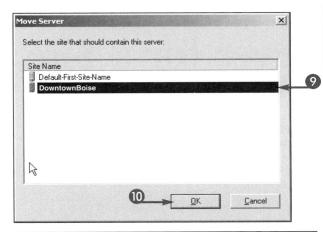

You have moved your server to the new site.

Are all Domain Controllers that you move to a new site located in Default-First-Site-Name?

▼ Only if the Default-First-Site-Name is the only site in existence when you first created the domain controller. When you have already created and configured more than one site, a new domain controller is automatically placed in the site that matches the subnet for which you have configured it. Also, you can move a domain controller from any one site to any other site if you have created multiple sites and have already populated them with Domain Controllers. You can do this for load balancing in the event that user resource requests are not being managed adequately.

Should I physically place the domain controller at the site location before moving it in the Active Directory Sites and Services snap-in?

▼ You can wait until after you move the domain controller in Active Directory before you move it physically to the new site. Although you can choose either option, your move location process is not complete until after you install the domain controller at the new location and connected it to your network. You must make the move both in Active Directory and physically within a short time span to avoid an inaccurate record of the Domain Controller location in Active Directory database.

Choose a Licensing Server for a Site

You must add a licensing server to each of the sites you create in Active Directory Sites and Services. A *licensing server* adds, deletes, and changes licensing options at your site and replicates licensing information to other licensing servers at other sites. The licensing server tracks licenses at each site, verifying that you own the appropriate number of licenses for each connection configured to your servers at each site you administer.

Your site cannot collect licensing information from a site until you designate a licensing server at your new site. You do not have to make your licensing server a domain

controller but it can be. You can make a licensing server on a member server in the Active Directory domain.

You must purchase licenses from Microsoft to legally allow the use of your Windows Server 2003 servers by the number of users or devices that connect to each server. By default, Windows Server 2003 comes with five licenses either per user or per device as part of the purchase price of the operating system. This means that a total of five users or devices are allowed to connect with your Windows Server 2003 server at any one time.

Choose a Licensing Server for a Site

① Click Start.

② Click Administrative Tools.

③ Click Active Directory Sites and Services.

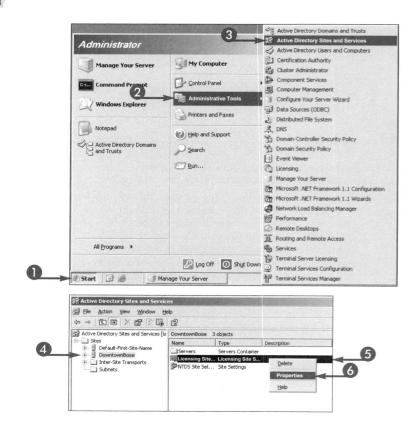

The Active Directory Sites and Services snap-in appears.

④ Click the new site.

⑤ Right-click Licensing Site Settings.

⑥ Click Properties.

The Licensing Site Settings Properties dialog box opens.

⑦ Click the Licensing Settings tab.

⑧ Click Change.

The Select Computer dialog box opens.

⑨ In the Enter the object name to select (examples): field, type the server name.

⑩ Click Check Names.

⑪ Click OK.

- The new licensing server is listed in the Licensing Site Settings Properties dialog box.

⑫ Click OK.

Your settings are applied.

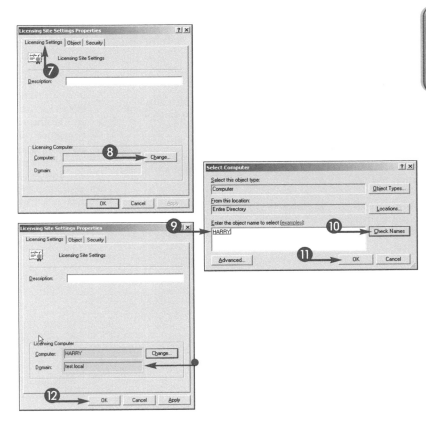

Is the first domain controller created in the first default site automatically listed as the licensing server for that site?

▼ No. You can follow steps 1 to 6 in this section to open the Licensing Site Setting Properties dialog box and see that there are not listings in the Licensing Computer section. You must use the same set of steps to select a domain controller or member server for the first default site just as you must for any site you create. The Licensing Server collects data within the site that is used by the Windows Server 2003 administration tool. You must add licenses directly to the licensing server for the site.

In the Select Computer dialog box, do you always select a computer from the Entire Directory?

▼ You can, but it is not required. If you choose not to select the licensing server from the Entire Directory, click Locations and select a more specific location. You can make your selection from a specific domain or even from the Domain Controllers folder. After you change Active Directory containers, you can continue with steps presented in this section.

Assign a Subnet to a Site

You must assign one or more subnets to a site in order for it to function. If you do not assign your site at least one subnet, your member servers and domain controllers cannot communicate over the LAN link within the site or over the WAN link between sites. Your site remains disconnected from the rest of the Active Directory domain tree and forest infrastructure.

You must configure all network devices to have a unique Internet Protocol (IP) address and either a default or custom subnet mask in order to communicate with other devices

on your network. Your Active Directory network infrastructure does not automatically detect your IP network addressing scheme or network topology. You must configure the subnet or subnets for each site to mirror your actual physical network structure. Once you configure your site with a subnet, any member server or domain controller you subsequently create with an IP addressing scheme matching one of your sites automatically moves to that site in Active Directory. You can then install that server in the physical location of that site.

Assign a Subnet to a Site

① Click Start.

② Click Administrative Tools.

③ Click Active Directory Sites and Services.

The Active Directory Sites and Services snap-in appears.

④ Right-click the Subnets folder.

⑤ Click New Subnet.

The New Object – Subnet dialog box appears.

⑥ Type the IP network address of your site.

Note: This address is not the IP address of any computer on the network, but rather the network address, which is created using trailing zero bits after the subnet mask.

⑦ Type the subnet mask for the network of your site.

⑧ Click the site name.

⑨ Click OK.

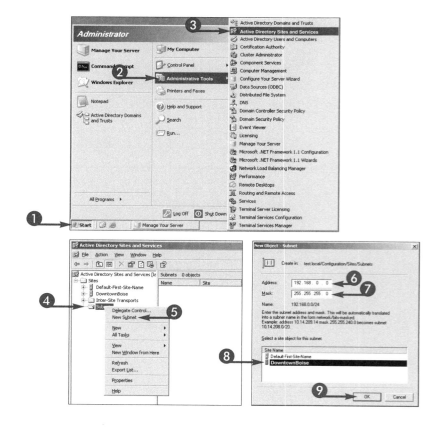

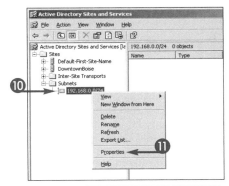

Your new subnet appears in the sidebar pane.

⑩ Right-click your subnet.

⑪ Click Properties.

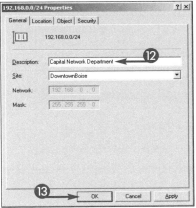

The subnet Properties dialog box appears.

⑫ In the Description field, type a name for your subnet.

⑬ Click OK.

Your new subnet is now assigned.

When you create more than one subnet for your site, do you have to populate all the subnets with servers and computers immediately after the subnet's creation?

▼ No. You can configure any number of subnets for your site even if you only currently use one subnet. You can anticipate the growth of your site by creating more subnets ahead of time and populating each subnet as your site grows. You must make sure that the overall IP addressing scheme of your network makes these subnets available and lets you reserve them for future use as your infrastructure grows.

Why is the subnet name not the same name as the site?

▼ You generally have numerous subnets in a single site. Each subnet represents a subnetwork at your location, with an individual office, team, or department using the subnetwork. Naming the subnet after the particular team or department using it allows you to easily identify it in the event that you need to locate it later. You can troubleshoot or change subnets more easily when you can locate them by name instead of by the subnet number.

Configure Site Links

reating a site link makes it possible for your site to communicate with other sites in the Active Directory domain forest. Without site links, your site becomes an isolated unit, only able to conduct Active Directory replication within the boundaries of that site.

You can lease WAN links from your local telco to physically connect one site to another. All of your network devices at one site can then successfully communicate with other sites and with the rest of the world over the Internet. A site link provides a logical pathway in Active Directory and allows the Active Directory database to replicate across the site link using the WAN.

You can configure a site link to use one of two intersite transport protocols. The most often used protocol is remote procedure call (RPC) over IP. This is the default protocol and is the only one of the two protocols that allows Active Directory replication within a single domain. The other protocol is Simple Mail Transport Protocol (SMTP). You configure SMTP as your intersite transport protocol when you are using a slow and unreliable WAN link between two sites. The most commonly used transfer protocol is RPC over IP.

Configure Site Links

1. Click Start.
2. Click Administrative Tools.
3. Click Active Directory Sites and Services.

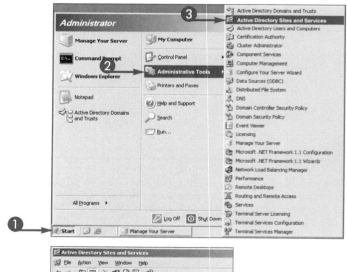

The Active Directory Sites and Services snap-in appears.

4. Expand the sites folder.
5. Expand the Inter-Site Transports folder.
6. Right-click IP.
7. Click New Site Link.

The New Object – Site Link dialog box appears.

8 Type the site link name.

9 Verify that the sites using this link appear in the Sites in this site link field.

10 Click OK.

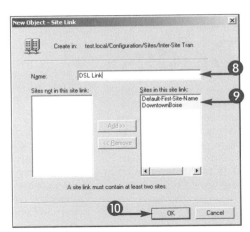

The New Object – Site Link dialog box closes.

11 Click IP.

● Your new site link appears in the main display pane.

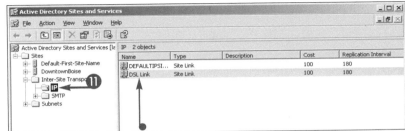

Are all available sites automatically placed in the "Sites in this site link" box in the Site Link Properties dialog box?

▼ No. Sites are automatically placed in the "Sites in this site link" box only if you previously constructed one or two sites. As you create more sites, they appear in the "Sites not in this site link" box. To add a site from that location to the "Sites in this site link" box, you can select the site name and click Add. To remove a site from the site link, you can select it and click Remove.

Can I configure any other site link features in the Site Link Properties dialog box?

▼ Yes. Two main features are cost and the replication schedule. *Cost* is reliability of the site link in terms of data rate and up time. You change cost if the reliability of the link physically changes due to an upgrade. The *replication schedule* is the frequency and duration at when AD replication occurs. By default, the cost is set at 100 and the Intersite replication schedule at every 180 minutes, but you can change both values. For more replication cost, see the section "Understanding Active Directory Sites and Services." For more on the Intersite replication schedule, see the section "Configure Intersite Replication."

Configure a Site Link Bridge

When you create and configure a site link bridge, you can collect a group of site links together that do not otherwise communicate with each other. You can bridge these otherwise separated Site Links and allow Active Directory replication to occur across the links. Without site link bridging, not all domain controllers can replicate their Active Directory data to the complete domain tree and forest. By default, site links are bridged automatically, but you can disable automatic site link bridging and create your own site link bridges. You must create a site link bridge when parts of your network are

separated. Separation causes include a network that is not completely routed and subnets that are separated by a firewall.

Active Directory configuration settings for site links automatically bridge all site links. Active Directory creates a chain of site links that let any two individual domain controllers replicate between each other, even when they are not directly, physically connected. Active Directory's automatic transitive site link bridging is not effective with every network topology. If the automatic site bridging function does not allow the domain controllers at all your sites to replicate with each other, you can create a site link bridge manually that allows full replication.

Configure a Site Link Bridge

① Click Start.

② Click Administrative Tools.

③ Click Active Directory Sites and Services.

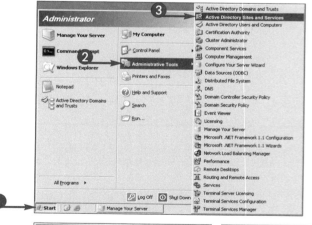

The Active Directory Sites and Services snap-in appears.

④ Expand the Inter-Site Transports folder.

⑤ Right-click IP.

⑥ Click Properties.

The IP Properties dialog box appears.

⑦ Click to deselect the Bridge all site links option (☑ changes to ☐).

⑧ Click OK.

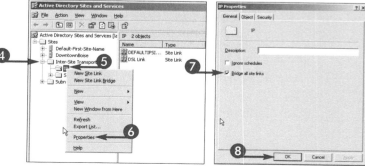

9 Right-click IP.

10 Click New Site Link Bridge.

The New Object – Site Link Bridge dialog box appears.

11 In the Name field, type the name of the site link bridge.

12 Verify that the site links you want are in Site link in this site link bridge box.

13 Click OK.

The new Site Link Bridge appears in the main window of the snap-in.

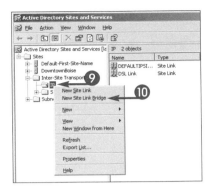
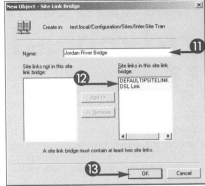
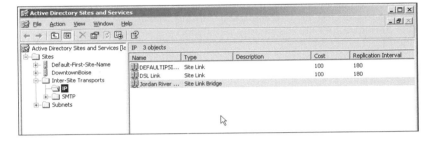

The example uses IP to create the site link bridges. Are all site link bridges created with IP as the transport protocol?

▼ No. IP is the most widely used transport protocol you can configure, and it is the one you use most often. However, you can also use SMTP as the transport protocol. For more on transport protocols, see the section "Create a Site Link" earlier in this chapter.

Is the name you assign a site link bridge important?

▼ You can give a site link bridge any name. Unlike naming a site link, there are no restrictions on naming a site link bridge. You should give the bridge a name that intuitively identifies the links the bridge contains. For more on site links, see the section "Configure a Site Link" earlier in the chapter.

What if I want to get rid of a bridge I made and let Active Directory automatically create a bridge?

▼ You can select the manually created bridge in the Active Directory Sites and Services snap-in, right-click the bridge and click Delete. Then go back into the IP Properties dialog box and check the Bridge all site links box. If the transport protocol is SMTP, you use the SMTP Properties box.

Designate a Preferred Bridgehead Server

When you designate a preferred bridgehead server, you can provide load balancing to your site by assigning one domain controller to send and receive Active Directory database replication between sites. The bridgehead server you make then replicates the database to the other domain controllers within the site.

By default, the Knowledge Consistency Checker (KCC) process automatically assigns the preferred bridgehead server role to a particular domain controller in a site. The KCC is also responsible for automatically creating both intersite and intrasite Active Directory replication topologies.

The purpose of the KCC assigning a particular domain controller the preferred bridgehead server role is to make sure that the Active Directory database is only replicated to other sites across the WAN link once. If all domain controllers at a site replicated across the WAN, it wastes a lot of network time and bandwidth.

You can manually assign a preferred bridgehead server if you want the role to go to a different domain controller other than the one selected by the KCC. You can do this if you have a server that has more resources for a replication-intensive role such as more RAM and a faster CPU.

Designate a Preferred Bridgehead Server

① Click Start.

② Click Administrative Tools.

③ Click Active Directory Sites and Services.

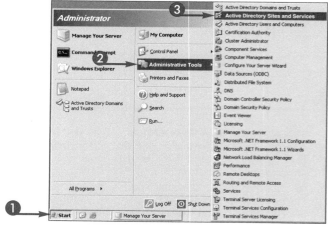

The Active Directory Sites and Services snap-in appears.

④ Expand Sites.

⑤ Expand the Site you want.

⑥ Expand the Servers folder.

⑦ Right-click the server you want.

⑧ Click Properties.

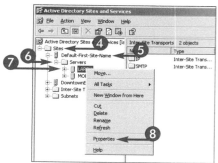

The server Properties dialog box opens.

9 Click the General tab.

10 Click a protocol.

11 Click Add.

The protocol is added to the "This server is a preferred bridgehead server for the following transports" box.

12 Click OK.

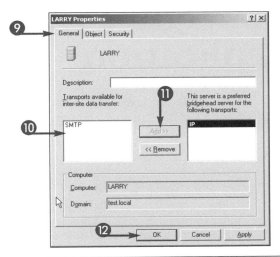

● The selected server is now the bridgehead server for that protocol.

Can I assign the same preferred bridgehead server for both IP and SMTP.

▼ You can select both protocols for the same preferred bridgehead server, but it is not recommended. You use IP and SMTP as transport protocols under completely different circumstances and with different types of WAN links. You can get better load-balancing results by assigning a different preferred bridgehead server to each of the different protocols. To perform this action you must be a member of the Domain Admins group or the Enterprise Admins group. For more information on transport protocols, see the section "Configure Site Links" earlier in this chapter.

What happens if the preferred bridgehead server goes offline?

▼ If you manually assigned the bridgehead server, you must assign the role to a different domain controller at the site. If the KCC process automatically assigned the role, it also makes the reassignment automatically. Keep track of your manually assigned bridgehead servers. You must know which bridgehead server you created manually so you know when you need to reassign the role in the event of a server failure. Assigning a bridgehead server manually can cause replication problems because it prevents the KCC from making an automatic failover assignment.

Configure Intersite Replication

Configuring replication intervals between sites allows you to control when the WAN links between your site and other sites are consumed with Active Directory intersite replication. Without a set schedule for replication, replication can tie up intersite WAN traffic causing problems for users who depend on the WAN link for business usage. Replication significantly slows down your link and your users cannot perform computer tasks.

Intersite replication has four basic characteristics you can configure: traffic is compressed, scheduled, uses either IP or SMTP, and connections are prioritized based on site link cost. All Intersite replication traffic on the WAN link is

compressed if the Active Directory database is larger than 50K. You can override compression if you have the available bandwidth, but not a lot of processing power on the preferred bridgehead server. You can read more about IP and SMTP in the sections "Configure a Site Link" and "Understanding Active Directory Sites and Services."

You cannot only control the time when Active Directory replication occurs, but you can also schedule how often replication occurs. The default settings for Active Directory intersite replication is 180 minutes (three hours), 24 hours a day, seven days a week. You must change this schedule for maximum efficiency of replication.

Configure Intersite Replication

① Click Start.

② Click Administrative Tools.

③ Click Active Directory Sites and Services.

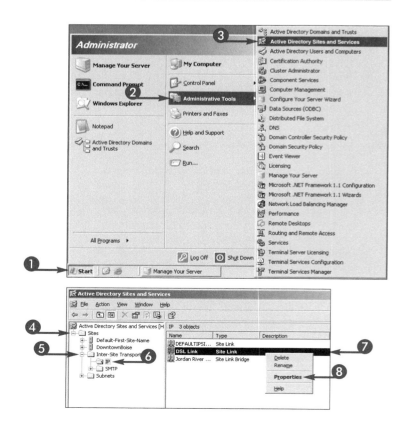

The Active Directory Sites and Services snap-in appears.

④ Expand the Sites folder.

⑤ Expand the Inter-Site Transports folder.

⑥ Click a transport protocol.

⑦ Right-click a link.

⑧ Click Properties.

The Link Properties dialog box opens.

9 Click here and type the number of minutes you want.

10 Click here and type the cost value you want.

11 Click Change Schedule.

The Schedule for Link dialog box appears.

12 Select the hours and days for no replication.

13 Click the Replication Not Available option (○ changes to ◉).

Replication does not occur during the selected days and times.

14 Click OK.

15 Click OK in the DSL Link Properties dialog box.

You have configured intersite replication.

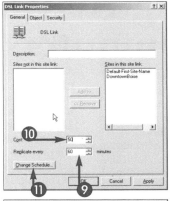

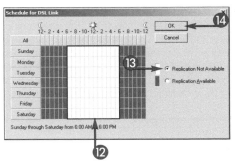

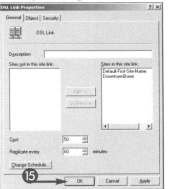

Do I have to make Active Directory intersite replication available and not available in a one-block time period?

▼ No. You can schedule Active Directory intersite replication to occur or not occur at any time on an hour-by-hour basis. However, you must allow enough time for replication to complete. In addition, your replication schedule must be consistant with the replication frequency interval you set. You want to schedule intersite replication so that you can control how much bandwidth it consumes. If you misconfigure the interval and the schedule, Active Directory replication does not occur.

Can I set replication internals and schedules for a site link bridge and have that configuration apply to all site links in the bridge?

▼ No. You must manually configure each site link for cost, replication frequency, and a replication schedule. You can open the Site Link Bridge Properties dialog box by right-clicking the bridge in the same way you open a Site Link Properties dialog box. Both Properties boxes look nearly almost identical. The configuration controls for link cost, replication interval, and replication schedule are not present. Configuring each site link separately allows you a high degree of control over the different connections available in a diverse set of site links.

Understanding Active Directory Users and Computers

The Active Directory Users and Computers snap-in in a Windows Server 2003 domain controller is where you can create, administer, and delete any device or user account in the domain tree or forest. You can also install these tools on a non-domain controller using ADMINPAK.NSI found in the i386 directory of the Windows Server 2003 installation CD. *Domains* are the basic logical container in Active Directory and *sites* are considered the basic physical container in Active Directory. *Users, computers, groups,* and *organizational units* are the individual elements and containers for those elements in Active Directory. Active Directory already created some objects when you promoted the first Windows Server 2003 member server to the first domain controller. You can manually create users, computers, groups, and other objects, place then in built-in containers, or custom make your own objects and containers. Any user on a local computer is automatically a member of the local users group. A user in a domain is also automatically a member of the domain users group. You can add users to almost any other group to give them additional access and permissions to resources or allow them to perform additional duties on a server or on the domain.

Built-In Users

All domain controllers contain a precreated set of built-in users located in the Users folder in the Active Directory Users and Computers snap-in. For the domain to function, built-in users are required in the Active Directory domain. Each built-in user provides a specific task in the domain and on domain controllers. If they did not exist, it would be impossible for you to do necessary tasks. A domain controller has three accounts in the Users folder; Administrator, Guest, and Support.

Administrator: Provides management services in the domain. The account automatically belongs to all domain local and enterprise administrative groups including the Schema Admins group. You configure the authentication credentials for this account when you create a server and promote it to domain controller.

Guest: This built-in user account is disabled by default. The Guests account allows for limited access to any Windows computer where the account is enabled. This account is disabled on Domain Controllers because only administrators have account access for purposes of domain security.

Support: This built-in user account is the vendor account for Help and Support. You use this account to allow a remote logon to your server for Remote Assistance.

Built-In Groups

This folder contains a list of domain-wide groups in the domain. They are all enabled by default. Active Directory assigns users to some built-in groups by default and a member of the Administrators account can manually add users to other built-in groups:

Account Operators: This built-in group has the authority to provide administrative services to domain users and domain user group accounts. This is a limited group in that members can provide assistance to the domain administrator but do not have the same rights.

Backup Operators:
This group has the authority to only conduct backup and recovery operations on domain controllers. For more on backup and recovery functions, see Chapter 21.

Incoming Forest Trust Builders: This group can create an incoming, one-way trust relationship to an Active Directory domain forest. By default, no users are automatically assigned to this group. Administrators do not belong to this group but do have the ability to create trusts as members of the Administrators group.

Network Configuration Operators: This built-in group has permission to change the TCP/IP network configuration settings on servers. As a group member, you can assign a server an IP address and subnet mask, and a preferred and secondary DNS server. You can also release or renew automatically assigned IP addresses at the command-line interface.

Print Operators: This group has the authority to administer all domain printers. For more on the functions of Print Operators, see Chapter 8.

Organizational Units

This is a special container that manages user and group permissions, privileges, and group policies. You primarily use organizational units (OUs) as security containers for other objects such as Users, Computers and Printers. Organizational units are another class of basic object in Active Directory. You can create organizational units to mirror the physical design or infrastructure of your company, or you can create them to represent a logical structure. For more on OUs, see the final three sections in this chapter. Each folder in the Active Directory Users and Computers snap-in represents built-in OUs.

Create a User

T he benefit of creating a user in Active Directory is that it allows you to manage the privileges of each person accessing domain tree and forest resources. You must create a user account for each individual in the domain. If you do not create individual accounts, as far as your system is concerned, the user does not exist and cannot log on to the domain, or access any domain-based services.

Each time your company hires an employee, you must create a user account for him or her. You must configure a

real name, logon name, and password for the user. You can configure a wide number of other user characteristics including address, phone number, e-mail address, Web site, password account options, and logon hours. Although most of these are optional parameters, you can assume a great deal of control over the user account and provide granular administration over each individual user. You can add a user to a group and assign privileges to the group instead of the user per the section "Add a User to a Group."

Create a User

1 Click Start.

2 Click Administrative Tools.

3 Click Active Directory Users and Computers.

The Active Directory Users and Computers snap-in appears.

4 Right-click Users.

5 Click New.

6 Click User.

The New Object – User dialog box appears.

7 Type the user's first name.

8 Type the user's last name.

The first and last names are automatically added to the Full name field.

9 Type a User logon name.

The domain name is already selected.

10 Click Next.

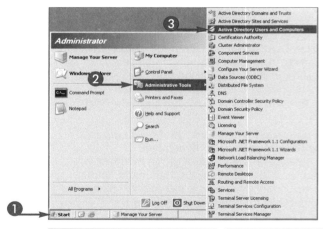

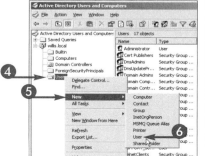

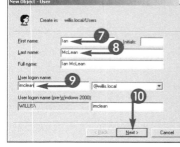

The password configuration box appears.

⑪ Type a password.

⑫ Type the password again.

⑬ Click the "User must change password at next logon" option (☐ changes to ☑).

⑭ Click Next.

The summary page appears.

⑮ Click Finish.

● The new user appears in the Users folder.

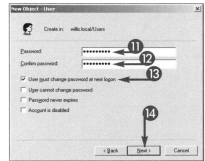

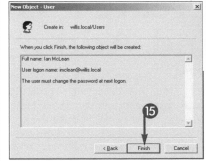

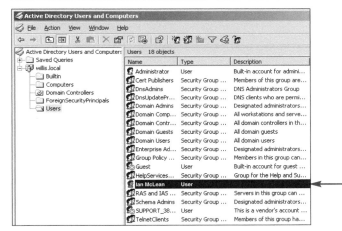

Do I always set the password so that users must change it at their next logon?

▼ Best business practices state that you should have users change their passwords the next time they log on. However you do not have to select the "User must change password at next logon" option (☐ changes to ☑). As an administrator, and to maintain domain security, you do not need to know user passwords. If users forget their passwords, you can reset the password for them in the Properties box of the individual user on the Account tab.

Do I create all new users in the Users folder in Active Directory Users and Computers?

▼ You can create a new user in any of the built-in folders in the Active Directory Users and Computers snap-in. You can also create a new user in one folder and move the user account to a different folder later. You do not want to move a user account into the Domain Controllers folder or the Computers folder only because it does not make good organizational sense.

Create a Group and Add a User

Creating a group allows you to collect all the users who need exactly the same type of access and permissions in the domain, place them in a group, and assign those permissions to the group instead of to each individual user account. This saves you time because you do not have to manually configure each user account one by one. You can assign permissions to a group, and everyone in the group automatically inherits those permissions.

You can create two different types of groups. A *security group* applies permissions to the users inside of the group. A *distribution group* collects specific users as recipients of

group e-mail messages. You can create a distribution group for members of the same team who receive broadcast e-mail messages from their supervisor.

You can create three different scopes of groups. A *domain local group* contains users, computers, and other groups from any domain in the domain forest. A *global group* contains users, computers, and other local groups from the same domain only. A *universal group* also contains users, computers, and groups from any domain in the forest but also grants members access to any resource in the forest.

Create a Group and Add a User

① Click Start.

② Click Administrative Tools.

③ Click Active Directory Users and Computers.

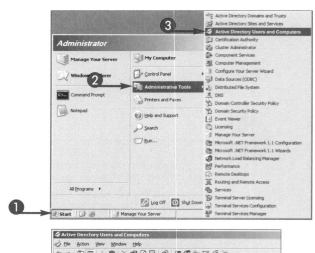

The Active Directory Users and Computers snap-in appears.

④ Right-click the Users folder.

⑤ Click New.

⑥ Click Group.

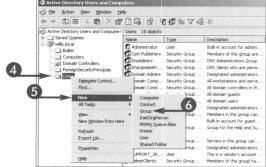

PART I

The New Object – Group dialog box appears.

⑦ Type the group name.

⑧ Click the Global Group scope option
(◻ changes to ◉).

⑨ Click the Security Group type option
(◻ changes to ◉).

⑩ Click OK.

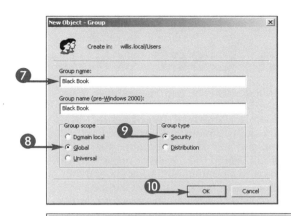

The new group appears in the display pane.

⑪ Right-click the new group.

⑫ Click Properties.

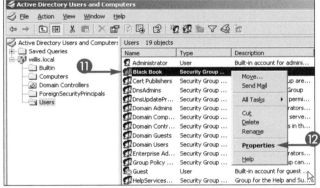

What is the Group Name (pre–Windows 2000) field in the New Object – Group box?

▼ This is the NetBIOS name for the group. The NetBIOS name is often, but not always, the same as the Group Name. Windows 2000 and Windows Server 2003 use DNS to resolve names and can use very long names for objects. Pre–Windows 2000 computers used WINS to resolve NetBIOS names and you can only make each object name 15 characters long. This field is included so that any pre–Windows 2000 computers using WINS can see and access this group in Active Directory.

When I create a group on a particular domain controller, can I add a user to it right away?

▼ In most cases, yes. If you create a group at one domain controller at a particular site and another administrator creates a user at a domain controller at a different site, the new user and group must be replicated to the domain controllers in the domain before you can see and add the user.

continued

Create a Group and
Add a User *(Continued)*

You can continue to create a group and give it any name to identify the purpose of the group in your organizational infrastructure. This makes the group easily identifiable for both administrators and users. You can also rename a group and add or remove rights and privileges to the group should the nature or purpose of the group change in your organization. Although you can create group structure using any design, you can best administer a set of groups by keeping the structure simple and preventing unneeded administrative effort.

To exercise a best practice model for group design, you can use domain local groups to control user access to resources. You can use global groups to organize several different groups of users that have a similar purpose in your organization. You can also use universal groups to either replace global groups or to place global groups as members of a universal group. To continue to use the best practice model, you can move users out of the default groups and into a custom group infrastructure while keeping the number of groups to the smallest number that still serves your purpose.

Create a Group and Add a User *(continued)*

The group's Properties dialog box opens.

⑬ Click the Members tab.

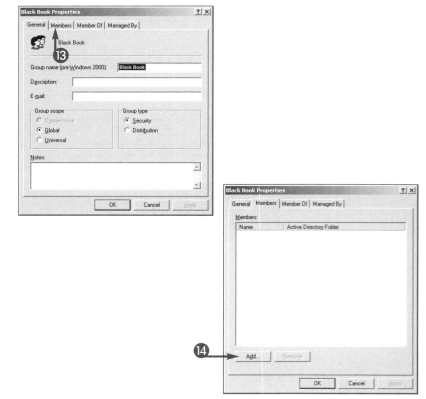

The Members dialog box appears.

⑭ Click Add.

The Select Users, Contacts, Computers, or Groups dialog box appears.

⑮ Type a user name.

⑯ Click Check Names.

The user logon name and domain is appended.

⑰ Click OK.

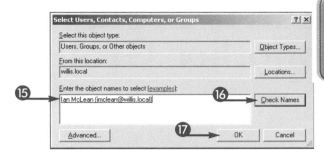

● The user is added to the group.

⑱ Click OK.

Windows Server applies your changes.

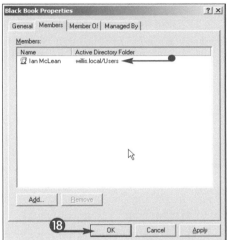

Do I always add a user to a group from the Group Properties dialog box?

▼ No. You can also add a user to a group in the following way: right-click the user name, and then click Add to a group. The Select Group dialog box appears. Type the group name, click Check Names, and click OK. An Active Directory box opens to say the user was added to the group. Click OK to apply your changes.

What is the Managed By tab on the Group Properties box?

▼ You can assign a particular user to manage the group on the Managed By tab. You can click the tab and click Change. The User or Contact dialog box appears. Type a user name and click Check Names, then click OK. The user now can administer this group only. You can give this user the ability to update the group membership list. Allowing users to manage groups and help you with administrative jobs in the domain frees you to do more critical tasks.

Add a Group to Another Group

The advantage of adding a group to another group is that you can assign and manage access policies and permissions to large numbers of users and groups in the domain tree or forest. Once you place the other groups in the one group, all the groups contained within it inherit the policies and permissions you assign to that group.

This is a similar process to assigning a user to a group and assigning that group permissions and policies. You can add a group to another group to expand the scope of your control over users, computers, and groups. You can make your administrative tasks simpler by administering the configuration of just a few groups rather than many groups. Your strategy can only work if the groups inside the primary group need the exact same permissions and policies.

You can add a group to another group to increase access to domain forest resources to domain members. You can place a global group inside a universal group to allow users in a single domain to access resources throughout the domain forest.

① Click Start.

② Click Administrative Tools.

③ Click Active Directory Users and Computers.

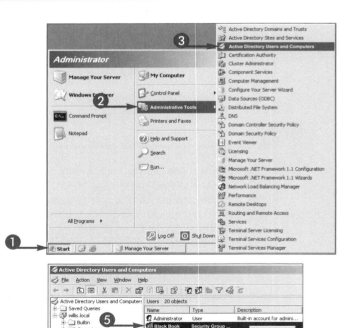

The Active Directory Users and Computers snap-in appears.

④ Click the folder the group is in.

⑤ Right-click the group.

⑥ Click Properties.

The Group Properties dialog box appears.

7 Click the Member Of tab.

8 Click Add.

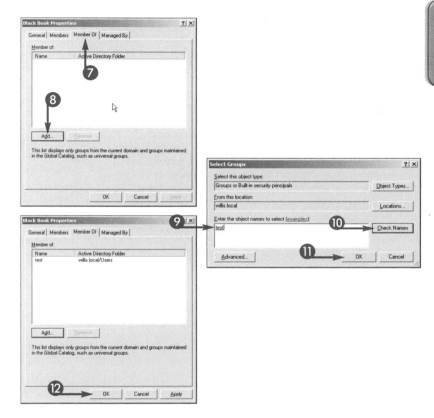

The Select Groups dialog box appears.

9 Type the name of the group you want to join.

10 Click Check Names.

11 Click OK.

The group is added to the group test.

12 Click OK.

Active Directory applies your changes.

How many groups can I add to other groups?

▼ You can add an endless number of groups to other groups. However, you should avoid making your group nesting structure too complicated. Your goal of adding a group to another group is to make it easier for you to administer your domain tree and forest. When you add too many groups to other groups, you may find it more difficult to keep track of the group nesting structure.

Can I add a global group to a universal group and access the resources in another domain without the knowledge of the administrator in the other domain?

▼ No. Before you can add a global group from a domain to a universal group and have members of the global group access resources in another domain, you must establish a trust relationship between your domain tree and the other domain tree. You cannot use a universal group to access another tree in the forest without permission. You can read more about this in Chapter 1.

Create an Organizational Unit and Add a Group

When you create an organizational unit (OU), you can organize your users and groups to match the departmental structure or administrative structure of your company. You can then apply group policies to organizational units to create particular working environments to the groups inside the OUs. You can also delegate authority over particular OUs to others so they can help you with your administrative tasks. For more about group policies and how you can apply them, see Chapters 14 and 15.

Organizational units are represented by the folder structure in the Active Directory Users and Computers snap-in on the left-hand sidebar menu. They are logical containers in Active Directory. You can structure your organizational units to match office locations or to match team or division structures. If you create organizational units to match office locations, a single site can contain one OU. If you create organizational units to match divisions, departments, or teams, you can have multiple OUs in one site.

With Windows NT you created a separate domain for each security or administrative requirement. With Windows Server 2003, you can replace Windows NT domains with organizational units and place all your organizational units in a single domain or domain tree.

Create an Organizational Unit and Add a Group

① Click Start.

② Click Administrative Tools.

③ Click Active Directory Users and Computers.

The Active Directory Users and Computers snap-in appears.

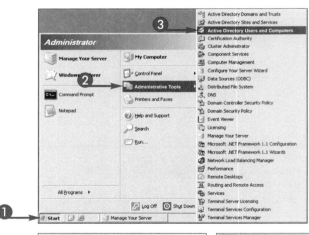

④ Right-click the domain container.

⑤ Click New.

⑥ Click Organizational Unit.

The New Object – Organizational Unit dialog box appears.

⑦ In the Name field, type the name of the organizational unit.

⑧ Click OK.

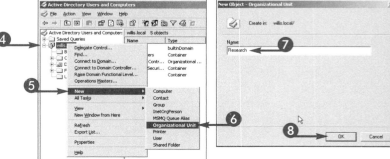

The new OU appears in the left-hand sidebar menu.

⑨ Click Users.

⑩ Right-click the group you want.

⑪ Click Move.

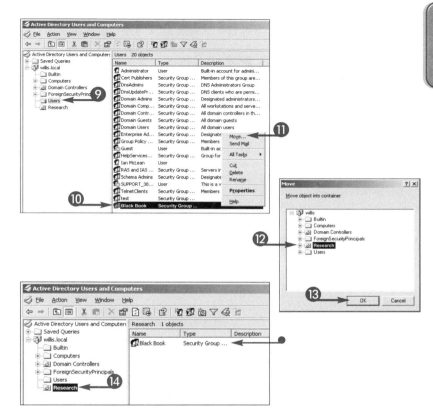

The Move dialog box appears.

⑫ Click the group you want.

⑬ Click OK.

The Move dialog box closes.

⑭ Click Research.

● The group is moved to OU.

Can I add an organizational unit to another organizational unit?

▼ Yes. However, you can only add an organizational unit to a domain. You can nest groups in other groups, but you cannot nest an OU in an OU. You can use OUs to mirror your organizational structure and nesting OUs lets you do this. You also cannot create an OU in a site container in the Active Directory Sites and Services snap-in. Organizational units are basic containers just like domains and sites.

If I create an organization unit based on departmental structure, how can I tell the difference between the same department at different sites?

▼ All members of a particular department belong to the same organizational unit regardless of which site they work at. Members of the finance department at Site A need the same permissions as members of the finance department at Site B. It does not matter where they work. You can place members of one department in an OU who physically work in any number of sites as long as they belong to the same domain.

Delegate Control of an Organizational Unit

The benefit of delegating control of an organizational unit is to spread administrative tasks to other domain users without granting them full administrative privileges in the domain tree. You can balance your need for help with administrative tasks with your need to preserve domain tree security. When you delegate authority of an organizational unit to another party, you allow it as much or as little ability to administer the organizational unit as you want.

There are 11 common tasks and you can assign as few or as many of these tasks as you want to any domain user. You

can delegate authority to an individual or a group. You can delegate authority of an organizational unit to members of the help desk group and allow them to reset passwords for any member of that OU. By giving control of this function to a non-administrative group, you can allow domain administrators to perform more critical domain-related tasks.

You can delegate control of custom tasks as well. Custom tasks cover a scope or range of task sets rather than individual common tasks. For example, you can delegate control of all computer objects, document objects, group objects, or site objects related to an organizational unit.

Delegate Control of an Organizational Unit

① Click Start.

② Click Administrative Tools.

③ Click Active Directory Users and Computers.

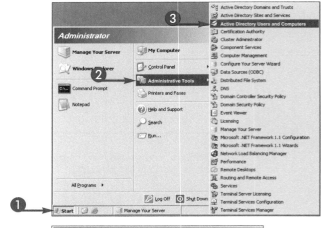

The Active Directory Users and Computers snap-in appears.

④ Expand the domain.

⑤ Right-click Research.

⑥ Click Delegate Control.

The Delegation of Control Wizard launches.

7 Click Next.

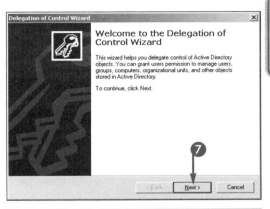

The Users or Groups page of the Wizard appears.

8 Click Add.

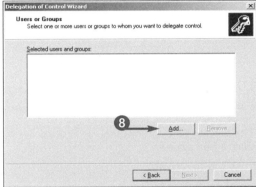

What does the Advanced button in the Select Users, Computers, or Groups dialog box access?

▼ You can search for a particular user, computer, or group when you click Advanced. If you only know what the name of the group starts with, you can type what you know in the Name field and click OK. Active Directory searches all users, groups, and security principals and produces the results. You can select the correct object in the Search results window.

How can I use the Object Types and Location buttons in the Select Users, Computers, or Groups dialog box?

▼ You can click the Object Types and select only the object or objects you want to find. They include built-in security principals, computers, groups, and users. When delegating authority of an OU, the Computers object is not selected. You can click Location to select a particular domain in the forest or limit your search to an organizational unit in a single domain.

continued

Delegate Control of an Organizational Unit *(Continued)*

Y ou can continue to delegate control of organizational units using the Delegation of Control Wizard and allow the group given rights over the selected OU as many or as few duties as necessary for them to accomplish their tasks. You can select any group to have authority over a specific OU including the Administrator group or a custom-made group, created just for a single administrative task. You can delegate administrative tasks to a group with a high degree of granularity including allowing a group to administer extremely limited tasks such as the ability to modify only OU member phone numbers or remote access settings.

When you administer older Windows domains such as Windows NT 4.0 domains, you can only delegate authority to different parts of your organizational structure at the level of the domain. You must create a separate NT resource domain to allow separate administration of an individual security container. Windows Server 2003 is able to use the Organizational Unit model to provide much more efficient control over more discrete structural units and provide that administration within a single domain.

Delegate Control of an Organizational Unit *(continued)*

The Select Users, Computers, or Groups dialog box appears.

⑨ Type a group name.

⑩ Click Check Names.

⑪ Click OK.

● The group appears in the Selected users and groups box.

⑫ Click Next.

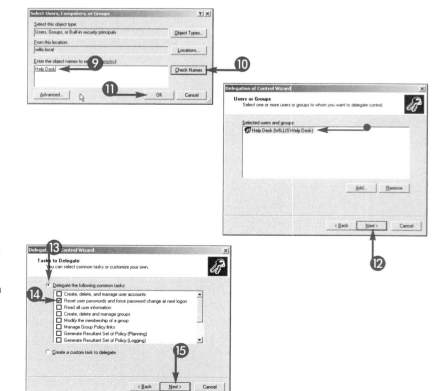

The Tasks to Delegate page of the Wizard appears.

⑬ Click the Delegate the following common tasks option (◯ changes to ◉).

⑭ Click the Reset user passwords and force password change at next logon option (☑ changes to ☐).

⑮ Click Next.

The Delegation of Control Wizard Summary page appears.

You can verify that all information is correct.

⑯ Click Finish.

The Delegation of Control Wizard closes.

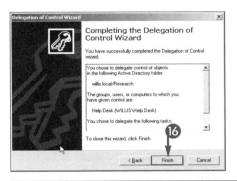

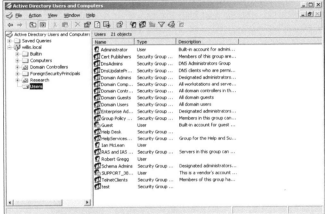

How can I change the specific tasks that are delegated to a user or group?

▼ You can run the Delegation of Control Wizard again to make those changes. When you run the wizard and select the same group, there is no indication that this group already has been delegated authority over the organizational unit. The selections you make in the Wizard will overwrite the previous settings made during the previous run.

How can I make sure that control of a common task was delegated to the group selected in the Delegation of Control Wizard?

▼ You can verify the success of the Delegation of Control Wizard by having a member of the selected group log on to the domain and attempt to perform the common task. For example, a member of the Help Desk can log on and reset the password of a member of the Research OU. You can notify the user who is the test subject that he or she can expect to log on with the reset password and change it as a result of your test.

Understanding Active Directory Command Line Tools

Active Directory command-line utilities let you administer the domain controller at which you are working, or remotely administrater other domain controllers in the domain tree. You can perform a variety of tasks more quickly at the command line. This saves you time because you do not have to enter Administrative Tools in the Start menu, select a particular Active Directory snap-in, and access the configuration controls from a particular container in the snap-in.

The Command Shell

The *Command Shell* is also known as the command prompt or command window. It is the basic user interface that allows you to enter information request and configuration instructions without having to access the GUI (Graphical User Interface). It is a software program that provides you with direct access to the operating system, using character-based applications and utilities. You can call this the DOS shell but this is not accurate. Every Windows operating system built on NT Technology no longer uses the MS-DOS command interpreter Command.com. The command shell is a DOS emulator using the command interpreter Cmd.exe. You can still use the same or similar commands and command syntax in the command emulator so any knowledge you have of DOS commands is still valid. The command shell is a non-graphical environment in which you can issue commands and view a printout of the result on the screen. You use the command shell to issue directives to the operating system. The shell translates your input into commands the operating system can interpret and carry out.

To find out more about Windows Server 2003 command shell commands, go to www.microsoft.com and search for command shell commands.

Syntax

Syntax is the order in which you must type a command and any of the parameters or switches that follow the command. If you do not use correct syntax in writing your command, you will receive an error message. A *parameter* or *switch* is a method of adding a specific command set to the particular command or utility you are using in the command shell. For any task you perform in the command shell, you can ask for help in finding the possible commands issued from a prompt and a brief explanation of what each command does. Help also provides examples of a command structure's syntax. The proper use of words, phrases, and special symbols in the command ensures the command's proper execution in the shell. If you make a mistake in your command syntax, the system returns an error message. For example, the correct syntax to ask for help with the where.exe command is "where /?". Because all commands use the same syntax, once you know the syntax, you can use it for all commands you issue in the Shell.

Nesting a Command Shell

You can issue multiple command sets in separate command shells. For example, you can issue a particular command set in one shell, then start a separate instance of the shell to issue a separate set of commands. This lets you issue the second command set without interrupting the shell environment running the first command set. You can do this from inside the command shell.

Remote Administration

You can use the `ntdsutil` command to connect to other domain controllers in the domain tree or forest to administer them from a single location, as shown in Chapter 3. Once you connect to a remote domain controller, you can issue the same command sets in the command shell just as if you were sitting in front of that specific domain controller. You must be a member of the Enterprise Admins group to access all domain controllers.

Scalability and Power

The command line syntax provides more options in issuing command arguments than in the GUI using a Wizard. This means you can include more variables in a command set and receive more varied configuration control than you can when using the graphical interface. You can use a wide variety of switches or parameters with the various command line utilities to execute commands

and configure your server. You can also run multiple commands from a single command line rather than having to open multiple MMC snap-ins in the GUI. You can use the command shell not only to issue more finely detailed commands, but also to issue commands having a significant impact on the domain controller and the domain, using just a few specific commands. You do not always receive an "are you sure" response from the operating system as you do in the GUI.

Automate Tasks with Scripts

You can create and edit batch files or scripts to automate routine and repeated tasks on the command line. A batch file is a text file that contains one or more commands. A batch file can be set to run whenever a user logs onto the domain and automatically configures the user environment as the script executes. A batch file has either a .bat or .cmd file extension. You can use the command shell to automate tasks involving all Active Directory objects using a Visual Basic (VB) script. You can write the script in a number of different programming languages including Microsoft Visual Basic, Perl, JavaScript, and C++.

You can write a script so that it executes once at some future date or runs on a regular basis on preset dates and times, automatically executing Active Directory object administration tasks.

Using dsadd.exe

Y ou can use a dsadd command to add Active Directory objects directly to the directory from the command shell. You can add computers, contacts, distribution groups, security groups, organizational units, users, and quotas. The command line helps you simultaneously add these objects, as well as multiple Active Directory objects, more quickly than when you use the graphical interface.

You must know Active Directory naming conventions to use the dsadd.exe command. Each object in Active Directory has a unique convention, such as CN for common name, OU for organizational unit name, and DC for domain component name. For example, you can indicate the common name for the group sales by typing **CN=Sales**. Command shell syntax requires you use Active Directory naming for not only the dsadd command, but also for all commands affecting Active Directory.

Using dsadd.exe

① Click Start.

② Click Command Prompt.

The Command Prompt window appears.

③ Type **dsadd /? | more**.

④ Press Enter.

The dsadd help page prints a single screen.

⑤ Press the space bar.

The next dsadd help screen appears.

⑥ Type **dsadd ou OU=?, DC=?, DC=?,** where *?* is the name of the OU or DC.

⑦ Press Enter.

```
Command Prompt                                              _|□|X|
dsadd ou - adds an organizational unit to the directory.
dsadd user - adds a user to the directory.
dsadd quota - adds a quota specification to a directory partition.

For help on a specific command, type "dsadd <ObjectType> /?" where
<ObjectType> is one of the supported object types shown above.
For example, dsadd ou /?.
Remarks:
Commas that are not used as separators in distinguished names must be
escaped with the backslash ("\") character
(for example, "CN=Company\, Inc.,CN=Users,DC=microsoft,DC=com").
Backslashes used in distinguished names must be escaped with a backslash
(for example,
"CN=Sales\ Latin America,OU=Distribution Lists,DC=microsoft,DC=com").
Directory Service command-line tools help:
dsadd /? - help for adding objects.
dsget /? - help for displaying objects.
dsmod /? - help for modifying objects.
dsmove /? - help for moving objects.
dsquery /? - help for finding objects matching search criteria.
dsrm /? - help for deleting objects.

C:\Documents and Settings\Administrator>dsadd ou OU=development,DC=willis,DC=loc
al
```

The OU development is added.

⑧ Type **dsadd group CN=?,OU=?,DC=?,DC=?,** where *?* is the name of the CN, OU, or DC.

⑨ Press Enter.

The Group developers are added to the OU development.

```
C:\Documents and Settings\Administrator>dsadd ou OU=development,DC=willis,DC=loc
al
dsadd succeeded:OU=development,DC=willis,DC=local
C:\Documents and Settings\Administrator>dsadd group CN=programmers,OU=developmen
t,DC=willis,DC=local
```

```
C:\Documents and Settings\Administrator>dsadd ou OU=development,DC=willis,DC=loc
al
dsadd succeeded:OU=development,DC=willis,DC=local
C:\Documents and Settings\Administrator>dsadd group CN=programmers,OU=developmen
t,DC=willis,DC=local
dsadd succeeded:CN=programmers,OU=development,DC=willis,DC=local
C:\Documents and Settings\Administrator>exit
```

How can I ensure that the Active Directory object I created on the command line has actually been created?

▼ You can check by accessing the graphical interface where the object is located. For example, check in the Active Directory Users and Computers snap-in to see if the OU developers was created, then open the OU to see if the group programmers is inside. Creating an Active Directory object on the command line is the same as creating it in the GUI.

Can I add Active Directory objects to other domains on the command line?

▼ Yes. If you set up your domain to have a trust relationship with another domain, you can add an Active Directory object to the other domain. You can specify the other domain canonal name such as CN=otherdomain, CN=com and the new Active Directory object is created in otherdomain.com. You can complete the same action in the GUI, but you perform additional steps to access the other domain.

How can I quickly get help when using dsadd **commands?**

▼ To receive help when using dsadd, you can type **dsadd /?.** For help with the object types, you type **dsadd computer /?** to see a list of all the commands used to add a computer. Type **dsadd user /?** to get help using the commands designed to add a user.

Using dsget.exe

You can use the dsget command to display the properties of a large number of objects in Active Directory. The GUI retrieves similar properties information but you have to go into Administrative Tools on the Start Menu, locate and open the Active Directory snap-in in which the object is contained, locate the object in the snap-in, and access its properties. On the command shell, you can access the same information in a single environment rather than toggle between numerous locations to find all these objects.

You can use the dsget command to look up the properties of such diverse objects as users, computers, groups, organizational units, subnets, servers, sites, quotas, partitions, and more. The dsget command can also verify an object after its creation or modification to ensure the variables you set for the object are correct. You can also check multiple objects at the same time. You can check related objects one after the other such as users, groups, and organizational units, or sites and subnets because you very often create these objects together.

Using dsget.exe

① Click Start.

② Click Command Prompt.

The command prompt window appears.

③ Type **dsget user "cn=?,ou=?,dc=?,dc=?"**, where *?* is the name of the CN, OU, or DC.

④ Press Enter.

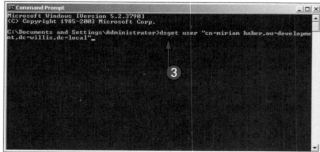

The properties data for the user is returned.

⑤ Type **dsget ou "ou=?,dc=?,dc=?"**, where *?* is the name of the OU or DC.

⑥ Press Enter.

The data for the OU is returned.

⑦ Type **exit**.

⑧ Press Enter.

Why do I use quotation marks in the `dsget` command?

▼ You must use the quotation marks to surround the distinguished name of the object you are locating if the object name or names have spaces in them. If you do not use the quotation marks, the command interprets any name with a space as two separate entries and returns a syntax error when you attempt to execute the command. Without the quotation marks, you must type each word with a preceding distinguished name indicator and equals sign such as CN=company, CN=Users. Also, you can use commas as separators between distinguished names but there must be no spaces after the commas.

Can I retrieve more detailed information about an object using the `dsget` command?

▼ Yes. For example, you can use a set of variables or parameters to gain detailed information about a site. After typing the `dsget` site command, you can type the parameter **–desc** to get a description of the site or **–autotopology** to see if automatic intersite topology generation is enabled. These are only two examples of the dozens of parameters available. You can find out more about sites in Chapter 4. To read all of the attributes of any object, you must use the `dsquery *` command. You can find out more about dsquery in the section "Using DSQUERY.EXE."

Using dsquery.exe

You can use the `dsquery` command line utility to ask Active Directory to find a particular object in the directory if you do not know the location of that particular object. You can also use `dsquery` in conjunction with other command line utilities such as `dsget`. For example, in the section "Using dsget.exe," in order to use the `dsget` command, you must know the location of the object. For an object with an unknown location, you can utilize `dsquery` to find the Active Directory object, and then input the results into the `dsget` command.

You use `dsquery` to find the same list of objects that you can apply to the `dsget` command. You can also use the asterisk (*) symbol as a wildcard symbol with the `dsquery`

command to retrieve objects for which you do not know the exact name. You can look for a user with the first name Phil and substitute * for his last name in `dsquery`. The `dsquery` command returns the results for all users in Active Directory with the first name Phil, no matter what their last names are.

You can use the `more` command and `pipe` (`|`) command with commands that produce a long stream of data in the result. You use the | symbol, which is called a pipe, to send the output of one command into the input of another. In the example in this section, the pipe sends the output of the `dsquery` command into the more command. You use the more command to view long results one screen at a time.

Using dsquery.exe

① Click Start.

② Click Command Prompt.

The Command Prompt window appears.

③ Type **dsquery * ou=?,dc=?,dc=? – attr * | more**, where *?* is the name of the OU or DC.

The example in these steps searches for all the attributes for a specific OU in a domain using the * symbol, which is as a "wildcard" symbol that returns all attribute data for the OU.

④ Press Enter.

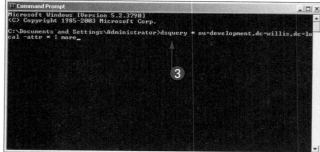

The attributes for OU development appear one screen at a time.

5 Press the Spacebar.

Note: Because you piped the output to a more command, data is shown only one page at a time. To scroll through the pages, press the spacebar.

Another screen of information appears.

6 Press the Spacebar twice.

The final screen of data appears showing all available attribute data regarding the OU.

7 Type **exit**.

8 Press Enter to close the command window.

What are some of the switches or parameters that I can use with the `dsquery` command and what do they do?

▼ There are too many switches that you can use with the `dsquery` command to list here. For example, you can use the `dsquery computer` command to find computers in the directory that match specific search criteria you can input. The –o switch specifies the format in which a list of entries located by the search will be presented. The –scope switch specifies the scope of the search. The –name switch searches for computers by their name attributes. The –desc switch searches for computers by their description.

Why would I want such a great deal of information about an Active Directory object?

▼ You can use the `dsquery` command to collect a large amount of data about a container when you are not sure what piece of information you want to use. For example, you can find out when the user object was created and modified as well as the organizational unit object, the distingushed name of any groups in the OU, and the last time the user logged on and off. You can use `dsquery` to search for a variety of different objects. For example, you can use the `dsquery computer` command, the `dsquery contact` command, the `dsquery group` command and so on.

Using dsmod.exe

You can use the dsmod.exe command-line utility to modify an object in Active Directory. The advantage is you can take an already created object and change the characteristics of the object. You can use the dsmod.exe command in combination with other commands that have an affect on Active Directory objects. For example, you can create an object in Active Directory and later change a quality about the object. When you make an error when you create an object, you can use the dsmod.exe command to correct your error.

You can change the scope of group membership for a group with the dsmod command. You can also reset the password of a user and force the user to change the password at his or her next logon. You can even disable the account of the user with the dsmod command. You cannot perform as wide a variety of tasks using dsmod as you can with other command-line utilities but you will use this command more often than other Active Directory command shell utilities.

Using dsmod.exe

① Click Start.

② Click Command Prompt.

The Command Prompt window appears.

③ Type **dsmod ou "ou=?,dc=?,dc=?" –desc "This is the development OU"**, where *?* is the name of the OU or DC.

④ Press Enter.

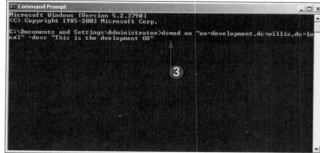

A success message appears displaying any errors.

5 Press the up arrow.

The previous command reprints.

6 Correct the spelling error.

7 Press Enter.

A success message prints that shows that you corrected the error.

8 Type **exit**.

9 Press Enter to close the command shell.

Can I use the dsmod utility to affect multiple computer accounts at the same time or do I have to use a separate command for each computer?

▼ You can use the dsmod command-line utility to have an affect on multiple computers using a single command string. For example, you can disable multiple computers with the following string:

dsmod comptuer CN=computer1,CN=computers, DC=mtech,DC=local CN=computer2,DC=mtech, DC=local — disabled yes.

You can also reset multiple computers by using the same string but replacing — disabled yes with — reset. When you use multiple entries, use a space between each entry to separate the values such as the list of distinguished names used in the above examples.

What are some other examples of modifications I can make with dsmod commands?

▼ You can set company information for multiple contacts by using the string shown in the following example:

dsmod contact "CN=Marie Perry, OU=Contacts,DC=MTech,DC=Local" "CN=Craig Robinson,OU=Contacts,DC=MTech,DC=Local" —company Mtech

You can add user Marie Perry to all administrator distribution list groups by using the following example:

dsquery group "OU=Distribution Lists, DC=MTech,DC=Local" — name adm* | dsmod group —addmbr "CN=Marie Perry,CN=Users, DC=MTech,DC=Local"

You can change the description of several organizational units at the same time using the following example:

dsmod ou "OU=Domain Controllers,DC= MTech,DC=Local" "OU=Research,DC=MTech, DC=Local" "OU=Development,DC=MTech, DC=Local" —desc "This is a secure OU"

7 Server Management

Manage Your Server Roles 98
Open the Manage Your Server Wizard 100
Configure a DNS Server 102
Configure a DHCP Server 106
Configure a File Server 110
Configure a Print Server 112
Configure a Mail Server 116
Configure a WINS Server 118

8 Printing

Understanding Printing..............................120
Configure Point and Print Services 122
Enable Web-Based Printer Management 124
Change the Location of the Print
    Spooler Folder 128
Set Printer Priority and Availability
    Levels 132
Working with Print Queues.........................134

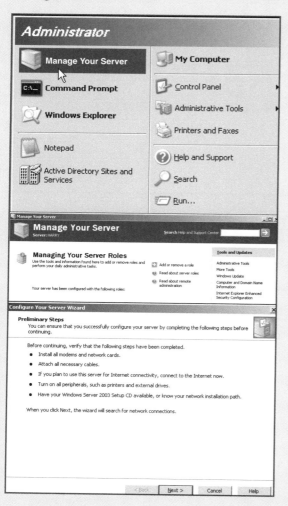

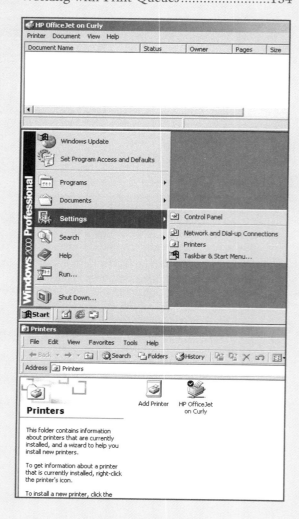

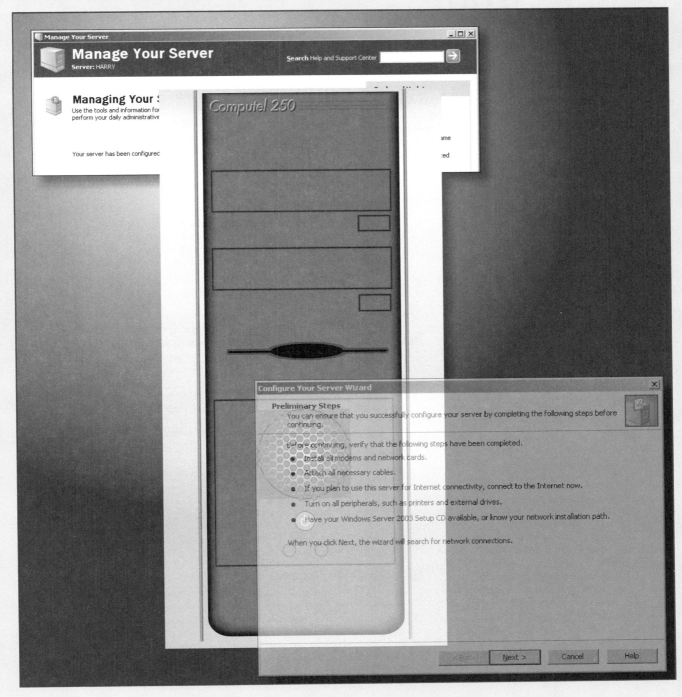

Manage Your Server Roles

You can manage all of your server roles from a single interface that launches every time you power up or log on to Windows Server 2003, saving you time and frustration. A server can provide many different kinds of services for a network and a domain. Each different service requires the server to take on a specific server role. A server can have more than one role at a time. The Manage

Your Server page contains links that help you search for the various locations of the interfaces that you must create as well as administer the most common roles your server can assume. You can use the same interface to configure roles that you used in both member servers and domain controllers. For more on opening the Manage Your Server page, see the section "Open the Manage Your Server Wizard."

A Add or Remove a Role

Starts the Configure Your Server Wizard, which configures the different roles Windows Server 2003 performs. You receive a report detailing what roles your server can and cannot fulfill at the present time. This information verifies what your server is already doing on the network and helps you plan what roles to assign different servers to balance the load evenly among all the machines you administer.

C Read About Remote Administration

Opens another help box that shows how remote management tasks on Windows Server 2003 operate. In this box, you can read the contents in a list, use the index, and search the contents for a specific word or topic. You can also print information for your future reference.

B Read About Server Roles

Opens a help page where you can read about how you can configure server roles, review an index of subjects related to server roles, search for words and topics, and add your frequently referred-to topics to the favorites list. You can also print information from this page.

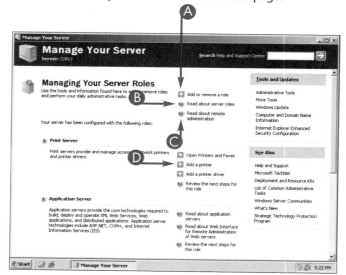

D Manage Configured Server Roles

You can also use similar links on the Manage Your Server page to administer roles your Windows Server 2003 server already has been assigned. If you have already assigned your server as a domain controller, you can click links to Manage Users and Computers in Active Directory, Manage Domains and Trusts, and Manage Sites and Services.

E Administrative Tools

Opens a list of shortcuts to all the Active Directory snap-ins and other server tools you normally see when you click Administrative Tools in the Start Menu. You can double-click any shortcut icon to open the snap-in or dialog box you use in administration.

F More Tools

Opens the Help and Support Center for the server, which is very similar to Help and Support Centers on other Windows operating systems, including Windows XP. You can search for a tool using the search window or expand topic trees in the left-hand sidebar window of the page.

G Windows Update

Opens a Web browser that allows you to download the latest security patches and hotfixes issued by Microsoft. Regularly updating your server prevents any potential security breaches.

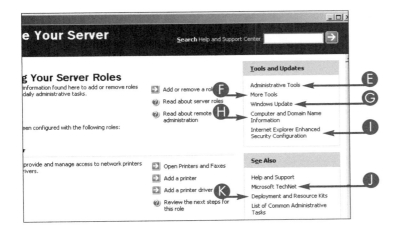

H Computer and Domain Information

Opens the System Properties box where you can view the server and domain name on the Computer Name tab.

K Deployment and Resource Kits

Links to a help page that contains various resources that you can use to configure your server and deploy software tools. You can view information on how to access additional tools located on the Windows Server 2003 installation CD.

J Microsoft Technet

Connects to the Microsoft technical network on the Internet. This searchable site has a wide variety of technical papers, notices and "how to" pages to help you find any instructions for configuring your server. You can also find out how to troubleshoot configuration problems on your server at Technet.

I Internet Explorer Enhanced Security Configuration

This link configures increased security features that come enabled by default in the Internet Explorer Web browser on your Windows Server 2003 server. Warnings appear when you open this link telling you that the enhanced security on the browser affects how some Web pages appear.

Open the Manage Your Server Wizard

You can use the Manage Your Server page to launch a wide variety of wizards that configure several server roles. The Manage Your Server Wizard, which is available on both Windows Server 2003 member servers and domain controllers, gathers information about your server and offers choices for which roles you want to assign your server.

You can immediately determine what roles your server already has when you open the initial Manage Your Server page. You can use the links accompanying the already-present server roles to continue to manage that role. You can also use the Wizard to safely remove any role your

server currently has. The one role you cannot remove with the wizard is the domain controller. You can only safely remove the domain controller role by running dcpromo.exe from the Run window of the server.

You can either use the Windows Server 2003 installation CD to install any extra components on the server when you add the role or you can point your server to the location on the network where these files are found by using Windows Explorer to navigate to the location.

This section only shows how to open the Manage Your Server Wizard. To install individual server roles, see the remaining sections in this chapter.

Open the Manage Your Server Wizard

1 Click Start.

2 Click Manage Your Server.

The Manage Your Server page appears.

3 Click the Add or remove a role link.

The Configure Your Server Wizard appears.

4 Click Next.

The Server role page of the Wizard appears.

5 Click the DNS server.

6 Click Next.

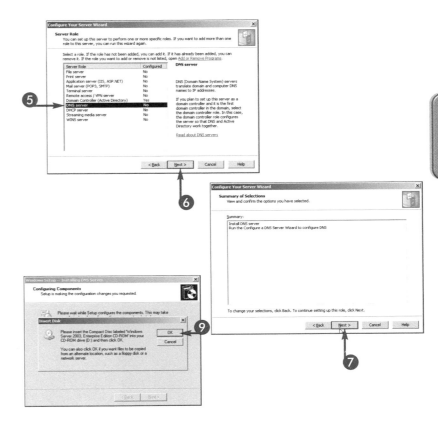

The Summary of Selections page appears.

7 Click Next.

8 Insert the Windows Server 2003 Installation CD.

9 Click OK.

A server-specific wizard walks you through the rest of the installation process.

Note: See the remaining sections in this chapter to add individual server roles.

Can I add more than one server role at a time to my Windows Server 2003 machine?

▼ No. The Manage Your Server Wizard is designed to add only one role at a time. Each set of server roles is unique and requires you to load a separate collection of components for you to enable the role. If you were to try and add two or more server roles at once, you can do irreparable harm to the server operating system. The remaining sections in this chapter detail how to add and configure each set of server roles.

What if I want to add a role to the server that is not present on the Server Role list?

▼ You can click Start, click Control Panel, and click the Add or Remove Programs applet. You can then click Add/Remove Windows Components. When the Windows Components Wizard launches, you can select the specific features you want to add to your server. To find out which features each role contains, you can select the role and click Details. Also, when you select a role or component, a brief desciption is displayed in the dialog box. You must insert the Windows Server 2003 Installation CD to complete the addition.

Configure a DNS Server

You use *Domain Name System (DNS)* to resolve network IP addresses to computer names. Active Directory natively depends on DNS to locate all objects in the domain tree and structure. Active Directory requires DNS, and, in fact, does not function without it. Although you do not have to have DNS running on a Domain Controller, or even on a Microsoft Windows server or computer, an AD must have access to DNS service on the network.

When you create the first domain controller in the first domain, if one of your member servers is not already running DNS on the network, Active Directory creates a DNS server on the first domain controller automatically as part of the domain controller promotion (dcpromo) process. You must create any other DNS servers required on the root domain or any child domain manually.

You can create additional DNS servers for load balancing and redundancy by placing them in each site in your infrastructure. You can then configure the DNS server located at each site to be the Primary DNS server for that site. Active Directory continually replicates changes to its topology to all the domain controllers in the forest and relies on DNS to keep up with the changes in resources.

You configure the DNS Server using the Manage Your Server Wizard. To access this Wizard, see the section "Open the Manage Your Server Wizard."

Configure a DNS Server

① Open the Manage Your Server Wizard, selecting DNS server from the Server Role list in step 5.

Note: *For more on the Manage Your Server Wizard, see the section "Open the Manage Your Server Wizard."*

The Configure a DNS Server Wizard appears.

② Click Next.

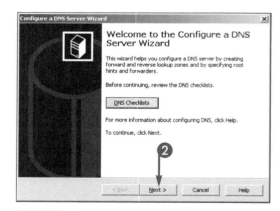

The Select Configuration Action page appears.

③ Click the configuration option that you want (◯ changes to ⦿).

④ Click Next.

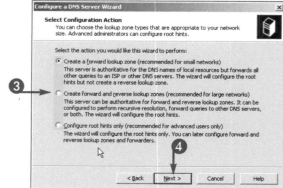

The Primary Server Location page of the Wizard appears.

⑤ Click the server option you want to use to maintain the DNS zone.

⑥ Click Next.

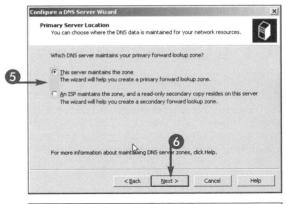

The Zone Name page of the Wizard appears.

⑦ Type the DNS zone name.

⑧ Click Next.

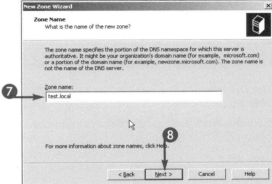

When the Configure a DNS Server Wizard opens, what does the DNS Checklist button do?

▼ You can click DNS Checklist to open a help window. The DNS Checklist help window lets you review all of the necessary tasks you can perform before assigning the role of DNS server to your Windows Server 2003 machine. If you are new to assigning DNS roles, you may find this checklist very helpful. You can also click the Read about DNS servers link on the Server Role page of the Wizard after you select the DNS server to learn more about the various DNS servers. You can choose to ignore the checklist if you have a lot of experience in assigning the DNS server role.

What is the difference between the server maintaining the lookup zone and the ISP server maintaining the zone?

▼ On the Primary Server Location window, you must decide which server you want in charge of the lookup zone. A DNS zone is the part of the namespace for which a DNS server is responsible. The test.local domain controller is configured to be responsible for the domain namespace in which it resides. If you chose to assign the ISP server as the responsible server, you must create a read-only copy of the zone data on the local server, and the server refers to the ISP server for zone changes.

continued

Configure a DNS Server *(Continued)*

The Windows Server 2003 DNS Server Wizard allows your server to perform Dynamic DNS (DDNS) updates on your domain tree. *Dynamic DNS* is a feature introduced with Windows 2000 Server that lets client computers on the network register and unregister their own host to IP address mappings on the DNS server. Without this capacity, you must manually configure these records on the DNS server. You can only use secure dynamic updates on a network that uses Active Directory.

You must configure your DNS server to accept only secure dynamic DNS updates, even on networks that do not run Active Directory due to the security risk.

You can use the wizard to determine whether you configure your DNS server to forward name to IP address queries. If you set your DNS server to forward client queries, you must specify the IP address of the upstream DNS server to which the query is sent. If you choose not to allow forwarding, your server still uses DNS root servers to resolve name-to-address mappings not in its database.

Configure a DNS Server *(continued)*

The Dynamic Update page of the Wizard appears.

⑨ Click the Allow only secure dynamic updates option (◯ changes to ◉).

⑩ Click Next.

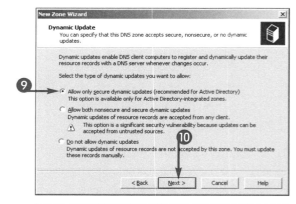

The Forwarders page of the Wizard appears.

⑪ Click a forwarding option (◯ changes to ◉).

If you click the Yes option, type the IP address to which DNS server queries are forwarded.

⑫ Click Next.

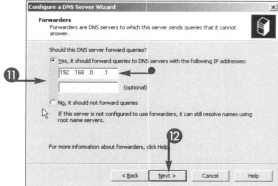

The Completing a DNS Server Wizard page appears.

⑬ Review the Settings information for accuracy.

⑭ Click Finish.

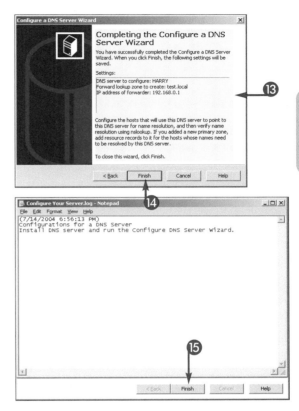

The Configure Your Server log appears.

⑮ Click Finish.

Your server is configured for DNS services.

How can a DNS server resolve name to IP address mappings if it cannot forward client queries to DNS servers authoritative for other namespaces?

▼ You can configure your DNS server not to forward client queries by clicking the "No, it should not forward queries" option (○ changes to ●) on the Forwarders page window. The DNS server still has the ability to forward requests to the DNS root domain servers on the Internet. You regularly use Internet DNS root servers to resolve top-level domains such as .com, .net, .org, .gov, and so forth. The main root servers are simply referred to as (.) "dot".

How does a DNS server know how to locate the root server system on the Internet.

▼ You must download an updated version of the root hints file from the Internet. Your DNS server automatically has a root hints file with the location of each DNS root-level server on the Internet and searches that file if it cannot resolve a query and cannot forward the request. The URL you can use to update the file is: ftp://ftp.rs.internic.net/domain/named.cache

DNS root servers are at the top of the DNS hierarchy and are represented by a dot (.). The next level down in the hierarchy are servers such as .com, .net, .gov. and so on.

Configure a DHCP Server

You can configure your server to provide DHCP services for your network, automatically assigning IP addresses to large numbers of networked computers. You need not configure each and every networked device in your system or domain to accept a manual assignment. You also do not have to keep records of which computer is assigned which particular IP address.

You provide your DHCP server with a block or pool of available IP addresses. No other device on your network can use any of the addresses in the address pool. If you include an IP address in your pool that is already statically assigned

to a server, printer, or switch, you cause an address conflict on the network resulting in one of the devices not connecting.

You can configure the amount of time your DHCP server assigns a particular IP address to a specific computer on the network. The amount of time you can set is called a *DHCP lease*. You can set the lease for any amount of time, but the typical time period is from a few days to a week.

Before you configure a DHCP server, you must first access the Manage Your Server Wizard. See the section, "Open the Manage Your Server Wizard" for more information.

Configure a DHCP Server

① Open the Manage Your Server Wizard, selecting DHCP server from the Server Role list in step 5.

Note: *For more on the Manage Your Server Wizard, see the section "Open the Manage Your Server Wizard."*

The Welcome to the New Scope Wizard of the Wizard appears.

② Click Next.

The Scope Name page of the Wizard appears.

③ Type a name for the scope.

● You can type an optional description.

④ Click Next.

The IP Address Range page of the Wizard opens.

⑤ Type the range of IP addresses for the scope.

● The default subnet mask and length are automatically entered.

⑥ Click Next.

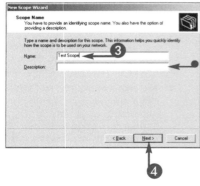

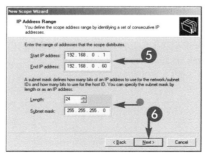

The Add Exclusions page of the Wizard appears.

⑦ Type the IP address range you want to exclude from the scope.

⑧ Click Add.

The addresses are added.

⑨ Click Next.

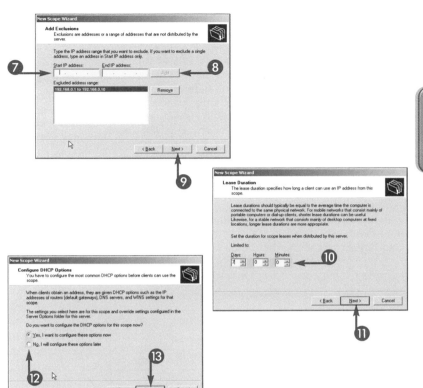

The Lease Duration page of the Wizard appears.

⑩ Type the amount of time for DHCP leases.

⑪ Click Next.

The Configure DHCP Options page of the Wizard appears.

⑫ Click to specify when you want to configure the options (○ changes to ⊙).

⑬ Click Next.

Why do I need to give my IP address scope a name and description?

▼ You can create several scopes on your DHCP server, and each scope can provide dynamic IP address assignments to different groups of computers. Giving each scope a name and description helps you keep track of which computer groups are using which address scopes. You use this information to resolve any issues if there is an IP address conflict on your network. *Lease durations* are how long a dynamic IP address is assigned to a particular computer are also configured in this part of the Wizard.

Why do I exclude IP addresses from the scope instead of creating a scope that does not have static addresses in it?

▼ You exclude blocks of IP addresses from your IP address scope for ease of configuration. You can configure a scope that contains all the IP addresses available on your subnet in order to provide as many addresses as possible for an enterprise-level network. From that scope, you can then decide which address ranges to use for static assignments, reserving not only blocks off addresses already assigned, but also other addresses in the block for equipment you add later.

continued

Configure a DHCP
Server *(Continued)*

The New Scope Wizard lets you determine whether to configure additional DHCP options now or at a later time. These options include configuring the address for the local default gateway router, the DNS server, and the WINS server. If you choose to configure these options, you can still select whether to activate the scope now or at a later time.

When you configure your DHCP server to automatically assign IP addresses to network nodes, you allow the computers on your network to communicate with each other and with other devices statically addressed. You have not told those computers where they can find other

necessary services. The default gateway router is a router specifically designated to provide a path out of the local subnet to other company subnets and the Internet. For more information on what a DNS server does on a network, see the section "Configure a DNS Server."

Along with dynamically assigning computers an IP address, subnet mask, default gateway and DNS server, DHCP can also assign a WINS server address. A WINS server is also known as a Windows Internet Service server. Older Windows operating systems such as Windows 95, Windows 98, and Windows NT require WINS to provide name-to-address resolution, and you must provide WINS services if your network contains legacy operating systems. For more on WINS servers, see the section "Configure a WINS Server."

Configure a DHCP Server *(continued)*

The Router (Default Gateway) page of the Wizard appears.

⑭ Type the IP address of the default gateway for the subnet.

⑮ Click Add.

The address is added.

⑯ Click Next.

The Domain Name and DNS Servers page appears.

⑰ Type the name of parent domain.

⑱ Type the name of the DNS server.

⑲ Click Resolve.

The DNS server IP address is automatically added.

⑳ Click Add.

The IP address is added to the box.

㉑ Click Next.

The WINS Servers page of the Wizard appears.

㉒ Type the WINS server name.

㉓ Click Resolve.

㉔ Click Add.

㉕ Click Next.

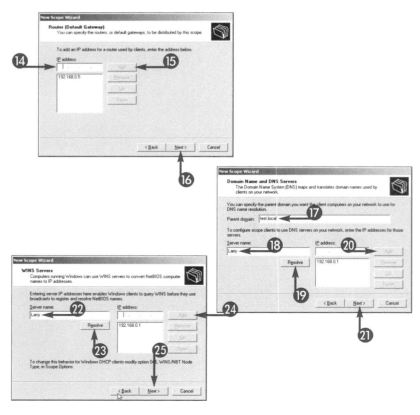

The Activate Scope page appears.

㉖ Click whether you want to activate your selection now (☐ changes to ☉).

㉗ Click Next.

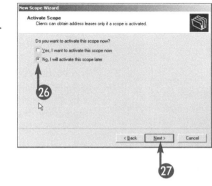

The Completing the New Scope Wizard page appears.

㉘ Click Finish.

The This Server is Now a DHCP Server page opens.

㉙ Click Finish.

The server now functions as a DHCP server.

Can I add more than one DNS or WINS server into the DHCP Server Scope configuration wizard?

▼ Yes. You can add as many DNS and WINS servers as you feel necessary to provide adequate services to your client base. You typically find two DNS servers and two WINS servers on most networks. You can add more if you feel that you require additional load balancing or failover. You can also change the position of each server IP address so that particular servers are queried for resolution services first, second, and so on.

When do I choose to not activate my DHCP scope immediately after configuring it?

▼ In the Activate Scope page, you can choose to activate a selected scope later (☐ changes to ☉). You can create a DHCP server and configure several scopes before the network is fully installed. You can choose to set up your server services in a new office before any workstation computers have even been installed. By leaving your scope inactive, you do not have IP addresses assigned to computers that are not ready to go on the network. You also can make adjustments to your network addressing scheme easier by not having live addresses on the LAN.

Configure a File Server

Y ou can use your Windows Server 2003 machine as a file server and allow client computers on your network to store their files and application data in a central storage device so you can administer the safety and security of all business information. Having network users store all of their work in a single location lets you manage all the company data rather than storing it on the hard drives of multiple computers in the enterprise network environment.

You can back up only your server information and secure company information in case of network or computer failure. You cannot back up hundreds or even thousands of

individual computers. If your business data is on a regularly backed-up server and an individual computer crashes, you can still recover the data. You can also recover data if your file server crashes because you back up server data to removable storage.

You can also share data from your file server to allow team members on your network to access common files and collaborate on a single file set. This helps you avoid saving individual and unsynchronized copies of data on specific workstations.

Configure a File Server

1 Open the Manage Your Server Wizard, selecting File server from the Server Role in step 5.

Note: *For more on the Manage Your Server Wizard, see the section "Open the Manage Your Server Wizard."*

The Share a Folder Wizard appears.

2 Click Next.

The Folder Path page of the Wizard appears.

3 Type the path to the shared folder.

4 Click Next.

The Name, Description, and Settings page of the Wizard appears.

5 Type the Share name.

6 Type a description for the shared folder.

7 Click Next.

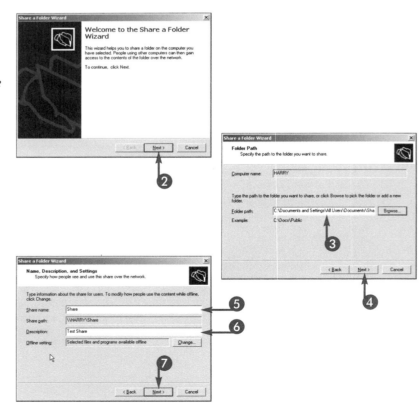

The Permissions page of the Wizard appears.

8 Click an option to set permissions for the shared folder (changes to).

9 Click Finish.

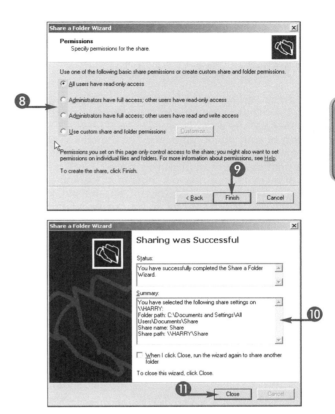

The Sharing was Successful page of the Wizard appears.

10 Verify that the information is correct.

11 Click Close.

The files are shared on the network.

What if I do not know the exact path to the shared folder on the server?

▼ You can click Browse on the Folder Path page of the Wizard and use Windows Explorer to browse the file structure until you find the particular folder where you want to create the share. If you have not created the particular folder yet, you can create a new folder on the fly in Windows Explorer before you designate it as the share location. Also, if you know the name of the shared folder, but are unsure how to browse for it, click Start, click Search, then click For Files or Folders. When the search window opens, click the Address menu and browse to My Network Places, click All Files and Folders and then type the name of the folder you are looking for and click Search.

On the Name, Description, and Settings page of the wizard, what happens if I click Change next to the Offline setting field?

▼ If you click Change, you open the Offline Settings dialog box. In this box, you can choose to make all shared files and programs available offline, make only selected files and programs available, or make no files or programs available offline. You also can choose to optimize all files and programs if you have automatically shared them. This means that a copy of the files that are on the server are available on your computer when you are not connected to the company LAN. This option is most often accessed by users with mobile computers who travel on business.

Configure a Print Server

Y ou can assign your Windows Server 2003 device the role of print server to allow the server to manage the print requests on your network. By organizing all your printing processes on a print server, you can centralize the print queues for multiple print jobs and multiple print devices. This gives you greater ease in setting up new printers on your network. Instead of loading printer drivers on each individual computer in your domain, you install all the printer software for all your networked printers on one server. Once users add a particular print device to their computers for use, users connect to the print server and the drivers automatically load onto their computers.

You can also avoid installing print devices onto individual computers using parallel or USB cables. Each print device you install is capable of connecting to the Local Area Network (LAN) with onboard network interface cards (NICs), and you must manually configure them with their own, unique IP addresses. You then connect your print server to each print device, creating print devices on your server just as you do on a computer. You can also connect printers directly to the print server to provide access to client workstations. For more on printers, see Chapter 8.

Configure a Print Server

① Open the Manage Your Server Wizard, selecting Print server in the Server Role list in step 5.

Note: *For more on the Manage Your Server Wizard, see the section "Open the Manage Your Server Wizard."*

The Add Printer Wizard appears.

② Click Next.

The Local or Network Printer page of the Wizard appears.

③ Click either the Local printer or Network printer option (◯ changes to ◉).

This example uses the Local Printer option.

④ Click Next.

The Select a Printer Port page of the Wizard appears.

⑤ Click the "Create a new port Type of port" option (◯ changes to ◉).

⑥ Click here and select Standard TCP/IP Port.

⑦ Click Next.

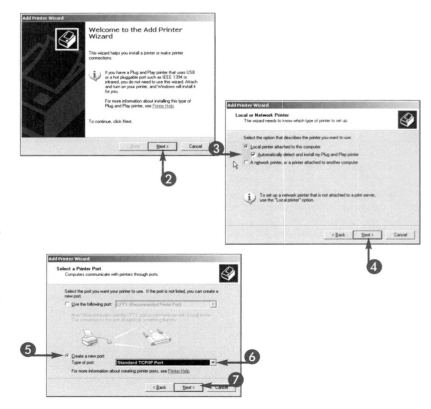

The Add Standard TCP/IP Printer Port Wizard appears.

8 Click Next.

The Add Port page of the Wizard appears.

9 Type the Printer Named or IP Address of the network printer.

10 Click Next.

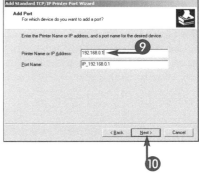

The Completing the Add Standard TCP/IP Printer Port Wizard appears.

11 Click Finish.

Do all print servers manage print devices connected by Ethernet cables to the network?

▼ No. You can configure your Windows Server 2003 print server to manage a print device in the same way that any other computer manages and shares a printer. You can attach a print device to the server with a USB or IEEE 1394 (FireWire) cable and the server automatically detects and installs the print device without using the Add Printer Wizard. Also, you can use wireless technology to connect a print server to an appropriately equiped printer using IEEE 802.11 a, b, or g compliant equipment. The wired LAN can connect to a wireless access point and transmit and receive data to and from a printer using a wireless network interface card.

Do I have to create a TCP/IP port to add a network print device to the network and manage it with my print server?

▼ No. On the Local or Network Printer page, you can select a network printer, and then click Next. On the next page, either specify the print device host name, IP address, or browse the network for the print device. You must have already installed the print device on the network and given it an IP address for the print server to detect it. You must also install the appropriate print drivers for the printer onto your print server. Otherwise, print jobs do not print correctly.

continued

Configure a Print Server *(Continued)*

Once you create a TCP/IP port for your print device and tell your print server the IP address of the print device you are creating, you create the specific print device. You must install the specific printer drivers on your Windows Server 2003 print server just as if it were a workstation on the network. You can install print drivers either from the driver CD that came with the print device or by connecting to Microsoft's Windows Update page on the Internet. You can also automatically install the drivers because your server operating software comes

equipped with thousands of device drivers. You can connect to the printer manufacturer Web site to download the latest drivers for the device to your server.

Once you complete the Add a Printer Wizard for the first time, your server becomes a print server. You can run the Wizard again to add a second network printer. You must run the Add a Printer Wizard each time you want to add a network printer to be administered by this particular print server. You can also create multiple print servers to manage groups of print devices in different locations or subnets.

Configure a Print Server *(continued)*

The Install Printer Software page appears.

⑫ Click a printer manufacturer.

⑬ Click a printer.

⑭ Click Next.

The Name Your Printer page of the Wizard appears.

⑮ Type your printer name.

⑯ Click Next.

The Printer Sharing page of the Wizard appears.

⑰ Click Share Printer (◯ changes to ◉).

⑱ Type the share name.

⑲ Click Next.

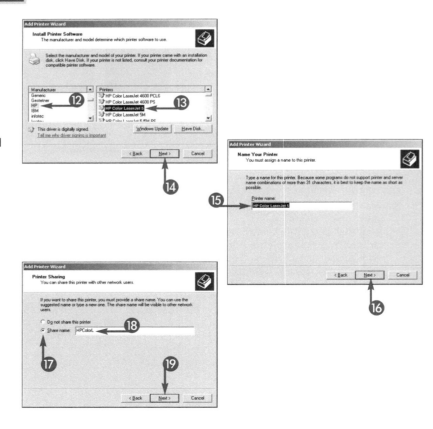

The Print Test Page of the Wizard appears.

⑳ Click an option to print a test page (⬭ changes to ⦿).

㉑ Click Next.

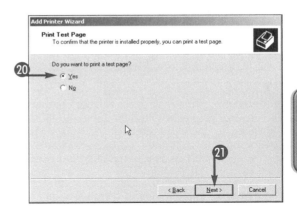

The Completing the Add Printer Wizard page appears.

㉒ Click Finish.

The Print device and Print Server are created.

PART II

Why is the printer name different than the share name?

▼ You can name your printer anything on the Name Your Printer page and your Windows Server 2003 print server uses the name as the basis for the Share Name. It is not necessary for the two names to be the same or even similar and you have the option to change the share name for the printer. The Share Name is eight characters long by default. You can create a print server to accommodate many different types of computers on the network. Older Windows computers can only use shorter Share Names. If your computers have only Windows 2000 and later installed, you can make the Share Name longer.

Can I create one print server to administer all the print devices on my network at all locations and subnets.

▼ Yes, you can, but you may experience some problems on the network. Your users may not be able to print as effectively because they may need to connect to the print server across one or more routers just to queue a print job at a print device next to them. Your configuration may cause delays and you may overload your print server causing the server to lose print jobs. Also, a large number of print jobs being sent through a gateway router from one subnet to another may bottleneck the gateway router, slowing down all traffic transversing that gateway.

Configure a Mail Server

You can control the receiving, storing, and delivering of e-mail traffic to your company by configuring your Windows Server 2003 as a mail server. Doing so gives you the ability to store e-mails for any period of time, back them up to a removable storage device for safety, and recover e-mails for your users when they accidentally delete them.

You configure an e-mail server to use several different protocols including Simple Mail Transport Protocol (SMTP), Post Office Protocol 3 (POP3), and Internet Mail Access Protocol (IMAP). Your mail server uses SMTP whenever you send a piece of e-mail and it passes mail between mail

servers. POP3 and IMAP are both used to connect mail client software such as Outlook to a mail server. IMAP is newer and more sophisticated than POP3 but POP3 is universally supported. You can use a number of mail clients including Outlook and Outlook Express to interact with the SMTP server. Your SMTP server receives your mail from your mail client across the network, queues the mail along with other mail it is sending, and transmits the mail across the LAN or the Internet to its destination. Your mail server can receive e-mails using both POP3 and IMAP. You can configure your mail server with either of these protocols to make user mailboxes and store e-mails. IMAP keeps the e-mails on your mail server even when users read them.

Configure a Mail Server

① Open the Manage Your Server Wizard, selecting Mail server (POP3, SMTP) in the Server Role list in step 5.

Note: *For more on the Manage Your Server Wizard, see the section "Open the Manage Your Server Wizard."*

② Click Next.

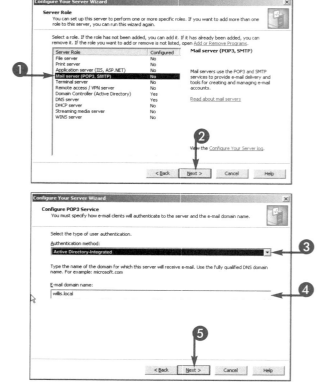

The Configure POP3 Service page of the Wizard appears.

③ Click here and select Authentication Method.

④ Type your e-mail domain name.

⑤ Click Next.

The Summary of Selections page of the
Wizard appears.

6 Review the data.

7 Click Next.

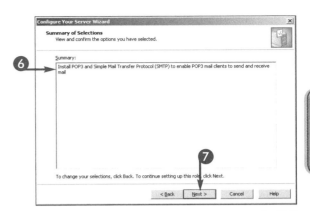

The components are installed.

The This Server is Now a Mail Server page
appears.

8 Click Finish.

The mail server is created.

**Are there any other tasks I need to do to ensure
that my users can send and receive e-mail?**

▼ Yes. On the Manage Your Server page, beside the
Mail Server (POP3, SMTP), you can click the
Manage this mail server link to open the POP3
Service window. In this window, you can expand
the server icon, right-click the domain name, click
New, and then click Mailbox. Now you can start
creating new mailboxes for your clients to use for
sending and receiving e-mail. POP3 has both client
and service components that work together so that
a mail server can retrieve and download e-mails and
then read and manage them on the client machine.

**Is there any help on my Windows Server 2003
Mail Server to provide additional information
about making and configuring user mailboxes?**

▼ Yes. On the This Server is Now a Mail Server page,
you can click the "View the next steps for this role"
link to open a help window containing detailed
instructions on creating mailboxes in your POP3
server. You can also use the Review the next steps
for this role link on the Manage Your Server page to
open the same help box. Also, you can click Start
and click Help and Support to open the Help and
Support Center page. Type "mail server" in the
search window and click the green arrow. Additional
information about mail server configuration
becomes available.

Configure a WINS Server

The advantage of configuring a WINS Server on your network is that you can provide names to address resolution for older Windows operating systems such as Windows 95, Windows 98, and Windows NT. Without running WINS on your network, your older clients cannot access some computers, servers, and resources on your network.

WINS stands for *Windows Internet Services* and is an earlier name resolution service designed specifically for Windows computers. WINS specifically resolves network addresses to NetBIOS host names. NetBIOS stands for *Network Basic*

Input/Output System and is a 15-character name with a hidden 16th character that carries additional information about the computer affiliation with a domain and server type.

You do not have to configure WINS if your entire network operates Windows 2000, Windows XP, and Windows Server 2003 machines because those operating systems use long host names and DNS for address-to-name resolution. You can also maintain a WINS server on your network if you use older applications that require NetBIOS names to function. For more on DNS server services, see the section "Configure a DNS Server" earlier in this chapter.

Configure a WINS Server

① Open the Manage Your Server Wizard, selecting WINS server in the Server Role list in step 5.

Note: *For more on the Manage Your Server Wizard, see the section "Open the Manage Your Server Wizard."*

② Click Next.

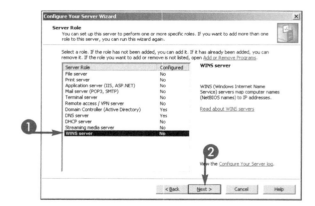

The Summary of Selections page of the Wizard appears.

③ Click Next.

Components begin to install.

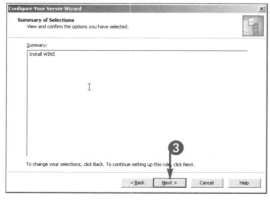

The Insert Disk dialog box appears.

④ Insert the Windows Server 2003 Installation CD.

⑤ Click OK.

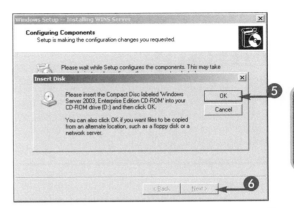

The This Server is Now a WINS Server page of the Wizard appears.

⑦ Click Finish.

Your WINS server is created.

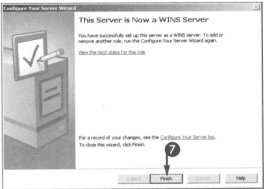

How do I access my WINS server to continue to configure and manage it?

▼ You can access it by clicking the Manage this WINS server link on the Manage Your Server page. You can also click Start, All Programs, Administrative Tools, and click WINS on the Administrative Tools menu. The WINS page appears and you can click the server name to see the Active Registrations and Replication Partners folders. You can also verify that WINS services are active by seeing that a green arrow is on top of the WINS server icon on this page.

How do I configure Active Registrations and Replication Partners on my WINS server?

▼ You can configure Active Registrations by right-clicking the Active Registrations folder and selecting Display Records, New Static Mappings or Import LMHOSTS file. You can use each of these methods to add NetBIOS host names into the WINS server database. You can configure Replication Partners by right-clicking the Replication Partners folder and selecting New Replication Partner. A window appears where you can type the host name or IP address of the partner, or browse the network for the partner server.

Understanding Printing

You can provide printing services on your network to allow all of your users to create hardcopies of their documents, graphics, presentations, and other forms that allow every person in business to display, store, and demonstrate their work. Your ability to install, configure, and maintain printing services on your network is one of your most important tasks. Your users may view a failure of printing services just as seriously as a failure of e-mail services. The concepts presented below are a broad overview of printing and print services.

Printer

A *printer* is not a machine or device that produces hard copies of text or graphics on paper. A printer is actually the software interface between the operating system and the printing device. The printer determines where the output from the computer issuing the print command goes — a local parallel or serial port, a TCP port, a network connection, or a file. The printer name you configure when you set up a print device points to the device.

Print Device

The *print device* is what you think of when you think of a printer. The print device is the actual, mechanical device that receives the input from the computer and printer, formats the information, and issues the output on paper using an ink medium. Print devices can be either directly connected to a computer or connected to a network.

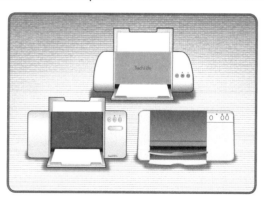

Print Server

A *print server* is a type of computer that manages print jobs from network computers to print devices. Instead of sending a print request directly to a print device from a computer, the request goes to the print server, which processes the request and sends it to the selected print device. You can use print servers to configure and share print devices on a network.

Printer Pooling

You can use printer pooling to use multiple printers as if they were a single print device. You can do this to provide load sharing among your pooled printers so that no one printer receives more print jobs than any other. Your print server will create the printer pool as a single printer with as many output ports as you assign. When you send a print job to the pool, the first available printer receives the job and prints it. You must use printers of the same kind and locate them in a central location together.

Print Driver

A *print driver* is a collection of small programming files that contain specific information. A Windows Server 2003 print server uses these program files to translate print requests into different printer languages. Each print device manufacturer writes print drivers that are specifically for each model of device it makes. You must already have the printer drivers on the print server as part of the Windows Server 2003 operating system, or you must install the drivers, before the print device can work.

Local Print Device

You can make any print device a *local print device* when you directly connect the device to a computer by either a parallel cable or a USB connection. You can either configure a local print device for dedicated use by one computer, or for shared use on a network so that other users can access it. You can only use the local print device when the computer is powered up and connected to the network because the local print device is configured for others to use on the network and is unavailable when the host computer is not running.

Network Print Device

You can use a network print device to provide print device services to a group of users on a workgroup or domain network. The device must be equipped with a network interface card (NIC). You can purchase a device with a NIC already installed, or you can install the NIC yourself if the device is equipped for a NIC installation. Because the device is not associated with an individual computer, you must install the printer and print drivers on a print server and create a share for the network print device so that users can access it.

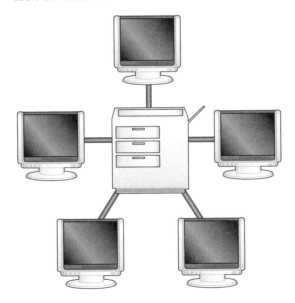

TCP/IP Port Print Device

You can use a NIC to configure a print device to connect to a network and not have the printer and print drivers installed on a print server. After you connect the print device to the network, you can configure each computer accessing the device with a port that is associated with the IP address you assign to the device. You can also configure a print server to connect to a device with a TCP/IP port. You can read more about this type of print device in Chapter 7.

Configure Point and Print Services

Y ou can configure Point and Print services on a Windows Server 2003 print server. This allows users on your network to print to a network print device without having to first manually install the print drivers for the device. You can use Point and Print to automatically install drivers. This speeds up the process of installing and using a print device because you do not have to install drivers on each individual computer using the driver installation disk that is packaged with the print device.

When you use Windows NT servers as print servers, the print drivers you load run on the server in kernel mode. Any driver error on the Windows NT print server crashes your

server, forcing you to restart the server so you can restore print services on the network. Windows 2000 Server and Windows Server 2003 print servers run print drivers in user mode, which isolates the print drivers on your print server from the operating system kernel. If a driver error occurs, the print server does not crash and you can restore print services for your network users by just restarting the print spool. You configure Point and Print services on a network client computer by connecting to a network print share on a print server. For more on print servers, see Chapter 7.

Configure Point and Print Services

① Click Start.

② Click Run.

Note: *The client computer used in this example is running Windows 2000 Professional. This method can also be used with Windows XP.*

The Run dialog box appears.

③ Type*servername\printername*, where *servername* is the name of the server and *printername* is the name of the printer.

④ Click OK.

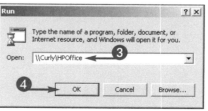

The Printers dialog box appears.

⑤ Click Yes.

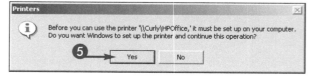

The network print device window appears.

6 Click the Close button (⊠) to close the window.

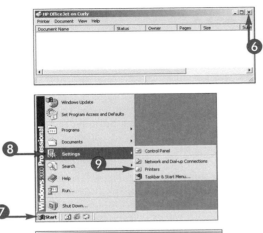

7 Click Start.
8 Click Settings.
9 Click Printers.

● The Printers window appears showing that a new network printer is added.

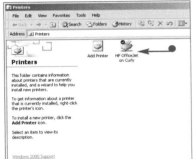

Are there any methods other than the UNC path that I can use to access Point and Print Services on a print server?

▼ Yes. You can use the Add a Printer Wizard and specify a network printer. You can then add the path to the print device share on the print server. You can also browse from either My Network Places or the Run window. In addition, you can right-click Start and select Explore to find the print server and the network print device shares on it. Then you open the share you want to add the device.

Does the Windows Server 2003 print server have print drivers that are compatible with all client computers?

▼ Not by default. You can set up a print server to provide print services to only Windows 2000 and Windows XP client computers, or you can specify that all Windows client computers have access. You can initially configure the print server for only 2000 and XP clients. Later, you can open the properties box of the print device on the server and, on the Sharing tab, click Additional Drivers to select the drivers you want to install for particular client computers.

Enable Web-Based Printer Management

You can configure your Windows Server 2003 print server to access and manage a print device using the server Web browser, which eases your job as administrator of your network printers. You can also let users connect their computers to a network print device with their computer's Web browser. You access the various print device controls in a browser environment the same way you remotely access another server or computer on your network, or configure other network devices, such as routers and switches. You can manage numerous devices using your Web browser. Even home users configure wireless access points and routers by a simple-to-use Web interface.

You can also set up Windows XP and Windows 2000 Professional computers to use Internet browsers to manage network print devices, turning them into print servers. You can set no more than 10 simultaneous client connections to a print device when you set up XP and 2000 Professional to be print servers.

You enable Web-Based Printer Management on Windows Server 2003 Print Servers by installing Internet Information Services (IIS) services. IIS is no longer installed on Windows 2000 Servers by default for security reasons. You can read more about remote management services in Chapter 18.

Enable Web-Based Printer Management

① Click Start.

② Click Control Panel.

③ Click Add or Remove Programs.

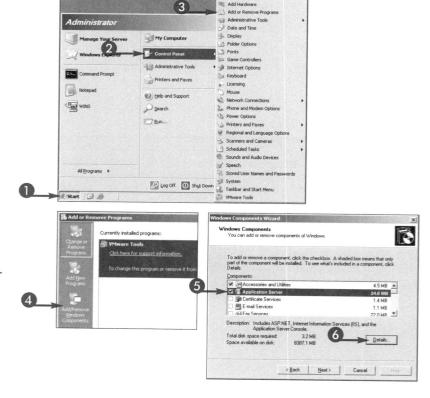

The Add or Remove Programs window appears.

④ Click Add/Remove Windows Components.

The Windows Components Wizard appears.

⑤ In the Components field, click Application Server (☐ changes to ☑).

⑥ Click Details.

The Application Server dialog box appears.

⑦ Click Internet Information Services (IIS) (☐ changes to ☑).

⑧ Click Details.

The Internet Information Services (IIS) dialog box appears.

⑨ Click the Internet Printing option (☐ changes to ☑).

⑩ Click the World Wide Web Service option (☐ changes to ☑).

⑪ Click Details.

The World Wide Web Service dialog box appears.

⑫ Click the Active Server Pages option (☑ changes to ☐).

⑬ Click OK.

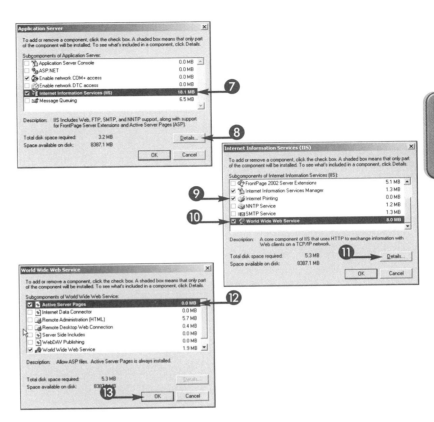

When I select all the different options in the Windows Components Wizard, do I click all of the check boxes for each component?

▼ No. You can select most of the components in this section by clicking once on each component so that it is highlighted in blue. If you inadvertently deselect a checked box, you can uninstall the component and disable your ability to set up and use Web-based printer management. Make sure you select the correct component or Windows will not take you to the correct options when you click Details. In this event, you will have to click the Back button to return to the page where you can correct the error.

Should these components have been installed when this server was made a print server?

▼ Not by default. You can make a server a print server, but you can never manage network print devices through a Web browser. Many Windows Server 2003 components are not installed when the server is installed or a role is assigned because you do not need most of those components. You can choose to install all Windows Components available, but you may bloat your server with unnecessary software programs. Also your server will become extremely vulnerable to outside intruders so this method is not recommended.

continued

Enable Web-Based Printer Management *(Continued)*

Once you specify the particular components you want installed in the Application Server boxes, you can use your Windows Server 2003 installation CD to install the programs you need to enable Web-based printer management. You can select Internet Printing in the Wizard to automatically install Active Server Pages (ASP) because both work together to enable Internet Print Management. If you set Active Server Pages to Allowed but Internet Printing to Prohibited in the IIS Manager, you can use Web-based printer management, but you prevent your users from connecting to any network print shares through their Web browsers.

You can allow users to do Internet Printing in two ways — by creating an IPP printer connection and using an HTTP printer port or by having Windows create a remote procedure call (RPC) and printer connection. Windows can create an IPP printer port if the Windows Explorer Web browser security settings for the Web content zone are set at medium or higher. Windows creates an RPC true-connect printer connection if the Web browser security settings are at medium-low or lower.

Enable Web-Based Printer Management *(continued)*

All open dialog boxes close and the Windows Components Wizard reappears.

⑭ Click Next.

The Configuring Components page of the Wizard and the Insert Disk dialog box appear.

⑮ Insert the Windows Server 2003 installation CD.

⑯ Click OK.

Components are installed from the CD.

The Completing the Windows Components Wizard page appears.

⑰ Click Finish.

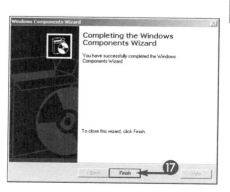

⓲ Click Start.

⓳ Click All Programs.

⓴ Click Administrative Tools.

㉑ Click Internet Information Services (IIS) Manager.

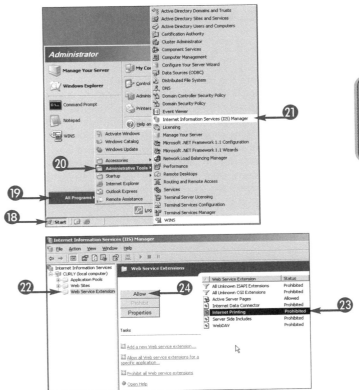

The IIS Manager appears.

㉒ Click Web Service Extensions.

㉓ Right-click Internet Printing.

㉔ Click Allow.

Print Server can now manage network print devices with a Web browser.

What are some of the improvements in IISv6 that ships with Windows Server 2003?

▼ Internet Information Services (IIS) is actually a group of services including FTP, HTTP, SMTP for e-mail and NNTP for news groups, and is the Microsoft product to create Web pages. You can use Active Server Page (ASP) to embed application software such as ActiveX into Internet Explorer (IE) Web pages. ASP allows server-side scripting and access to COM objects. IISv6 improvements including Http.sys, WAS, Application Handlers/Worker Processes, and IIS Admin Service. Microsoft also improved the scalability, security, and manageability of IISv6 over prior versions.

What are Web Service Extensions, including ASP and Internet Printing?

▼ You can use Web Service Extensions to provide any of the services that make up IIS including ASP and Internet Printing. You can have any number of different extensions loaded into IIS and then allow or prohibit those Web Service Extensions that fit the task you are using. Another important extension is Internet Server Application Program Interface (ISAPI), which is similar to CGI and SSI interfaces that run under other Internet server platforms. You can use command-line scripts to configure and manage Web Service Extensions on any Windows Server 2003 computer.

Change the Location of the Print Spooler Folder

Y ou can change the location of the Print spooler folder on your Windows Server 2003 print server to improve both server performance and increase the speed at which print jobs process and complete. By moving the spooler folder to a location with more hard drive space, the spooler can accommodate a greater print job load and process jobs more quickly. Print spooling stores print jobs sent from each user computer to the print server so that the user computer does not have to wait for the print job to process before going on to other tasks. In addition, you can add more RAM to the print server and ensure that it has a

high-capacity hard drive to enable the server to process all of the print jobs sent to it in a timely manner. Otherwise, a bottleneck can form, especially if a large number of users assess your server, or if your users print large files.

You can also increase resources on your print server because print spooling uses more space than the actual data being printed. Spooling requires that you send print jobs through the printer device drivers so they can prepare the data sets for actual printing. The size of the print spooler folder dictates the number of print jobs the server can accept.

Change the Location of the Print Spooler Folder

① Click Start.

② Click Run.

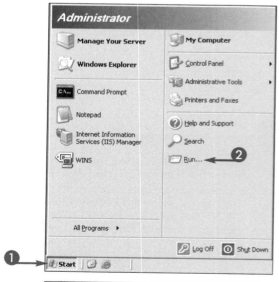

The Run dialog box appears.

③ Type the path to where you want to place the new spooler folder.

④ Click OK.

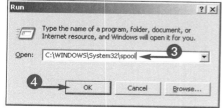

The Windows Explorer window appears.

5 Right-click in the window.

6 Click New.

7 Click Folder.

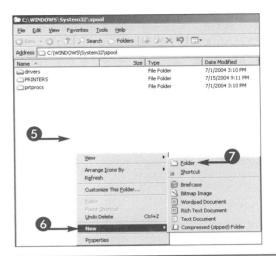

A new folder appears.

8 Type a name for the new folder.

9 Click ✕.

The Windows Explorer window closes.

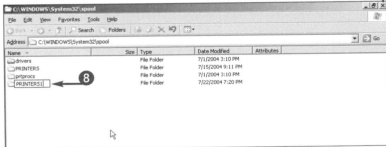

Do I have to use the Run dialog box to access the location where I intend to place the new spooler folder?

▼ No. You can click Start, My Computer, and then the C drive, and then continue clicking the folder structure until you arrive at the place where you want to create the folder. You can also right-click Start, click Explore, use Windows Explorer to navagate the file structure to the proper location, and then create the new spooler file. You can also use the same method to right-click the appropriate drive rather than the Start button and use Windows Explorer.

Why do I have to create a new spooler folder ahead of time and not when I am ready to move the spooler from the old location to the new one?

▼ You can only move the spooler folder to an already created location. You cannot execute any sort of move command that automatically moves the spooler folder and creates the new folder at the same time. Attempts to move the spooler folder to a nonexistant location will fail. This feature does not support "on the fly" creation of a new spooler folder location.

continued

Change the Location of the Print Spooler Folder *(Continued)*

After you create the new location for the Print Spooler folder, you can start the process of moving the spooler from the old folder to the new folder by accessing the Print Server Properties. You can configure other functions from the Print Server Properties dialog box including the type and size of forms your server can manage, the printer ports your server is configured to use, and the print drivers that are loaded on your Print Server.

On the Advanced tab in the Print Server Properties dialog box, you cannot only change the path to the spooler folder, but you can also set up a number of spooler log

notifications including spooler errors, warning events, and informational events. You can have these settings recorded in the Print Server Event Log. For more on viewing Event Logs, see Chapter 23.

Before you change the location of the Print Spooler folder, you should notify all your users not to send any print jobs to the print server. Any print jobs that are pending when you change the location of the print spooler do not print. Alternatively, you can take the printer offline and wait for the print queue to empty before moving the folder.

Change the Location of the Print Spooler Folder *(continued)*

⑩ Click Start.

⑪ Click Printers and Faxes.

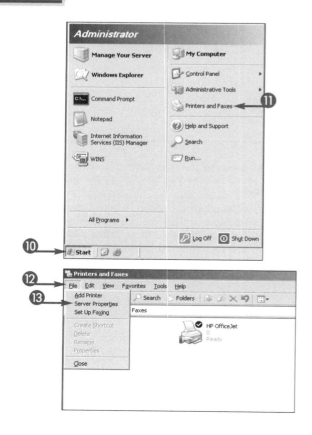

The Printers and Faxes window appears.

⑫ Click File.

⑬ Click Server Properties.

The Print Server Properties dialog box appears.

⑭ Click the Advanced tab.

⑮ Type the complete path to the new spooler folder.

⑯ Click OK.

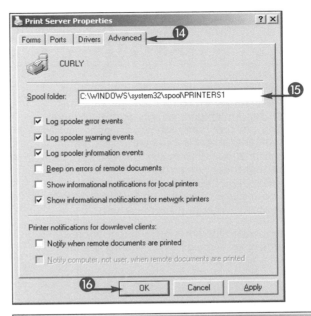

A warning box appears.

⑰ Click Yes to apply the changes.

The Print Spooler folder is moved.

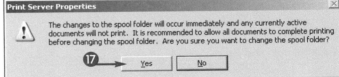

Is there anything I need to check to ensure the move was successful?

▼ You can make sure that the print spooler services are still running. Click Start, Administrative Tools, and then Services. When the Services window appears, scroll down the list to Print Spooler and click it. You should see a notation indicating whether the print spooler is started or stopped. You can also start and restart print spooler services here if you think the print server did not record the changes. You can stop print spooler services if it appears the move was successful, but is still not functioning, then restart services.

Does each print device associated with a print server have a separate spooler folder?

▼ No. You can direct print jobs only to one location in the Windows Server 2003 print server for print job spooling. You must make sure that the spooler folder is on a disk volume large enough to manage all the print requests from all users accessing the server and all the print devices the server manages. You can even install an additional hard drive and place the Print Spooler folder there to ease the load. You can move the spooler folder to a large area if you anticipate that it will receive a great number of print jobs, such as those that a printer pool processes.

Set Printer Priority and Availability Levels

Y ou can set printer priority levels for the different printers that your print server manages so that print jobs sent to a higher priority print device are processed first. You can configure high-priority print devices so that only mission-critical teams, or departments that must have immediate access to print services, can use them. This means that these groups do not have to wait for print jobs from other departments to print before they access the same print server. You set print priorities on print devices using the same printer port on the server.

You can set printer availability times for different printers that the same print server manages. This enables you to create two or more virtual print devices on the same

physical print device in the Printers and Faxes page so that you can offload excessively large print jobs during peak business hours.

You can use both options to maximize your printer and print device resources to meet printing service demands in a business environment. You can also configure printer pooling, so that print jobs can be assigned round robin to the first available print device in the pool. However, you can only configure printer pooling for print devices that have the same make and model.

Set Printer Priority and Availability Levels

① Click Start.

② Click Printers and Faxes.

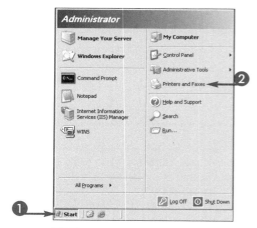

The Printers and Faxes page appears.

③ Right-click a printer.

④ Click Properties.

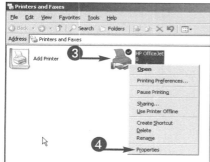

The printer's Properties dialog box appears.

5 Click the Advanced tab.

6 Click the Available from option (⊙ changes to ⊙).

7 Type a start and stop time.

8 Click in the Priority field and type a priority number.

9 Click OK.

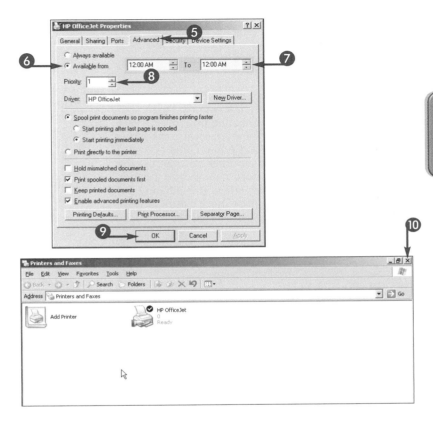

10 Click ⊠.

The Printers and Faxes page closes.

Windows Server changes the printer priority and availability levels.

How do I know which priority number is higher than another and what range I can choose from?

▼ You can set your print device priority level anywhere from 1 to 99. 1, which is the default setting, is the highest priority you can set. Although you can choose to set up to 99 different settings, it is more likely that you will choose priority settings for just a few printers attached to the print server because the printers must be using the same printer port. For example, you can set one group's printer to a priority level of 50 and another group's printer to a level 75.

How can changing the availability settings on a printer create several virtual printers available at those different times?

▼ In this context, a virtual printer is created when you change availability settings for the physical printer. Each printer, which is available only at a certain time, becomes a separate entity from the other virtual printers, which are available at different times, even though they are the same physical device. You can set a print device based on shifts to track print device usage, for example. Once you set the first print device for a particular time range, you can then use the Add Printer feature to create another printer using the same physical print device, but with a different name. You can then set the availability level for the second print device to a different time frame than the first.

Working with Print Queues

You can use a print device Print Queue to control a number of different print job functions. These functions include troubleshooting print job problems, monitoring print device use, reviewing the type of documents and other forms being printed, and even pausing or canceling print jobs at a printer. You can use the Print Queue to open a particular document sent to a print device to view the document's properties. This is handy when you want to determine whether specific print job qualities are causing problems in the Print Queue.

It is easy to confuse a print spooler and a Print Queue because they are similar to each other. Basically, a *Print Queue* lines up print jobs in a sequence so that they process in a particular order. A print spool stores print jobs that the print server receives from client's computers. The print spool stores print jobs waiting in queue to free up disk space and RAM on the client computers. Print jobs move from the spooler into the queue so you can send each print job to the print device to which they are addressed.

Working with Print Queues

① Click Start.

② Click Printers and Faxes.

The Printers and Faxes page appears.

③ Double-click a printer.

The Print Queue window appears displaying any print jobs that are being processed.

④ Click a queued document.

⑤ Click Document.

⑥ Click Pause.

Document printing pauses.

⑦ Click Document.

⑧ Click Resume.

Windows resumes printing the document; when the print job is finished the queue is empty.

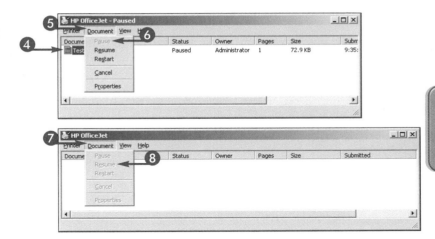

What options do I have when I click Printer on the Print Queue window?

▼ Clicking Printer opens a menu with various options. These options include setting a printer as the default printer, opening printer preferences and setting the layout and paper quality, pausing all print jobs instead of just one document, canceling all print jobs, changing printer sharing, choose the Use Printer Offline option, access Printer Properties, or close the Print Queue window. By clicking Advanced in the layout tab, you can select Paper Output options, Graphic quality, Document options and Printer features. You must be granted the necessary access to perform this function.

What can you tell about a document when it is in the Print Queue?

▼ You can tell the name of the document, who the Owner is, how many pages the document is, the size of the document, and when the user submitted it. By double-clicking the document while it is in the queue, you can open the document properties box, reset the document priority, schedule when it can print, and notify the user when the job prints. The Document Properties dialog box also has Layout and Paper Quality tabs but you cannot adjust these settings if you are not assigned the appropriate access.

9

**Data Storage
Disk Systems**

Understanding Data Storage
Disk Systems 138
Convert a Basic Disk to a Dynamic
Disk Manually 140
Convert a Basic Disk to a Dynamic
Disk on the Command Line.....................142
Increase Disk Performance on
a Dynamic Disk 144
Reactivate a Missing or Off-Line Disk 146
Create a Partition or Logical Drive 148
Create a Simple Volume 152
Add a New Hard Drive and Initialize
the Drive 156
Create a Spanned Volume 158
Extend Simple and Spanned
Volumes...162
Create a Striped Volume 164
Create a Mirrored Volume 168
Create a RAID 5 Array 172

10

**Shared and
Redirected Folders**

Understanding Shared and
Redirected Folders 176
Create a Shared Folder with Windows
Explorer 178
Create Shared Web Folders 180
Create Shares with the Shared
Folders Snap-In 182
Enable Windows File Protection
with Group Policy 186
Restrict Offline File Usage
with Group Policy 188
Enable a Computer to Use Offline Files 190

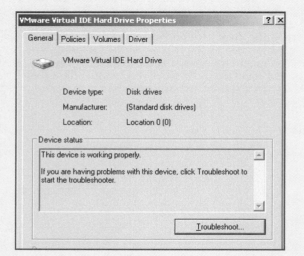

PART III
MANAGING STORAGE AND HARDWARE

11   NTFS Share Permissions

Understanding NTFS Share Permissions 192

Set Basic Share Permissions 194

Set NTFS Disk Quotas 196

Set NTFS File Compression 198

Set NTFS Data Encryption 200

Set Up Shadow Copies 202

Assign NTFS Permissions to Users
and Groups 204

Determine NTFS Effective Permissions 206

Change Ownership of Files
and Folders 210

12   Manage Devices and Device Drivers

Understanding Manage Devices
and Device Drivers....................................214

Install PnP Devices 216

Troubleshoot Installed Devices 218

Troubleshoot with Device Manager............220

Configure Automatic Updates....................222

Manually Update Device Drivers.................224

Roll Back Device Drivers............................226

Identify Unsigned Device Drivers
with sigverif.exe 228

Set Driver Signing with System
Properties 230

View USB Hub Power Allocations 232

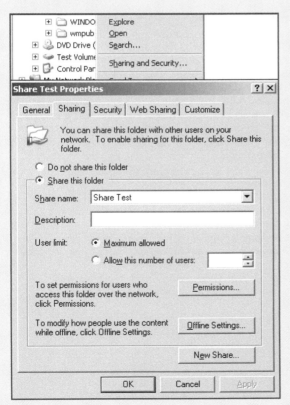

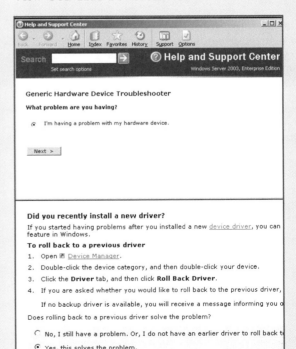

Understanding Data Storage Disk Systems

You can utilize disk storage management to manage the storage of data on your Windows Server 2003 server. When you utilize disk storage management you can create file system fault tolerance, which insures that all your business databases and file systems are available for work upon request and that they are protected from loss. Starting with Windows 2000 Server systems and continuing with Windows Server 2003, Microsoft created a number of file system features that create fault tolerance for disk systems, formatting disk volumes for file systems such as NTFS (New Technology File System), data compression, data encryption, directory-based security, and file-based security. The following concepts present a broad understanding of the nature of server data storage.

Fault Tolerance

Fault tolerance is the capacity of a computer operating system and a server hardware system to prevent the loss of data stored on the device in the event of any type of incident such as a power outage, hardware failure, or catastrophic crash of the operating system. You can use a wide variety of fault tolerance systems including uninterruptible power supplies, data backup systems, and data duplication systems.

File Management Systems

A *file management system* organizes all the files and folders on your data server. A hierarchical file system is the most commonly used. You can use it to store your data in directories and organized in a tree structure with the root directory at the top and all subdirectories located underneath. Elements under the root are called branches; smaller elements beneath the branches are called leaves. Your data are stored in files and folders organized inside your directory tree structure. You can use NTFS as well as FAT (File Allocation Table) 32 to organize your file system. FAT, commonly used in Windows 95 and Windows 98, is a table that Windows operating systems uses to track the various segments of any disk that stores data. MS-DOS supports FAT on any computer running a Windows operating system. NTFS, a newer file storage system, adds reliability to disk storage, a greater ability to recover from hard drive failures, the capacity to compress and encrypt data, and improved file-level security. Windows NT 4.0 Service Pack 4 or higher, Windows 2000, Windows XP, and Windows Server 2003 all support NTFS.

Data Compression

Data compression reduces the size of the files that store your data. This enables you to store more data in a limited space, which may help you avoid adding additional hard drives in your server system to store your growing data store. You can transmit compressed data more quickly because compressed data uses fewer bits than uncompressed data. ZIP files are an example of data compression and backup devices commonly used to compress data for storage. Windows 2003 can create ZIP files or compressed folders. Alternatively, you can flag a file for storage in a compressed format. For more about backing up your data, see Chapter 21.

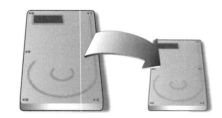

Data Encryption

You can use data encryption to store your sensitive data in a form that users cannot read unless they decrypt it. Your data is protected even if an unauthorized person accesses it because it is not stored in plain text but cipher text. You must use a secret key or password to decrypt the data. The secret key is an algorithm that converts plain text into cipher text in data encryption. For more on NTFS data encryption, see Chapter 11.

File and Directory Based Security

You can use file-based security to secure an individual file in the server data storage structure against everyone except the person who created the file. All other files in the folder and data directory structure are accessible and not affected when you set security on one file. Directory-based security is similar except you can prevent unauthorized personnel from accessing an entire branch of your data directory or just a folder containing a set of sensitive files. For more on File and Folder security and to set basic share permissions, see Chapter 11.

Redundant Array of Independent Disks (RAID)

You can use RAID to provide different types of fault tolerance to the data stored on your Windows Server 2003 file server and prevent data loss in the event of an accident affecting your server. You can implement RAID either as a hardware or a software solution in your file servers. Windows 2003 makes only the software RAID solution available. Hardware RAID provides better performance. Only use software RAID when a hardware solution is not available. You can also offload your data to the RAID controller for load balancing and reduce the responsibility of the operating system to manage your data sets. The RAID hardware solution works on many different kinds of server hardware and server operating systems, and can use any one of five levels of fault tolerance providing a mixed degree of performance, reliability, and cost. You can use RAID to combine two or more independent hard drives together to improve performance and data safety more effectively than a single disk can. You can set up RAID configurations so that different parts of the same data set are written to different disks. This increases the speed of accessing the data because separate disk reads can occur on the two disks at the same time. RAID can also make data more available to your users because if one disk is damaged or malfunctions, the data is still available from another disk. You can construct RAID in arrays, which are a collection or group of hard drives and configure them in a single RAID implementation. RAID can use both IDE and SCSI technologies. Windows Server 2003 also implements a software RAID solution using dynamic disks.

Convert a Basic Disk to a Dynamic Disk Manually

Disk sets on Windows Server 2003 are basic disks by default, and you can use a basic disk to support data created and stored on any Windows operating system. You can segment a basic disk into as many as four separate partitions or three primary partitions and one extended partition. Primary partitions are treated together as a single disk volume while you can use an extended partition to create numerous logical drives. Each logical drive you make appears as a separate drive and has a separate drive letter in the My Computer window under Hard Disk Drives on your server.

You can convert a basic disk to a dynamic disk to improve disk performance, security, and fault tolerance, and to add an increased layer of protection for your stored data sets on your file servers. You can segment a dynamic disk into numerous logical drives that are also called dynamic volumes. Your Windows Server 2003 operating system can manage your dynamic volumes with Virtual Disk service. You can only mount a dynamic disk onto a Windows Server 2003 server and Windows 2000, but users with any Windows operating system can access data on the dynamic disk. The steps in this section assume that you are converting a disk that you have already used for data storage. You cannot convert a dynamic disk back to a basic disk without losing all of your data. Perform this procedure only if it is absolutely necessary.

Convert a Basic Disk to a Dynamic Disk Manually

① Click Start.

② Right-click My Computer.

③ Click Manage.

The Computer Management snap-in appears.

④ Click Disk Management.

⑤ Right-click the basic disk.

⑥ Click Convert to Dynamic Disk.

The Convert to Dynamic Disk dialog box appears.

⑦ Click the disk that you want to convert.

⑧ Click OK.

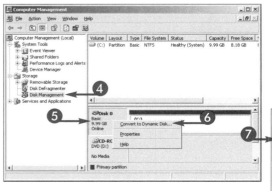

The Disks to Convert dialog box appears.

9 Click Convert.

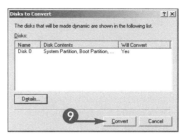

A confirmation box appears.

10 Click OK.

The server restarts.

Note: *The server restarts here automatically because the disk is not empty and has already been used for data storage.*

● The basic disk is converted to a dynamic disk.

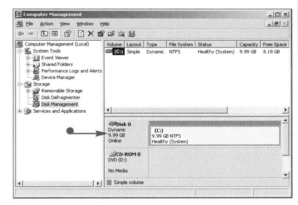

Do I always have to restart my Windows Server 2003 server when converting any basic disk to a dynamic disk?

▼ No. If you convert a completely empty basic disk to a dynamic disk, you do not have to restart your server. You only have to restart your server if you convert a disk from basic to dynamic that you have already used for data storage. However, when you use Windows NT 4.0, you must select a special Commit Changes command before you can restart the server or close the Disk Management snap-in. When you convert a disk from basic to dynamic that is not empty, the server restarts automatically after you click OK in step 10 in this section.

Can I access the Computer Management snap-in on my Windows Server 2003 device another way?

▼ Yes. You can create a stand-alone mmc console to create a Computer Management snap-in. Click Start, click Run, type **mmc** in the Run dialog box, and click OK. The mmc console manager appears. Click File, the Add/Remove Snap-in, and when the Add/Remove snap-in opens, click Add. Click Computer Management from the list and click Add. Close the snap-in then name and save your new snap-in. You can then open your new snap-in on the Administrative Tools menu by clicking Start, All Programs, Administrative Tools, or just click Start, Administrative Tools to locate the snap-in.

Convert a Basic Disk to a Dynamic Disk on the Command Line

You can convert a basic disk to a dynamic disk to improve disk performance, security, and fault tolerance. You can convert a basic disk to a dynamic disk using the command shell. This allows you to perform the conversion quickly, and without having to access the Computer Management snap-in through the GUI. Although you can use the Graphical User Interface and the numerous snap-ins to configure your Windows Server 2003 server, the command shell offers you a way to accomplish the same tasks without having to locate the specific snap-in or console in charge of that process.

You perform the conversion of a disk from Basic to Dynamic when you use the `diskpart` command in the command shell. The `diskpart` accomplishes a wide range of disk management activities besides basic-to-dynamic disk conversion. `Diskpart` can create or delete a new volume or partition, extend a volume, import a disk group, remove a drive letter or mount point assignment, repair a RAID 5 volume, and many other tasks.

When you convert a basic disk to a dynamic disk either with the Computer Management snap-in or at the command line, you can only convert the dynamic disk back to a basic disk by losing all your data. Avoid this procedure unless it is absolutely necessary.

Convert a Basic Disk to a Dynamic Disk on the Command Line

① Click Start.

② Click Command Prompt.

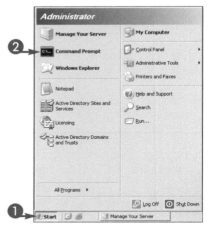

The Command Prompt window appears.

③ Type **diskpart**.

④ Press Enter.

The diskpart cursor appears.

⑤ Type **select disk 0**.

⑥ Press Enter.

● The disk 0 message appears.

7 Type **convert dynamic**.

8 Press Enter.

● A message appears instructing you to reboot to complete the operation.

9 Type **exit**.

10 Type **quit** to close Command Prompt window.

11 Click Start.

12 Click Shut Down to restart the computer.

After the computer restarts, the basic disk converts to a dynamic disk.

Can I still use FAT and FAT32 file systems on a dynamic disk or does the disk only support NTFS?

▼ You can use FAT, FAT32, or NTFS on both basic disks and dynamic disks on your Windows Server 2003 machine. You can also use the command-line tool `fsutil.exe` to manage any of the above file systems including managing disk quotas, managing mount points, and managing volumes. For example, you can type **fsutil volume** to either dismount a volume or query the free space of a volume. You can access the Windows Command Line reference at www.microsoft.com/windowsxp/home/using/productdoc/en/default.asp?url=/windowsxp/home/using/productdoc/en/ntcmds.asp

Can I use the diskpart command to convert a dynamic disk back to a basic disk?

▼ Yes. You can open a command window, type **diskpart**, click the dynamic disk you want to convert, and then type **convert basic** to initiate the conversion process. You must back up all the data on the disk before conversion or it will be lost. Once you convert the disk and restore the data, only Windows 2000, Windows XP, and Windows Server 2003 operating systems can access.the disk. You should only want to convert a dynamic disk back to basic if you need the disk to be mounted by a system other than Windows Server 2003.

Increase Disk Performance on a Dynamic Disk

You can increase the read and write performance on a dynamic disk to speed data access for users who frequently need to quickly create, modify, and save file information. You can improve performance of a dynamic disk by enabling the advanced performance features, but you must only do this on a server with a backup power supply. Enabling advanced performance can result in data loss if the hard drive loses power due to a power outage or other electrical or mechanical accident.

With the advanced performance feature, you can enable write cache to have the hard drive write the most recent transactions to a cache in temporary memory for quicker recovery by a server user. You can also lose this data during a power failure because the last several write operations are stored in RAM rather than on the hard drive. There are other features you can enable in advanced performance, but some are only available for SCSI drive arrays and not IDE.

Using a redundant power system, such as an uninterruptible power supply (UPS), can save the data cached in RAM by continuing electrical power to your server during a power outage.

Increase Disk Performance on a Dynamic Disk

① Click Start.

② Right-click My Computer.

③ Click Manage.

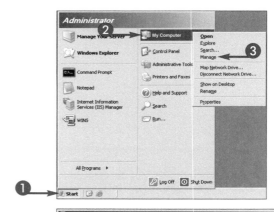

The Computer Management snap-in appears.

④ Click Disk Management.

⑤ Right-click the dynamic disk.

⑥ Click Properties.

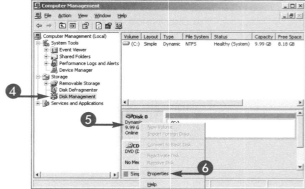

The hard drive's Properties dialog box appears.

7 Click the Policies tab.

8 Click the Enable advanced performance option (☐ changes to ☑).

9 Click OK.

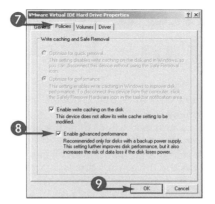

● Advanced Performance is enabled.

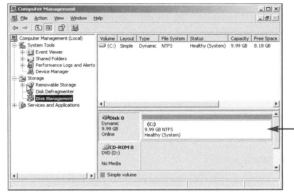

Can I disable Advanced Performance for my dynamic disk?

▼ Yes. You can change the dynamic disk back to the default performance setting, especially in situations where you do not have adequate protection of the server power supply system or your geographic area is prone to electrical power outages. Your data is at risk of loss in an electrical accident because at least some of the data is stored in cache electrically. In a power failure, any data not saved to the hard drive will be lost. You can access Disk Management in the Computer Management snap-in, right-click the disk, click Properties, and on the Policies tab, click the Enable advanced performance (☑ changes to ☐), then click OK.

In order to enable Advanced Performance on my hard drive, do I also have to click the "Enable write caching on the disk" option?

▼ No. The "Enable write caching on the disk" option is selected by default so you can enable Advanced Performance with a single action once you are at the Policies tab. If you deselect the "Enable write caching on the disk" option (☑ changes to ☐), the Enable advanced performance check box grays out and Advanced Performance is disabled if you have already activated it on your dynamic disk. Advanced Performance works by caching frequently requested data in temporary memory making the data more quickly available.

Reactivate a Missing or Off-Line Disk

You can reactivate a disk volume that is missing in the Disk Management snap-in or that is off-line due to some form of damage. Reactivating a disk volume allows you to regain access and use of that disk and the data stored on it. You can lose a disk from the Computer Management snap-in due to damage involving the hard drive or a volume on the drive. Your disk is physically present in the machine and even powered and active, but you cannot access the drive or the data on it. A disk can go off-line due to a power outage, a disconnected data cable, or a fault on the server motherboard.

You can only reactivate a missing or off-line disk if it is a dynamic disk. The reactivate option is not available for use on basic disks. You must first correct the physical problem that caused the disk to go off-line, such as restoring electrical power to the server or reconnecting the ribbon cable between the hard drive and the hard drive controller on the motherboard. The disk still reads as off-line until you use the reactivate feature in the disk management console.

① Click Start.

② Right-click My Computer.

③ Click Manage.

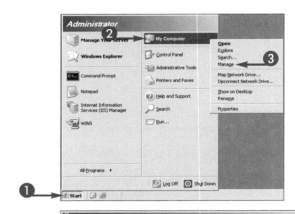

The Computer Management snap-in appears.

④ Click Disk Management.

⑤ Right-click the disk volume.

⑥ Click Reactivate Volume.

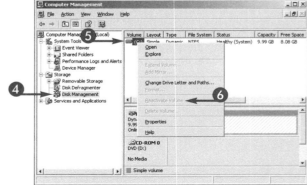

Disk volume is now Healthy.

7 Right-click Disk 0.

8 Click Properties.

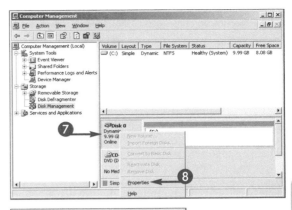

The hard drive's Properties dialog box appears.

● The Device status section indicates that the device is working properly.

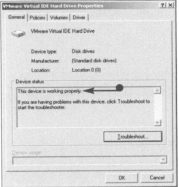

What happens if I have a basic disk that goes off-line or is missing?

▼ You can recover an off-line or missing basic disk either by repairing the physical disk or replacing the disk. If you cannot repair the disk, you can replace the disk with a new hard drive and use your backup tapes to restore any data that you may have lost when the drive failed. You can only restore the data that you have previously backed up. Any data stored on the damaged disk that you did not back up is lost. It is recommended that you store your backup tapes offsite rather than in the same area as the server.

Are there any times when I cannot use the Reactivate Volume option to restore a dynamic disk?

▼ Yes. If the disk is physically damaged and you cannot repair the damage, the Reactivate Volume option does not work. You can then replace the damaged disk and recover the data from backup. Also, if your server is an Active Directory domain controller, Active Directory replication restores the lost database information, but only after you replace the damaged disk with a new hard drive. Active Directory does not immediately restore the data but only as AD replication occurs.

Create a Partition
or Logical Drive

Y ou can create a partition or logical drive on a disk in your Windows Server 2003 server to separate data, applications, and the system folder information on a single, physical drive. This protects each different type of data from corrupting any other type, which easily occurs when you store all your data on a single partition on just one hard drive. You also can create a separate partition or logical drive and place the data you want to back up from the drive in the specific location you designate. You, thus, save time and server resources by only backing up desired information rather than everything on the physical drive.

You can create a primary partition, an extended partition, or logical drives only on a basic disk. A *primary partition* contains the operating system and is the only partition that is bootable. You can subdivide an *extended partition,* which is created from free space on the hard drive, into one or more logical drives. Downlevel Windows operating systems such as Windows NT, Windows 98, and Windows 95 can all access shared resources on the network as well as Windows 2000 and later operating systems. A significant percentage of networks that use Windows Server 2003 servers also use some legacy operating systems, and you can maintain services on a mixed operating system environment by using basic disk partitions rather than dynamic disk volumes.

Create a Partition or Logical Drive

① Click Start.

② Right-click My Computer.

③ Click Manage.

The Computer Management snap-in appears.

④ Click Disk Management.

⑤ Right-click the unallocated region of the Basic Disk.

⑥ Click New Partition.

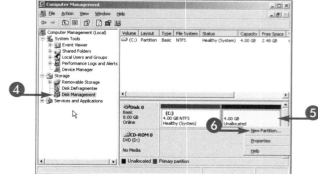

The New Partition Wizard appears.

7 Click Next.

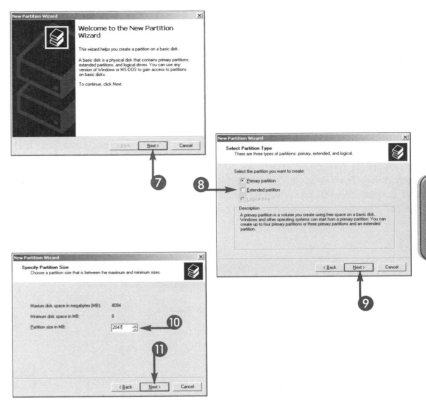

The Select Partition Type page of the Wizard appears.

8 Click a partition option (○ changes to ◉).

This example uses the Primary partition option.

9 Click Next.

The Specify Partition Size page of the Wizard appears.

10 Type a size for the partition.

Note: Create a partition the size you will need for the amount of information you plan to store.

11 Click Next.

When I am on the Select Partition Type page, why is the Logical drive option grayed out?

▼ You must first create an extended partition before you create a logical drive. Once you create an extended partition, you can create one or more logical drives using the space in the extended partition. You can create as many logical drives as you want as long as you do not exceed the space available in the extended partition. You can create one extended partition and three primary partitions or four primary partitions if you do not create an extended partition.

Can I allocate only part of the unallocated space in the Computer Management snap-in instead of using the New Partition Wizard?

▼ No. You must select the entire unallocated partition space and launch the New Partition Wizard to adjust the size and type of partition you create. You can use the `diskpart` command shell utility to create a new volume or partition on a disk in Windows Server 2003 using the `create` command, but that is your only other option besides using the wizard. If you use the command shell, you must use the diskpart utility to accomplish this task.

continued

Create a Partition or Logical Drive *(Continued)*

Y ou can either assign a drive letter to your new partition or logical drive or mount the drive to an empty NTFS folder in order to determine if users can access the data stored in the new partition as a standard drive or as a folder in the file system directory tree. In a Windows Server 2003 Active Directory environment, you can create partitions as a series of folders your users can access rather than drive letters for ease of use. Your domain users do not need to know where resources are located physically in your server system. You can create partitions

and use them as folders to place particular files in the folders. Users can use Active Directory to locate any shared resources they need in the directory tree.

You can also choose to format the partition with any available format type — usually FAT, FAT32, or NTFS — or not format the partition at all. You can create a partition now and wait to format it until you need to place data on it. That way, you can partition drive space in the particular structure that meets your needs, but not make use of it until your need for storage space sufficiently grows.

Create a Partition or Logical Drive *(continued)*

The Assign Drive Letter or Path page of the Wizard appears.

⑫ Click the "Assign the following drive letter" option (◯ changes to ◉).

⑬ Click here and select a drive letter.

● Alternatively, you can select the "Mount in following empty NTFS folder" option.

⑭ Click Next.

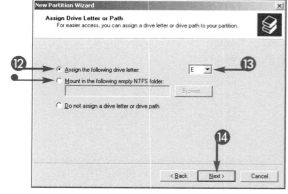

The Format Partition page of the Wizard appears.

⑮ Click the "Format this partition with the following settings" option (◯ changes to ◉).

⑯ Click here and select a file system type.

⑰ Click here and select an allocation size or leave it at the Default setting.

⑱ Type a name for the volume label.

⑲ Click Next.

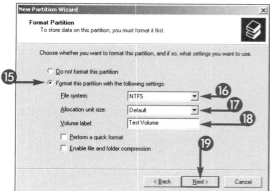

The Completing the New Partition Wizard
page of the Wizard appears.

⑳ Click Finish.

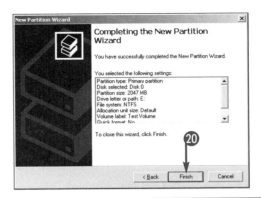

● The new primary partition is created.

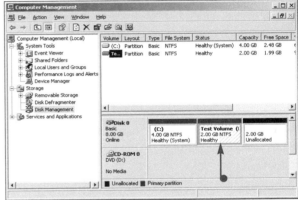

What other options can I select in the New Partition Wizard?

▼ You can choose to perform a quick format of your partition or to enable file and folder compression on the Format Partition page of the New Partition Wizard. You use the quick format option when you need to make a partition available for use quickly. You can use File and Folder compression to store a greater amount of data in a partition of limited size by compressing the data at the level of the file and folder structure. You can use this method to conserve hard drive space when adding a larger drive is not an option.

What is a mounted drive?

▼ You can use a mounted drive to attach an NTFS partition or volume to an empty folder on your Windows Server 2003 server rather than assign the partition a drive letter. You give the NTFS folder a label or a name rather than assign it a drive letter. You can then access the mounted drive by using the full path name to the folder location such as C:\MyMounts\MountPath1, or you can use Windows Explorer and browse to the location. You can have both a drive letter and one or more mount pathes to the same partition.

Create a Simple Volume

Y ou can create a simple volume on unallocated space on a dynamic disk in your Windows Server 2003 server to separate data, applications, and the system folder information on a single, physical drive. You use a simple volume on a dynamic disk in a similar way that you use a partition on a Basic Disk. For more information, see the section "Convert a Basic Disk to a Dynamic Disk." Only Windows 2000, Windows XP, and Windows Server 2003 operating systems can access data on a simple volume. Therefore, if your server provides resources for

downlevel Windows operating systems such as Windows NT, Windows 98, or Windows 95, you cannot use simple volumes on dynamic disks.

Also, unlike an extended partition on a basic disk, a simple volume on a dynamic disk cannot contain partitions or logical drives. The simple volume is a single, undividable container on your hard drive. Additionally, you cannot make a simple volume fault tolerant the way other types of volumes are on a dynamic disk. You cannot install the Windows Server 2003 operating system on a simple volume on a dynamic disk that was created directly from unallocated space on your hard drive.

Create a Simple Volume

① Click Start.

② Right-click My Computer.

③ Click Manage.

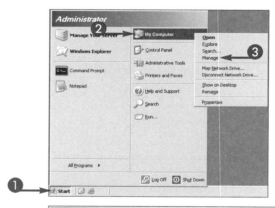

The Computer Management snap-in appears.

④ Click Disk Management.

⑤ Right-click the unallocated space.

⑥ Click New Volume.

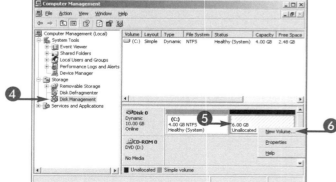

The New Volume Wizard appears.

⑦ Click Next.

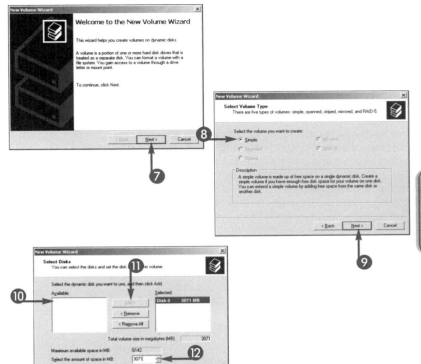

The Select Volume Type page of the Wizard appears.

⑧ Click the Simple option (⊙ changes to ⊙).

⑨ Click Next.

The Select Disks page appears.

⑩ Click in the Available section and select a dynamic disk.

⑪ Click Add.

⑫ Type the amount of space you require for use.

Note: The amount of space you select is limited by the disk space available and you can designate the amount of space you need for the purpose of this volume.

⑬ Click Next.

On the Select Volume Type in the New Volume Wizard, why is Simple the only volume type that is not grayed out?

▼ You can only create the other volume types on an already formatted simple volume. You can choose unallocated space on the disk in which to create the simple volume; you cannot create any other volume type in the unallocated space. You can use the first partition on the dynamic disk to create other types of volumes. When you convert a basic disk to a dynamic disk, any space already formatted as a primary partition is automatically converted to a simple volume.

On the Select Disks page in the New Volume Wizard, why were there no disks initially in the Available box?

▼ You can choose different disks in the Available box on the Select Disks page only if you have more than one dynamic disk created on your Windows Server 2003 server. You only have one dynamic disk on this server so the New Volume Wizard automatically selected Disk 0 as the only choice. You can select the disk and click Remove to place it in the Available box, but you cannot proceed with creating a simple volume. If you choose more than one dynamic disk, you can create a single volume from them.

continued

PART III

Create a Simple Volume *(Continued)*

Y ou can only format a dynamic volume on a dynamic disk with NTFS when you use the New Volume Wizard in the Disk Management console. A dynamic volume is subdivided into smaller areas that can be sized and resized according to your needs. You can use the `format.exe` command line utility at the command prompt to format the same Dynamic Volume with FAT or FAT 32 file systems. You must first create the dynamic volume in the Wizard, select a drive letter for the volume, but do not select a file system to format the volume. Then you can open a command shell and use the `format.exe` command set to specify fat, fat32, or ntfs as the format for the dynamic volume.

A simple volume cannot support logical drives inside the volume space because each volume is considered an independent logical drive. You use a simple volume when the server has sufficient disk space on a single hard drive to contain the entire volume. The Windows Server 2003 operating system can use the Virtual Disk service to manage dynamic disks, but the Virtual Disk service adds to the processing load of the server. Although you can configure any number of volumes on a dynamic disk, Microsoft recommends that you use only up to 32 volumes so as not to overload your server.

Create a Simple Volume *(continued)*

The Assign Drive Letter or Path page of the Wizard appears.

⑭ Click the "Assign the following drive letter" option (⬚ changes to ◉).

⑮ Select a drive letter from the drop-down list.

- Alternatively, you can select the "Mount in the following empty NTFS folder" option.

Note: *For more on this option, see the section "Create a Partition or Logical Drive.*

⑯ Click Next.

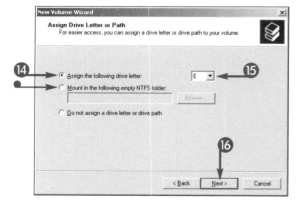

The Format Volume page of the Wizard appears.

⑰ Click the "Format this volume with the following settings" option (⬚ changes to ◉).

⑱ Click here and select NTFS.

⑲ In the Allocation unit size list, click Default or select another size.

⑳ Type a name for the volume label.

㉑ Click Next.

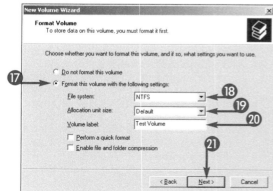

The Completing the New Volume Wizard page appears.

㉒ Click Finish.

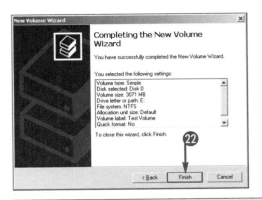

● The new simple volume is created.

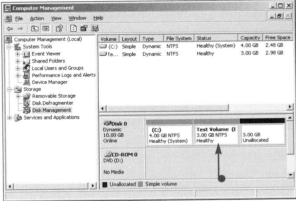

Can I use the command line to convert a basic disk to a dynamic disk, create an additional simple volume, and format the simple volume with FAT 32?

▼ Yes. You can use the `diskpart.exe` command to both convert a basic disk to a dynamic disk and create a volume on the dynamic disk with the create subcommand of `diskpart`. Then you can use the `format.exe` command to format the Dynamic Disk with FAT 32. You can avoid using the New Volume Wizard and the GUI altogether and accomplish all your goals in the command shell. You can confirm that you have accomplished your tasks by checking in the Disk Management console.

Can I choose any drive letter for my new simple volume on the dynamic disk?

▼ Almost. You cannot use a drive letter that is already in use on your Windows Server 2003 system. Drive letter C is assigned to your first hard drive and drive letters A and B are both reserved for floppy diskette drives, although B is rarely used anymore. A CD or DVD drive on your server usually is assigned drive letter D leaving drive letter E as the first available letter. You can use any other letter not mentioned, but make sure you do not use a particular letter for a mapped drive.

Add a New Hard Drive and Initialize the Drive

You can add a new Hard Drive to your Windows Server 2003 computer to increase the storage space of the computer and enable more fault tolerance solutions using dynamic disks. You can administer a number of servers for your business environment and as your business — and your storage needs — grow. Adding a new hard drive or hard drive array is both a hardware and operating system task. You can use the utilities in Windows Server 2003 to immediately configure a blank hard drive after you install it.

You can install up to four IDE drives on the two IDE controllers available on your server motherboard. All servers need hardware upgrades to meet changing storage and processing needs on your network. You can purchase additional physical disks as you need them. In addition, you can purchase and store disks as your budget allows so that you have them available when you need them.

With Windows NT or other Microsoft downlevel operating systems, after you install a hard drive, you use command line utilities, such as `fdisk` or `format`. This prepares the newly installed disk to receive a file system, applications, and data files.

Add a New Hard Drive and Initialize the Drive

① Click Start.

② Right-click My Computer.

③ Click Manage.

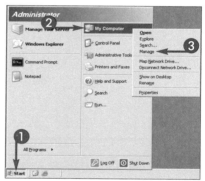

The Computer Management snap-in appears.

The Initialize and Convert Disk Wizard appears.

④ Click Next.

The Select Disks to Initialize page appears.

⑤ Click the Disk box (☐ changes to ☑).

⑥ Click Next.

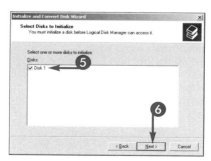

The Select Disks to Convert page of the Wizard appears.

⑦ Click the Disk box if want to convert the disk (☐ changes to ☑).

If you do not want to convert the disk, leave the box empty (☐).

⑧ Click Next.

The Completing the Initialize and Convert Disk Wizard appears.

⑨ Click Finish.

● The new disk is initialized and online.

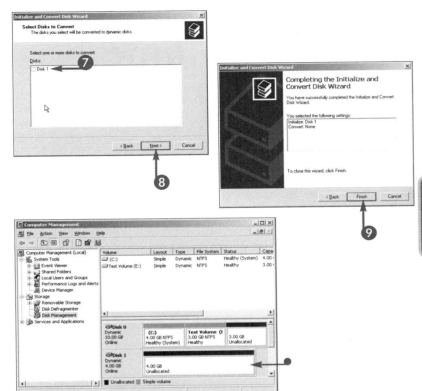

Why does the Convert Disk Wizard start without me doing anything to launch it?

▼ You start the wizard automatically when you open the Computer Management snap-in and click the Disk Management console. When you select the Disk Management console, Windows always initiates a scan of the hard drives on your server and, using the Virtual Disk server, determines what types of partitions and volumes you have. The Virtual Disk service discovers the newly installed hard drive, determines that it is not initialized or formatted, and then launches the Convert Disk Wizard without any other action by you in the snap-in.

What happens when I choose to initialize and convert the new hard drive in the Convert Disk Wizard?

▼ The entire area of the basic disk converts, but you can still determine how much space you want to leave unallocated and how much you want to allocate to a new volume. You can also leave the new disk as a basic disk if you need to store data on your server that you want available to downlevel Windows operating systems, such as Windows NT or Windows 98. For more on converting disks, see the sections "Convert a Basic Disk to a Dynamic Disk," and "Convert a Basic Disk to a Dynamic Disk on the Command Line."

Create a
Spanned Volume

You can create a spanned volume on a dynamic disk on your server. This enables a single volume to span more than one physical hard drive and allows you to store data in one logical container, without limiting you to the size of a physical hard drive. You can only create and use a spanned volume when you need to exceed the physical size limits of one hard drive because spanned volumes are slow to read from and write to. You use a spanned volume when you cannot move application from the volume containing the application software and you are running out of hard drive space.

You cannot create a spanned volume in unallocated space on a dynamic disk. You must have at least two dynamic disks to create a spanned volume, and you can use up to 32 dynamic disks for a single spanned volume. The only advantage you gain when using a spanned volume is increased storage space because the spanned volume cannot be mirrored or striped and does not provide fault tolerance for your data.

Create a Spanned Volume

① Click Start.

② Right-click My Computer.

③ Click Manage.

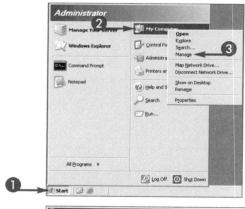

The Computer Management snap-in appears.

④ Click Disk Management.

⑤ Right-click the unallocated space on dynamic disk.

⑥ Click New Volume.

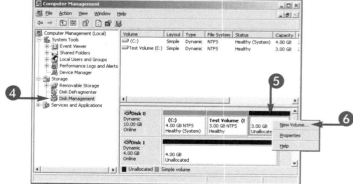

The New Volume Wizard appears.

7 Click Next.

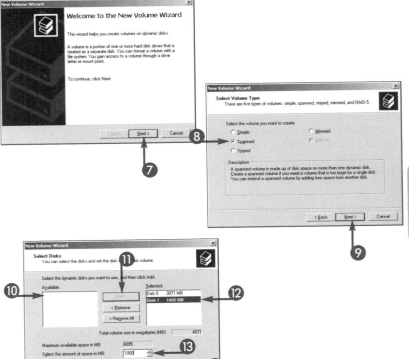

The Select Volume Type page appears.

8 Click the Spanned option (☐ changes to ☑).

9 Click Next.

The Select Disks page of the Wizard appears.

10 Click Disk 1 in the Available section.

11 Click Add.

Disk 1 appears in the Selected section.

12 Click Disk 1.

13 Type an amount of space to allocate based on disk size and how much space you need to accomplish your goals.

14 Click Next.

What happens if I change the amount of space on Disk 0 instead of Disk 1 on the Select Disks page?

▼ You cannot create a spanned volume if you select less than the maximum amount of space available on the volume on Disk 0. You can only achieve your goal to span the space from Disk 0 to Disk 1 by using a single volume to create one virtual drive using two physical hard drives. This means you must use all the available space on the volume on Disk 1 and at least some of the volume on Disk 2. The wizard allocates all of the space on Disk 1 so you can only decrease space on Disk 2.

Why were all the selections for Select Volume Type, except RAID-5, available when they were not available with only one or two dynamic disks?

▼ You can create all of the different dynamic disk volume types when you create two dynamic disks except for RAID 5. You must have at least three dynamic disks to configure a RAID 5 array. You can read more about RAID 5 as a software solution in the section "Create a RAID 5 Array." The other selections on the Volume Type page, besides Simple and Spanned, are considered RAID arrays because they can provide fault tolerance for your data, but neither simple or spanned volumes are fault tolerant.

continued

Create a Spanned Volume *(Continued)*

Although the spanned volume occupies the area on two separate physical hard drives, you can still assign the volume with a single drive letter or mount the volume to a single, empty NTFS folder because it is a single, logical container for data. Your network users will be totally unaware they are accessing separate physical containers when they open, modify, and save information on the spanned volume on your Windows Server 2003 server.

However, if one of the hard drives containing the spanned volume suffers from a hardware failure, you cannot recover the information on the entire volume. You can only restore

data that you have preserved on the most recent tape backup of your server. Any information that users added or changed on the spanned volume since the last backup is lost unless the server is also a domain controller. You can use Active Directory database replication to restore the lost AD database as it is replicated from the other domain controllers.

You can still delete the spanned volume, however this means that you will delete the volume from both hard drives and that you will lose the data on it unless you previously back it up.

Create a Spanned Volume *(continued)*

The Assign Drive Letter or Path page of the Wizard appears.

⓯ Click the "Assign the following drive letter" option (◌ changes to ◉).

⓰ Click here and select a letter to assign to the empty NTFS folder.

⓱ Click Next.

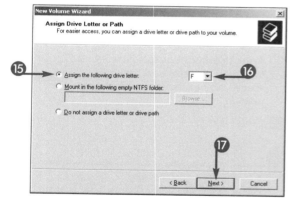

The Format Volume page of the Wizard appears.

⓲ Click the "Format this volume with the following settings" option (◌ changes to ◉).

⓳ Click here and select a file system.

⓴ Click here and select an Allocation unit size or select Default.

㉑ Type a name for the Volume label.

㉒ Click Next.

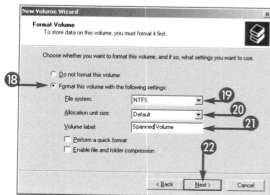

The Completing the New Volume Wizard
page appears.

㉓ Click Finish.

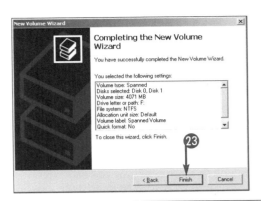

● The spanned volume is created.

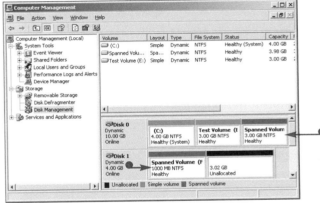

When I right-click a spanned volume or other volumes on a dynamic disk, I receive the option to format. What happens when I select the format option?

▼ You can click Format and open the Format page, but when you click the list, the only option available is NTFS. You cannot format FAT on any volume on a dynamic disk from the Computer Management console, only from the command shell using the `format.exe` utility. You can change the Allocation unit size of the volume on the Format page, but this is not recommended; if you remove the formatting from part of the volume, you cannot recover the data on any of the volume.

After I create a simple or spanned volume, what information is on it?

▼ When you create a simple or spanned volume, it remains completely empty until you load application programs or place and save data files and folders on it. The volumes require no additional preparation in order for you to add data or software onto them. Unlike a primary partition, they do not contain any operating system or program files. You can save a Word file on a new spanned volume, for example, by clicking File, Save As, and in the Save in window, browsing to the new drive letter and creating a folder for your data, then click Save.

Extend Simple and Spanned Volumes

You can extend a simple or a spanned volume to increase storage space on your Windows Server 2003 server. This allows you to store data on more than one hard drive by creating a single logical container spanning two or more physical drives. You can either extend the space a spanned volume occupies into unallocated space on one or more drives, or you can extend a simple volume beyond a single hard drive onto a second drive. When you extend a simple volume to more than one drive, you automatically create a spanned volume. For more on creating a simple or spanned volume, see the sections "Create a Simple Volume," and "Create a Spanned Volume."

You can extend a volume only if it is formatted with NTFS. You cannot extend simple or spanned volumes formatted with FAT or FAT 32. You cannot use an extended volume as a mirrored volume, a striped volume, or a RAID 5 volume after the volume has extended to two or more drives. You cannot extend volumes that are already designated boot volumes, striped volumes, mirrored volumes, or RAID 5 volumes. You also cannot delete any part of an extended simple or spanned volume without deleting the entire volume on all hard drives along with all of the data in it.

Extend Simple and Spanned Volumes

① Click Start.

② Right-click My Computer.

③ Click Manage.

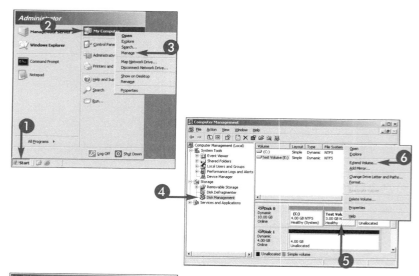

The Computer Management snap-in appears.

④ Click Disk Management.

⑤ Right-click the volume you want to extend.

⑥ Click Extend Volume.

The Extend Volume Wizard appears.

⑦ Click Next.

The Select Disks page appears.

⑧ Click to select the disks you want to use to extend the volume.

⑨ Click Add.

⑩ Click here to select the amount of space to use to extend the disks.

⑪ Click Next.

The Completing the Extend Volume Wizard page appears.

⑫ Click Finish.

● The volume is extended.

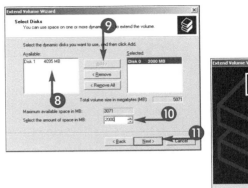

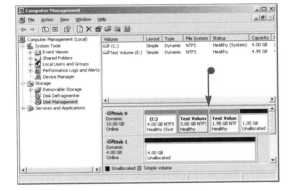

Why do I not have to select a drive letter for the extended simple or spanned volume on the dynamic disk?

▼ You can create an extended volume without choosing a new drive letter because you are not creating a new, independent volume. You can use the same drive letter for the extended volume because you are extending an already existing volume, not creating a new volume. You can select the size and even the disk you use to extend the volume so the extended volume either stays on the same individual hard drive or becomes spanned to the next drive. In either case, you can still use the same drive letter.

Can you extend an already extended volume without damaging the data already on the volume?

▼ You can extend an extended volume as long as it is formatted with NTFS. The volume does not have to be empty of data for you to extend it. You can extend a volume already in use, but you cannot reduce the size of an extended volume unless you delete the entire volume. You should extend a volume only as large as you need it. You can make it larger later, but you cannot recover the space without significant work in backing up and restoring data.

Create a Striped Volume

You can create a striped volume to improve a user's access speed to data on the volume. On a striped volume, data is alternately written in *stripes* on two or more hard drives so those separate hard drives are writing and reading different sections of one data set simultaneously. A striped volume is also known as RAID 0, but RAID 0 cannot provide fault protection for your data. If one of the drives that contains part of the striped volume fails, you cannot retrieve any of the data stored anywhere on the volume, even on the healthy hard drives.

Because data is written alternately in stripes from one dynamic disk to the other, you must create an equal amount of space on each of the two dynamic disks. For example, you can create a Striped Volume 6GB in size by using 3GB of unallocated space on each dynamic disk.

Windows Server 2003 can create striped volumes using a software solution, but you can also create striped volumes and other RAID array configurations as hardware solutions. The hardware solution for a striped volume requires a separate physical hard drive instead of a separate dynamic disk.

Create a Striped Volume

① Click Start.

② Right-click My Computer.

③ Click Manage.

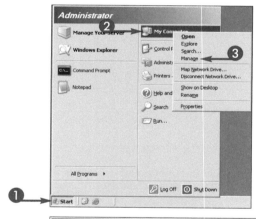

The Computer Management snap-in appears.

④ Click Disk Management.

⑤ Right-click the unallocated space.

⑥ Click New Volume.

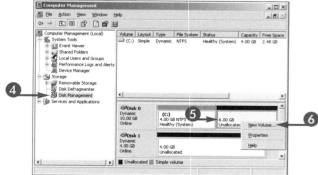

The New Volume Wizard appears.

7 Click Next.

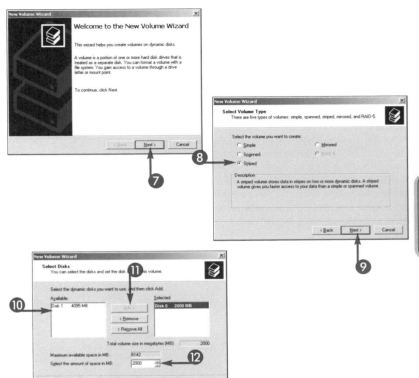

The Select Volume Type page of the Wizard appears.

8 Click the Striped option (○ changes to ◉).

9 Click Next.

The Select Disks page of the Wizard appears.

10 Select Disk 0.

11 Click Add.

12 Click here to select an amount of space.

PART III

How many disks can I use to create striped volume on.

▼ You can use up to 32 separate dynamic disks on which to create striped volumes, but the only thing you gain is fast read and write speeds for your users. Your data is not protected by a fault-tolerant solution; regularly backing up your data is the only way you can protect it. In fact it is a less reliable solution as you add disks. Also, you can only make a stripe on a particular hard drive as big as the smallest area available on any drive. You can improve data storage and retrieval by using hard drives made by the same manufacturer and using similar models.

Why do I only have to set the size of the first dynamic disk on the Select Disks page?

▼ You can select the size of the amount of space you want to use for the striped volume on Disk 0, and when you choose Disk 1 and add it to the Selected box, the Virtual Disk service detects the amount of space you selected and automatically configures the same amount of space for the second dynamic disk and does so for any other disks you add. The striped volumes have to be the same size on all of the drives in order to work.

continued

Create a Striped Volume *(Continued)*

You cannot make a striped volume any larger than you originally create it by extending the volume or creating a mirrored volume, and you cannot enlarge the striped volume by adding another physical hard drive to the server. If you need to make your striped volume larger, you can only delete the entire volume, add additional hard drives, or free up more space on existing hard drives, then re-create the striped volume in the new dynamic disk space with the new physical drives. You must either accept the loss of your data or recover it from tape backups if backups have been made.

A striped volume uses all the dynamic disk space you can create for it and not just the space occupied by the data and programs loaded onto the volume. When you create a striped volume, you cannot use all of the space allocated because the formatting that allows for striping occupies some of each volume on each dynamic disk. For example, if you create a striped volume of 2GB on each dynamic disk, you can only use 1.65GB of the space of each volume.

Create a Striped Volume *(continued)*

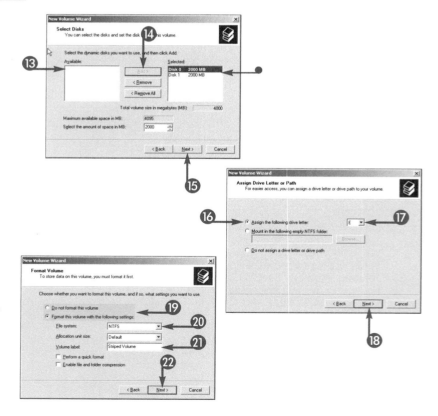

⑬ Select Disk 1.

⑭ Click Add.

- The same amount of space automatically appears for Disk 1 as is set for Disk 0.

⑮ Click Next.

The Assign Drive Letter or Path page of the Wizard appears.

⑯ Click the Assign the following drive letter option (○ changes to ⦿).

⑰ Click here and assign either a drive letter or path.

⑱ Click Next.

The Format Volume page of the Wizard appears.

⑲ Click either the "Do not format this volume" option (○ changes to ⦿) or the "Format this volume with the following settings" option.

This example shows the "Format this volume with the following settings option" selected.

⑳ Click here and select a file system.

㉑ Type a name for the Volume label.

㉒ Click Next.

The Completing the New Volume Wizard page appears.

㉓ Click Finish.

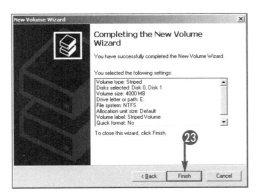

● The striped volume is created.

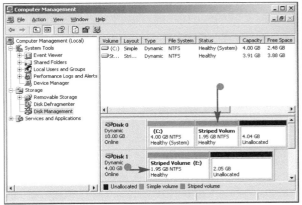

What do I have to do as a user to access my data on a striped volume that spans two or more dynamic disks?

▼ You can save your data to the particular drive letter that is assigned to the spanned volume just as you save data to any physical disk. When you view the spanned volume as either a mapped drive or as a single hard drive in your network shares section of My Network Places on your Windows XP or Windows 2000 computer, you cannot tell that it is a striped volume. You can write or read to a striped volume just as easily as you can on the local hard drive of your PC.

If I do not know which types of volumes are fault tolerant and which ones are not. How can I tell except by looking them up?

▼ You can find out which volumes on a dynamic disk are fault tolerant by checking the main window of the Disk Management console. You must either click the window button on the upper left-hand corner of the Computer Management snap-in, or use your mouse cursor to drag the right side of the window wider. You can then see more of the catagories at the top of the window including File System, Capacity, and Fault Tolerance, which are listed as Yes or No.

Create a Mirrored Volume

You can create a Mirrored Volume on two dynamic disks on your Windows Server 2003 server to provide fault tolerance for your data by literally creating a mirror image of the data from the first drive onto the second drive. If one drive suffers a catastrophic failure, you can access all of your data on the other drive. If one of your mirrored drives should fail, you can retrieve all of your data from the remaining mirrored drive. If you lose a mirrored drive, you also lose fault tolerance until you replace the damaged drive and re-create the mirrored volume.

You must use two, and only two, dynamic disks for the mirroring process. Both disks have data written to them, modified, and retrieved from them at the same time. This can cause your users to experience a performance slowdown, especially in writing data because the hard drives must both be writing at the same time. If possible, you should connect the two drives to different disk controllers for best performance. Another issue you experience with mirrored volumes is that you must use twice the amount of hard drive space for your data than if you do not use mirroring.

Create a Mirrored Volume

① Click Start.

② Right-click My Computer.

③ Click Manage.

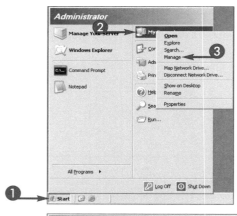

The Computer Management snap-in appears.

④ Click Disk Management.

⑤ Right-click the unallocated space.

⑥ Click New Volume.

The New Volume Wizard appears.

⑦ Click Next.

The Select Volume Type page of the Wizard appears.

⑧ Click the Mirrored option (○ changes to ⊙).

⑨ Click Next.

The Select Disks page of the Wizard appears.

⑩ Select Disk 0.

⑪ Type the amount of disk space.

continued

What if I attempt to select more than two disks to add to the selected box in the Select Disks page of the New Volume Wizard?

▼ You cannot choose to add more than two disks to the Selected box because a mirrored volume uses only two dynamic disks to write duplicate information to and then read from the same two identical disks. Mirrored volumes, or, as they are also called, RAID 1, can only be comprised of an array to two disks. There is no RAID software or hardware solution that allows you to mirror data to three or more disks.

Is there another way to create a mirrored volume on a dynamic disk besides using the New Volume Wizard in Disk Management?

▼ You can use the `diskpart.exe` command line utility to add a mirror to a simple volume using the `add` subcommand. You can open a command prompt from the Start menu, type **diskpart** at the prompt and the diskpart prompt appears. Then you can type **add** and specify the simple volume and dynamic disk to which you want to add a mirror. You can also eliminate a mirrored set using `diskpart` by using the `break` subcommand, so you can use the space for normal data storage again. Technicians or administrators, who have a great deal experience configuring servers at the command line, can best use this method.

PART III

Create a Mirrored Volume *(Continued)*

You can create a mirrored volume using two IDE disks, two SCSI disks, and even a mix of one IDE and one SCSI disk to make the widest use of available hard drives in your Windows Server 2003 server. You can also mirror a hard drive containing the system partition of the operating system, but you must take certain precautions to avoid problems booting if one disk fails. Although you can mirror an IDE and a SCSI disk, Microsoft recommends you do not do this because you can have boot problems if one disk fails. Also, you can make a boot

disk in case one mirrored disk containing the system partition fails and the server has a problem booting after the failure.

You can avoid unanticipated boot problems related to a failed mirrored disk by simulating a mirrored disk failure and observing how your server responds when you reboot it. You can simulate a disk failure by opening the server case and disconnecting the power cable leading to one of the mirrored drives. You should use a test lab for this process rather than a server in a production environment.

Create a Mirrored Volume *(continued)*

⑫ Select Disk 1 in the Available box.

⑬ Click Add.

● Disk 1 is added to the Selected box.

Disk 1 is automatically allocated the same disk space as Disk 0.

⑭ Click Next.

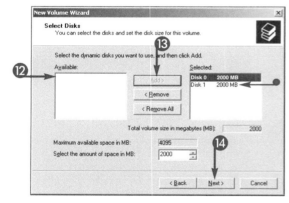

The Assign Drive Letter or Path page of the Wizard appears.

⑮ Click the "Assign the following drive letter" option (○ changes to ⊙).

⑯ Click here and select a drive letter.

⑰ Click Next.

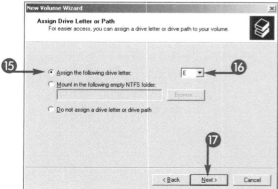

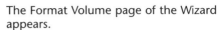

The Format Volume page of the Wizard appears.

18 Click either the "Do not format this volume" option or the "Format this volume with the following settings" option (⬜ changes to 🔘).

This example shows the "Format this volume with the following settings" option selected.

19 Click here and select a file system.

20 Type a name for the volume label.

21 Click Next.

The Completing the New Volume Wizard page of the Wizard appears.

22 Click Finish.

● The mirrored volume is created.

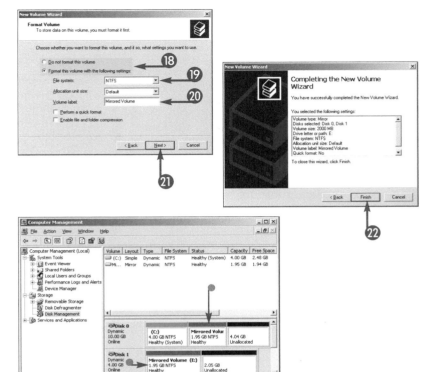

Can I reverse the mirroring process without losing my data?

▼ Yes. You can *break* the mirrored volume using either the `diskpart` command line utility or the Disk Management console. You can break a mirror in Disk Management by opening Disk Management, right-clicking one of the mirrored volumes and clicking Break Mirrored Volume. The areas that you have mirrored function like independent disks again and the data stays intact. However, all of the data is the duplicate data that you wrote before you broke the mirror. You can use the same process of right-clicking a mirrored volume and choosing Remove Mirror, but you must back up your data first.

When I mirror two physical dynamic disks together, how should I configure them, and is there a difference in configuration between IDE and SCSI drives?

▼ You can use either IDE or SCSI drives to create a mirrored pair of drives. Although you can use two separate IDE or SCSI controllers and still create a successful mirrored set, you can achieve better results from using the same type of controller for both mirrored disks in order to improve read and write speeds. If you choose to use two separate controllers, you should use controllers from the same manufacturer and of the same or similar model types.

Create a RAID 5 Array

You can create a RAID 5 dynamic disk array to provide the most effective RAID fault tolerance solution for data stored on your Windows Server 2003 server. RAID 5 also provides your users with faster read speeds. RAID 5 is best for "write once and read many" situations. You must use three or more hard drives to create your RAID 5 array but you cannot use more than 32 disks. RAID 5 works like RAID 1 or mirrored volumes because you must use a volume of equal space on each of the drives you configure for your array. You lose the equivalent space of

one hard drive using RAID 5, because this solution uses disk striping with parity, and parity information is stored in areas on all three (or more) disks.

You can suffer the loss of one RAID disk and your server still performs without losing any data. The parity information on the two surviving disks can rebuild the information that was lost when the third drive failed. You can then replace the failed drive, and the parity information on the first two drives rebuild the complete data set on the new third drive.

Create a RAID 5 Array

① Click Start.

② Right-click My Computer.

③ Click Manage.

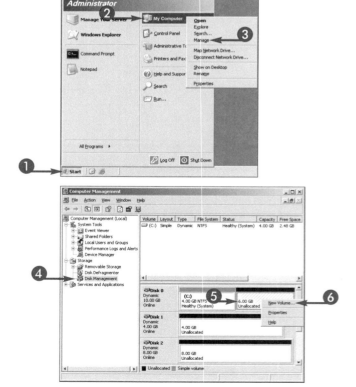

The Computer Management snap-in appears.

④ Click Disk Management.

⑤ Right-click an area of unallocated space.

⑥ Click New Volume.

The New Volume Wizard appears.

7 Click Next.

The Select Volume Type page of the Wizard appears.

8 Click the RAID-5 option (⊙ changes to ⊙).

9 Click Next.

The Select Disks page appears.

10 Select Disk 0.

11 Type an amount of disk space to use on Disk 0 for the RAID-5 array.

PART III

Do I have another way to set the amount of space for use in the RAID 5 array on each disk besides typing the amount to allocate on the first disk selected?

▼ You can choose how much space to use per disk when you select Disk 0 or the first disk to be used in the array, and type the amount on the Select Disks page in the New Volume Wizard. Each disk you choose to add to the Selected box after you configure the space on the first disk automatically allocates the same amount of space for use in the RAID 5 volume.

Is the only way to make the RAID 5 option available in the New Volume Wizard to physically install at least three IDE or SCSI drives in the Windows Server 2003 server?

▼ Yes. The Virtual Disk service can detect the number of hard drives installed on your system and determine if you have the resources available on your server to allow the RAID 5 option or any of the other volume types on your dynamic disks to be configured. None of the other types of volumes you can configure on a dynamic disk requires a minimum of three hard drives to be available, although many of them can use three or more drives.

continued

Create a RAID 5 Array *(Continued)*

Ymou can improve the percentage of space available in a RAID 5 array by adding more hard drives to your Windows Server 2003 server, thereby giving your users more space per disk to store their data. When you use three hard drives to construct your array, you can only use the total space available on two of the disks — or 66 percent of the available disk space — due to parity striping. For example, if you use three drives of 30GB each, although the total space that is available before they are configured is 90GB, after you set them as a RAID 5 array, only 60GB is actually useful for storing data.

You can add five hard drives of 30GB each but the space equaling one disk is still used for parity striping. That means you have the total space available of four out of the five drives you installed so that 80 percent of the total disk space is used for data instead of 66 percent. You can get more space savings for your data as you increase the number of disks, but you must have a need to potentially store more data as you add disks. RAID 5 can only manage a single disk failure. The more disks you add, the greater the chance a second disk will fail before the first failed drive is rebuilt. 5 to 7 disks is usually the maximum number to use safely in a RAID 5 array.

Create a RAID 5 Array *(continued)*

⑫ Select Disk 1.

⑬ Click Add.

⑭ Select Disk 2.

⑮ Click Add.

All three disks appear in the Selected box and use the same amount of disk space.

⑯ Click Next.

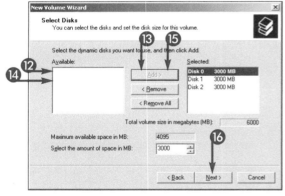

The Assign Drive Letter or Path page of the Wizard appears.

⑰ Click either the "Assign the following drive letter" option, and assign a drive letter, or select "Mount in the following empty NTFS folder" option (○ changes to ◉).

This example shows the "Assign the following drive letter" option selected.

⑱ Click Next.

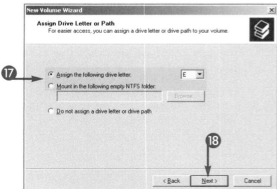

The Format Volume page of the Wizard appears.

⑲ Click either the "Do not format this volume" option or the "Format this volume with the following settings" option (☐ changes to ☑).

This example shows the "Format this volume with the following settings" option.

⑳ Click here and select a File system.

㉑ Click here and select either an Allocation unit size or Default.

㉒ Type a name for the Volume label.

㉓ Click Next.

The Completing the New Volume Wizard page appears.

㉔ Click Finish.

● The RAID 5 volume is created.

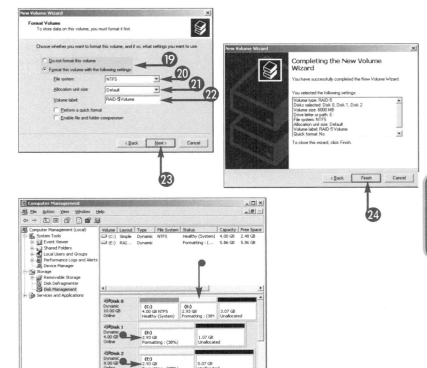

Is there any way to recover the disk space that a RAID 5 volume uses besides deleting the volume?

▼ No. While there are two ways to recover space from a mirrored or RAID 1 volume, the only way you can recover dynamic disk space from a RAID 5 set is to delete the volume. Because RAID 5 is very effective as a method of fault tolerance and is widely used on data storage servers, you can delete RAID 5 but your data is no longer protected except for periodic tape backup. Once you delete a RAID 5 volume, you can only recover your data by restoring it from your backup tapes.

Is there any other way to calculate how much space RAID 5 parity information actually uses in a hard drive array?

▼ Yes. You can use the following formula to calculate the space used by parity data: $(N-1)*S=T$ where N is the total number of disks used, S is the size alloted to each disk, and T is the total space available for data storage on the disk. For example, if five disks each allocate 30GB for the RAID 5 set, total disk space for the array is $(5-1)* 30GB=120GB$ with 30GB of space reserved for parity information.

Understanding Shared and Redirected Folders

With your Windows Server 2003 server, you can create and administer shared and redirected folders to manage the resources on your network. You can allow users network access to the same resources, and have them save their data to a central location for increased security. You can create file shares by using volumes formatted with FAT, FAT32, and NTFS. Although NTFS offers the best security, you can use FAT or FAT32 formatted drives, but these drives only receive the protection you set for the share. The FAT and FAT32 shares do not have Access Control List (ACL) protection. You can read more about NTFS file shares in Chapter 11.

Disk Management

You can place shared folders on either the basic or dynamic disks located on your File Server. Before you create a shared file structure on a disk and allow network users to access it, you should first verify the condition of the disk partition or volume that you intend to use. If you use a faulty volume, then any data that your users save to it can become corrupted and even lost. You can check the condition of your disk by using the Disk Management console in the Computer Management snap-in.

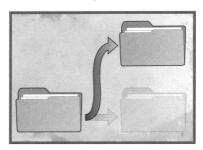

Workgroups and Domains

You can create file shares on a network that is either a workgroup or an Active Directory Domain. File shares in a workgroup are available to all members of the workgroup, although access to all of the resources may be limited. In addition, you cannot set up a workgroup-wide security set, which means that anyone can connect to the network and can log in locally to access the entire workgroup from their desktop. You can only protect data on the server by requiring a separate login to the server and then setting file level permissions.

Active Directory Domain structures allow the sharing of resources to a wider group of users, including users in the local domain, the child domain, and the domain forests. However, you can limit access to ensure that domain resources are secure by implementing a specific user login to the domain network.

Types of Shares

You can use different methods to create a variety of shares to share different types of folders, including Web folders and standard folder shares on a server. You can create shares in Windows Explorer, from the command line, or using the Shared Folders snap-in.

Folder Redirection and Group Policy

You can implement folder redirection to allow users to save their data to a server on the network. When a user saves data, it is as if they are saving it to the local hard drive on their computer. You can only set up folder redirection on a Windows 2000 or Windows Server 2003 Active Directory Domain using Group Policy. Group Policy is a collection of

settings applied to an Active Directory object, and which determines the behavior of that object. You can read more about Group Policy in Chapters 13 and 14.

Universal Naming Convention and Root Paths

To start the folder redirection process, you can create a shared folder by creating different types of paths to the shared folder. A Universal Naming Convention, or UNC, path is the full path to a network share, including notation for the username and folder name, for example, \\server\share\%username%\MyDocuments.

You can also use an easier method called a root path. This method uses the notation, \\server\share, and allows the folder redirection process to automatically add the username and folder name when you apply Group Policy.

Special Path

You can specify an alternative path to redirect the user folder data. The alternate location can be on a user's local hard drive, or in any partition on any hard drive of the server that you select. You can use this option on both Windows 2000 and Windows Server 2003 servers.

Home Directory

You can redirect a user's My Documents folder to the user's Home directory. You can use either a UNC path, such as \\server\share\path\filename, or a local path, such as C:\share. Keep in mind that you can only use this option if you have already configured a server environment to include Home directories for all users. You can also only use this option with Windows Server 2003 servers.

Local User Profiles

You can redirect a user's My Documents folder to the Local User Profile, which is configured on the Windows Server 2003 server. This method allows you to redirect a special folder for your network users to a single location rather than to the My Documents folder, for example, using the notation %username%\share.

Create a Shared Folder
with Windows Explorer

You can create shared folders and resources in your Windows Server 2003 server in much the same way that you can in Windows XP or Windows 2000. Windows Explorer allows network users to easily access the resources and the entire file structure of all drives on your server. It allows you to locate a particular folder without having to know the exact path and without having to open several windows to find the location of the folder.

You can launch Windows Explorer from any location on your Windows Server 2003 server. These locations include the Start button, My Computer, any type of drive on your server, and any part of the file structure on your computer.

You can even use Windows Explorer to navigate to the shared file structure on another computer in your network. You can do this by using My Network Places on Windows Server 2003, Windows XP, and Windows 2000 computers. You can also use Network Neighborhood for down-level operating systems, such as Windows 98 and Windows 95.

Create a Shared Folder with Windows Explorer

① Click Start.

② Right-click My Computer.

③ Click Explore.

The My Computer window appears.

④ Right-click the drive you want to share.

⑤ Click Explore.

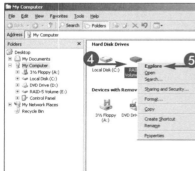

The file structure appears for the drive that you selected.

⑥ Right-click the folder you want to share.

⑦ Click Sharing and Security.

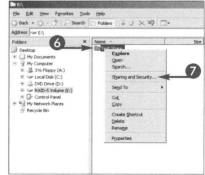

The Test Share Properties dialog box appears.

8 Click the Share this folder option (○ changes to ⊙).

9 Click OK.

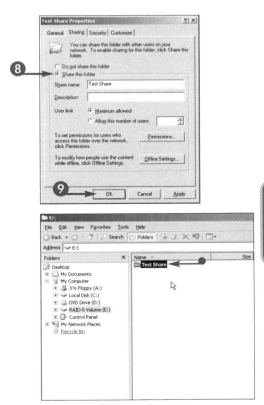

● The shared "hand" symbol appears ( ), indicating that the folder is shared.

Does the share name of the shared folder have to be the same as the name of the folder?

▼ No. You can assign any name you want to your shared folder, and this name does not have to be related to the actual name of the folder on the server. This is also the case when you share any resource on a network. When you specify a name for a folder or other resource, the name should easily identify the resource for any users who need to access it. For example, if you are sharing an application that is specifically for the marketing department, you can name it Market_App. You can also use a different name when downlevel clients, who can only use access names of up to eight characters, access your share.

When I share a folder on the network from my server, can I limit access to it?

▼ Yes. You can limit access to a shared folder on the network in many ways. For example, you can limit the number of users who can access the shared folder at any one time by opening the Shared Folder Properties box. Click the Sharing tab and under User limit, click the "Allow this number of users" option (○ changes to ⊙). In the dialog box that appears, type the maximum number of users that you want to connect to the share folder at once, and click OK.

Create Shared Web Folders

Y ou can create Web Folders that users can share on your Windows Server 2003 server. Please be aware that a Web share exposes Port 80 to the Internet and potentially makes your files accessible to intruders. Remote users can access these folders with the Internet Explorer Web Browser instead of through a standard folder format. This offers you an advantage when you create shared content that uses HTML or XML languages rather than other file language types.

Users can access shared Web folders using Hypertext Transfer Protocol, or HTTP, over Port 80, exactly as they would access a Web page on the Internet or on a company Intranet. To access a file, users can open Internet Explorer

and type the URL of the shared Web folder in the Browser address bar. You can still access a typical non-Web network share on a standard server standard tree structure; to do this, you need to use the Server Message Block, or SMB, Protocol, which is the typical transport protocol for network shares.

To enable shared Web folders, you must install Internet Information Services, version 6 (IISv6) — also known as Application Services — and the World Wide Web component. Without these additional Windows components, the Web Sharing tab option is not available when you try to share a Web folder. See Chapter 19 to install IISv6.

Create Shared Web Folders

① Click Start.

② Right-click My Computer.

③ Click Explore.

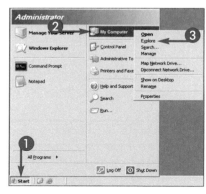

The My Computer window appears.

④ Right-click a drive.

⑤ Click Explore.

The folder structure appears for the drive that you selected.

⑥ Right-click the folder you want.

⑦ Click Sharing and Security.

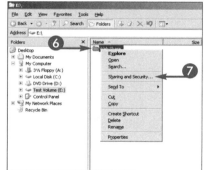

The Web Share Properties dialog box appears.

⑧ Click here and select a Web site you want to share.

This example uses the Default Web Site option.

⑨ Click the Share this folder option (◯ changes to ◉).

The Edit Alias dialog box appears.

⑩ Type an alias name for the share.

⑪ Click the options for the access permissions you want (☐ changes to ☑).

⑫ Click the Application permissions option you want (◯ changes to ◉).

⑬ Click OK.

⑭ Click OK in the Web Share Properties dialog box.

The Web folder is now shared.

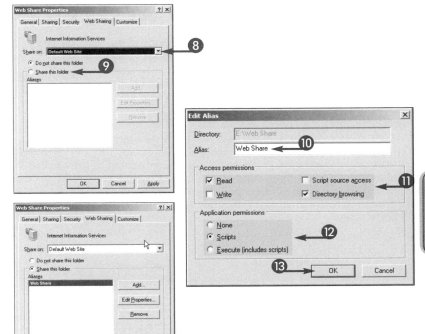

PART III

When I share a folder as a Web Folder, is it also shared as a regular network share folder?

▼ No. You can create a shared Web folder that is accessible to network users with a Web Browser and still not share the folder on the network in any other way. If you open the Folder Share Properties dialog box and click the Sharing tab after sharing the folder as a Web Share, the Do not share this folder option is still selected (◉). You can select the Share this folder option to share the folder as both a network share and a Web share. The network share uses the same folder name as the shared Web folder.

Why do I have to type an alias for the shared Web folder?

▼ An alias works in the same way as the share name for a folder. You can even make the name from the name of the folder. You can give a Web folder any alias or share name that you want people to use in order to access the Web share. They cannot access the Web folder by any other name. You can even add and remove aliases so that users can reference the Web share by several names.

Create Shares with the Shared Folders Snap-In

You can use a stand-alone Microsoft Management Console (MMC) snap-in to create folders that you want to share on your network. You can easily create folders using the Wizard format. You can also use the MMC console as a way to manage your shared folders by placing them in a single location on your Windows Server 2003 server. The Share a Folder Wizard is a new component of Windows Server 2003 that allows you to configure both share permissions and NTFS folder permissions. You must create the folder share in an NTFS drive in order to set NTFS permissions.

In addition to creating a stand-alone MMC console snap-in for the Shared Folders snap-in, you can access it in the Computer Management snap-in. This snap-in also allows you to access utilities such as the Disk Management Console, Disk Defragmenter, and Event Viewer.

You can publish shares from the Shared Folders snap-in to the Active Directory. However, you cannot publish to the Active Directory if you create a share from either Windows Explorer or a My Computer window. When you publish a share to the Active Directory, your network users can find the share by using a wide range of search methods.

Create Shares with the Shared Folders Snap-In

① Click Start.

② Right-click My Computer.

③ Click Manage.

The Computer Management window appears.

④ Click Shared Folders.

⑤ Right-click Shares.

⑥ Click New Share.

The Share a Folder Wizard appears.

⑦ Click Next.

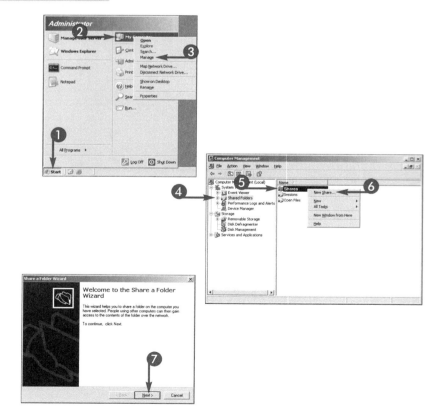

The Folder Path page of the Wizard appears.

8 Click Browse.

The Browse for Folder dialog box appears.

9 Click a drive.

10 Click Make New Folder.

11 Type a new share name.

12 Click OK.

The Folder Path page of the Wizard appears.

13 Click Next.

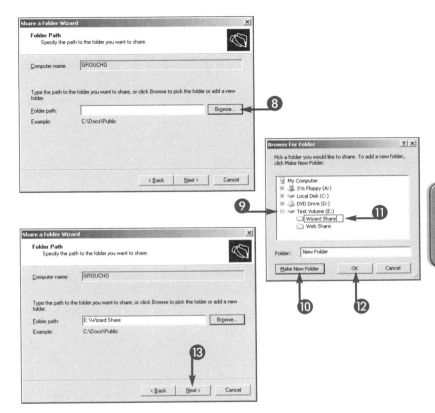

Is there any other way for me to find the share path other than by using the Browse button in the Wizard Folder Path page?

▼ Yes. If you know the path to the share, you can type the path in the Folder path window, and then click Next. You do not have to create a new folder by clicking Make New Folder if the folder that you want to share already exists. You can either make the folder before running the Share a Folder Wizard, or you can select a folder that already exists but that you did not yet share.

In addition to using the Share a Folder Wizard, creating a share with Windows Explorer, and by accessing a drive in My Computer, is there any other way to make a share?

▼ Yes. You can use the command shell to make a share using the net share command. You can find the net share command line utility on many Windows operating systems. Open a command prompt and type **net share /?** to locate all of the commands that are available under net share. To share a folder, type **net share sharename= drive:path** and then grant users permissions such as read, change, and full. You can also limit the number of users who can access the share at any given time.

continued

Create Shares with the Shared Folders Snap-In *(Continued)*

When you are creating a shared folder, you can access the offline settings of the folder in the Name, Description, and Settings page of the Share a Folder Wizard. This page allows you to specify whether users can access the share when they are offline, as well as how they can use the offline folder. Offline folders are useful to portable computer users who travel frequently and who are not connected to the home network through a virtual private network (VPN) or other connection.

By setting offline permissions in the Wizard when you create the share, you can prepare the folder for offline use while it is still being created. You can also go back later and specify or reconfigure offline settings by accessing the Properties dialog box for the share.

You can specify that only the files and folders specifically requested by a user are available, or that all files and folders that users open are available for offline use. The Properties dialog box also allows you to prevent the share from being available offline. You can use this option to ensure the security of information in the folder share.

Create Shares with the Shared Folders Snap-In *(continued)*

The Name, Description, and Settings page of the Wizard appears.

⑭ Type a share name.

⑮ Click Next.

The Permissions page of the Wizard appears.

⑯ Click the permissions option you want (▢ changes to ◉).

⑰ Click Finish.

The summary page of the Wizard appears.

⑱ Click Close.

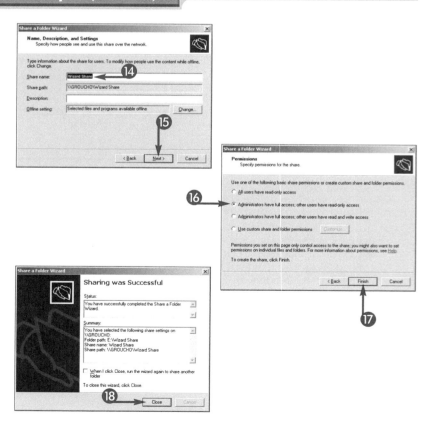

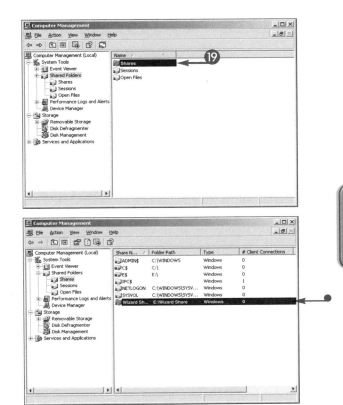

⑲ Double-click Shares.

● The new share appears with other shared folders.

How can I use the Shared Folders console in the Computer Management snap-in to publish a folder share in the Active Directory?

▼ You can access the share by clicking Shares under Shared Folders in the Computer Management Console and clicking the share you want to publish. You can then right-click the share and click Properties in the menu that appears. In the Properties dialog box, click the Publish tab. Click the Publish this share in Active Directory option (☐ changes to ☑). You can add an optional description to the share, and specify an owner. You can add keywords to help the Active Directory users to locate the share by clicking Edit, typing a keyword, clicking Add, and then clicking OK.

After I have created a share with the Share a Folder Wizard, do I have to run the Wizard again to remove the share?

▼ No. You can remove the share by clicking Shares under Shared Folders in the Computer Management console, and then right-clicking the shared folder you want to remove from the list. When you click Stop Sharing in the menu that appears, the folder is no longer shared. You can also click Properties in the same menu to open the Properties dialog box for the folder, and then click the Sharing tab to add or remove user access to the share. You can click the Publish tab, and then click the Publish the share in Active Directory option (☐ changes to ☑).

Enable Windows File Protection with Group Policy

Y ou can use Windows Server 2003 Active Directory Group Policy to enable file protection for shared files and folders on a server and in a domain. This feature prevents an unauthorized user from modifying your files. It helps you to ensure file integrity on the network and to add security to sensitive business information.

File integrity is your ability to monitor the files and folders on your network and in your domain and to ensure that only authorized users can change them. These users can include the owner of a folder or a system administrator.

You can set permissions so that even a system administrator cannot access files if the information is particularly sensitive. You can also prevent these files from being changed. You can guard file integrity not only from outside intruders such as hackers but also from any users who have authorized access to the domain, but not to the protected files.

You can use Group Policy to exercise very specific control sets over the behavior of any object in the Active Directory. For more information about Group Policy, see Chapters 13 and 14.

Enable Windows File Protection with Group Policy

① Click Start.

② Click Administrative Tools.

③ Click Active Directory Users and Computers.

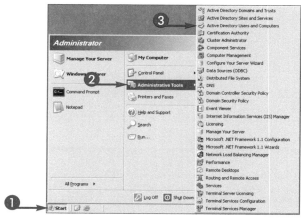

The Active Directory Users and Computers window appears.

④ Right-click a domain.

⑤ Click Properties.

The Properties dialog box appears for the domain you selected.

⑥ Click the Group Policy tab.

⑦ Click Edit.

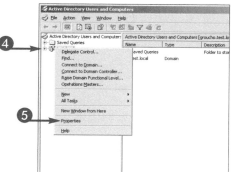

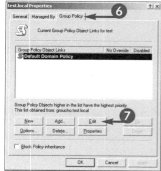

The Group Policy Object Editor window appears.

8 Under Computer Configuration, expand Administrative Templates.

9 Expand System.

10 Click Windows File Protection.

11 Double-click Set Windows File Protection scanning.

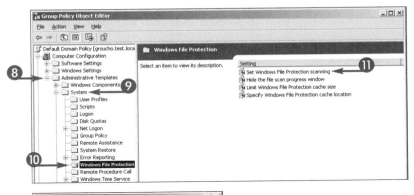

The Set Windows File Protection scanning Properties dialog box appears.

12 Click the Enabled option (⬭ changes to ⬤).

13 Click here and select Scan during startup.

14 Click OK.

Windows file protection is enabled.

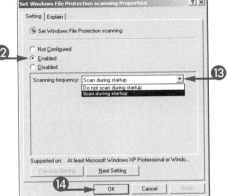

What happens if I do not enable file scanning during startup?

▼ You can configure either setting in the Set Windows File Protection scanning Properties dialog box for the level of security you want. If you choose the Scan during startup option, then file integrity is scanned each time you restart the server and also causes scans to occur whenever a Windows XP computer with offline copies of shared files on the server synchronizes the offline files with the shared files. This happens to verify that any changes to online and offline files were made by an authorized user. If you do not select this option, then the scans are only conducted during startup. Only Windows XP and Windows Server 2003 computers can take advantage of this option.

What other options can I set in the Group Policy Object Editor in the Windows File Protection pane?

▼ You can configure the Hide the file scan progress setting, which prevents users from seeing that a file scan is in progress. You can set the Limit Windows File Protection cache size, which limits the amount of disk space that is used to add protected files to the File Protection cache. You can also specify the Windows File Protection cache location, to indicate an alternate location for Windows file protection cache files. To read a description of what each setting does, select the setting in the Windows File Protection pane in the Group Policy Object Editor window. An explanation appears to the right of the sidebar menu.

PART III

Restrict Offline File Usage with Group Policy

You can increase security of the shared files and folders in your domain as well as gaining more specific control over offline files, by using the Group Policy Object Editor. The Group Policy Object Editor allows you to configure over 20 different options that affect the behavior of offline files. You can only set a few options for offline folder use, such as enabling and disabling offline folders in the Shared Folder Properties dialog box.

While Windows XP and Windows 2000 Professional are both set by default to use offline files, both Windows 2000 Server and Windows Server 2003 computers are not. To change the behavior of offline files, you must manually change the default settings in the Group Policy Object Editor.

The settings that you change in the Group Policy Object Editor can affect how users throughout your domain use offline folders. You can also use the Group Policy Object Editor to apply offline-file settings that target a particular physical site, a single domain or child domain, or an Organizational Unit.

You cannot use the Offline files option if your Windows Server 2003 computer is the Terminal Server. To learn more about the Terminal Server, see Chapter 18.

Restrict Offline File Usage with Group Policy

① Click Start.

② Click Administrative Tools.

③ Click Active Directory Users and Computers.

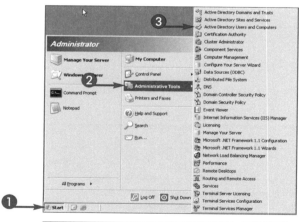

The Active Directory Users and Computers window appears.

④ Right-click a domain.

⑤ Click Properties.

The domain's Properties dialog box appears for the domain you selected.

⑥ Click the Group Policy tab.

⑦ Click Edit.

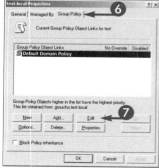

The Group Policy Object Editor window appears.

8 Under Computer Configuration, expand Administrative Templates.

9 Expand Network.

10 Click Offline Files.

11 Double-click Allow or Disallow use of the Offline Files feature.

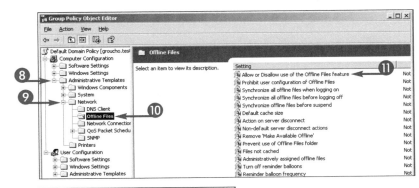

The Allow or Disallow use of the Offline Files feature Properties dialog box appears.

12 Click the Enabled option (⃝ changes to ⦿).

13 Click OK.

The Offline files feature is enabled.

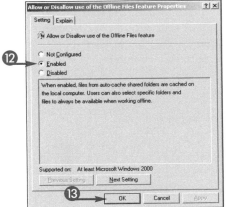

What other options can I configure for offline file behavior in the Group Policy Object Editor.

▼ You can configure a wide variety of settings in the Group Policy Object Editor. For example, you can prohibit user configuration of offline files, specify when to synchronize offline files with the shares on the server, specify the default cache size allotted for offline files, and allow the encryption of the offline file cache. You can access the settings in the Group Policy Object Editor in your Windows Server 2003 Domain Controller. Simply open a particular setting and select the Explain tab to review the function of each one.

Why would I want to encrypt an offline file?

▼ You can set offline files to be encrypted on the client computer for additional protection. Shared folders reside on a protected server inside your network and domain. If an offline file is cached on a client computer and the computer leaves the building, then the information may be vulnerable if an unauthorized person accesses that computer. When you enable this feature, an unauthorized person who attempts to read an offline file cannot access the file, as the data is not readable. This includes all of the data when the file is originally cached as well as data that is added later after more information is cached from the shared folder.

Enable a Computer to Use Offline Files

Y ou can manually configure a client computer in your domain to use offline files. For example, a traveling business user may want to cache network file shares on their portable computer and continue to work with those files without having to connect to the business network. These files change as the traveling user works with them, and the original network share also continues to change as network users at the office access the information and modify it.

When the traveling user returns to the office, or when they access the network from a secure remote connection such as a VPN, the information between the portable computer

cache and the network share is synchronized so that they are both identical again, with all changes intact.

While you can enable a file server or domain controller to make offline files available, you must configure the client computer to use offline files. Only Windows 2000 and Windows XP client computers can use offline files on a Windows Server 2003 server. You cannot configure a down-level operating system such as Windows NT or Windows 98 to use offline files.

Please note that the example in this section uses Windows 2000 Professional as the client computer.

Enable a Computer to Use Offline Files

① Click Start.

② Click Settings.

③ Click Control Panel.

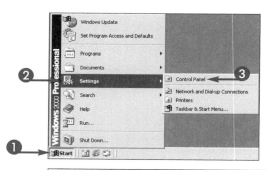

The Control Panel window appears.

④ Double-click Folder Options.

The Folder Options dialog box appears.

5 Click the Offline Files tab.

6 Click the Enable Offline Files option
(☐ changes to ☑).

7 Click the "Synchronize all offline files before
logging off" option (☐ changes to ☑).

8 Click and drag the slider bar to specify the
amount of disk space you want to use for
temporary offline files at 10 percent of the
total hard drive space.

9 Click Advanced.

The Offline Files - Advanced Settings dialog
box appears.

10 Click the "Notify me and begin working
offline" option (☐ changes to ☉).

11 Click OK.

12 Click OK in the Folder Options dialog box.

Offline files are enabled.

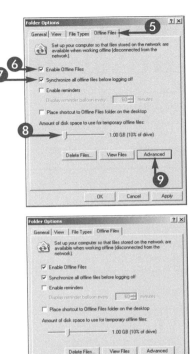
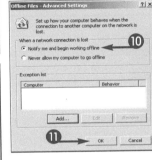

Do I enable offline file usage for a Windows XP computer differently than for a Windows 2000 computer?

▼ The process is almost identical for both operating systems. For example, the way in which you access the Offline Files tab in the Folder Options dialog box is the same. However, when you click the Offline Files tab, you may find that the controls are not available if Fast User Switching is enabled in Windows XP. Fast User Switching allows different users who use the same computer to quickly change logins. You must disable this feature to use offline files. When you have disabled Fast User Switching, the Offline Files configuration settings become available. One of the other differences is that Windows XP offers an Encrypt Offline Files option.

Does the way in which I set up a client computer to access and manage offline files stay the same regardless of which server I use to get those files?

▼ Yes, but only if you configure an exception rule. Both Windows 2000 and Windows XP offer a setting in the Folder Options dialog box that you can access by clicking Advanced and then clicking Add in the Exception list area. In the Offline Files - Add Custom Action dialog box, you can either type the pathname, or browse to a particular server and then select whether to allow your computer to work with offline files from this server.

Understanding NTFS Share Permissions

You can configure your Windows Server 2003 server to use New Technology File System, or NTFS, as your file management system. NTFS supports long filenames, provides greater access control to files and folders, and uses very large disk partitions for data storage.

You can use NTFS to protect your data because it is less prone to corruption than FAT or FAT32. NTFS is also more likely to recognize and repair errors and bad sectors on a hard disk drive and provides options for disk compression and data encapsulation.

NTFS or FAT

Although NTFS is almost exclusively associated with Windows 2000 Server and Windows Server 2003, it was introduced with Windows NT 4.0 Service Pack 4. NTFS offers more features and better security than FAT32; however, you may find situations where you prefer to use FAT32 on your Windows server. For example, you may need to dual boot your Windows Server 2003 server to another operating system that must use FAT — such as Windows 98 — and still have the Windows 98 system to access files. You may also need to boot your server from a floppy disk using Windows 98.

File Size, Disk Size, and Clusters

In theory, you can use FAT32 on partitions of up to 2 Terabytes (TB). However, Windows Server 2003 limits the size of FAT volumes to only 32GB, and any individual file on FAT32 can only be 4GB in size. On FAT16, the maximum allowable file size is only 2GB. On Windows Server 2003, NTFS supports both volume and individual file size limits of 16TB. Like FAT, NTFS uses clustering on hard disk drives and supports all cluster sizes from 512 bytes to 64KB, although 4KB is the standard cluster size on disks.

Master File Table

NTFS must use the first 12 percent of a hard disk drive for the Master File Table, or MFT. The MFT is the master record that is used to locate data in any NTFS partition. If you destroy or cannot access the MFT, then you cannot locate any of the files on the NTFS partition, even if the NTFS data is perfectly intact. The MFT can grow as you create more files on the NTFS partition. The MFT file can also become fragmented, thus increasing the access time for the MFT file. Initially, the first 2 percent is reserved, but you can return for use if all other space has been allocated and the MFT no longer needs the space. Also, you can have more than one NTFS partition, each containing its own MFT, on your hard disk.

Metafiles

Metafiles are part of the MFT system and constitute the first 16 files in the NTFS partition. The MFT is the very first of these 16 metafiles. NTFS uses metafiles to control different aspects of system operation. The 16 metafiles must occupy a very specific location on the partition. You cannot move it manually or by using a defragmentation operation.

The first three metafiles must be located in the very middle of the partition. Although metafiles have a fixed location on the disk, they are not all located together. As a result, they do not represent a single point of failure if a particular area of the disk becomes damaged or corrupt. Some of the metafiles are part of the MFT: the root directory, the boot sector, and a list of file attributes on the disk. You cannot normally access metafiles either with Windows Explorer or from the command line. However, you can use a particular command in the command shell window — dir /ah <filename> — to read metafile information regarding that particular file. The name of each metafile is preceded by a dollar sign ($), for example, $BITMAP or $MFT.

NTFS and Operating Systems

You can use NTFS as a file system structure on Windows NT 4.0 (Service Pack 4 or higher), Windows 2000, Windows XP, and Windows Server 2003. When you do a fresh install of Windows 2000, Windows XP, and Windows Server 2003, you have the option of selecting FAT32 or NTFS Version 5 file systems. If you upgrade a

Windows NT 4.0 computer with Service Pack 4 or higher that is running an earlier version of NTFS, then NTFS automatically upgrades to NTFS Version 5 without your intervention.

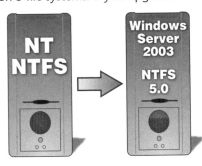

NTFS Command Line Management

You can create and manage NTFS files and partitions from the command line using format.exe and windisk.exe. You can specify a precise size for your disk drive clusters, or you can accept the default selection. The file system bases the default selection on the physical size of the disk that you are formatting.

Directories

NTFS uses a root index system to organize its file directory system. Each NTFS directory entry contains the filename and the file standard attribute data. The root index in the MFT describes where the file is located on the disk, and NTFS can provide index buffers when the directory outgrows the MFT metafile.

Set Basic Share Permissions

Y ou can set Basic Share Permissions on a FAT32 volume. This enables you to limit access to the data on a particular file or folder to a certain group of users on your network or domain. It also enables you to prevent unauthorized persons or groups from reading or changing restricted data.

When you first create a shared folder on your network, the share permissions for that folder are set by default to allow the Everyone group to read what is in the folder. Any user who can authenticate onto the network and access shared folders is a member of the Everyone group. Therefore, you must manually restrict their access to information on the network shares, and you cannot use the more powerful and specific access control lists that are available in NTFS. You can use Basic Share Permissions on both FAT and NTFS, but NTFS has access to its own data protection system.

Share permissions only apply to users who access the shares over the network. If you access the shared file or folder directly from the server where the data resides, you can open and read the data; the share permission has no effect on you.

Set Basic Share Permissions

① Click Start.

② Right-click My Computer.

③ Click Explore.

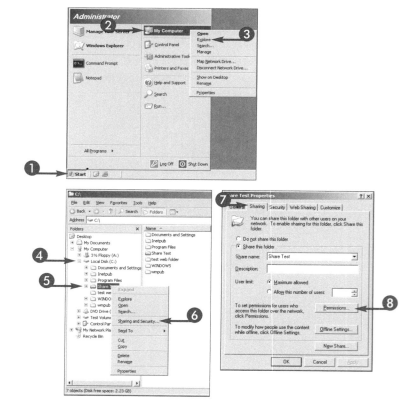

The My Computer window appears.

④ Navigate to the hard drive you want.

⑤ Right-click the shared folder.

⑥ Click Sharing and Security.

The Properties dialog box appears for the shared folder.

⑦ Click the Sharing tab.

⑧ Click Permissions.

The Permissions dialog box appears.

9 Click Add.

The Select Users, Computers, or Groups dialog box appears.

10 Type the name of the group you want to add.

11 Click Check Names.

12 Click OK.

The Permissions dialog box appears for the shared folder.

13 Click the new group.

14 Click the Allow or Deny check boxes that you want in the Permissions for Security area (☐ changes to ☑).

15 Click OK.

Windows applies the new basic file permissions set to the group.

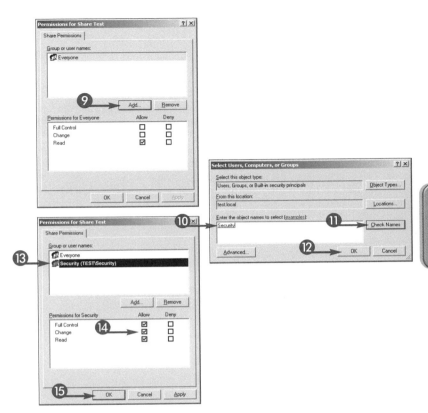

Why is there only one default group that has access to the shared folder permission?

▼ The Everyone group includes all other groups, but you cannot separate the permissions for the Everyone group from any other group on the network or domain. You must add another group if you want to give them more or less permissions to share than the Everyone group. You can also increase the security access to the shared folder by removing the Everyone group from the Share Permissions area and adding only those groups that you want to allow permissions for the shared folder.

What is the difference between the types of permissions and between Allow and Deny?

▼ Permission types include Full Control, Change, or Read. With Read permission, a user can read information but cannot change it. Change permission allows a user to modify and save information in the folder. Full Control permission includes both Read and Change permissions and creating and deleting files. If you select the Deny setting for any one of the permissions (☐ changes to ☑), it overrides any Allow settings. Therefore, if you select Allow under Full Control, but select Deny under Change for a particular group, that group can only read but not change or save information. Use Deny with the Everyone group with caution as it denies access to the file owner and system admins.

Set NTFS Disk Quotas

You can control disk usage on an NTFS volume. This enables you to limit the amount of hard disk space that a user may access, or to limit the amount of hard disk space that is used on a drive. This feature allows you to conserve storage resources and prevents a server from overextending the hard disk storage system. You can set up an NTFS volume so that it controls disk usage on a per-user and per-volume basis. This means that any authorized user can only save a certain amount of information on the drive, regardless of the location of the folder in which the user is saving data.

You can set different quotas for different NTFS volumes, even if the volumes reside on the same hard disk drive. You can assign each volume a separate drive letter, thus causing each volume to look like a separate hard drive to network and domain users.

You can only use NTFS Disk Quotas for Windows 2000, Windows XP, and Windows Server 2003 systems. You can assign each user a disk quota. A user cannot use file compression to gain more disk quota space because the quota reads the original amount of file space.

Set NTFS Disk Quotas

① Click Start.

② Double-click My Computer.

The My Computer window appears.

③ Right-click a drive.

④ Click Properties.

The Properties dialog box appears for the disk you selected.

⑤ Click the Quota tab.

⑥ Click the Enable quota management option (☐ changes to ☑).

⑦ Click Limit disk space to option (☐ changes to ⊙).

⑧ Type a value to specify a disk space limit and a warning level.

⑨ Click Log event when a user exceeds their quota limit (☐ changes to ☑).

⑩ Click OK.

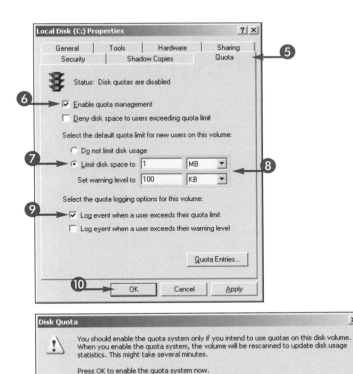

The Disk Quota dialog box appears.

⑪ Click OK.

Windows enables the disk quota.

How can I set a disk quota entry for a specific user for a particular NTFS volume?

▼ To set a disk quota entry, you can access the Disk Properties dialog box by right-clicking the disk and clicking Properties in the menu that appears. When the Properties dialog box opens, click the Quota tab and then click Quota Entries. Click Quota on the toolbar and then click New Quota Entry. In the Select Users dialog box that appears, type the name of the user and click Check Names. Click OK. The Add New Quota Entry dialog box appears. Click the Limit disk space to option (☐ changes to ⊙), type the amount of disk space for the user quota, and specify a warning level. Click OK to apply your changes.

If I set a disk quota limit option (☐ changes to ⊙) in the Hard Disk Properties dialog box, but do not select the "Deny disk space option for users who exceed their limit" option (☐ changes to ☑), what happens?

▼ You can set a quota limit without restricting a user from exceeding that limit. This feature is useful when a user makes a mistake and attempts to save a very large file that exceeds the disk quota limit. You can set disk quotas to send warnings to a user as they are approaching their limit, when they have exceeded their limit, or both. You can set disk quotas to log these events in the Event Viewer to help you to manage user folders that exceed their limits.

Set NTFS File Compression

Y ou can set file and folder compression on an NTFS volume. This feature allows you to store more data on a particular hard disk drive or volume so that you can save more data in a limited storage area. You can use compression when you manage older storage server devices with smaller hard disks. Compression is also useful when the network storage needs of your company grow and you cannot purchase additional disks or servers to meet these needs.

You can access compressed files and folders in an NTFS volume from a computer running any Windows operating system or from MS-DOS without having to first decompress

the data. The data that you access automatically decompresses when you open the file to read it and automatically recompresses when you close the file.

You can compress individual files and folders, or you can compress an entire NTFS volume on your Windows Server 2003 server. For best server performance, limit the number of compressed files that are accessed frequently, because the compression and decompression process requires increased processing power. Any compressed files that you move from an NTFS volume to a FAT32 volume are automatically decompressed.

Set NTFS File Compression

① Click Start.

② Double-click My Computer.

The My Computer window appears.

③ Double-click the drive you want.

The window appears for the drive that you selected.

④ Right-click a folder.

⑤ Click Properties.

The Properties dialog box appears for the folder.

6 Click Advanced.

The Advanced Attributes dialog box appears.

7 Click the "Compress contents to save disk space" option (☑ changes to ☐).

8 Click OK.

Windows enables compression for the folder.

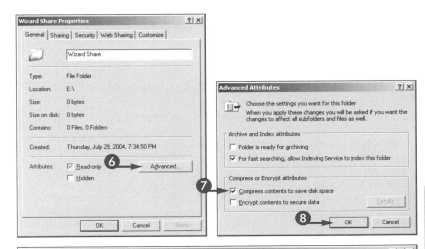

● The folder text appears blue to indicate that it is compressed.

Note: *To see the blue color, you may need to select the "Show encrypted or compressed NTFS files in color" option in the Window's Explorer's Folder option dialog box in the View tab.*

What happens if I move a compressed folder on an NTFS volume to another NTFS folder?

▼ You can move a compressed folder to another folder on an NTFS volume, but what happens to the compressed folder depends on the state of the other folder to which you are moving it. For example, if you move or copy a compressed folder to another compressed folder on an NTFS volume, the original folder stays in a compressed state. A compressed folder that you move or copy to a decompressed folder on an NTFS volume becomes decompressed. A decompressed folder that you move to a compressed folder on an NTFS volume becomes compressed.

What types of files or data I should not compress?

▼ Although you can compress almost any file type, some file types compress more than others. For example, bitmap files contain less redundant information and compress less than application files. As a result, you can compress more information onto an NTFS volume if you store application files. You cannot compress files on an NTFS volume if they are already compressed. For example, if you place a compressed file, such as a ZIP file, into an NTFS compressed folder, it does not compress any further, although NTFS attempts to compress it, thereby wasting server resources. Do not compress files that a server application, such as AD data files and SQL Server data and log files, constantly opens and uses.

PART III

Set NTFS Data Encryption

Y ou can set NTFS Data Encryption on your Windows Server 2003 server to protect the data by preventing unauthorized personnel from accessing and reading the data. This means that only users who own the information or who are otherwise authorized to read protected data can access the data. NTFS Data Encryption uses Encrypting File System, or EFS, data encryption designed by Microsoft to increase the security of sensitive business information. EFS can use public key and private key encryption, but it only works on NTFS Version 5 volumes. Only Windows 2000, Windows XP, and Windows Server 2003 operating systems can use EFS data encryption.

You can create an encrypted folder on an NTFS volume and then move unencrypted files and folders into the encrypted folder. The encrypted folder automatically encrypts the unencrypted information once the data is inside. You can rename, move, and even back up the encrypted files without changing their encrypted state.

You can encrypt and unencrypt files and folders either from the Graphical User Interface, or GUI, or when you use the command shell with the cipher.exe command line utility. You cannot apply both compression and encryption to the same file or folder.

Set NTFS Data Encryption

1 Click Start.

2 Double-click My Computer.

The My Computer window appears.

3 Double-click a drive you want to encrypt.

The window appears for the drive that you selected.

4 Right-click a folder.

5 Click Properties.

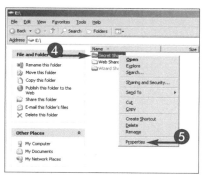

The Properties dialog box appears for the folder.

6 Click Advanced.

The Advanced Attributes dialog box appears.

7 Click the "Encrypt contents to secure data" option (☐ changes to ☑).

8 Click OK.

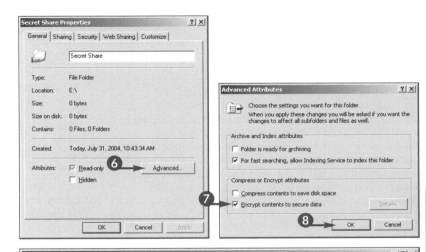

● The folder text appears green to indicate that it is encrypted.

Note: *To see the green color, you may need to select the "Show encrypted or compressed NTFS files in color" option in the Window's Explorer's Folder option dialog box in the View tab.*

How can I perform data encryption on the command line?

▼ You can use the cipher.exe utility at the command line to encrypt or decrypt folders and the files they contain. Click Start, click Command Prompt. The command shell opens. To encrypt a directory only, type **cipher /A /pathname** where *pathname* is the path to the directory you want to encrypt. Press Enter. The directory or folder is encrypted, but files added to the directory are not. To encrypt a directory and any files added to it afterwards, type **cipher /E /pathname**, for example **cipher /E /C:/encrypt**. To unencrypt a directory type **cipher /U /pathname**.

What happens when an unauthorized user tries to access an encrypted file?

▼ If you try to access an encrypted file and you are not authorized to read it, then you receive an Access Is Denied message from NTFS. However, if you have NTFS access permissions, then even though you cannot read the file, you can still move it to another location on the same NTFS volume or even delete the file. You can prevent file movement and deletion by carefully assigning and monitoring who has NTFS access list permissions to any sensitive, encrypted data files and folders. No one can access encrypted data on Windows Server 2003 from Windows NT 4.0.

Set Up
Shadow Copies

You can configure Shadow Copies on an NTFS volume to make automatic copies of shared folders at scheduled times in order to add fault tolerance. You can use Shadow Copies to restore data that was deleted from a volume on a local drive or a mapped network drive. You can only use Shadow Copies on volumes that are formatted with NTFS. The Volume Shadow Copy Service (VSS) is only available on Window Server 2003 systems.

NTFS volumes can use the VSS service to create a point-in-time backup of the contents of the volume, and even back up the contents of open files in the volume. The VSS service

can operate quickly compared to typical tape backups. You can back up the data to another local NTFS volume or hard disk drive using a Shadow Copy, also called a *snapshot*, of the volume data. You can also use the Task Scheduler, located in the Control Panel on your server, to schedule regular backups using the VSS service for one or more volumes.

The built-in Windows Server 2003 backup program can back up the Shadow Copy data to tape, leaving the live NTFS volume data available for use.

Set Up Shadow Copies

① Click Start.

② Double-click My Computer.

The My Computer window appears.

③ Right-click an NTFS volume.

④ Click Properties.

The Properties dialog box appears for the NTFS volume that you selected.

⑤ Click the Shadow Copies tab.

⑥ Click Enable.

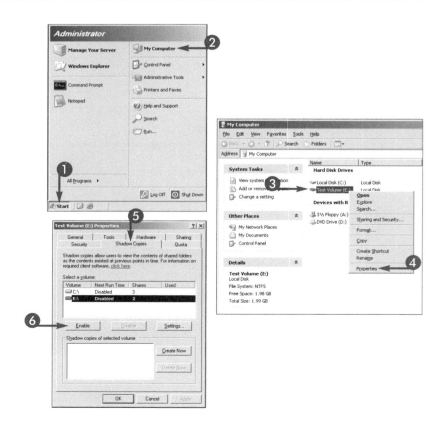

The Enable Shadow Copies dialog box appears.

⑦ Click Yes.

Windows automatically creates a Shadow Copy.

⑧ Click Settings.

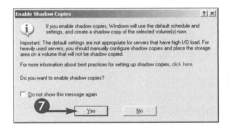

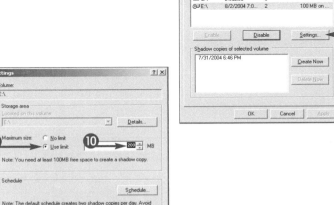

The Settings dialog box appears.

⑨ Click the Use limit option (◌ changes to ◉).

⑩ Type the volume size you want for the Shadow Copy.

⑪ Click OK.

Windows enables Shadow Copying.

Can I create a schedule for the VSS service to create Shadow Copies from the volume's Properties dialog box?

▼ Yes. You can click Settings in the Shadow Copies tab of the Properties dialog box. In the Settings dialog box, click Schedule. By default, the setting for making a Shadow Copy of the volume is every day, from Monday through Friday at 7:00 A.M. Frequency options include Weekly, Daily, Monthly, Once only, and At System Startup. You can select any of the daily options to change the settings and time (◌ changes to ☑). You can also click Advanced to access the Advanced Schedule Options dialog box.

Are there any other advanced options that I can use with Shadow Copies?

▼ Yes. In the Properties dialog box for the volume, you can click Create New to manually create a Shadow Copy of the volume. Click Schedule. In the Shadow Copy Schedule dialog box that appears, you can click New to create a new schedule or Delete to delete the current schedule for making a Shadow Copy. In the volume's Properties dialog box, you can also disable Shadow Copying by clicking Disable. You can also use the Disk Management console in the Computer Management snap-in to access an NTFS volume and set up Shadow Copies. To do this, right-click an NTFS volume, click Properties, and then click the Shadow Copies tab.

Assign NTFS Permissions to Users and Groups

You can assign NTFS Permissions to users and groups for Active Directory Object resources such as folders, files, printers, and computers. This allows you to restrict general security access and to set more specific security permissions to the resources. You can use Access Control Lists, or ACLs, and Access Control Entities, or ACEs, to set very specific types of access to any shared resource object. Although you have access to more detailed permission controls than simply Read, Modify, and Full Control, you can set NTFS permissions using these settings as a basis.

When you first create an NTFS volume on your Windows Server 2003 server, NTFS default permissions are created for the users and groups that are available on your system rather than simply the Everyone group. For more on the Everyone group, see the section "Set Basic Share Permissions."

NTFS permissions are inherited, and you can specify that the file objects inside a folder also inherit the permissions that you assign to the folder. You can remove permissions inheritance from a folder and set individual NTFS permissions to separate file objects inside the folder. NTFS permissions are cumulative, and you can add permissions that are set to a folder to any permissions that are separately set to file objects inside the folder.

Assign NTFS Permissions to Users and Groups

① Click Start.

② Double-click My Computer.

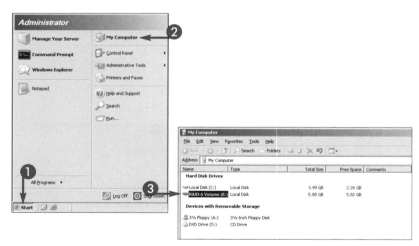

The My Computer window appears.

③ Double-click an NTFS volume.

The window appears for the volume you selected.

④ Right-click a shared folder.

⑤ Click Properties.

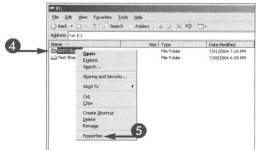

The Properties dialog box appears for the folder you selected.

6 Click the Security tab.

7 Click Add.

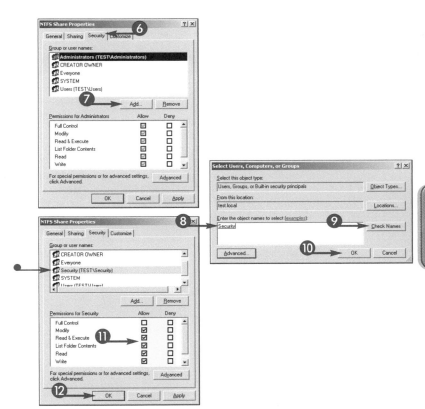

The Select Users, Computers, or Groups dialog box appears.

8 Type the name of a user or group.

9 Click Check Names.

10 Click OK.

- The new group appears in the Access List.

11 Click the permissions you want for the group (☐ changes to ☑).

12 Click OK.

The new NTFS permissions are applied to the group.

How can I set up more specific permissions settings for users and groups on an NTFS share?

▼ You can right-click the NTFS folder, then click Properties to open the shared folder Properties dialog box, and then click Advanced. The Advanced Security Settings dialog box displays a list of each group and their relative permissions. Select a group by clicking it, and then click Edit. The Permission Entry dialog box appears for the group, displaying a detailed list of specific permissions for that group. This list includes Full Control, Traverse Folder/ Execute File, and Create Folders/Append Data. You can click the Allow and Deny option (☐ changes to ☑) to set more specific permissions.

How can I set up or change the inheritable permissions involving parent and child objects in an NTFS share?

▼ You can access the shared folder Properties dialog box by right-clicking the folder and clicking Properties in the menu that appears. Click Advanced to open the Advanced Security Settings dialog box for that folder. There are two options (☐ changes to ☑) at the bottom of the dialog box. The first option, which is selected by default (☑), allows inheritable permissions to propagate to the shared object and all child objects. The other option, which is not selected (☐), allows you to replace permission entries on all child objects with entries that you can create.

Determine NTFS Effective Permissions

You can determine the NTFS Effective Permissions for each set of users and groups for an NTFS share. This enables you to determine which settings are applied, whether any settings conflict with each other, and whether any settings that you want to apply conflict with the current effective permissions.

You may find it difficult to manually determine and keep track of the NTFS permissions that each user or group has for a particular NTFS share. This difficulty increases if you or other users change or modify the inheritance of those

permissions. Windows Server 2003 can calculate all applied effective permissions and then provide a list to enable you to quickly assess NTFS permissions status.

NTFS permissions are cumulative, meaning that you can set a Deny permission at one level that conflicts with an Allow permission that you set at a different level in the parent-child share hierarchy. If a user or group complains that they do not have access to a share to which they should have access, then you can use this feature to determine whether a conflict exists. You can then use it to correct the permission settings for the NTFS share.

Determine NTFS Effective Permissions

① Click Start.

② Double-click My Computer.

The My Computer window appears.

③ Double-click an NTFS volume.

The window appears for the NTFS volume you selected.

④ Right-click an NTFS folder.

⑤ Click Properties.

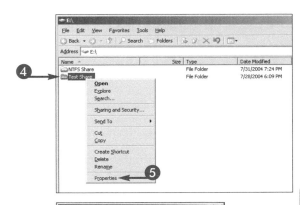

The Properties dialog box appears for the shared folder you selected.

⑥ Click the Security tab.

⑦ Click Advanced.

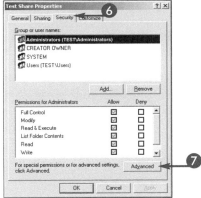

How can I learn more about Access Control functions that relate to NTFS share permissions?

▼ You can open the Properties dialog box of a shared folder with NTFS permissions and click Advanced. Click the Permissions tab, and at the bottom of the Advanced Security Settings for Test Folder area, click the "Learn more about access control" option (☐ changes to ☑). The Access Control Help dialog box appears, and a general statement about Access Control appears in the right-hand pane. The dialog box also displays links that you can click, including User Rights, Permissions, Best Practices, Concepts, and a How to link. You can also click the Index and Search tabs for more information.

What does Access Control allow you to do?

▼ It controls how users, groups, and computers access Active Directory objects in a domain. The key concepts in Access Control are Permissions, User Rights, and Object Auditing. User Rights, which include priviledges and logon rights, are the tasks a user can perform on a computer system. Object Auditing lets you review all security-oriented access events for a server in a log in the Event Viewer. With Object Auditing, you can log and review events, such as when a file is opened, modified, saved, and deleted. You can enable auditing in the Auditing tab of the Advanced Security Settings dialog box for an NTFS share. See the section "Assign NTFS Permissions to Users and Groups" for more information.

continued

Determine NTFS Effective Permissions *(Continued)*

You can only use the NTFS Effective Permissions tool to receive a report of the approximate Effective Permissions that a user, group, or computer has for a particular NTFS shared object. This is because the actual permissions that a user has may be different, based on how that particular user logs in when they access the share. You can have different permissions when you log in locally to the server and access the file share compared to when you log in to a remote computer to a network or domain. The four categories that affect how you can access an NTFS share are Global Group Membership, Local Group Membership, Local Permissions, and Local Privileges.

You must have sufficient permissions in order to read the NTFS Effective Permissions that a user or group has for a shared object. These permissions may vary, depending on the nature of the object. For example, if you assess a domain object, you must log in as a Domain Administrator to read the Effective Permissions. Domain users can only read group membership information when the domain is using pre-Windows 2000 security.

Determine NTFS Effective Permissions *(continued)*

The Advanced Security Settings dialog box appears for the share you selected.

⑧ Click the Effective Permissions tab.

⑨ Click Select.

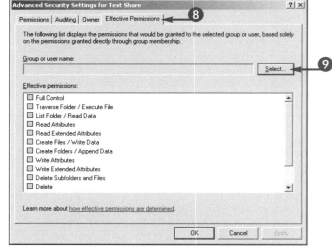

The Select User, Computer, or Group dialog box appears.

⑩ Type a user or group name.

⑪ Click Check Names.

⑫ Click OK.

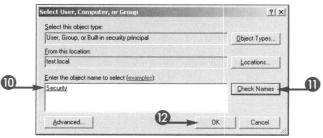

The Effective Permissions display for the group.

⑬ Click the "Learn more about how effective permissions are determined" link.

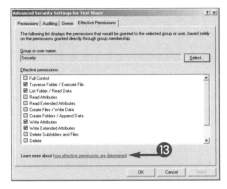

The Access Control help window appears.

● You can navigate to the Effective Permissions tool page for more information.

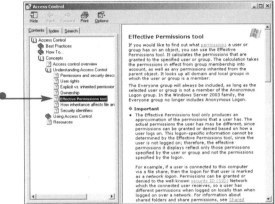

How can I search more specific locations on the Windows Server 2003 server?

▼ In the Select User, Computer, or Group dialog box, you can click Locations to search more specific locations on your Windows Server 2003 server. When you type a name in the Object Name dialog box that appears, and click Check Names, the computer searches all of the user, group or computer objects in the database to verify that the name is valid in the domain. You can also narrow the search to a particular location on the server or select a child domain to broaden the search for the Active Directory object.

Can I type the group or username directly in the Group or user name field in the Advanced Security Settings dialog box?

▼ No. Although the cursor is blinking and appears to be active, you cannot make an entry into the name field. You can only make a valid entry by clicking Select and typing the entry in the Enter the object to select field. If you are not sure what to type, you can click the examples link; when you do so, a menu appears with examples, such as how to type in a Display Name, an Object Name, and a User Name.

Change Ownership of Files and Folders

Y ou can change ownership of NTFS files or folders. This allows you to assign an owner of a system-created object, other than the Administrator, or to reassign an owner to a file or folder object if the original owner is no longer available. The user who created the object owns each file or folder object by default. Your Windows Server 2003 system also creates file objects and automatically assigns the Administrator as the owner. The owner has complete control over how to assign NTFS permissions to the file or folder object, as well as which users, groups, and computer objects to assign permission to the object.

File and folder owners can retain complete control of the object that they own, even if they do not have sufficient permissions to access the object, read it, write to it, or delete it. When an employee owner of a file or folder object leaves the company, the object becomes orphaned and does not have an owner until someone else takes ownership of the object. Administrators can take ownership of an object as well as a user or group that is assigned the Allow Take Ownership permission to a specific object.

Change Ownership of Files and Folders

① Click Start.

② Double-click My Computer.

The My Computer window appears.

③ Double-click an NTFS volume.

The window appears for the NTFS volume
that you selected.

④ Right-click an NTFS folder.

⑤ Click Properties.

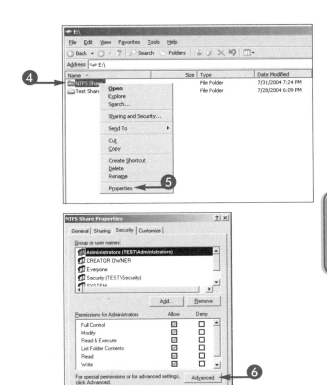

The Properties dialog box appears for the
NTFS share that you selected.

⑥ Click Advanced.

What is the difference between taking ownership of an object and transferring ownership?

▼ Before Windows Server 2003, you could only take ownership of an NTFS file or folder object, and only if you had sufficient permissions to do so. With Windows Server 2003, you can now change the ownership of an object from yourself to another user or group in the domain. You no longer have to grant special permission to the user or group for the user or group to take ownership of an object and become the new owner. Any owner of a file or folder object can specifically assign another owner, regardless of the permissions that the other user or group holds.

Who can initiate the process of voluntarily reassigning ownership of an NTFS file or folder?

▼ You can reassign ownership of an NTFS file or folder if you are an Administrator, the current owner of the object, or a user who has been granted the Restore Files and Directories permission. You can also still give a particular user or group the Allow Take Ownership permission; however, that user or group must then take ownership rather than have it assigned to them. Once you have voluntarily given up ownership of the file or folder object, you no longer have the authority to make more ownership reassignments.

continued

Change Ownership of
Files and Folders *(Continued)*

As an administrator, you can take ownership of a file or folder from the current owner. This enables you to change permissions on the file or folder object or to conduct any necessary repair operations on a damaged data file. You can also assign another user the Restore Files and Directories permission and give them the ability to take ownership of the file or folder object without giving them full administrative rights over the server, network, or domain.

A user with Restore Files and Directories permissions can completely bypass any file or directory permissions in order to restore backed-up files or directories on a server or server network. When a data file is damaged or corrupted, you can restore the data from a tape or other media backup so that you can continue to use it. A user with Restore Files and Directories permissions is automatically given the Traverse Folder/Execute File and Write permissions to the NTFS share. With this permission, you can also overwrite settings to the registry, hide data, and take ownership of system-related objects. As a result, although you do not have the rights of an Administrator, you can still have significant authority over the system.

Change Ownership of Files and Folders *(continued)*

The Advanced Security Settings for NTFS share dialog box appears.

7 Click the Owner tab.

8 Click Other Users or Groups.

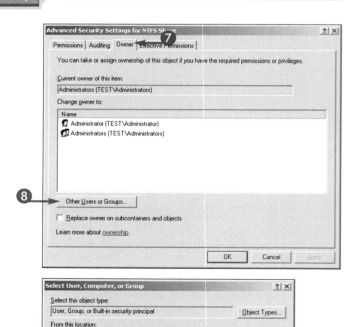

The Select User, Computer, or Group dialog box appears.

9 Type the name of a user or group.

10 Click Check Names.

11 Click OK.

- The new group appears in the Change owner to field.

⑫ Click Apply.

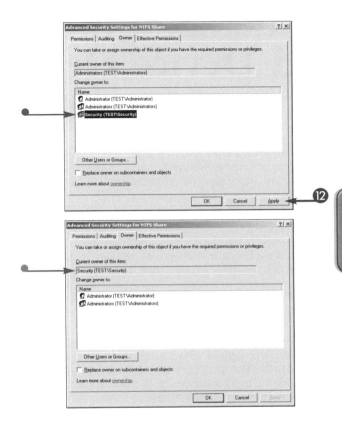

- The new group appears in the Current owner of this item field, indicating that you have changed the owner.

What happens when I click the "Replace owner on subcontainers and objects" option (☐ changes to ☑), in the Owner tab of the Advanced Security Settings dialog box?

▼ Although you can own a particular NTFS folder, as well as all files and subfolders inside the folder, each sub-object inside the folder can also have a separate owner. For example, as an owner or an Administrator, you can give another user or group permission to create, modify, and save files inside a folder that you own. Whoever creates those files owns them, not the owner of the folder. Although you can change the owner of the folder, the owner of the contents does not change. With this option, you can change the owner of the contents of the folder.

What are the exact permissions of the Creator Owner of an NTFS file or folder?

▼ As Creator Owner of an NTFS share, you have special permissions over the object. In the Security tab of the NTFS share Properties dialog box, all of the Allow and Deny options are empty (☐), except for the Special Permissions box, for which Allow is selected (☑). To read the Special Permissions, you can click Advanced, select the Creator Owner, and then click Edit. You can then see that the Special Permissions grant Allow permissions to the Creator Owner over all of the fourteen different specific permissions that are available in the NTFS share.

Understanding Manage Devices and Device Drivers

You can install and manage new devices and device drivers on your Windows Server 2003 computer. Additional devices and device drivers allow you to expand and improve the general performance of your server and to improve the delivery of services on your network. You can perform several types of hardware installations and upgrades. For example, you can install additional IDE or SCSI hard disk drives, upgrade the Central Processing Unit (CPU) or install more than one CPU, and install additional Random Access Memory (RAM) modules. You can also upgrade the Network Interface Card (NIC) to increase the speed at which your server transmits data to and from the network, install a second NIC card to multi-home your server, and upgrade other PCI cards, such as sound and video cards.

Device Drivers

When you install a device, such as a new NIC card, in your server, you must also install a piece of software that helps you to use the new device. This software is called a device driver. Device driver software provides a programming interface that allows the device to communicate and interact with the other computer or server components, including the CPU.

The motherboard of every computer contains a basic set of programming instructions called a Basic Input Output System, or BIOS. The BIOS controls the basic hardware components of the computer, such as the keyboard, mouse, and monitor. However, the BIOS cannot contain all of the operating instructions for every possible device that you may install in or connect to your computer or server.

Device drivers contain additional operating instructions that the BIOS does not have. Not only must you install device drivers for any internal device that you install in your server, but you must also install drivers for many peripheral devices, such as printers, fax machines, and scanners. These devices often ship with a CD-ROM that contains the device driver software. You can also download the software from the device manufacturer Web site or from Web sites such as www.download.com.

Hardware Compatibility List

Although Windows Server 2003 supports full Plug and Play (PnP) functionality and can accommodate a wide range of hardware devices and manufacturers, you may encounter some devices that cannot interact with your server. To determine whether Microsoft has tested and approved a device under consideration for use on or with a server running Windows Server 2003, review the Hardware Compatibility List (HCL) at www.microsoft.com/hwdq/hcl. Keep in mind that your Windows Server 2003 computer may also support limited non-PnP devices.

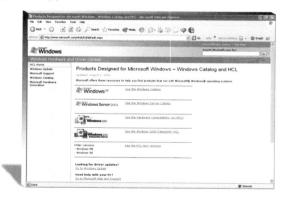

Plug and Play

When you install a new PnP device, you can use it immediately, often without having to restart your Windows Server 2003 computer. PnP is a combination of technologies that allows your computer to immediately recognize when you have installed a new device. PnP also allows your computer to interact with the device, to search for the drivers that are associated with it, and to install the drivers and enable the device for immediate use.

PnP technology can automatically configure the IO, IRQ, DMA, and other required settings so that you do not experience any resource conflicts on the server. While this technology is not perfect, it is very reliable, and you can quickly upgrade your server by using PnP devices.

Electrostatic Discharge

You must take precautions against electrostatic discharge, or ESD, when you install new devices in your server. An ESD is a damaging or catastrophic electrical discharge inside your server that can render it completely inoperable. You can carry an electrostatic potential on your body that, if not managed beforehand, can discharge inside the server while you are installing a device. Although the charge may be so slight that you cannot feel it, it may still be powerful enough to damage the sensitive electrical components inside the server, including the motherboard.

To guard against ESD, you can use equipment such as an anti-ESD wrist strap, workbench mat, and floor mat. This equipment is designed to drain the electrostatic potential from your body so that you can safely work inside the server. You must always take measures against ESD when working inside any computer.

Add Hardware Wizard

Windows Server 2003 comes with an Add Hardware Wizard, which you can use to add hardware to your server. You can also use the wizard process that comes with the manufacturer's CD-ROM; Microsoft recommends using the CD-ROM before using the Add Hardware Wizard. You can use the wizard to install devices that are non-PnP, to diagnose a malfunctioning device, and to safely disable and remove a device from the server. When you launch the wizard, it searches for new hardware that you have recently installed. If it does not find the new hardware, it guides you through a manual process of locating and installing the new device, along with the device drivers.

Installation Management

Your Windows Server 2003 computer can track each time the server shuts down along with the reasons for the shutdown. When you shut down the computer, Windows Server 2003 prompts you to choose a reason for the shutdown from a supplied list, and allows you to enter additional comments regarding the shutdown. Your server adds this information to a log, which you can access in the server's Event Viewer as a record of all maintenance-related shutdown procedures that you have conducted on your server.

Install PnP Devices

You can install PnP devices in your Windows Server 2003 computer to upgrade your server more quickly and to make additional functions and services more readily available to your network users. Your Windows Server 2003 computer can manage the entire detection and installation of your new device with little intervention from you.

The Windows Server 2003 operating system often includes drivers for devices that you install. As a result, you may not need the drivers that accompany the new device on the

CD-ROM. For example, although most keyboards and mice come with a driver disk, you never use the disk unless the driver becomes corrupt and you need to reinstall it.

To install any internal device, you must first shut down your Windows Server 2003 computer by issuing a shutdown command. Unlike Windows 2000 or Windows XP computers, your Windows Server 2003 computer does not shut down before it prompts you to enter the reason for the shutdown command. You can select a reason and then shut down the computer in order to install the device.

PnP technology is available for you to use on Windows 2000, Windows XP, and Windows Server 2003 computers. However, it is unavailable on Windows NT computers.

Install PnP Devices

① Click Start.

② Click Shut Down.

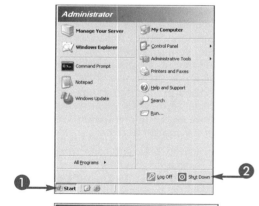

The Shut Down Windows dialog box appears.

③ Click here and select Shut down.

④ Click the Planned option (☐ changes to ☑).

⑤ Click here and select Hardware: Maintenance (Planned).

● You can type an optional comment.

⑥ Click OK.

Windows shuts down.

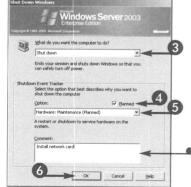

7 Install the new device after disconnecting the server's power supply cord.

8 Restart Windows after you install the device.

Windows automatically detects and installs the drivers for the new device.

9 Click Start.

10 Right-click My Computer.

11 Click Properties.

The System Properties dialog box appears.

12 Click the Hardware tab.

13 Click Device Manager.

The Device Manager window appears.

14 Expand the Network Adapters.

Windows installs the new device.

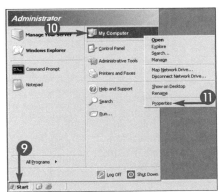

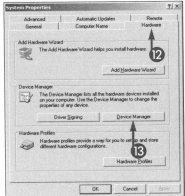

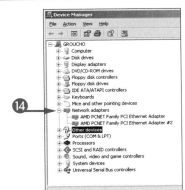

PART III

How can I verify that my new device is not only installed but functioning properly?

▼ You can open the System Properties dialog box by right-clicking My Computer or by clicking Start, then clicking Control Panel, and then clicking System. Click the Hardware tab and then click the Device Manager button. Right-click the newly installed device and click Properties. When the device Properties dialog box appears, click the General tab. In the Device Status dialog box, a message should appear, stating that the device is working properly. However, a yellow question mark (🕮) or red X (🗷) next to the device in the Device Manager window, usually indicates that the device is malfunctioning. If the device is missing from the Device Manager window, then your computer does not detect it.

What is a resource conflict, and how can I determine whether a conflict is causing a device malfunction?

▼ In order to function, most devices that you install on your server use different resources on the server to send calls to the CPU, receive processing instructions, and even access memory space on the server. To avoid conflicts, different devices must not use resources at the same time. Although PnP can configure non-conflicting resources most of the time, a conflict may still occur, causing your device not to function. To check a new device, right-click the device in the Device Manager window and click Properties in the pop-up menu. In the Properties dialog box for the device, click the Resources tab and see if there is a message in the Conflicting device list.

Troubleshoot Installed Devices

The Plug and Play enumeration normally detects an installed device automatically. However, when you have a problem, you can use the Add Hardware Wizard to determine why a newly installed device has not automatically installed, or why a device does not function after installation. You can also use the Add Hardware Wizard to install non-PnP devices, to uninstall hardware devices, and to diagnose problems with an installed device.

To troubleshoot, you require the Windows Server 2003 installation CD-ROM, as well as the CD-ROM that contains the drivers for the malfunctioning hardware device. They may be necessary if you need to install driver software from either disc.

Although most hardware devices used to require manual configuration, Windows Server 2003 automatically configures most devices for you. You can use the Add Hardware Wizard to install and troubleshoot older server hardware that is not PnP compatible. These devices are no longer common and are known as *legacy devices*. Because your Windows Server 2003 computer cannot always detect non-PnP devices, you can use the Wizard to manually install and configure these devices.

① Click Start.

② Click Control Panel.

③ Click Add Hardware.

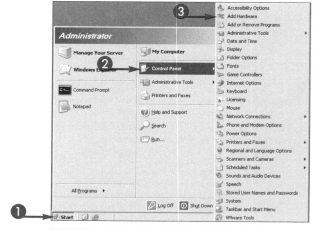

The Add Hardware Wizard appears.

④ Click Next.

The Wizard searches for new hardware.

The next page appears, asking you to confirm that the hardware is connected.

5 Click the "Yes, I have already connected the hardware" option (⦿ changes to ⦿).

6 Click Next.

The next page appears, with a list of installed hardware.

7 If the malfunctioning hardware appears in the list, then click the hardware icon.

8 Click Next.

● The Completing the Add Hardware Wizard page appears with troubleshooting results.

9 Click Cancel.

The wizard closes.

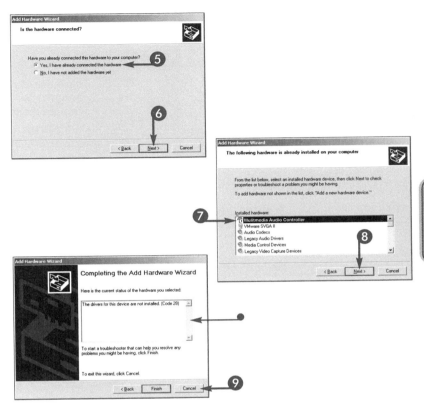

If the Add Hardware Wizard discovers that the problem is due to the device drivers, then what should I do?

▼ If you know that you must install the device drivers for the device to work properly, then you can use the CD-ROM that contains the device drivers for the new device. Insert the CD-ROM in the CD-ROM or DVD drive, and install the drivers. If you do not have the CD-ROM that contains the device drivers, then you can go to the Web site of the device manufacturer and download them. Click Finish when the Add Hardware Wizard is done to launch another wizard that helps you to install the drivers. A missing device driver is a commonly occurring issue.

What happens if I click the "No, I have not added the hardware yet" option on the Is the hardware connected page of the Add Hardware Wizard?

▼ Plug and Play functionality and the Add Hardware Wizard can only detect and install a device that you have already physically installed in your server or attached as a peripheral device. You can select this option (⦿ changes to ⦿) and click Next to access the Cannot Continue the Add Hardware Wizard page. The only option that you have at this point is to select the "Turn off the computer when I click Finish" option (☐ changes to ☑) to safely open the server and install your new device.

Troubleshoot with Device Manager

You can use Device Manager in your Windows Server 2003 computer to diagnose as well as manage malfunctioning devices that you have just installed. Device Manager can monitor a variety of different information about the installed devices on your computer, including how the device is functioning, what the specific installed drivers are, when you need to update the drivers, and what computer resources the device uses.

You can also disable or uninstall the device in Device Manager. This enables you to remove a device that you suspect is causing the system to malfunction without

powering down the server. Please note that you must still power down the computer completely to open the computer case and physically remove any internal device.

You can use Device Manager to list devices by different characteristics, including device type, connection, resources type, and resources connection. By default, Device Manager displays devices by type, and lists devices such as disk drives, display adapters, and keyboards. You can view devices by connection to see which data bus they are using. Viewing resources by type allows you to see the four resource types: DMA, IO, IRQ, and Memory. When you view resources by connection, the data appears very similar.

Troubleshoot with Device Manager

① Click Start.

② Right-click My Computer.

③ Click Properties.

The System Properties dialog box appears.

④ Click the Hardware tab.

⑤ Click Device Manager.

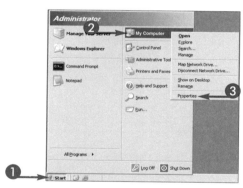
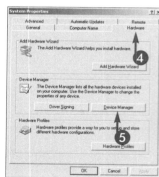

The Device Manager window appears.

⑥ Expand to the device category you want to troubleshoot.

⑦ Right-click a device.

⑧ Click Properties.

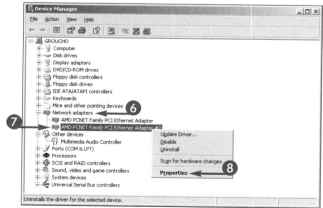

The Properties dialog box appears for the device you selected.

⑨ Click Troubleshoot.

The Help and Support Center window appears, displaying the Generic Hardware Device Troubleshooter page.

⑩ Click Next.

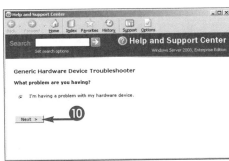

The Generic Hardware Device Troubleshooter page presents a solution.

⑪ Click one of the options that the troubleshooter presents (○ changes to ◉).

Note: How the troubleshooter responds depends on the selection you choose.

⑫ Click Next.

The Help and Support Center window closes.

Are there any other hardware troubleshooters besides the generic troubleshooter in Device Manager?

▼ Yes. When you open the troubleshooter for your disk drives on your server, the Drives and Network Adapters Troubleshooter opens. With this troubleshooter, you can diagnose and possibly treat malfunctions to your optical drives, hard drives, floppy drives, tape drives, and network adapters. Depending on which selection you make at the beginning of this troubleshooting wizard, you can take various paths to solve different device problems. For example, if you select tape drives, you can diagnose a problem with a SCSI drive or a tape backup device.

What is the difference between disabling a device and uninstalling it in the Device Manager?

▼ When you disable a device, you turn it off from the point of view of the operating system, although the device drivers remain installed. You can disable a device if you suspect that the operation of the device is causing a malfunction in the system. When you uninstall the device, you are actually uninstalling the drivers; the device is still physically in the server. You can do this if you suspect that the device drivers are causing a problem. An extreme measure is to restart the server in Safe Mode, which boots the operating system with minimal drivers loaded. You can then see if this corrects the problem.

Configure
Automatic Updates

You can protect your Windows Server 2003 computer from viruses, worms, Trojans, and other outside attacks that exploit vulnerabilities in the operating system or an integrated component by maintaining a regular schedule of downloading and installing the necessary patches from the Microsoft Web site. Although you can also download and install these patches manually, you can configure the updates to occur automatically, allowing you to perform other server maintenance tasks.

Microsoft provides a special Web site to download all of the critical patches, hotfixes, recommended upgrades, and updated device drivers for your Windows Server 2003 operating system on a regular basis. Although critical updates are the most important downloads, you can also

download most or all of the software updates that are necessary for complete server maintenance. You can manually run an update scan from the Start menu on your server or by going online and accessing http://windowsupdate.microsoft.com.

You can specify various degrees of autonomy for the Automatic update process. For example, full autonomy — not recommended for production servers — updates installations without your knowledge. Always test updates on a test server before deploying them and then deploy them at a pre-scheduled time so you can back out, if necessary. Windows can also download updates automatically for you to install, or can send a notification of new updates for you to download and install them manually.

Configure Automatic Updates

① Click Start.

② Right-click My Computer.

③ Click Properties.

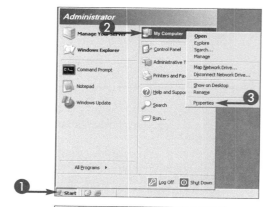

The System Properties dialog box appears.

④ Click the Automatic Updates tab.

⑤ Click the "Automatically download the updates, and install them on the schedule that I specify" option (○ changes to ⊙).

⑥ Click here and select a schedule.

⑦ Click here and select a time.

● You can click this link to learn more about scheduled installing.

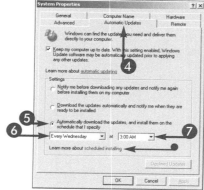

The Windows Automatic Updating window appears.

⑧ Click the Close button (⊠).

The Windows Automatic Updating window closes.

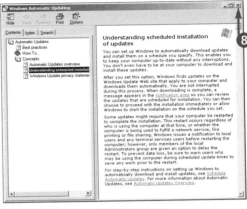

⑨ Click OK.

Windows now automatically updates your computer.

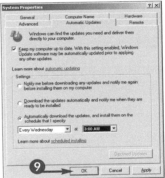

What is the difference between a Critical Update and a Service Pack?

▼ A critical update is usually a response to the discovery of a single vulnerability in the Windows operating system code or in the code of an integrated system, such as the Internet Explorer Web browser. You can download and install a critical update as soon as Microsoft makes it available in order to quickly patch a vulnerability in your system before it can be exploited. A service pack is a collection of critical updates and hotfixes that you can download and install in one package. Service Packs are only issued periodically, the most recent one being Windows XP Service Pack 2.

Why would I choose one type of download and installation strategy over another in the Automatic Updates tab in the System Properties dialog box?

▼ You can select the type of download and installation strategy that most closely meets the needs of your Windows Server 2003 servers and your administrative system. On occasion, the installation of a patch or hotfix has caused problems with the subsequent operation of Windows computers. You may want to first download and install updates to a test network and to monitor the response before you update your production environment. For more on installing manually, see the section "Manually Update Device Drivers."

Manually Update Device Drivers

Although the Microsoft Windows Update Web site can automatically update the device drivers on your Windows Server 2003 server, you can also manually control the updates. This enables you to ensure that new drivers do not cause any operational problems in your network.

Although most device drivers interact well with other software on your server, you may sometimes encounter a driver that causes a conflict with other software on your computer. This can result in a malfunction, or even a serious system crash. To prevent this, you can manually download

and install device drivers so that you can monitor their operation firsthand and ensure that they do not cause problems.

You can maintain a small server lab in your office to which you can manually download device drivers first. This allows you to leave your server production environment untouched and operational until you have tested the new drivers in the lab.

Depending on your requirements, you can also go to different Web sites to manually download device drivers. For example, you can go to the Microsoft Windows Update Web site, a manufacturer's Web site, or a Web site such as www.download.com.

Manually Update Device Drivers

① Click Start.

② Click Windows Update.

The Windows Update page appears.

③ Click Scan for updates.

Windows Update locates updates for your computer.

④ Click Driver Updates.

The available driver updates appear.

⑤ Click Add.

⑥ Click Review and install updates.

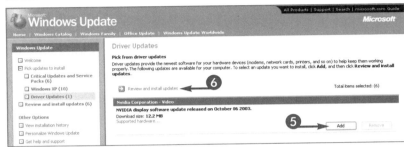

The Total Selected Updates pane appears.

⑦ Click Install Now.

The download and installation begins.

You must restart the server after the installation is complete.

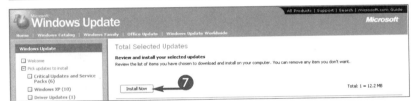

Can I update device drivers from the Device Manager?

▼ Yes. You can either allow Windows to automatically search for the drivers or specify a particular location such as a file on the server, the CD-ROM drive or a location on the Internet. To update drivers in the Device Manager, click Device Manager in the Hardware tab of the System Properties dialog box. In the Device Manager window, locate the device you want to update. Expand the category, right-click the device, and then click Update Driver in menu. In the Hardware Update Wizard, you can either allow Windows to manage the software installation, which is recommended, or you can install from a list or specific location. Make your selection and click Next to follow the Wizard instruction set.

Why go to a Web site such as www.download.com rather than download device drivers from the Microsoft Web site or the manufacturer's Web site?

▼ You can go to a Web site that "collects" drivers for a wide variety of devices if you only want to download drivers from one convenient Web site. For example, you may need the latest drivers for a device that was manufactured by a company that is no longer in operation. You may also need to find drivers for a legacy device that provides a function to your server that no newer device can provide. It is important to ensure that the Web site you select is considered reputable.

Roll Back Device Drivers

You can roll back or uninstall a new device driver on your Windows Server 2003 server if the new driver causes a problem in the functioning of the server. The rollback procedure uninstalls the new driver and "rolls back" to the previous driver that operated properly on your server.

If you cannot roll back from a new device driver to an older driver, then you must uninstall the new driver and reinstall the older driver. If you do not revert to the older driver, then you may not be able to resume using the device, or

perhaps even the server. If you do not already have a copy of the older driver to reinstall on the server, then you can download it from the Internet.

You can only use device driver rollbacks on Windows XP and Windows Server 2003 computers. Some device drivers do not function well with different types of software on your server or computer. This can result in either the specific device suddenly not working, or a more general malfunction in the server. You can roll back the new driver if you suspect that it is the problem.

Roll Back Device Drivers

① Click Start.

② Right-click My Computer.

③ Click Properties.

The System Properties dialog box appears.

④ Click the Hardware tab.

⑤ Click Device Manager.

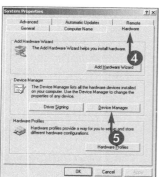

The Device Manager window appears.

⑥ Expand to the device category.

⑦ Right-click the device.

⑧ Click Properties.

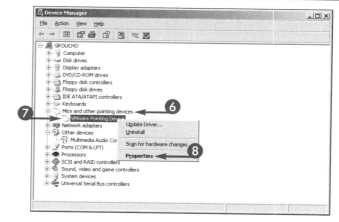

The Properties dialog box appears for the device you selected.

⑨ Click the Driver tab.

⑩ Click Roll Back Driver.

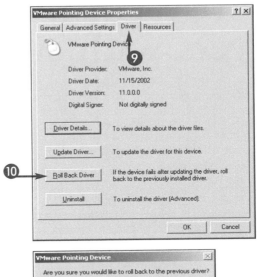

A dialog box appears asking you to confirm the rollback.

⑪ Click Yes.

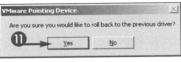

The System Settings Change dialog box appears.

⑫ Click Yes.

The server restarts, and the driver rolls back.

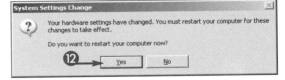

When can I not roll back a device driver?

▼ You cannot roll back if Windows Server 2003 does not have a record of a previous driver being installed for the device. This happens when you have installed a device and installed the drivers for the first time and have never updated the drivers. It may also happen when the older driver is corrupt or missing and Windows cannot find it. The older driver can become damaged or missing if you have downloaded a virus or other type of malware that has rewritten or deleted the driver or related files on your server. Whatever your situation, consider rebooting the server into safe mode, which loads only a minimal set of drivers, and attempt the roll back.

Why would I not want to roll back to a previous driver?

▼ You download new drivers for the devices that you install on your server in order to provide the best possible performance for your device. Older drivers generally provide less functionality for the device and the server as a whole. You should only roll back a device driver if you are reasonably sure that the driver is the problem. You can install a newer driver to fix a problem that you have with a device; by rolling back to the older driver, the problem may resume and be as bad as, or worse than, the problem that you are trying to fix.

Identify Unsigned Device Drivers with sigverif.exe

You can use the sigverif.exe utility to locate and identify device drivers that Microsoft did not sign, and therefore did not test for your operating system, to determine which device drivers are a problem on your Windows Server 2003 server. You can install different types of devices that different companies make for the devices on your server.

Most device drivers operate and interact well with other software processes on your computer. Microsoft has developed a procedure of testing device drivers and verifying those that are approved to function on a particular Windows operating system. Microsoft "signs" these drivers

digitally to verify them. You can still use a device driver that is not signed. Unsigned device drivers are not automatically dangerous. Microsoft has just not tested them.

You can specify that your Windows operating system notify you when you download device drivers that Microsoft has not signed. An unsigned device driver may work quite well with your Windows computer, even though Microsoft has not signed it. After the warning, you can often proceed with the download with no further incident, and the device functions adequately. You can verify unsigned drivers only in Windows 2000, Windows XP, and Windows Server 2003. For more information, see the section "Roll Back Device Drivers."

Identify Unsigned Device Drivers with sigverif.exe

① Click Start.

② Click Run.

The Run dialog box dialog appears.

③ Type **sigverif.exe**.

④ Click OK.

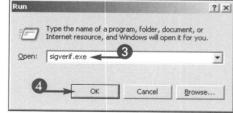

The File Signature Verification dialog box appears.

5 Click Start.

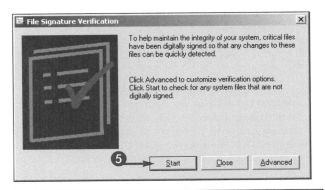

The File Signature Verification utility builds a list.

A list of unsigned drivers appears.

Note: *Unsigned device drivers are not automatically dangerous; once you review the list, you can determine if you want to keep these drivers or roll back any drivers.*

6 Click Close.

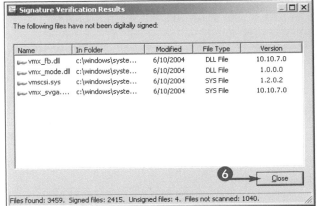

What happens if I click Advanced in the File Signature Verification dialog box?

▼ If you click Advanced, the Advanced File Signature settings dialog box appears. You can click the Search tab to look for any other drivers that are not digitally signed and specify the file type that you want to look for as well as the location where you want to search. You can also tell the system to notify you of any system files that are not digitally signed. You can click the Logging tab to request a log file of the results of the sigverif.exe scan, to decide whether you want additional scan logs to append the current log, or to overwrite it and name the new log file.

How can I find the log file of any sigverif.exe searches on my Windows Server 2003 computer?

▼ You can open the utility by typing **sigverif.exe** in the Run dialog box. When the utility opens, you are prompted to click Start to begin a scan, but you do not have to do so. Instead, you can click Advanced to open the Advanced File Signature settings dialog box, then click the Logging tab, and then click View Log. The log file sigverif.txt opens in Notepad and shows you a record of all of the drivers on your system. The results box from the scan in this section only showed a list of unsigned drivers. In actuality, the log shows all signed drivers and unscanned files on the server.

Set Driver Signing with System Properties

Y ou can control the Windows Server 2003 driver signing behavior in the System Properties dialog box to keep track of when your system downloads drivers that are unsigned by Microsoft. You can then determine the risk to your server system from these unsigned drivers and decide whether to download them.

Microsoft does not sign drivers either because they have not been tested or because they have been tested and are not compatible with a particular Microsoft operating system. Although untested, a programmer can still have written a driver for the operating system, and the driver

may function well. A driver that is tested and found incompatible for Windows Server 2003 may have been written for a different Windows operating system, or may have been written for an operating system such as UNIX, Linux, or Novell and not designed to work with Windows. In this event, you may have downloaded the wrong driver, overlooking the one written specifically for Windows Server 2003.

When Microsoft digitally signs a device driver, it includes the driver in a catalog of other drivers that it has signed. You can identify these drivers by their *.cat file extension.

Set Driver Signing with System Properties

① Click Start.

② Right-click My Computer.

③ Click Properties.

The System Properties dialog box appears.

④ Click the Hardware tab.

⑤ Click Driver Signing.

The Driver Signing Options dialog box appears.

⑥ Click the action you want Windows to take with unsigned drivers (○ changes to ⊙).

⑦ Click the "Tell me why this testing is important" link.

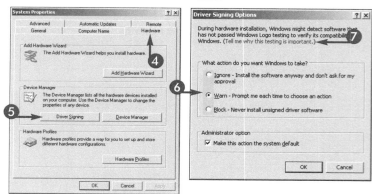

The Help and Support Center appears, displaying the Driver signing for Windows page.

8 Click Driver signing for Windows.

9 Review any relevant information about Windows driver signing.

10 Click ☒.

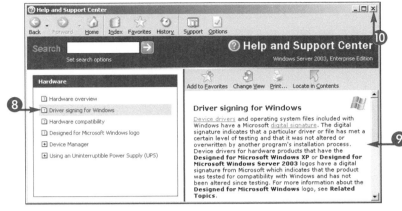

11 Click OK in the Driver Signing Options dialog box.

The Driver Signing options are enabled.

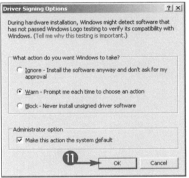

When should I enable the "Block – Never install unsigned driver software" option in the Driver Signing Options dialog box?	How are downloads affected by the "Make this action the system default" option in the Driver Signing Options dialog box?
▼ If your server is extremely critical to your business operation and you cannot take the risk of even minimal downtime on the server, then you can select this option (◯ changes to ◉). Your system will not download device drivers that Microsoft has not signed to your Windows Server 2003 server. Your system does not even give you the option to decide whether to download; it automatically blocks the driver. Most server systems have a failover process so that another server takes the place of a failed server. You can choose the Block option if a critical server has no failover process.	▼ You can specify a particular action when your system tries to download an unsigned driver. If you select the "Make this action the system default" option (☐ changes to ☑), then Windows applies the action, regardless of who logs in. If you deselect the option, then the action is different for each person who logs into the server or computer. Each user can specify Ignore, Warn, or Block; most users leave it at the default Warn setting.

View USB Hub Power Allocations

You can view USB hub power allocations on your Windows Server 2003 server to determine whether all of the USB devices associated with the server are receiving enough electrical power to operate correctly. Windows Server 2003 uses a built-in USB host controller on the motherboard to direct all USB traffic to the USB devices on the server. The USB root hub uses a self-powered or bus power system. When you install a USB keyboard or mouse on your server, they work well with bus power, although larger USB devices such as printers and scanners require additional power supplies.

Any USB device that uses power from the root hub, shares this power with all other attached devices. The more devices you attach to the hub, the less power that any one device has for its operation. The USB standard supports up to 127 USB devices on one USB host controller. However, to ensure that they work, you must locate each device no more than 5 meters or approximately 16 feet away from the USB hub by cable.

USB devices are fully Plug and Play. Both Windows XP Service Pack 1 and Windows Server 2003 support the USB 2.0 standard.

View USB Hub Power Allocations

① Click Start.

② Right-click My Computer.

③ Click Properties.

The System Properties dialog box appears.

④ Click the Hardware tab.

⑤ Click Device Manager.

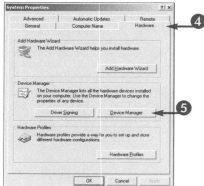

The Device Manager window appears.

⑥ Expand the Universal Serial Bus Controllers.

⑦ Right-click USB Root Hub.

⑧ Click Properties.

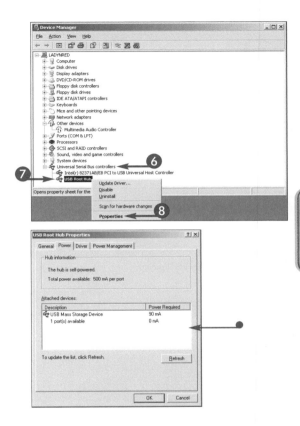

The USB Root Hub Properties dialog box appears.

⑨ Click Power tab.

● The Root hub power allocation displays for the device you selected.

What other options can I access on the USB Root Hub Properties dialog box?

▼ In the General tab, you can see whether the device is operating properly, open the troubleshooter, and enable or disable the hub. You can determine whether the root hub is self-powered or bus-powered in the Power tab. In the Driver tab, you can review driver details, update the driver, roll back the driver, or uninstall the driver. You can also determine the date of the driver, the version number, and who digitally signed the driver. In the Power Management tab, you can specify that the computer turn off the hub to save power and enable the hub to bring the computer out of standby mode.

What is listed under the Universal Serial Bus controllers in the Device Manager window?

▼ When you expand Universal Serial Bus controllers in the Device Manager window, you can see the USB Root Hub and all devices that are attached to the USB controller. This list may change often because USB devices are so easily attached and detached to and from a computer or server. Device Manager treats any USB device just like any other device that is attached to your computer. For example, the menus and Properties dialog boxes offer the same options as for any device that attaches to the PCI bus. When you right-click a USB mass storage device, you can then choose to click either Update Driver, Disable, Uninstall, Scan for hardware changes, and Properties in the pop-up menu, just like any other device.

13 — Creating and Editing Group Policy

Understanding How to Create
and Edit Group Policy 236

Create a Standalone GPO Editor................238

Create an Unlinked GPO 240

Open the Group Policy Object Editor........242

Link a GPO to an Organizational Unit 244

Create a New GPO in an
Organizational Unit..................................246

Edit a GPO in an Organizational Unit 248

14 — User and Computer Configuration

Understanding User and Computer
Configuration 250

Deploy a Software Package 252

Configure Web Browser Proxy Settings
with Windows Settings..............................254

Configure Windows Automatic Updates
with Administrative Templates 256

Add Administrative Templates
in the GPO Editor 258

Configure Loopback Policy Mode..............260

Configure Block Policy Inheritance 262

Configure No Override Option....................264

Modify the GPO Policy Application
Sequence 266

Configure Filtering on a GPO....................268

Disable a GPO Node 270

Disable a GPO 272

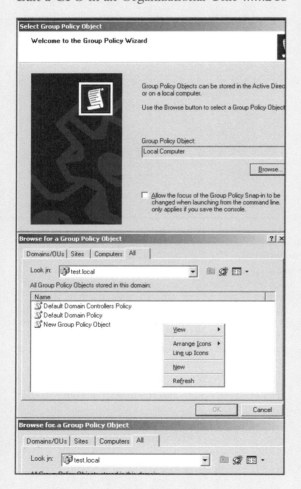

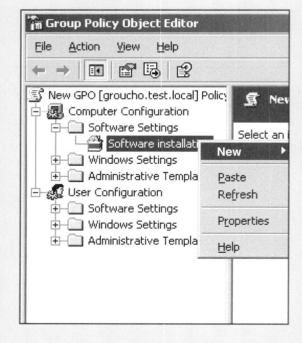

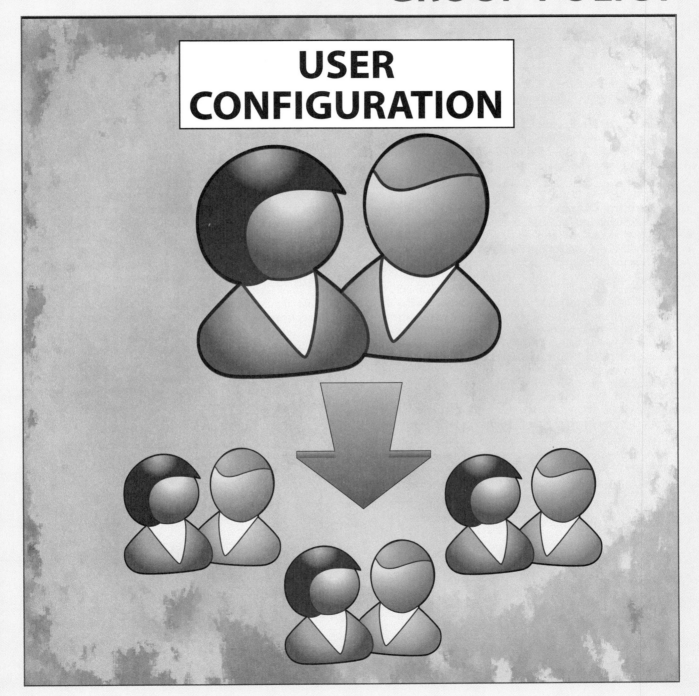

Understanding How to Create and Edit Group Policy

You can use Group Policy to apply a wide variety of granulated configuration settings on Active Directory User and Computer objects. *Group Policy* is a collection of configuration settings applied to an Active Directory Object that defines the behavior of that object. Group Policy eases the burden of administration, improves Active Directory security, and allows you to deploy software packages such as Critical Updates, Service Packs, and anti-virus software. You can also control the domain user environment, including desktop and menu settings. Group Policy settings allow you to exercise a fine degree of control over how computers and users interact with the domain. Without Group Policy, you can only use limited security access and environmental controls in the domain structure.

Group Policy Object

A Group Policy Object (GPO) is a collection of Group Policy settings or rules that are applied to a single Active Directory object. These rules control the access to and behavior of the Active Directory object to which you apply them. By applying a GPO to a site, domain or OU, you can exercise a high degree of administrative control over those objects to enhance the security of each one. Each local server has a Local Security Policy that is applied first before any other GPOs, but is then overwritten by the other listed GPOs. Each domain has a Default Domain Group Policy. You can either use the Default Domain Group Policy as the basis for your GPO by modifying it, or you can create a brand new GPO and apply it to your target object. You can apply GPOs to Active Directory objects such as sites, domains, and Organizational Units (OUs). You can either create or modify a GPO by using the GPO Editor.

Group Policy Object Inheritance

In a hierarchy, child-level objects inherit the Group Policy rules that you apply to a parent-level object. For example, if you apply a GPO to a Site object, then the settings automatically apply to the domain below, as well as to any parent and child OUs under the domain. As a result, you can create a specific combination of settings, apply them to only one Active Directory container object, and have the GPO implemented to all of the downstream objects.

You can also block Group Policy Object Inheritance at any level to prevent upper-level rules from affecting a lower-level container. You can then create a separate set of rules that apply only to the lower container object. When you add GPOs to lower-level objects without blocking, you can combine settings that are linked at different object levels. The lowest-level object is then affected by all of the rule sets that are linked to all levels above it. Group Policy Objects reside in Group Policy Containers and Group Policy Templates.

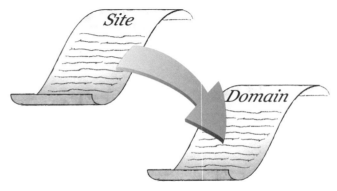

Group Policy Containers

Group Policy settings fall into the separate categories of Computer Objects and User Objects in the Active Directory. Group Policy Containers separate GPOs that apply primarily to user objects versus computer objects and contain the attributes and version data for each GPO. Computer or User subcontainers use Group Policy Containers (GPCs) to store GPOs. Each subcontainer holds the attributes and version data for each GPO. GPCs are Active Directory objects and are replicated throughout the domain with Active Directory replication.

Group Policy Templates

A Group Policy Template is a hierarchy of folders that contain all the information for a given GPO. Group Policy Templates (GPT) reside in the shared SYSVOL folder under C:\WINDOWS. They contain the policy settings for each GPO in the domain, regardless of the level of their creation. Inside each GPT folder is a set of subfolders for the Computer and User settings. Each Computer and User subfolder contains other subfolders with text files. The text files are processed and apply settings to the Windows Server 2003 Registry when the server starts up and when a user logs in. It is File Replication Service, and not the Active Directory, that performs GPT replication in the domain. Both GPCs and GPTs must exist in order for you to apply the GPOs to the domain structure.

Group Policy Environment

You can use Group Policy to control every aspect of the domain user computer and network environment. As the domain administrator, you have almost absolute control over what a user can and cannot do on their computer, both in the local network and in the domain.

You can use Group Policy to not only define the computer work environment, but to also enforce your configuration settings so that users cannot make any changes to their work environment. You can do this in one of two ways. The first way is to restrict user access to a variety of control utilities that are normally available on a Windows computer, such as Control Panel Applets. The second way is to allow users to make changes, but to not allow their changes to be saved after the user logs out of the domain.

You can set up completely different environments for different domain users that access the same server. For example, users from two different departments can log in to the same server at different times, resulting in two completely different computer and network environments. You can also enforce whether to allow a user to download any software from the network or the Internet.

You can link environmental settings to top-level containers, and add them to settings that are configured at lower levels. This results in an environment that consists of all of the rule sets that link to the current and upper layers. You can configure the exact environment that your IT department supports without domain users adding extra, unsupported elements.

Create a Standalone GPO Editor

You can use a Standalone Group Policy Object Editor to create a new GPO and apply it to an Active Directory container object, or to modify a pre-existing GPO. This allows you more convenient administrative control when you create policy configuration rules for each of your target container objects. Using the Microsoft Management Console (MMC), you can create a GPO Editor specifically for the GPO rule set that you want to create. You can read more about MMCs and how to register and install a schema snap-in in Chapter 3. As a result, you can easily access one set of isolated controls in the Administrative Tools menu, rather than navigating to the particular snap-in console in the Administrative Tools menu and accessing the GPO by Active Directory container object type.

When you create a domain, Windows automatically creates a Default Group Policy Object and applies it at the domain level. However, the Default GPO does not apply any particular rule set, or change the way in which the domain functions. To use the Default GPO to apply your security and environmental policy plan, you must use a GPO Editor to access the GPO and change the configuration settings for the domain. Other Active Directory container objects, such as sites and OUs, do not have Default GPOs.

Create a Standalone GPO Editor

① Click Start.

② Click Run.

The Run dialog box appears.

③ Type **mmc**.

④ Click OK.

The MMC console window appears.

⑤ Click File.

⑥ Click Add/Remove Snap-in.

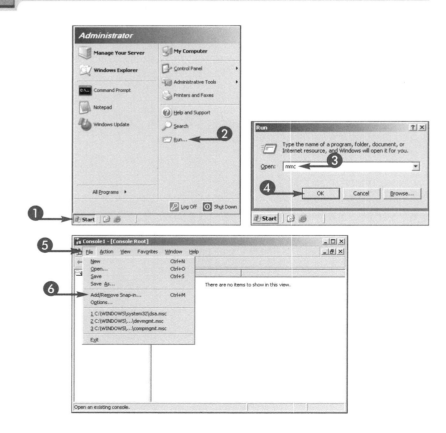

The Add/Remove Snap-in dialog box appears.

⑦ Click Add.

The Add Standalone Snap-in dialog box appears.

⑧ Click Group Policy Object Editor.

⑨ Click Add.

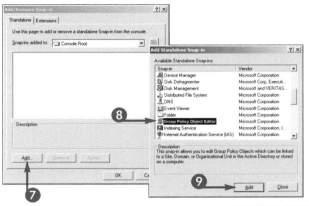

The Group Policy Wizard appears.

⑩ Click Browse.

⑪ Click Active Directory Group Policy Type for the target.

⑫ Click Finish.

● The Wizard creates the Standalone Group Policy Object Editor.

⑬ Click OK.

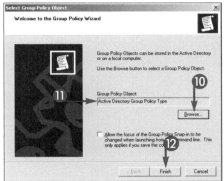

When I browse for a Group Policy Container Object in the Group Policy Wizard, which objects can I select?

▼ You can select from the following categories: Domains/OUs, Sites, Computers, or All. Under Domains/OUs, you can select the Default Domain Policy, the Domain Controllers OU, or any other OU that you have created in the domain. Under Sites, you can select any site that you have created. If you have not yet created any sites, then you can only choose the Default-First-Site-Name. Under Computers, you can select the server on which you are working, or browse to select any other server or computer on the domain. Under All, you can select any Domain Policy or select New GPO.

Is there a command-line utility that I can use to create and edit Group Policy Objects?

▼ Yes. Several command-line utilities query Group Policy and enact changes. Two command-line tools are gpresult, which provides a query result on which policies are applied to an object, and gpupdate, which refreshes Group Policy settings. gpupdate is new with Windows Server 2003, and replaces the Windows 2000 Server command secedit /refreshpolicy. You can also use the Group Policy Wizard to change the focus of the target object on the command line after you create the target object in the Wizard.

Create an Unlinked GPO

When you are planning how to apply group policies to your domain, you can create various standard rule sets before you create all of the container objects. You can create an Unlinked GPO in order to manufacture a rule set that you want to link to one or more Active Directory container objects either now or later. When you create GPOs that are not yet linked to any container, you can implement your plan without having to wait until you complete the domain infrastructure.

There are two steps that you must follow in order to create and implement Group Policy on a domain. The first step is to create a GPO, and the second step is to link it to one or more Active Directory container objects in the domain.

You can link an Unlinked Group Policy Object to any site, domain, or Organizational Unit. However, you must first be a member of a group that has the right to create and link a GPO to an Active Directory container, and the container must have the right to read and execute the Group Policy before it can take effect.

Create an Unlinked GPO

① Click Start.

② Click Run.

The Run dialog box appears.

③ Type **mmc**.

④ Click OK.

The MMC console window appears.

⑤ Click File.

⑥ Click Add/Remove Snap-in.

The Add Standalone Snap-in dialog box appears.

Click Add.

⑦ Click Group Policy Object Editor.

⑧ Click Add.

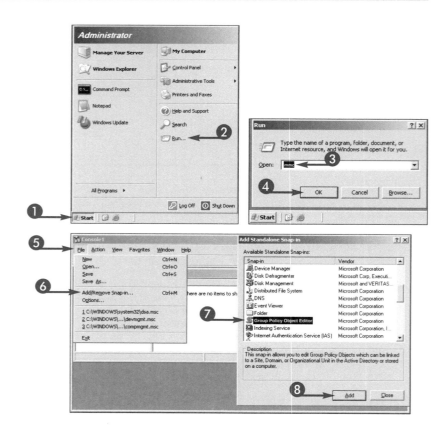

The Group Policy Wizard appears.

⑨ Click Browse.

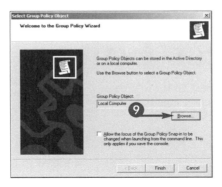

The Browse for a Group Policy Object window appears.

⑩ Click the All tab.

⑪ Right-click a blank part of the Name area.

⑫ Click New.

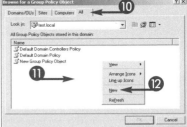

The Wizard creates the New Group Policy Object.

⑬ Type a name for the Unlinked GPO.

⑭ Click OK.

The Wizard creates a new Unlinked GPO.

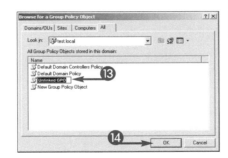

Is there another way to create an Unlinked GPO in the Group Policy Wizard?

▼ Yes. You can create an Unlinked GPO in the Wizard either by creating an entirely new GPO or by renaming a pre-existing GPO in the Browse for a Group Policy Object dialog box. The objects already in the dialog box are the Default Domain Controllers Policy, the Default Domain Policy, and the New Group Policy Object. When you click New, the Wizard creates a second New GPO that you can then rename. You can also right-click the original New GPO, select rename from the pop-up menu, and type a new name for the Unlinked GPO.

When I right-click a GPO in the Browser for a Group Policy Object dialog box, what other options can I select?

▼ You can right-click a GPO and select Edit, which opens the Group Policy Object Editor for that GPO. You can then click Delete to delete the GPO, then click Refresh to update any changes you made to the GPO, and then click Properties. When you click Properties, you can select either the General, Links, Security, or WMI Filter tabs. General shows summary information. Links searches for Active Directory objects that use the same GPO. Security enables you to configure access to the GPO. WMI Filter enables you to filter the users and computers to which the GPO applies.

Open the Group Policy Object Editor

You can use the Group Policy Object Editor to create or edit a GPO for an Active Directory container object. You can do this in either the Active Directory Users and Computers snap-in or the Active Directory Sites and Services snap-in. When you edit a GPO directly in the particular snap-in where you are configuring a container object, this reduces administrative effort because you can both create an object and apply the GPO in one environment.

The GPO Editor is the primary tool that enables you to configure the specific rule sets that you apply to Active Directory container objects. As a result, very specific controls are enacted over the user and computer environments in your Active Directory domains.

The GPO Editor enables you to modify the standard GPO Software settings, Windows scripts and Security settings, and Administrative Template settings. This applies to both Computer Configurations and User Configurations in a site, domain, or Organizational Unit. Although the settings appear the same for Computer and User Configurations, the details under each folder structure in the GPO Editor are different for each environment. For more information regarding these GPO Editor options, see Chapters 14 and 15.

see Chapters 14 and 15.

Open the Group Policy Object Editor

① Click Start.

② Click Administrative Tools.

③ Click Active Directory Users and Computers.

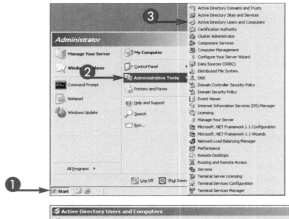

The Active Directory Users and Computers snap-in window appears.

④ Right-click a domain.

⑤ Click Properties.

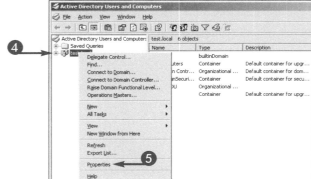

The Properties dialog box appears for the domain you selected.

⑥ Click the Group Policy tab.

⑦ Click Default Domain Policy.

⑧ Click Edit.

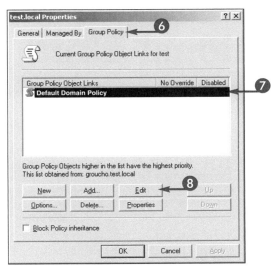

The Group Policy Object Editor appears for the Default Group Policy Object.

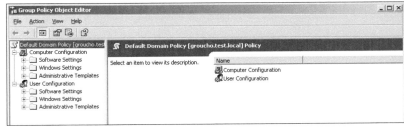

Can I only use the GPO Editor to edit GPOs that are created on one particular server?

▼ No. However, when you access the GPO Editor, the Default Domain Policy references the Domain Controller that you are using to access the GPO Editor and the Default Domain Policy; the policy is replicated to the entire domain, and you can use the GPO Editor to modify any GPO that is available in the domain. If you open the GPO for an Organizational Unit in Users and Computers or for a site in Active Directory Sites and Services, then by default, no policy is created; you must either create a new policy or link a GPO that has already been created.

What are some of the features that I can use when I open the GPO Editor?

▼ You can use the toolbar at the top of the GPO Editor. If you click File, then you can select either Options or Exit. Exit closes the Editor, while Options enables you to perform disk clean-up operations that are related to the Editor. Clicking Action lets you export a list of policies to a specified location such as My Documents. Clicking Properties opens the Editor Properties dialog box. Clicking Help opens the Help dialog box. Clicking View allows you to add or remove columns in the Editor, select the type of display icons, select Domain Controller options, and customize the MMC snap-in.

Link a GPO to an Organizational Unit

L inking a GPO to an Organizational Unit (OU) allows you to apply the rule set of the GPO to the OU, as well as any objects inside the OU, to make administration easier. You can apply the rule set of the GPO to other OUs, groups, computers, and users.

You cannot use a GPO effectively until you link it to an Active Directory container object. When you link a GPO rule set to an OU, you can define the precise environment in which the business unit can operate as an Active Directory container object. Chapter 5 covers how OUs are the most

basic logical container for enabling you to administer collections of Active Directory objects by workgroup, office, department, division, or other business unit.

Each OU represents a different workgroup with different needs, authority, and priorities in the company and in the domain infrastructure. You can accommodate the needs and restrictions of each OU by linking a different GPO to them. This makes administration easier because you only have to link and apply one GPO to one OU in order to affect a particular department, all of the groups inside the department, or all of the individual domain users and computers.

Link a GPO to an Organizational Unit

① Click Start.

② Click Administrative Tools.

③ Click Active Directory Users and Computers.

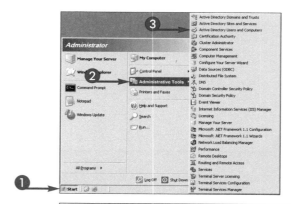

The Active Directory Users and Computers snap-in window appears.

④ Expand the domain.

⑤ Right-click an OU.

⑥ Click Properties.

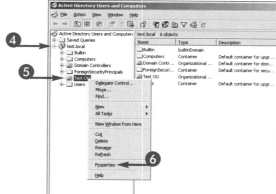

The Properties dialog box appears for the OU you selected.

⑦ Click the Group Policy tab.

⑧ Click Add.

The Add a Group Policy Object Link dialog box appears.

⑨ Click the All tab.

⑩ Click Unlinked GPO.

⑪ Click OK.

⑫ Click Apply.

Windows links the GPO to the OU.

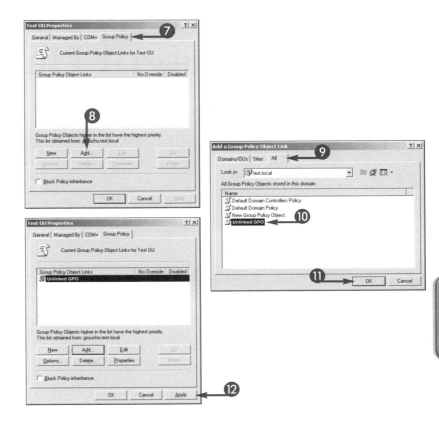

What type of users or administrators can create a GPO and link it to an Active Directory object?

▼ Any member of the Domain Admins or Enterprise Admins groups have these privileges. You can also delegate the right to another group, if necessary. Another global security group that has the right to create GPOs is called the Group Policy Creator Owners group. However, although this group has the right by default to create GPOs, it cannot link them to any Active Directory container object. You can use this group if you want to delegate the task of creating new GPOs without having that group acquire any additional rights in the domain.

If a GPO has been previously applied to one particular Active Directory object, can I apply it to another object? Also, how do I find what other objects are using the same GPO?

▼ You can link one particular GPO to several Active Directory container objects. To find out the other objects to which the GPO is linked, right-click the Active Directory object, such as a domain or OU, and click Properties in the menu. When the Properties dialog box appears, click the Group Policy tab, select the GPO, and click Properties. Click the Links tab in the Properties dialog box, select the domain, and click Find Now. All of the other objects that are linked to the GPO appear in the Sites, Domains, or Organizational Units found field in the properties box.

Create a New GPO in an Organizational Unit

You do not have to link a pre-existing Group Policy Object to an Organizational Unit or to another Active Directory container object. Instead, you can create a new GPO in the Group Policy Object Editor dialog box. This makes it easier for you to create a GPO that is tailored for the OU or any other object to which you are applying it.

Although you can apply one set of rules to many different objects, some objects, such as an OU, are unique in your company and domain, and therefore require that you apply

a unique set of rules. You can create a rule set for that individual object in the GPO Editor, rather than link a GPO to the OU from elsewhere.

You can create a new GPO in any of the applicable Active Directory snap-ins, such as Sites and Services, and Users and Computers. You can create any number of new GPOs, regardless of whether or not they are linked or were created by default. You can also delete or unlink GPOs that are created in the editor. This gives you control of the rule sets that apply to your Active Directory objects.

Create a New GPO in an Organizational Unit

① Click Start.

② Click Administrative Tools.

③ Click Active Directory Users and Computers.

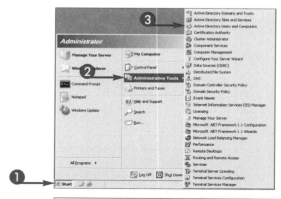

The Active Directory Users and Computers snap-in window appears.

④ Right-click an OU.

⑤ Click Properties.

The Properties dialog box appears for the OU you selected.

6 Click the Group Policy tab.

7 Click New.

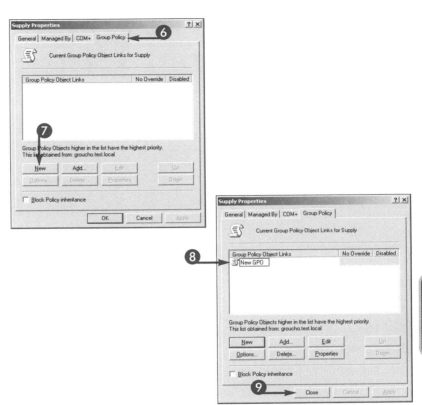

The New GPO appears in the Group Policy Object Links area.

8 Type a name for the new GPO.

9 Click Close.

Windows creates the new GPO.

Is the new GPO created in the OU any different than a GPO I create independently and then link to the OU later?

▼ No. Any new GPO is the same as any other GPO until you configure the specific rule sets. You can add or link dozens of generic new GPOs to a particular Active Directory object and have absolutely no difference in terms of how they affect that object. When you create a new GPO in the GPO Editor, you can immediately click Edit in order to configure the specific rule sets in the new GPO. After you apply the rule sets, the new GPO then implements whatever rules you configured.

Can I re-edit a GPO, or are there situations where I must create a new GPO and add it rather than reconfigure an existing GPO?

▼ You can re-edit a GPO as many times as you like. You may occasionally have to create two GPOs that are unique to a particular Active Directory container object. For example, you may need to create one set of GPO rules for Active Directory Users and another set for Active Directory Computers. Because users and computers have different rule set options in the GPO Editor, you can create a different GPO for each of them.

Edit a GPO in an Organizational Unit

You can edit the GPO for an Organizational Unit or other Active Directory container object, either when you first create it or at any other time. When you edit the GPO, you can configure and apply a unique rule set to the object. This gives you the maximum flexibility over objects on your domain because you can adjust the rule set for any object at any time. As the needs of your organizational work units change and grow, you can change the rule sets of each unit to meet the needs of your company.

You can also edit a GPO to either block an upper-level policy from being inherited by a lower-level Active Directory container, or to ensure that a lower-level container cannot override the inheritance rules. However, if the upper level is forcing inheritance and the lower level tries to block, the upper level always wins. This gives you more opportunities to set granular controls on objects such as parent and child OUs, or on inheritance betweens sites and domains. You cannot selectively block a single rule set from an upper-level GPO to allow the other rules to continue to inherit downwards. You must either allow all policies to inherit, or you must block them all.

Edit a GPO in an Organizational Unit

① Click Start.

② Click Administrative Tools.

③ Click Active Directory Users and Computers.

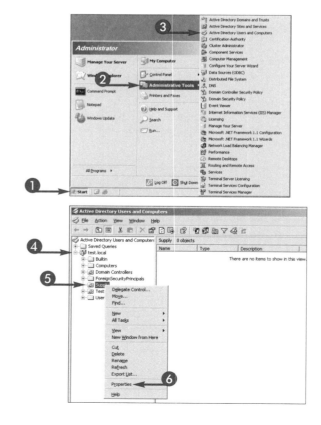

The Active Directory Users and Computers snap-in window appears.

④ Expand a domain.

⑤ Right-click an OU.

⑥ Click Properties.

The Properties dialog box appears for the OU you selected.

7 Click the Group Policy tab.

8 Click New GPO.

9 Click Edit.

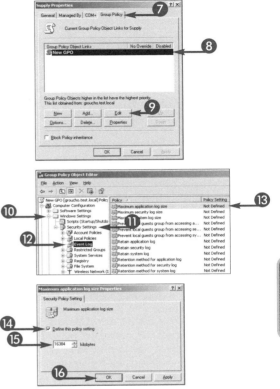

The Group Policy Object Editor window appears.

10 Expand the Windows Settings under Computer Configuration.

11 Expand the Security Settings.

12 Click Event Log.

13 Double-click Maximum application log size.

The Maximum application log size Properties dialog box appears.

14 Click the Define this policy setting option (☐ changes to ☑).

15 Type a maximum size for the application log.

16 Click OK.

Windows applies your GPO edits to the OU.

How many different rule sets can I configure for a GPO in the GPO Editor?

▼ Although you can theoretically configure all of the available rule sets, this is inadvisable, because the rule sets number in the hundreds. If you configure too many different rule sets, you may forget which ones apply to a particular GPO and you can lose control of your User and Computer environment configuration. You can control your domain environment more effectively by creating a GPO to affect a specific set of policies on an Active Directory object, rather than taking a scattered approach to GPO creation and editing. You may also experience conflicts if two GPOs link to the same object that have the same configuration, but different values.

If I make a mistake and configure a single feature incorrectly in the GPO Editor, can I correct it without having to delete and recreate the entire GPO?

▼ Yes. You can always go back and reverse what you have done to your GPO. This is helpful when you have configured several features and only want to correct a setting on one or two of them. Simply open the feature that you want to edit and deselect the "Define this policy setting" option (☑ changes to ☐). Click OK. The policy setting no longer applies. Remember that not all GPO features are configured the same way and that the above instructions do not apply to all of them.

Understanding User and Computer Configuration

You can apply Group Policy Object (GPO) rule sets to either Computer Configuration environments or User Configuration environments, or both, in Active Directory sites, domains, or Organizational Units (OUs). When you apply rule sets, you achieve greater control over these two major components of your domain. You can set rules that do one of two things: they either affect domain users regardless of which computer they log in to in the domain, or they affect computers regardless of who has logged in to them. This chapter reviews many of the concepts introduced in Chapter 13 and expands on how you apply those concepts to user and computer environments.

User and Computer Configuration folders are the two major nodes that make up GPOs. Both nodes contain the three identical subnodes, Software settings, Windows settings, and Administrative Templates. However, each subnode does not offer the exact same options under Computer Configuration as they do under User Configuration. Software settings control the distribution of software packages under both Computer and User Configurations. Windows settings and Administrative Templates only have a passing resemblance to each other, depending on which node you are accessing. By default, the settings in each node of the GPO apply to all users in the site and domain, as well as to all OUs to which the node is linked.

Windows Settings

Under Computer Configuration, Windows settings contain all of the security settings that you can apply to a computer. These include start-up and shut-down scripts, which run when you first power up the computer or when you send it the signal to power down. Because you apply these settings at the server level, the settings take effect regardless of who is using the computer.

Under User Configuration, you can configure similar scripts called logon and logoff scripts. These scripts are associated with the user who logs in to or logs out of the domain. A computer is often powered up for days or weeks and repeatedly runs these types of scripts, depending on who logs in to and out of the domain. By comparison, the start-up script only runs once at startup and does not execute again until you restart the computer.

Logon and logoff scripts affect the particular user environment, such as access to the Control Panel, start-up menu, and desktop environment. On the other hand, start-up and shut-down scripts affect the overall behavior of the server while it is in operation. The actual text files that contain the scripts reside in the SYSVOL folder under Domain\Policies. You can write scripts in a text editor such as Notepad and then add them by using the GPO Editor.

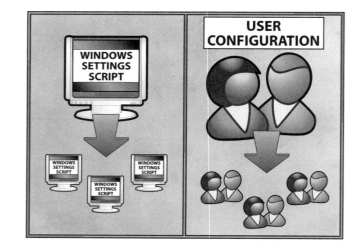

Administrative Templates

Under both Computer and User Configuration nodes, Administrative Templates have the Windows Components and System subnodes in common. You can use Windows Components to apply rule sets to many of the features that are integrated into Windows Server 2003, Windows XP, and Windows 2000. These features include NetMeeting, Internet Explorer, Terminal Services, Windows Messenger, and Windows Update.

Under both Computer Configuration and User Configuration nodes, the System controls User Profiles, Scripts, Logon, and Group Policy. There are also many other subnodes that are different under the Computer and User Configuration nodes. You can also add templates because the Administrative Template nodes are designed to be configurable.

It is not possible to include all potential combinations of rule sets in Windows Server 2003. You can create and add your own customized templates to the GPO Editor so that you can further design and control the exact nature of how your Computer and User environments behave. You cannot add any configuration subnodes or items to either the Software settings or Windows settings subnodes under either Computer or User Configuration.

Configuration Node Items

You can configure very specific settings for each node and subnode by opening one of the nodes and then opening one of the items that it contains. To determine what the item affects, you can select it; the requirements and description text display, and describe the item as well as the operating system and application software that it affects. You can double-click the item to open and configure it. Because there are such a wide variety of items that you can apply to very different systems, there is not a standard way to configure all of the items.

Software Settings

You can set software distribution and restrictions under both Computer and User Configuration nodes in the GPO Editor. This means that you can decide what kinds of software applications you want to distribute and run on computers in your domain. You can also create and enforce settings that affect certificate, hash, and registry-path rules.

Your ability to control the behavior of executable software on your network is very important because of the danger posed by viruses, trojans, and other types of malware that can affect your domain. Although anti-virus software can help protect your network, you can also use Software settings to set rules that restrict user activities. This helps to protect your network infrastructure from users who commonly open and execute e-mail attachments, along with other risky kinds of file transfers.

Deploy a Software Package

You can either assign or publish software packages to the computers in your network environment. This ensures that only appropriate software downloads and runs on your network, and it prevents users from uninstalling software that your company requires.

You can assign software packages to either users or computers, but you can only publish software packages to users. When you assign software to a computer, upon start up, the software automatically downloads onto each computer that the GPO affects. The software remains on that computer, regardless of who logs in to it. When you

assign software to users, the software automatically becomes available to the users, regardless of which computer they log in to, but it is not available to unauthorized users, even if they log in to a computer where that software package was available earlier.

When you publish software, the software does not automatically install on a computer. The user to which you publish the software has the option to go to the Add/Remove Programs applet in the Control Panel and install it. This way, you can make software available to qualified users, but not compel them to install or use it.

Deploy a Software Package

① Click Start.

② Click Administrative Tools.

③ Click Active Directory Users and Computers.

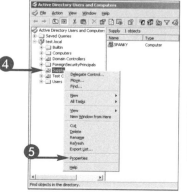

The Active Directory Users and Computers snap-in window appears.

④ Right-click an OU.

⑤ Click Properties.

The Properties dialog box appears for the OU you selected.

⑥ Click the Group Policy tab.

⑦ Click New GPO.

⑧ Click Edit.

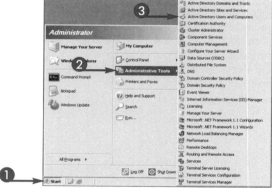

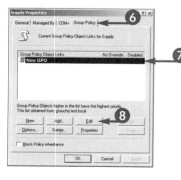

The Group Policy Object Editor appears.

9 Expand to Software Settings under Computer Configuration.

10 Right-click Software installation.

11 Click New.

12 Click Package.

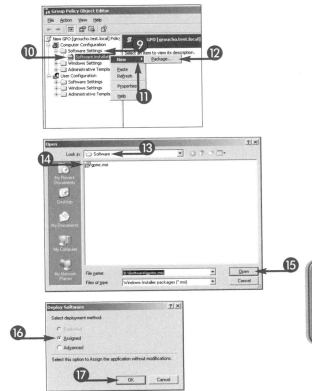

The Open dialog box appears.

13 Navigate to the software package.

14 Click the software package.

15 Click Open.

The Deploy Software dialog box appears.

16 Click Assigned (☐ changes to ⊙).

17 Click OK.

Windows deploys the software.

How can I verify that Windows has deployed the software that I have assigned to computers in the Active Directory Container Object?

▼ You can open the GPO Editor, navigate to Software Settings under Computer Configuration, and click Software installation. The assigned software appears in the display pane by name, version number, deployment state, and source. You can also navigate to one of the computers located in the affected OU, click Start, and then click Programs. The distributed software package that you assigned should appear. Another place to look is in Add/Remove Programs applet in Control Panel. Keep in mind that the software package may not install until after you restart the computers in the affected OU.

Can I ever uninstall assigned software packages with the GPO Editor?

▼ Yes. In the GPO Editor, under Computer Configurations, expand Software Settings and then select Software installation. Right-click the software package that you want to uninstall in the display pane, and click Remove. The Remove Software dialog box appears and allows you to choose either the "Immediately uninstalling the software" or the Allowing users and computers to continue to use the software, but preventing any new installations" options (☐ changes to ⊙). In the same menu that contains the Remove option, you can also select the Redeploy the application option (☐ changes to ☑) if something goes wrong with the initial deployment.

Configure Web Browser Proxy Settings with Windows Settings

Y ou can configure proxy settings for Internet Explorer Web browsers. The Windows computers in an Active Directory container object use these Web browsers to control, which Web sites users can and cannot access on the Internet.

You can improve user efficiency by preventing unauthorized Web surfing to sites that are not work-related. The proxy server also caches the html files of frequently accessed Web sites; users can increase their speed when they access these pages on the local proxy server rather than on the Internet. You can use transparent proxy to automatically configure

each computer that is affected by the GPO to use the proxy server. This frees you from having to manually configure each computer to point to the proxy server.

Configuring proxy settings is one of many GPO configuration settings that you can enable under Windows Settings in the User Configuration node of the GPO Editor. You have control of several other Web browser policies, including Browser user interface, Connection settings, Browser security, and Programs. You can also configure Folder Redirection and Security. You can read more about Group Policy security in Chapter 15.

Configure Web Browser Proxy Settings with Windows Settings

① Click Start.

② Click Administrative Tools.

③ Click Active Directory Users and Computers.

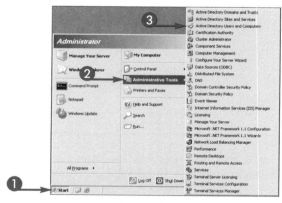

The Active Directory Users and Computers snap-in window appears.

④ Right-click an OU.

⑤ Click Properties.

The Properties dialog box appears for the OU you selected.

⑥ Click the Group Policy tab.

⑦ Click New GPO.

⑧ Click Edit.

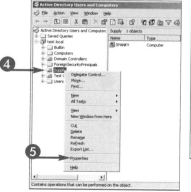

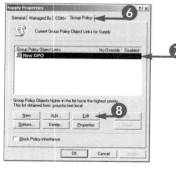

The Group Policy Object Editor appears.

9 Expand Windows Settings under User Configuration.

10 Expand Internet Explorer Maintenance.

11 Click Connection.

12 Double-click Proxy Settings.

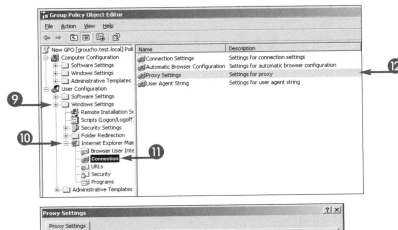

The Proxy Settings dialog box appears.

13 Click Enable proxy settings (☐ changes to ☑).

14 Type the IP address of the proxy server in the HTTP field.

15 Type **80** in the Port field.

16 Click OK.

Windows applies your proxy settings.

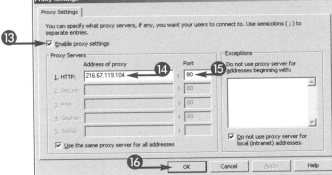

When I configure proxy settings for HTTP, do the same settings apply for all other protocols?

▼ Under the Proxy Servers address fields in the Proxy Settings dialog box, you can allow all other protocols — including HTTPS (Secure), FTP, Gopher, and Socks — to use the address that you set up for HTTP. Use port 80 by selecting the option "Use the same proxy server for all addresses" option (☐ changes to ☑). When you select this option, the configuration boxes for the other protocols appear greyed out. When you deselect this option (☑ changes to ☐), you can configure each of the other protocols to point to a different server address and to use different port numbers.

Can I configure any other proxy settings in the GPO Editor?

▼ Yes. You can create a list of exceptions so that computers affected by the GPO Editor do not point to the proxy server when they try to connect to certain IP addresses. In the Proxy Settings dialog box, you can type the addresses in the Exceptions field. You must use semi-colons (;) to separate IP address entries. You can also select the "Do not use proxy server for local (intranet) addresses" option (☐ changes to ☑). This allows computers on the network to bypass the proxy server and to directly access the business intranet sites that you maintain.

Configure Windows Automatic Updates with Administrative Templates

Y ou can use the Administrative Templates node to allow Windows Automatic Updates to automatically distribute from your Windows Server 2003 Domain Controller to any computer that is affected by the GPO. Periodically, Microsoft discovers vulnerabilities in Windows operating systems and application software, both of which can result in unauthorized users taking control of computer systems. Microsoft makes Hotfixes, Critical Updates, Service Packs, and other software distributions available for all supported Windows software. Individual users can visit the

Automatic Update Web site at Microsoft.com. However, enforcing mandatory Automatic Updates in an organization can be challenging.

You can use Administrative Templates to ensure that when your server system is notified of new available updates from Microsoft, these updates distribute to every computer in your domain; this means that your computers are protected from the latest outside threats to your network. You can configure this feature to notify the user when a new update is available, or you can configure the feature to be totally transparent, running in the background. The Windows Automatic Updates Template only supports the distribution of updates to the Windows XP operating system.

Configure Windows Automatic Updates with Administrative Templates

① Click Start.

② Click Administrative Tools.

③ Click Active Directory Users and Computers.

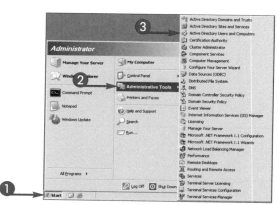

The Active Directory Users and Computers snap-in window appears.

④ Right-click an OU.

⑤ Click Properties.

The Properties dialog box appears for the OU you selected.

⑥ Click the Group Policy tab.

⑦ Click the GPO.

⑧ Click Edit.

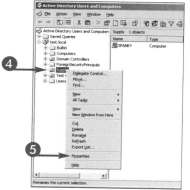

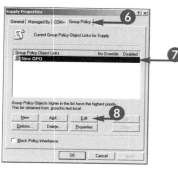

The Group Policy Object Editor appears.

9 Expand the Administrative Templates folder under User Configuration.

10 Click System.

11 Double-click Windows Automatic Updates.

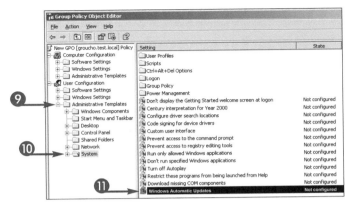

The Windows Automatic Updates Properties dialog box appears.

12 Click Enabled (○ changes to ◉).

● You can click Disabled (○ changes to ◉) to disable Windows Automatic Updates.

13 Click OK.

● Windows enables automatic updates.

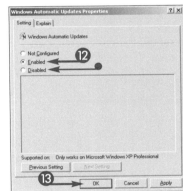

How can I find more information about Windows Automatic Updates, and how to configure them in the GPO Editor?

▼ In the Windows Automatic Updates Properties dialog box, you can click the Explain tab. An explanation dialog box appears, describing how to search for Windows updates, and how to download and distribute them to computers that the GPO affects. In the display pane of the GPO Editor, you can click Windows Automatic Updates in the Settings list, and then click the Extended tab at the bottom of the GPO Editor. A requirements and description statement appears in the display pane. A Properties link in the text also allows you to open the Administrative Template item by clicking it.

What happens if I disable Windows Automatic Updates in the GPO Editor?

▼ The Windows XP computers in your network individually search for automatic updates when they connect to the Internet, but only if you have configured them to do so on the local server. If you do not configure this feature, then each Windows XP server searches for updates if it has been configured to do so. You can enable Automatic Updates in the GPO Editor to prevent each individual Windows XP computer that is affected by the GPO from searching for updates. As a result, your Windows Server 2003 server provides the updates for them.

Add Administrative Templates in the GPO Editor

You can use the GPO Editor to add or remove specific templates in Administrative Templates under either Computer or User Configuration nodes. This allows you to create customized configuration settings for domain users and computers. Administrative Templates are stored in files with the .adm extension and contain all the categories and subcategory items that define how user interface settings display and how the settings are written to the Windows Server 2003 Registry key.

You can create a customized ADM file in a text editor, save it, and then add it to a GPO using the GPO Editor. If you want to add the customized template to several or all of

your GPOs, then you must add it to each GPO manually. Windows Server 2003 does not have an automated process that allows you to simultaneously add the customized file to multiple GPOs.

When you add a customized template, Windows adds the node and any necessary subnodes under the Administrative Templates folder in the GPO Editor. Because you write customized templates in a text editor, you can also open any existing ADM file with a text editor, such as Notepad, and examine its contents.

① Click Start.

② Click Administrative Tools.

③ Click Active Directory Users and Computers.

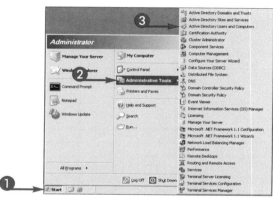

The Active Directory Users and Computers snap-in window appears.

④ Right-click an OU.

⑤ Click Properties.

The Properties dialog box appears for the OU you selected.

⑥ Click the Group Policy tab.

⑦ Click New GPO.

⑧ Click Edit.

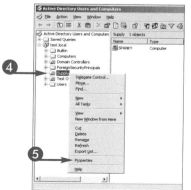

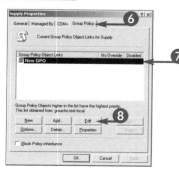

The Group Policy Object Editor appears.

9 Right-click Administrative Templates.

10 Click Add/Remove Templates.

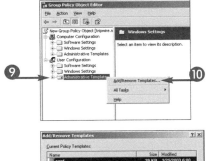

The Add/Remove Templates dialog box appears.

11 Click Add.

The Policy Templates dialog box appears.

12 Click a template.

13 Click Open.

Windows adds the template to the GPO.

What do I have to do to remove a template?

▼ You can right-click Administrative Templates in the GPO Editor, and then click Add/Remove Templates in the menu that appears. In the Add/Remove Templates dialog box, click the template that you want to remove and then click Remove. Windows removes the template. When you navigate to the Administrative Templates folder, the nodes and subnodes that were previously associated with the ADM file are now gone. If you remove a template that you are currently using in a GPO, then the GPO can no longer apply whatever settings were configured in the Administrative Template to the container object.

How can I actually read what is in an ADM file?

▼ The ADM files reside in C:\WINDOWS\inf. Navigate to that location using Windows Explorer and locate the ADM file that you want to examine. Right-click the file and then click Open in the menu. You are offered the option either of choosing a utility on the Internet to open the file or choosing from a list of applications on the local computer (◯ changes to ◉). Click local computer and then in the Open With list, choose Notepad. The ADM file appears as a Notepad document. You can edit the file in Notepad or write a new file and save it to this default location.

Configure Loopback Policy Mode

You can apply loopback processing to protect your network and domain from computers that you put in public places, such as kiosks and lobbies. *Loopback processing* reverses the normal precedence of GPO rule processing, allowing computer policy rules to override any privileges that the user may have. When you do this, the GPO applies only computer-based rule sets, regardless of which user logs in to the server. As a result, user-based rule sets cannot override computer Group Policies that are designed to restrict access to the internal network from public computers.

Normally, when you configure GPOs with both Computer Configuration and User Configuration components, User Configuration components override any conflicting Computer Configuration settings. When you place a group of computers in a public area, such as the lobby of a building, you offer a convenience to customers, but also increase the risk of unauthorized access to the domain. For example, a user who has rights to the domain may log in to a public computer, but may not log out afterwards. Any subsequent user can then access the network with the privileges of the former user.

Configure Loopback Policy Mode

① Click Start.

② Click Administrative Tools.

③ Click Active Directory Users and Computers.

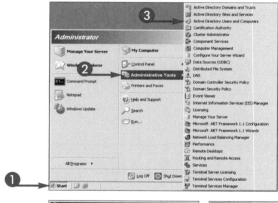

The Active Directory Users and Computers snap-in window appears.

④ Right-click an OU.

⑤ Click Properties.

The Properties dialog box appears for the OU you selected.

⑥ Click the Group Policy tab.

⑦ Click the GPO.

⑧ Click Edit.

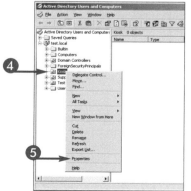

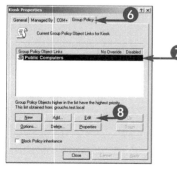

The Group Policy Object Editor appears.

9 Under the Computer Configuration folder, expand the Administrative Templates folder.

10 Expand the System folder.

11 Click Group Policy.

12 Double-click User Group Policy loopback processing mode.

The User Group Policy loopback processing mode Properties dialog box appears.

13 Click Enabled (⬜ changes to ⦿).

14 Click here and select Replace.

15 Click OK.

● Windows enables the loopback processing mode.

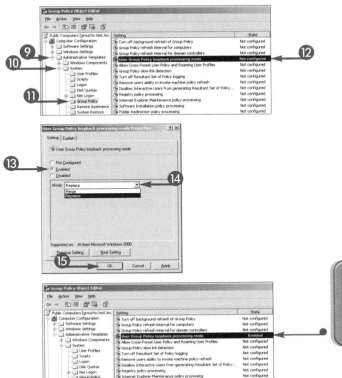

What is the difference between Merge and Replace in loopback processing?

▼ When you choose Merge in the User Group Policy loopback processing mode Properties dialog box, you simultaneously apply both computer policies to the public computer OU as well as to any user policies that the user may have. In the event of a conflict, the computer policies override the user policies. When you choose Replace, computer-based policies replace any user-based policies that the user who logs in to the computer may possess. The user-based policies are not so much replaced as they are not read or applied. Only computer policies are applied to the computer.

To keep my network safe, what settings can I apply to a computer that I place in a public area, but which still connects to the network?

▼ You can restrict user access to the Internet and to a set of intranet pages that are provided to inform the public user about the company. You can also restrict users from accessing the Start menu, Control Panel, and Run dialog box, as well as any other Windows utility that allows users to exercise too much control over the local computer and the network. You can apply settings to any public computer, such as those that you place in coffee shops and public libraries; you must make these computers domain members for Group Policies to apply.

Configure Block Policy Inheritance

You can use Block Policy Inheritance to prevent a GPO rule set that is linked to an upper-level Active Directory Container from automatically applying to a lower-level container. This allows you to customize rules for specific objects and to avoid GPO rule conflicts. As a result, you can exercise a fine degree of control over the rules that apply to a single object, and prevent other rule sets from interfering or conflicting with a low-level container object. For example, the Managers Organizational Unit needs a set of privileges that allow them more freedom on the domain than the larger population of domain users.

If you want a GPO to apply to all users in a domain, you must link it to the domain-level container object. Although you can enforce rules over all domain users, if you want to create exceptions at the OU level, then you can use Block Policy Inheritance.

Sites are above domains in the GPO policy inheritance hierarchy. A site can contain more than one domain, and you can prevent any rules that you set at the site level from applying to one or more associated domains. For more information about sites, see Chapter 4.

Configure Block Policy Inheritance

① Click Start.

② Click Administrative Tools.

③ Click Active Directory Users and Computers.

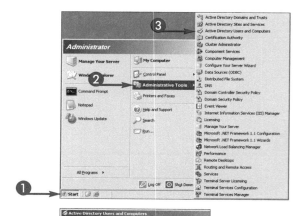

The Active Directory Users and Computers snap-in window appears.

④ Right-click the OU.

⑤ Click Properties.

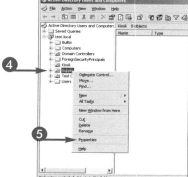

The Properties dialog box appears for the OU you selected.

⑥ Click the Group Policy tab.

⑦ Click the GPO.

⑧ Click Block Policy inheritance (☐ changes to ☑).

⑨ Click OK.

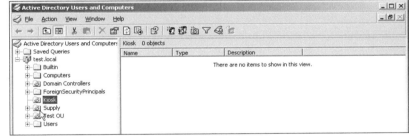

The upper-level policies no longer apply to the OU you selected.

Can I apply some items from an upper-level GPO to a lower-level object but not others?

▼ No. You must either allow all upper-level GPO items to apply to lower-level containers or you must not allow any of them to apply. You also cannot use the Block Policy Inheritance option (☐ changes to ☑) at the site level. This is because sites are at the top of the GPO policy inheritance hierarchy, and there are no container objects above them. If you have a group of users that have particular access and configuration needs, then you can place them in an OU and configure an independent rule set for them that includes all of the various items that they require.

If I use Block Policy Inheritance at an OU, how does policy inheritance operate at any subcontainers inside the OU?

▼ If you create an OU inside another OU, then the child OU object still inherits the policies that you apply to the parent OU object. However, any policies that you apply above the parent OU object are still blocked. If you do not want the child OU to inherit the GPO rule sets that you apply to the parent OU, then you must still go into the Properties dialog box of the child OU and click the Block Policy Inheritance option (☐ changes to ☑). This prevents rule inheritance from the parent OU to the child OU.

Configure No Override Option

You can use the No Override option in Group Policy to ensure that that child container objects inherit the policies you apply to a parent Active Directory container object. This guarantees uniformity of policy settings throughout the sites, domains, and OUs that you administer. It is often important in the corporate environment for all domain users, regardless of their department or workgroup, to operate in a uniform environment for security and support reasons. The No Override option prevents any subcontainers from blocking GPO rule sets that you apply and link to higher-level container objects.

You can also apply the No Override option to lower-level container objects — such as top-level OUs — if you want their GPO settings to apply to sub-OU containers without being blocked. For example, the Research OU may want a uniform set of policies to apply to the sub-OU containers Programmers, Engineers, and Technicians. You can apply the No Override option at the Research OU level to guarantee that the rules are inherited without having to rely on upper-level GPO rule sets.

Configure No Override Option

① Click Start.

② Click Administrative Tools.

③ Click Active Directory Users and Computers.

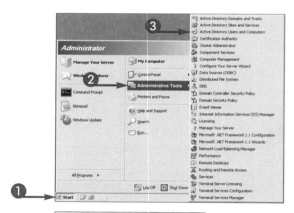

The Active Directory Users and Computers snap-in window appears.

④ Right-click an OU.

⑤ Click Properties.

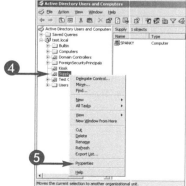

The Properties dialog box appears for the OU you selected.

6 Click the Group Policy tab.

7 Right-click New GPO.

8 Click No Override.

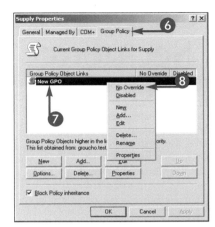

- The No Override field is checked (☑).

9 Click OK.

Windows applies the No Override option to your policies.

When I select the No Override option for a GPO, does it automatically apply to all of the subcontainers to which the GPO is linked?

▼ No. The No Override option actually affects the particular link rather than the actual GPO. If you have a GPO that links to several container objects, then you must select the No Override option for each of the links so that the rule set applies to the subcontainers. Otherwise, subcontainer objects can still block Policy Inheritance and remain unaffected by the upper-level GPO rule set. If a lower-level object applies the No Policy Inheritance in the Properties dialog box of the OU or another container, then this has no effect on the No Override option.

Is there any other way to set the No Override option?

▼ Yes. Instead of right-clicking the GPO in the Properties dialog box for the container, click the GPO and click Options. The GPO Options dialog box appears and offers two different selections. You can click the No Override option (☐ changes to ☑) to prevent GPO rule set override by lower-level containers that are using the GPO link. You can also select another option that is presented in the section "Configure No Override Option" later in this chapter. The No Override option prevents other GPOs from overriding policy set the current GPO you are working with. Selecting this option (☐ changes to ☑) has the same effect as right-clicking the GPO and selecting No Override.

Modify the GPO Policy Application Sequence

You can modify the sequence in which multiple GPOs are applied to a particular Active Directory container object. This controls which GPO rule sets apply to the container in the event of a conflict between different GPOs. This way, you can ensure that the correct rules are implemented on the container object, and make adjustments if the GPO Policy Application Sequence results in undesired effects.

You can link multiple GPOs to a single Active Directory container object, such as a site, domain, or Organizational Unit. When you link two or more GPOs to one object, the

GPO rule sets apply from the bottom up. For example, if Rule A is at the top of the list and Rule B is below Rule A, then Rule B applies first and Rule A applies second. In a conflict between Rule A and Rule B, Rule A wins because it applies afterwards and therefore overrides any rule that applies before it. If an item in Rule A overrides an item in Rule B, and you want the Rule B item to take precedence, then you can change the order in which the rules apply.

Modify the GPO Policy Application Sequence

① Click Start.

② Click Administrative Tools.

③ Click Active Directory Users and Computers.

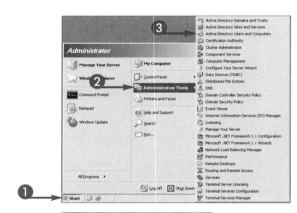

The Active Directory Users and Computers snap-in window appears.

④ Right-click an OU.

⑤ Click Properties.

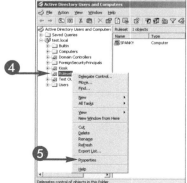

The Properties dialog box appears for the OU you selected.

⑥ Click the Group Policy tab.

⑦ Click the GPO you want to change.

⑧ Click Up or Down to change the GPO's order in the list.

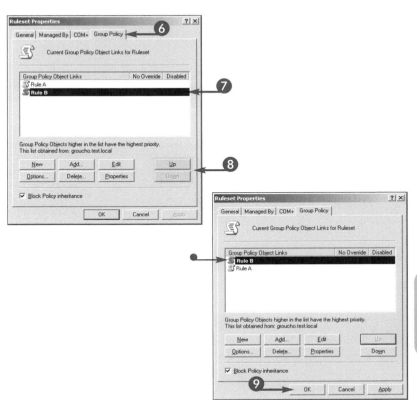

● The GPO moves to a different position in the list.

⑨ Click OK.

Your changes are implemented.

How can I use the method shown in the steps when more than two GPOs are linked to one Active Directory container object?

▼ You can use this method to recombine the position of the various GPOs to ensure that they follow the sequence that you find most effective. When you have too many GPOs, this results in an unruly combination of rule sets, the effects of which you may not anticipate. You can minimize this problem by linking no more than three GPOs to a single container object to maintain control over how the rule sets combine.

When I use more than one GPO linked to an Active Directory container object, do I always encounter a conflict between GPOs?

▼ Not necessarily. However, you must always anticipate that a conflict may occur. In the User Configuration and Computer Configuration nodes alone, there are hundreds of different GPO item combinations, and you may find it difficult to prevent conflicts from occurring. GPO planning is very complex; even when you plan an implementation that you believe is free of conflicts, you may be surprised at the outcome. Windows Server 2003 provides you with tools to manage GPO conflicts when they arise, but it cannot prevent conflicts from occurring in the first place.

Configure Filtering on a GPO

You can configure filtering on a GPO to lock down the desktop or other features on the servers of domain users while still allowing certain groups, such as managers and the system administrator, access to all of the available features. While it is important to limit the access of the general population of domain users to configuration tools on their computers, some groups still need to have access to all of these utilities to perform their jobs. You can create a GPO to impose all of your security

requirements, link the GPO to a site or domain, and still exempt some groups from having the rule sets apply to them.

For any user or group to have a GPO apply to them, they must first have certain permissions to read and execute those permissions. If you remove those permissions from select groups, such as the Managers group, the Group Policy rule sets cannot apply to these groups, and they are not limited by the GPO configuration. This means that you do not have to create a separate GPO and apply it only to the selected OU.

Configure Filtering on a GPO

① Click Start.

② Click Administrative Tools.

③ Click Active Directory Users and Computers.

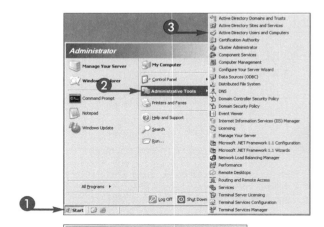

The Active Directory Users and Computers snap-in window appears.

④ Right-click the domain you want.

⑤ Click Properties.

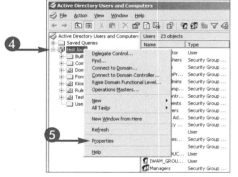

The Properties dialog box appears for the domain you selected.

⑥ Click the Group Policy tab.

⑦ Click a GPO.

⑧ Click Properties.

The Properties dialog box appears for the GPO you selected.

⑨ Click the Security tab.

⑩ Click the exempt group.

⑪ Click all of the selected Allow check boxes (☑ changes to ☐).

⑫ Click the Deny check box for Apply Group Policy (☐ changes to ☑).

⑬ Click OK.

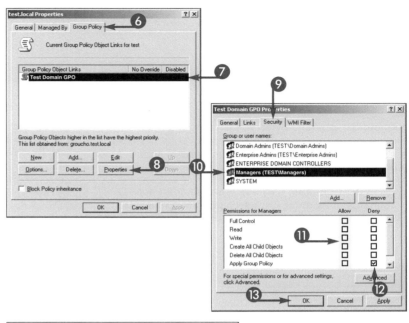

The Security dialog box appears.

⑭ Click Yes.

Filtering is configured on the GPO.

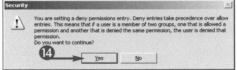

What happens if I only clear all of the Allow check boxes in the GPO Properties Security dialog box for a group, but do not check the Deny check box for Apply Group Policy?

▼ If you do this, the GPO rule set still does not apply to the exempt group, but an explicit Deny overrides any Allow permissions. It is best to click the Deny check box (☐ changes to ☑) to ensure that the group is really exempt. You should also select Deny for the Read permissions (☐ changes to ☑), although this is not absolutely necessary. Occasionally, a Group Policy rule set may inadvertently apply when you do not want it to if you do not explicitly configure the Access Control List with Deny permissions.

By default, do all groups have their Read and Apply Group Policy permissions set to Allow?

▼ No. By default, only the Authenticated Users group has these settings selected for Allow (☑). The Domain Admins and Enterprise Admins groups have Allow permissions for Read, Write, Create All Child Objects, and Delete All Child Objects so that they can access the GPO rule sets and modify them without having the rule sets apply to them when they log in to the domain. Enterprise Domain Controllers is another group in the Access Control List that has only Read permissions selected for Allow because Domain Controllers must be able to read the GPO to process the rule sets.

Disable a GPO Node

You can disable either the Computer Configuration node or the User Configuration node in any GPO to allow for quicker processing of the rule sets throughout the domain. When you do this, you save network bandwidth, server memory, and CPU processing cycles, as well as being able to run your domain and network more efficiently.

Every GPO has Computer and User Configuration nodes, and regardless of whether you have configured rule sets in one or both, Windows Server 2003 processes the list of

rules in both nodes by default. You can disable one of these nodes, if not in use, to allow only the rules in the other node to process.

If you suspect that you have a conflict between the rule sets of the two GPO nodes, then you can disable first one and then the other to see where the problem lies. Disabling GPO nodes can let you troubleshoot and diagnose some rule set conflict problems that you experience in your Active Directory container objects. You can also use this process to disable either start-up and shut-down scripts, or login and logout scripts for your computers and users.

Disable a GPO Node

① Click Start.

② Click Administrative Tools.

③ Click Active Directory Users and Computers.

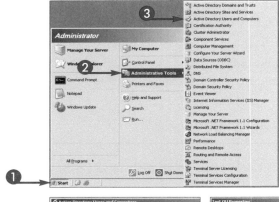

The Active Directory Users and Computers snap-in window appears.

④ Right-click an OU.

⑤ Click Properties.

The Properties dialog box appears for the OU you selected.

⑥ Click the Group Policy tab.

⑦ Click a GPO.

⑧ Click Properties.

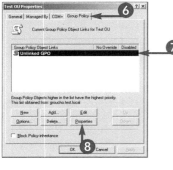

The GPO Properties dialog box appears.

⑨ Click the General tab.

⑩ Click Disable Computer Configuration settings (☐ changes to ☑).

The Confirm Disable dialog box appears.

⑪ Click Yes.

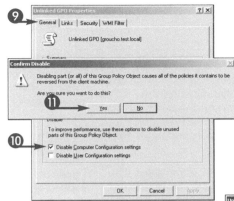

⑫ Click OK.

GPO Node is disabled.

What happens if I select both the "Disable Computer Configuration settings" and the "Disable User Configuration settings" options (☐ changes to ☑)?

▼ This completely disables the GPO, and none of the rule sets apply. These options are an "either, or" proposition, and you are not meant to use them at the same time. You can easily undo a Disable configuration by going back into the Properties dialog box of the GPO and deselecting the check box (☑ changes to ☐). If you are troubleshooting, then you can go in, select one option, and observe the results. You can then deselect the option, and select the other option to observe the results.

Can I use the Disable Configuration feature to disable individual GPO nodes in multiple GPOs that are linked to a container?

▼ Yes. However, you must be careful because when you use the Disable Configuration feature for a GPO, it applies to all of the Active Directory container objects that are linked to the GPO. You can mix and match which GPOs apply to which node rule sets to a container. However, if you have a GPO linked to multiple containers, then all of the containers are affected. You must plan and then document your GPO configurations so that you can keep track of how rule sets apply in the event of an unforeseen conflict or problem.

Disable a GPO

You can disable a GPO to prevent all of the rule sets in the GPO from applying. You may find this helpful when you want to diagnose a potential problem that the GPO is causing, yet without deleting the GPO. By using this method, you can enable and apply the GPO when you have resolved the problem.

Of course, you can simply delete any GPO if you think that it is causing a problem in the domain; however, this means that all of the work you have done to configure the GPO is also deleted. Instead of deleting a GPO, you can easily disable it while you correct any problems with the configuration of the rule sets.

To avoid many of the problems that are typically associated with using GPOs, you should limit the number of GPOs that you create and link on your system; you should use only the number of GPOs that accomplish your security goals. This prevents rule set conflicts and increases the processing speed of the rule sets on the network. It is also best to avoid using Block Policy Inheritance, No Override, and Group Policy filtering.

Disable a GPO

① Click Start.

② Click Administrative Tools.

③ Click Active Directory Users and Computers.

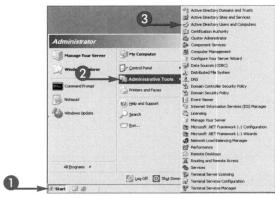

The Active Directory Users and Computers snap-in window appears.

④ Right-click an OU.

⑤ Click Properties.

The Properties dialog box appears for the OU you selected.

⑥ Click the Group Policy tab.

⑦ Right-click a GPO.

⑧ Click Disabled.

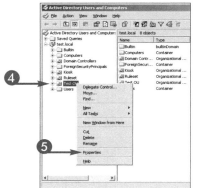

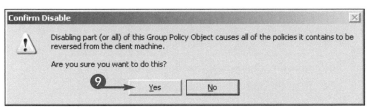

The Confirm Disable dialog box appears.

⑨ Click Yes.

⑩ Click OK.

● A check (☑) appears in the Disabled column.

Windows disables the selected GPO.

Can I enable and disable GPOs only on domains or OUs that I create, or can I use any of the built-in OUs?

▼ By default, GPOs cannot configure any OUs that are created in your Domain Controller, such as Builtin or Computers. When you right-click these OUs and click Properties in the menu that appears, only a General tab appears, displaying a description label without controls. The exception is the Domain Controllers OU. A default Domain Controller Policy GPO exists that you can configure. If you choose to change the default settings here, then you should ensure that you make a copy of it first. If you want to change back to the default settings later, you can use the copy for this purpose.

Because I can disable the GPO that applies to the domain in the Active Directory Users and Computers snap-in, can I also disable the GPO in the Domains and Trusts snap-in?

▼ No. Although the domain icon appears in the sidebar menu in both Active Directory snap-ins, when you right-click the domain in the Active Directory Domains and Trusts snap-in and click Properties in the menu that appears, the only tabs that appear are the General, Trusts, and Managed By tabs. You can only access the GPOs that are linked to the domain in the Active Directory Users and Computers snap-in. You can also only access GPOs that are linked to any sites in the Active Directory Sites and Services snap-in.

Understanding Windows Settings and
Security Settings in Group Policy 276

Set Password Policies 278

Set Account Lockout 280

Set Audit Policy For Event Viewer 282

Set User Rights Assignment 284

Set Security Options 286

Set Event Log Security 288

Configure Restricted Groups 290

Configure System Services 292

Configure Registry Security 294

Configure File System Security 296

Configure Wireless Network Security 298

Set Software Restriction Policies 302

Set IP Security Policies 304

Understanding Server Security
Configurations 308

Create a REG File 310

Create a Reserve File 312

Enable Monitoring for Anonymous
Active Directory Access 314

Rename the Default Administrator
Account 316

Create a Decoy Administrator Account 318

Deny Logon Access to the Domain 320

Install Certificate Services 322

Lock Down Your Server with
Trust-No-Exe 326

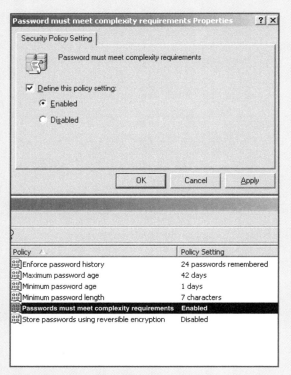

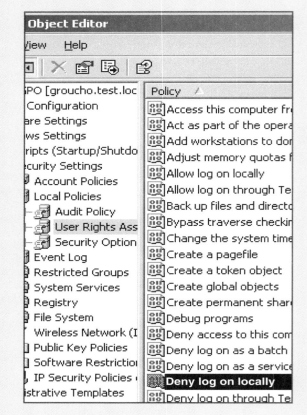

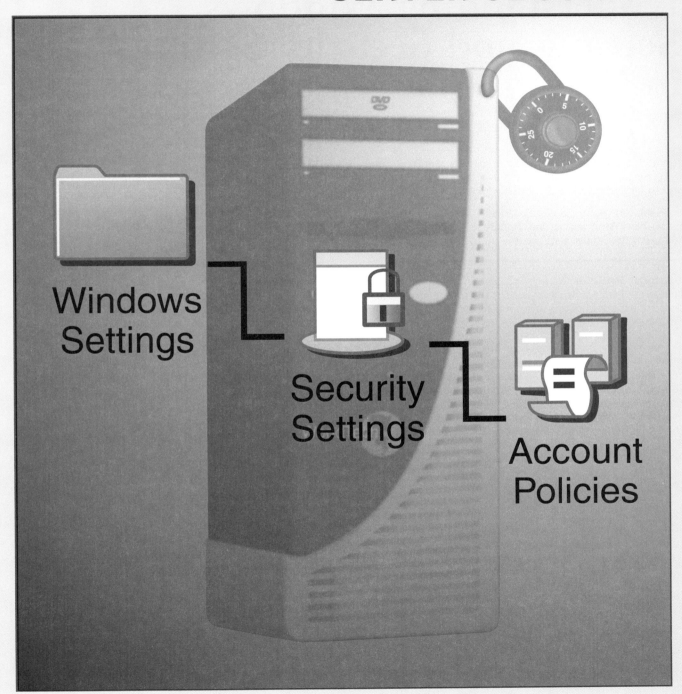

Windows Settings

Security Settings

Account Policies

Understanding Windows Settings and Security Settings in Group Policy

You can configure multiple settings in Group Policy in the Windows Settings and Security Settings nodes. This allows you to set detailed security conditions for your Windows Server 2003 Active Directory Domain, to prevent unauthorized access to the network, and to protect sensitive systems and data.

Both the Computer Configuration and User Configuration nodes have Windows Settings and Security Settings subnodes that implement security policies in the domain.

You can set security policies for a wide variety of computer and network elements, such as password policies, as well as the security for Event Logs, file systems, and wireless networks. You can use Group Policies as your primary tool to impose domain-level security features on your Windows network devices. The exceptions to this are non-Windows computers such as UNIX or Linux boxes, switches, and routers. Group Policy protects only Windows devices or devices that respond to Windows AD security measures.

Account Policies

You can only apply Account Policies to computers in your domain. Account Policies allow you to configure and protect password access to the network by imposing specific limits on password elements. Account Policies are unique because they are the only Group Policy Object (GPO) that does not comply with the normal GPO rules. Normally, when you set a GPO at the domain level, unless you set the No Override option, Group Policies that link to lower-level objects, such as Organizational Units (OU), can override the GPO. Any GPO that links to a lower-level Active Directory container object cannot override Account Policies. You must link Account Policies at the domain level. Although you can configure Account Policies for any container object, the policies will be ignored unless the container is a Domain.

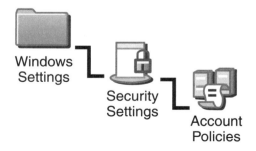

Local Policies

You can configure Local Policies to audit a variety of network events so that you are notified of potential security breaches. Auditing helps you to monitor and configure activities that are related to user rights on the domain. You can also configure many security options, such as network access domain controller security, domain member account elements, and system settings.

Local Policies refers to the behavior of Local Security Groups in the Active Directory, and not just security on the local Windows Server 2003 server. You can also set Audit Policies to only audit events on the local server rather than all of the network computers; this allows you to monitor any attempts to breach a server or domain controller security barrier. You can access Audit Policies that you set to monitor the local server from the desktop of the server, and not remotely from another device.

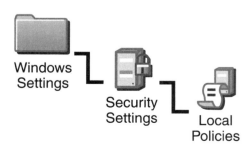

Importing and Exporting Security Templates

Rather than configuring many individual items in the GPO subnodes under Windows Settings and Security Settings, you can import a pre-configured set of security profiles. Using pre-configured security profiles can save you considerable time and work.

Security Templates are text files that you can import into a GPO from a default location on your Windows Server 2003 server. You can select from a set of INF files and import them under the Security Settings subnode in the GPO Editor. This option is only available under the Computer Configuration node in the GPO editor. There are three basic security levels that you can select from the Security Templates: Compatible, Secure, and High Security. The following section discusses each of these levels in more detail.

You can configure and modify a wide variety of security settings under the Windows Settings and Security Settings subnodes in the GPO Editor. To save a backup of your settings, you can export them to the default location that stores your default Security Templates, thereby creating a new customized template. Afterwards, if you alter your security settings and want to return them to a previous state, then you can easily import your customized template back into the GPO Editor and apply it.

SECURITY TEMPLATES

Compatible

You can use the Compatible-level Security Template when you want to set the minimum level of security for your server system and domain. This setting actually decreases the level of security from the default level that the Default Domain-Level GPO provides. Members of the Users group can access non-Windows Server 2003-compliant applications with Power Users privileges and permissions. You use this level when your network runs applications that only users with elevated privileges can execute. You should use this option sparingly.

Secure

You can use this Security Template level when you want users to access network applications and resources without any elevated privileges. This security level primarily affects Operating System and Network Protocols, and specifically applies configuration settings to password and audit policies under Account Policies and Audit Policies in Local Policies. A user or system administrator can receive a notification that the system is about to implement a security policy; the user can opt to override implementation when you set this level.

High Security

You can use this level of security if you want to implement domain security without any consideration for functionality. All security settings are implemented automatically once you set this level. The user is not notified of any implemented activities at this level and cannot override security.

Set Password Policies

Y ou can control how password security is set and implemented on your domain computers and servers. This ensures that users are required to use passwords that hackers cannot easily guess, preventing unauthorized personnel from authenticating onto the domain.

In order to authenticate onto the domain, you usually require a domain user to input two types of information into the logon interface: username and password. Although the username rarely changes, good password management policy requires that users change their passwords often,

that they repeatedly use a particular password once a password change is enforced, and that they can only use the password for a specific length of time.

Password Policies allow you to configure several specific items in order to apply granular control over the use of passwords on your network. For example, you can enforce password history, which allows the system to remember a particular number of passwords. If the password history remembers ten passwords, then the user must have used all ten different passwords before they can use the first one over again. The maximum value you can use is 24. A value of 0 means no passwords are remembered.

Set Password Policies

1 Click Start.

2 Click Administrative Tools.

3 Click Active Directory Users and Computers.

The Active Directory Users and Computers snap-in window appears.

4 Right-click a domain.

5 Click Properties.

The Properties dialog box appears for the domain you selected.

6 Click the Group Policy tab.

7 Click the GPO.

8 Click Edit.

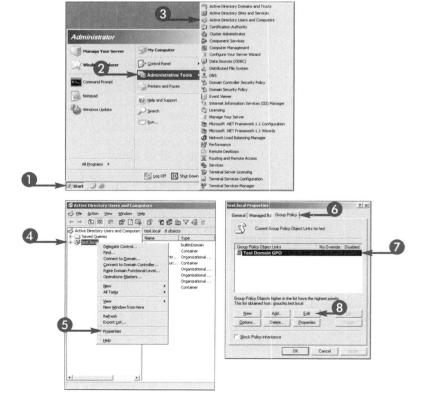

The Group Policy Object Editor appears.

9 Under Computer Configuration, expand Windows Settings.

10 Expand Security Settings.

11 Expand Account Policies.

12 Click Password Policy.

13 Double-click the password policy that you want.

The Password must meet complexity requirements Properties dialog box appears.

14 Click Define this policy setting (☐ changes to ☑).

15 Click Enabled (◯ changes to ◉).

16 Click OK.

● Windows enables the password policy.

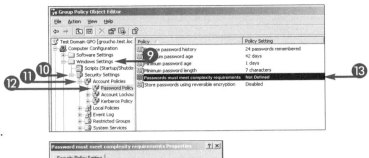

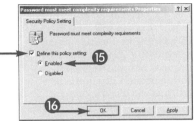

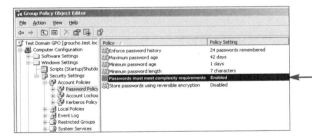

PART V

If I set a password to meet complexity requirements, what exactly are the requirements?

▼ When you click the "Password must meet complexity requirements" option, you prevent domain users from choosing passwords that a dictionary attack can reveal. Password complexity requirements state that a password must not contain part or all of the username, and must contain a combination of upper- and lower-case alphabetical characters, numbers zero through nine, and non-alphanumeric characters such as !, $, #, and %. By default, password complexity requires a password to be at least six characters long. Also by default, password complexity is enabled on domain controllers, but disabled on standalone servers.

Can I make my network more secure from intruders by enabling the "Store passwords using reversible encryption" option?

▼ You click this option primarily when you have applications on your network that use protocols that require access to user passwords to authenticate and run on the system. Using this option to store passwords in reversible encryption is no different than storing them in plain text. You should not use this option unless you have applications that require it because you risk the password security on your domain when you use it. Several common protocols require that you enable this option, including Challenge-Handshake Authentication Protocol (CHAP) and Internet Authentication Services (IAS).

Set Account Lockout

You can use Account Lockout policies to lock a user account and prevent the account from authenticating onto the domain when someone tries to type an incorrect password a certain number of times. For example, an unauthorized user may try to guess another user's password based on their knowledge of that user and what types of passwords the user is likely to use. To keep this intruder from endlessly guessing and possibly stumbling onto the correct password, you can limit the number of incorrect password attempts before the system locks the account. After the account is locked, the intruder can no longer make password attempts until some predefined action takes place.

You can only set three default items under Account Lockout: the account lockout duration, the account lockout threshold, and the conditions under which the account lockout counter is reset. The *account lockout duration* is the number of minutes that an account is locked before it automatically resets and the user can attempt to log on to the domain. The *account lockout threshold* is the number of times that a user can try to log on with an incorrect password before Windows locks the account.

Set Account Lockout

① Click Start.

② Click Administrative Tools.

③ Click Active Directory Users and Computers.

The Active Directory Users and Computers snap-in window appears.

④ Right-click the domain.

⑤ Click Properties.

The Properties dialog box appears for the domain you selected.

⑥ Click the Group Policy tab.

⑦ Click the GPO.

⑧ Click Edit.

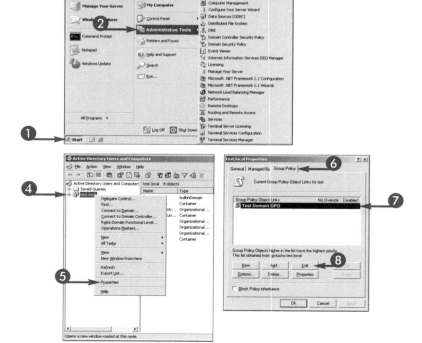

The Group Policy Object Editor appears.

9 Under Computer Configuration, expand Windows Settings.

10 Expand Security Settings.

11 Expand Account Policies.

12 Click Account Lockout.

13 Double-click the desired account lockout policy item.

The Lockout policy Properties dialog box appears.

14 Click Define this policy setting (☐ changes to ☑).

15 Type the value that is relevant to the lockout policy you are setting.

This example shows the Account lockout threshold option being enabled.

16 Click OK.

- The selected account lockout option is now set.

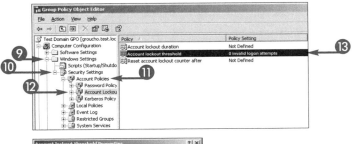
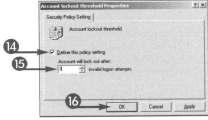
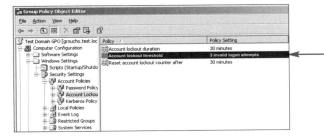

When I configure Account Lockout, is the lockout automatically reset after a certain number of minutes so that the user can automatically log on again?

▼ Not always. You can configure your system so that after a certain amount of time, such as 30 minutes, the account is automatically unlocked and the user can then log on. However, you can also set your Account Lockout policy so that the user cannot log on unless an administrator manually unlocks the account. The most typical reason for a computer lockout is that the user has forgotten their password. If your network requires high levels of security, then you can prevent any automatic logon by requiring that the user contact you to unlock the account and reset the password.

If users locks themselves out of their account, how can I unlock the account and reset the password manually?

▼ In the Active Directory Users and Computers snap-in window, locate and right-click the user account and click Properties in the menu that appears. When the User Properties dialog box appears, click the Account tab. The "Account is locked out" option is selected by default (☑). Deselect this option (☑ changes to ☐) to unlock the account. Under Account options, click the "User must change password at next logon" option (☐ changes to ☑). Create a new, temporary password for the user. You can now tell the user that they can log on using the temporary password. Remember to tell the user that they must change their password next time they log on.

Set Audit Policy for Event Viewer

Yer ou can set Audit Policy so that a number of network security events are written to the security logs in the Event Viewer. This helps you to monitor any attempts to breach the security of your Windows Server 2003 system or your domain.

You typically use the Event Viewer to view several default Event Logs that are kept by your Windows Server 2003 server. A server device keeps Application Logs, Security Logs, and System Logs. Other logs are automatically added as you add server roles. For example, when you make your

server a DNS server, a DNS Server log is automatically added. Also, if you promote your server to a Domain Controller, then Directory Service and File Replication Service logs are added.

You can also add logs that record a particular variety of audit events that occur on your server and in your domain. You can then view these log files through the Event Viewer. These logs record the success or failure of an attempt to access the network in some manner. You can set Audit Policy to record one or both types of events.

Set Audit Policy for Event Viewer

① Click Start.

② Click Administrative Tools.

③ Click Active Directory Users and Computers.

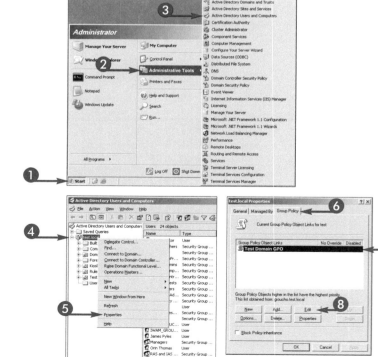

The Active Directory Users and Computers snap-in window appears.

④ Right-click the domain.

⑤ Click Properties.

The Properties dialog box appears for the domain you selected.

⑥ Click the Group Policy tab.

⑦ Click the GPO.

⑧ Click Edit.

The Group Policy Object Editor appears.

⑨ Under Computer Configuration, expand Windows Settings.

⑩ Expand Security Settings.

⑪ Expand Local Policies.

⑫ Click Audit Policy.

⑬ Double-click the Audit event.

The Audit event Properties dialog box appears.

⑭ Click Define these policy settings (☐ changes to ☑).

⑮ Click Success (☐ changes to ☑).

⑯ Click Failure (☐ changes to ☑).

Note: *If you are configuring other types of Local Policies such as User Assignment Rights or Security Options, steps 15 and 16 are performed differently.*

⑰ Click OK.

● Windows defines the audit event.

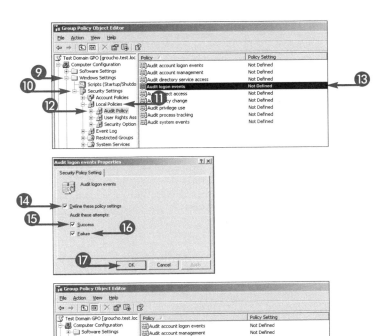

Is there another way besides using the GPO Editor that I can verify that the Audit Policy has been configured?

▼ Yes. You can verify the application of a security policy by going into the Event Viewer. From the Start menu, click Administrative Tools and then click Event Viewer. Open the Application log and then open the most recent Information entry. A notation appears, saying that the Security policy in the GPOs has been applied successfully. You eventually see successful and failed logon attempts as users log on to the domain, but this mostly occurs during the morning hours in a typical business.

Where can I view successful or failed logon attempts in the Event Viewer?

▼ Successful and failed logon attempts are recorded in the default Security log, and you can view that log file in the Event Viewer. You may have a difficult time distinguishing between user logon attempts and device logons; they display as Success Audit or Failure Audit. You must open the log entries to determine the account type. For example, under object type in the Event Properties dialog box, SAM_USER indicates a user logon attempt. The only type of policy that you can add that does not create a new log in Event Viewer is Security Policy.

Set User Rights Assignment

Y ou can configure User Rights Assignment in the GPO Editor to delegate a wide variety of rights to servers and domain controllers to a particular Active Directory container object and all of its contents. This relieves your administrative duties and enhances the rights of special work groups. In the User Rights Assignment node, you can configure many items that fall under two general categories: privileges and logon rights. These two categories are not specifically delineated in the User Rights Assignment subnode.

By default, built-in user and group accounts are assigned some of the rights and privileges that appear in the User Rights Assignment subnode. These groups include the

Administrators account, the Backup Operators account, the Print Operators account, and the Windows Authentication Access Group.

Both users and computers require some of these rights and privileges on the network and in the domain. To execute certain commands and to process application data, Domain Controllers require rights in the domain that are elevated above Member Servers and user Computers. Therefore, accounts such as the Terminal Server License Servers automatically possess some of the rights that you can add to users and groups in your domain.

Set User Rights Assignment

① Click Start.

② Click Administrative Tools.

③ Click Active Directory Users and Computers.

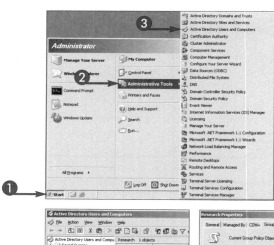

The Active Directory Users and Computers snap-in window appears.

④ Right-click an OU.

⑤ Click Properties.

The Properties dialog box appears for the OU you selected.

⑥ Click the Group Policy tab.

⑦ Click the GPO.

⑧ Click Edit.

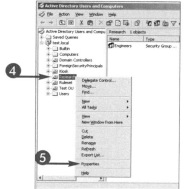

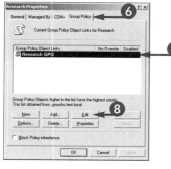

The Group Policy Object Editor appears.

⑨ Under Computer Configuration, expand Windows Settings.

⑩ Expand Security Settings.

⑪ Expand Local Policies.

⑫ Click User Rights Assignment.

⑬ Double-click the policy item.

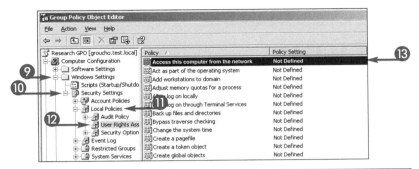

The Properties dialog box appears for the policy item you selected.

⑭ Click Define these policy settings (☐ changes to ☑).

⑮ Click Add User or Group.

The Add User or Group dialog box appears.

⑯ Type the name of a user or group.

⑰ Click OK.

Windows adds the group or user to the Security Policy Setting for the Policy Item.

⑱ Click OK.

The group now has the new privilege or right.

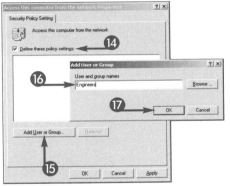

Can I give a user or group more than one User Rights Assignment at a time?

▼ No. However, you can give a particular Rights Assignment to multiple users and groups at a time. To do this, open a particular policy item and click Add User or Group. Then type the name of the user or group and click OK. You can open the Add User or Group dialog box as many times as is necessary to add all the users or groups that require a particular Security Policy Setting. When you are done, click OK in the Properties dialog box of the policy item. You must open and edit the list of IDs for each assignment separately within the same GPO.

Is there another way that I can add a user or group, other than typing the name?

▼ Yes. In the Add User or Group dialog box, you can click Browse to open the Select Users, Computers or Groups dialog box. You can then type the name of the user or group in the "Enter object names to select" field. To verify that you have correctly typed the name, click Check Names. If the name is correct, it appears underlined. You can also click Advanced to open a Common Queries search box if you are unsure of the user or group name that you want to add.

PART V

Set Security Options

You can set Security Options to restrict access to and improve the security of any computer in the Active Directory container object that links to a particular GPO. The Security Options subnode contains a large number of policy items that allow you to provide a high degree of granularity to the security settings for computer objects in your domain. Computers requiring more security are placed in a particular domain or OU, after which all of the necessary security options are configured in a GPO. You can link that GPO to the container object for those computers.

A number of logon policies are assigned in this subnode, including those that do not require the Ctrl+Alt+Delete keyboard combination, those that require smart card authentication, and those that do not display the username of the last user to log on or log off the computer. Other categories that you can configure in the Security Options subnode are Device access, Domain Controller access, Network access, System Shutdown settings, and System cryptography settings. You can also configure settings that affect only users who log onto the computer system locally.

Set Security Options

① Click Start.

② Click Administrative Tools.

③ Click Active Directory Users and Computers.

The Active Directory Users and Computers snap-in window appears.

④ Right-click an OU.

⑤ Click Properties.

The Properties dialog box appears for the OU you selected.

⑥ Click the Group Policy tab.

⑦ Click the GPO.

⑧ Click Edit.

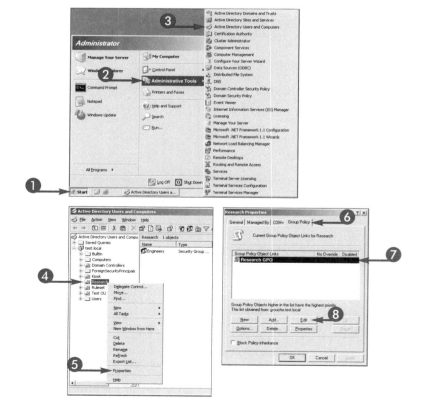

The Group Policy Object Editor appears.

9 Under Computer Configuration, expand Windows Settings.

10 Expand Security Settings.

11 Expand Local Policies.

12 Click Security Options.

13 Double-click the policy item.

The Properties dialog box appears for the policy item you selected.

14 Click Define this policy setting (☐ changes to ☑).

15 Click Enabled (○ changes to ⊙).

16 Click OK.

● Windows enables the Security Option item.

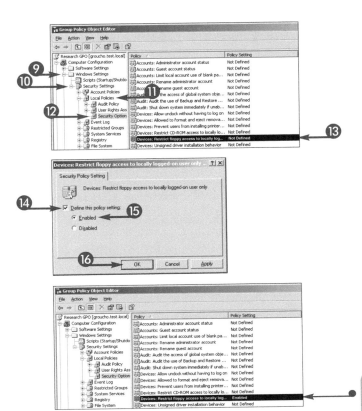

If I am configuring Security Options that affect the logon access of users, then why am I configuring the options under Computer Configuration?

▼ You can use the Security Options subnode to define how a user logs onto a particular group of computers or servers and how access to the various resources and attributes of those computers are restricted. As long as a Security Option under the User Configuration nodes does not override the Computer Configuration security settings, it does not matter which user logs on, or the privileges that user has, based on the group to which they belong.

Do all of the Security Option items that I can configure improve security access to computers and servers on the network?

▼ No. For example, you can configure options, such as "Let Everyone permissions apply to anonymous users" and "Do not require CTRL+ALT+DEL." Both of those settings actually decrease network security when you configure them in Security Options. You may use the "Do not require CTRL+ALT+DEL" option for users who cannot physically perform the three-finger maneuver to open a logon interface. You can use the "Let Everyone permissions apply to anonymous users" in a public environment where security is not an issue.

PART V

Set Event Log Security

Y ou can set Event Log Security to set rules that affect how some or all Event Logs are recorded and to prevent access to the Event Logs to stop intruders from accessing confidential data about your server system operations. Although some Event Logs are created when you add a service to a server, such as promoting it to a Domain Controller, you can manually configure attributes of various Event Logs on your Windows Server 2003 server.

The three default log types are application, security, and system logs. You can simultaneously configure restrictions for all three log types, or for individual Event Log types. You

can configure logs to be overwritten after a certain period of time or have logs continually appended without overwriting previous log entry data. You can also define the maximum size of any log type before it is overwritten.

Although you commonly use these logs to monitor the behavior of your server system, an intruder can also use the data that they contain, which can compromise a server or server network. You should balance the need to keep your data for reference with overwriting it to protect your servers.

Set Event Log Security

① Click Start.

② Click Administrative Tools.

③ Click Active Directory Users and Computers.

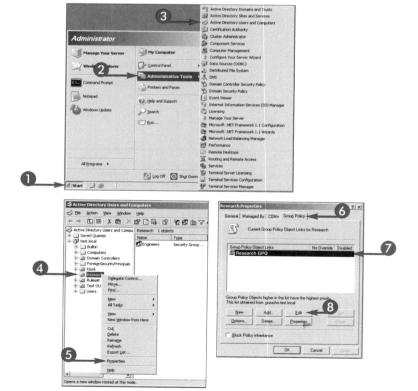

The Active Directory Users and Computers snap-in window appears.

④ Right-click the OU.

⑤ Click Properties.

The Properties dialog box appears for the OU you selected.

⑥ Click the Group Policy tab.

⑦ Click the GPO.

⑧ Click Edit.

The Group Policy Object Editor appears.

9 Under Computer Configuration, expand Windows Settings.

10 Expand Security Settings.

11 Click Event Log.

12 Double-click the policy item.

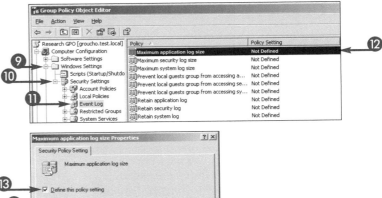

The Properties dialog box appears for the policy item you selected.

13 Click Define this policy setting (☐ changes to ☑).

14 Type in a value appropriate for the task you want to accomplish.

15 Click OK.

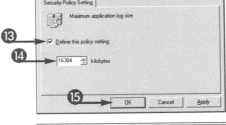

● The log policy item is set.

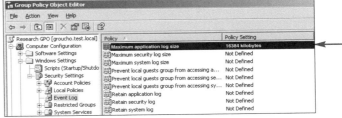

What restrictions can I configure to prevent user accounts from accessing Event Logs on the server?

▼ You can configure Event Log Policy Items to prevent members of the Local Guests Group from accessing the application, security, and system logs on your server systems. These particular settings affect only operating systems that are earlier than Windows Server 2003 server systems. Although your Windows Server 2003 server has new security options to prevent access to the log files by the local guest account, Windows XP and Windows 2000 do not come with this feature. You can protect older server operating systems by configuring these security items.

Is there any way that I can automatically configure these Security Option settings on my server?

▼ Yes. You can use the secedit.exe command line utility to automate the creation and application of security templates and other settings, rather than set them manually in the GUI. You can do this by using a batch file or automatic task scheduler. You can use secedit.exe when you must analyze and configure security settings for several computer systems, and you can perform these tasks when users are off duty. Common secedit commands include /analyze, /configure, and /validate. The command secedit/rerfreshpolicy has been replaced by gpupdate.

Configure Restricted Groups

You can create Restricted Groups that only allow you to add particular users to them. This protects your network resources from unauthorized personnel who may add themselves to groups because they have elevated privileges. You can determine who to make a member of a particular group and limit group membership to only those individuals. If users who you have not authorized to be a part of a restricted group are already members of a group you make restricted when you apply this Group Policy Object, they are automatically removed from the group.

As a system administrator, you control access privileges by assigning permissions to groups rather than to individual users. After you assign the appropriate permissions to a particular group, you can add the users who need those permissions to that group rather than having to configure permissions for each user account.

Security can be breached on a network when a user determines how to add themselves to a group with permissions they are not allowed to have. This can occur when a user is a member of a group that has this authority or has been delegated this authority. Once a user is a member of the group, they can access any resource to which the other group members have rights. When you configure restricted groups, you make it impossible for such a user to add themselves to the group.

Configure Restricted Groups

① Click Start.

② Click Administrative Tools.

③ Click Active Directory Users and Computers.

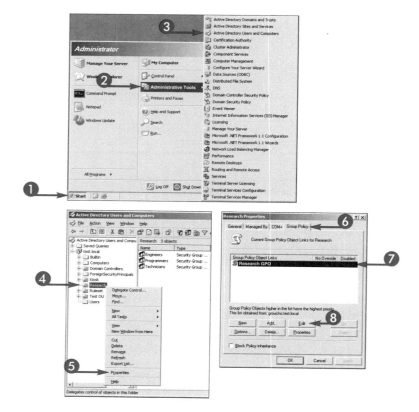

The Active Directory Users and Computers snap-in window appears.

④ Right-click the OU.

⑤ Click Properties.

The Properties dialog box appears for the OU you selected.

⑥ Click the Group Policy tab.

⑦ Click the GPO.

⑧ Click Edit.

The Group Policy Object Editor appears.

9 Under Computer Configuration, expand Windows Settings.

10 Expand Security Settings.

11 Right-click Restricted Groups.

12 Click Add Group.

The Add Group dialog box appears.

13 Type the name of the group.

14 Click OK.

The Properties dialog box appears for the group you selected.

15 Click Add.

The Add Member dialog box appears.

16 Type the name of a group member.

17 Click OK.

18 Click OK.

The user is added to the restricted group.

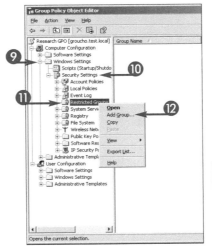

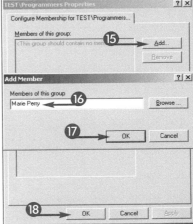

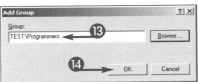

Why are there two "Add" fields in the Configure Membership for Group Properties dialog box?

▼ One field allows you to add users to the restricted group. The other field allows you to add other groups to the restricted group. You may have several groups containing members who all need specific privileges and access rights that the restricted group has. Instead of adding individual users, you can add entire groups to the restricted group. This allows you to add many users with just a few actions. Remember, however, that all members of the added group are accepted in the restricted group.

When I double-click Restricted Groups or right-click and then select Open, why does the subnode not open?

▼ You cannot open the Restricted Groups subnode if the subnode does not contain users or groups. This happens when you first configure restricted groups. However, as you add groups to this subnode, you can open it to view the groups that it contains. You can then open specific restricted groups and add or delete users from these groups. You can also delete entire groups from the Restricted Groups subnode through the GPO Editor.

Configure System Services

You can configure system services in the GPO Editor to restrict how users and groups access the different services that run on your Windows Server 2003 domain and to prevent unauthorized personnel from altering the configuration settings for those services. By definition, a server provides different services to the network and the domain, with each service having a vital function. If some services, such as DNS, are not functioning, then Active Directory does not work in the domain infrastructure. Also, some services must start automatically when the server boots, while you can start other services manually.

When you configure system services, you can determine which mode each service is in when the server boots. In most cases, you can allow your server system to follow the default action for each service. You can also override the default action. When you override, you can specify whether the service starts automatically, manually, or is disabled when the server boots. You can also determine access permissions for each service. Although the services already have default access rights set, you can override these settings or add access privileges to special users and groups.

Configure System Services

① Click Start.

② Click Administrative Tools.

③ Click Active Directory Users and Computers.

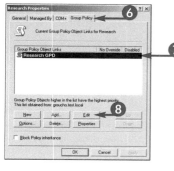

The Active Directory Users and Computers snap-in window appears.

④ Right-click the OU.

⑤ Click Properties.

The Properties dialog box appears for the OU you selected.

⑥ Click the Group Policy tab.

⑦ Click the GPO.

⑧ Click Edit.

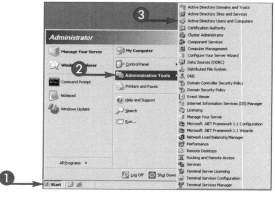

The Group Policy Object Editor appears.

⑨ Under Computer Configuration, expand Windows Settings.

⑩ Expand Security Settings.

⑪ Click System Services.

⑫ Double-click the service name.

The service's Properties dialog box appears.

⑬ Click Define this policy setting (☐ changes to ☑).

⑭ Click a service startup mode (◯ changes to ◉).

⑮ Click Edit Security.

The Security dialog box appears for the service you selected.

⑯ Click a group.

⑰ Click Allow or Deny (☐ changes to ☑).

⑱ Click OK.

⑲ Click OK.

Security Policy Setting is defined and applied.

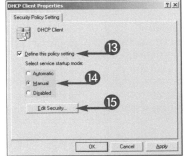

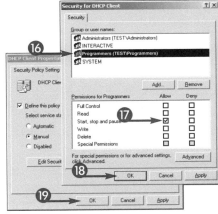

In the Security dialog box for the service that I am configuring, what can I configure by clicking Advanced?

▼ You can configure additional permissions and auditing for the particular service that you are modifying. In the permission entries dialog box, you can select a group and click Add to configure a more detailed set of permissions than you can in the Security dialog box. You can allow or deny permissions to the Query template and the Change template, as well as the User-defined control, and Take ownership among other attributes. You can also set which events regarding the service are audited on a group-by-group basis.

Can I only modify the permissions of the groups in the Access Control List in the Security dialog box for the service?

▼ No, you can add or delete any group in the domain to or from the Access Control List. In the Security dialog box, click Add. The Select Users, Computers, and Groups dialog box appears. You can type in the user, group, or computer that you want to have access to this service in the "Enter the object names to select field" and click Check Names. Then click OK to Add the user, group, or computer. You can then select that object and configure the Access Control List to determine what access the user, group, or computer can have to the service.

PART V

Configure Registry Security

Y ou can configure Registry Security to prevent an unauthorized user from altering or deleting a Registry key on the Windows Server 2003 server. This prevents unauthorized users from altering the critical configuration settings of your server.

The configuration settings for any Windows operating system are stored in a hierarchical database known as the Registry. The Registry stores all hardware and software configuration settings in its database. The most common way of changing the Registry is through the Control Panel on your Windows server. You can also directly change Registry keys using the regedit or regedt32 editing tools.

You can do a tremendous amount of damage if you change Registry settings without being careful. For example, if you improperly configure a part of the Registry, then you can permanently disable your server or computer, thus preventing it from booting.

When you configure Registry security, you can control which users and groups have access to which particular Registry key, ensuring that only authorized users can edit the Registry. You can also determine which services have authority to alter the Registry. This is important because malicious software, such as viruses or spyware, sometimes attempts to alter a computer Registry to take control of certain functions.

Configure Registry Security

① Click Start.

② Click Administrative Tools.

③ Click Active Directory Users and Computers.

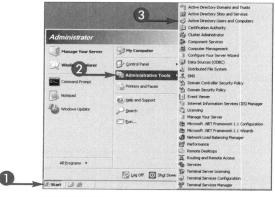

The Active Directory Users and Computers snap-in window appears.

④ Right-click the OU.

⑤ Click Properties.

The Properties dialog box appears for the OU you selected.

⑥ Click the Group Policy tab.

⑦ Click the GPO.

⑧ Click Edit.

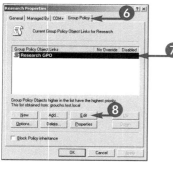

The Group Policy Object Editor appears.

⑨ Under Computer Configuration, expand Windows Settings.

⑩ Expand Security Settings.

⑪ Right-click Registry.

⑫ Click Add Key.

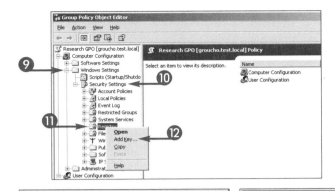

The Select Registry Key dialog box appears.

⑬ Click a Registry Key.

⑭ Click OK.

The Database Security dialog box appears.

⑮ Click a group.

⑯ Click Allow or Deny (☐ changes to ☑).

⑰ Click OK.

Windows applies permissions to the Registry key.

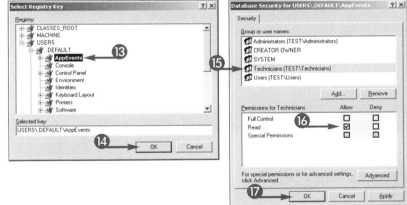

When I configure the Access Control List to a Registry key, can I only modify how users, groups, and computers access the Registry?

▼ No. There are actually two Access Control Lists. You use the Discretionary Access Control List to grant or deny a user or group permission to a Registry key or to another object in the Active Directory. The second list, the System Access Control List, is part of the object security descriptor, and it specifies which events are audited on either a per-user or a per-group basis. Access Control Lists are part of the object security descriptor, which holds the security information that is linked to the particular object.

If editing the Registry is so risky, then what procedures should groups with rights to Registry keys follow to correctly edit it?

▼ Of the many "best practices" procedures that you can follow, the primary one is to back up the Registry before you edit it. If you then misconfigure the Registry, then you can restore it to the Last Known Good Configuration (LKGC) so that your server returns to its previous state before you edited it. LKGC can only restore parts of the Registry. You can also limit the number of users or groups that have permission to edit the Registry. You can disallow the Administrator account from editing the Registry and you can assign that right to a special account.

Configure File System Security

Y ou can use Group Policy to control the security of specific files and folders on your Windows Server 2003 server. This centralizes your file security and reduces your administrative effort.

Although you can configure security for each file or folder on your file server, you can save time and energy by using Group Policy to assign access permissions to data that is stored on your servers. By using GPOs that are linked to any Active Directory container object, you can configure the security settings for a file to control auditing and ownership of files and folders as well as access to those files and folders.

You can use the File System Security subnode to create security templates for files and folders. A security template acts as a "blueprint" or a model for how specific permissions are configured. You can apply the template to different container objects so that you do not have to recreate file and folder access settings for each file that you are storing on your server. The templates also ensure that the access settings that you configure remain the same as when you originally set them up.

Configure File System Security

① Click Start.

② Click Administrative Tools.

③ Click Active Directory Users and Computers.

The Active Directory Users and Computers snap-in window appears.

④ Right-click the OU.

⑤ Click Properties.

The Properties dialog box appears for the OU you selected.

⑥ Click the Group Policy tab.

⑦ Click the GPO.

⑧ Click Edit.

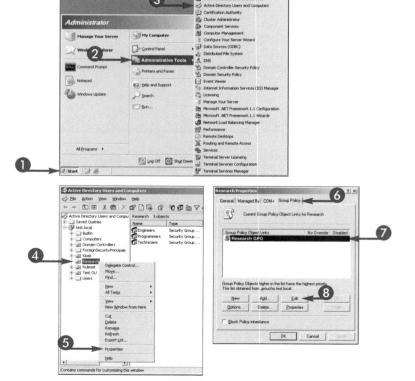

The Group Policy Object Editor appears.

⑨ Under Computer Configuration, expand Windows Settings.

⑩ Expand Security Settings.

⑪ Right-click File System.

⑫ Click Add File.

The Add a file or folder dialog box appears.

⑬ Expand a drive.

⑭ Expand a folder.

⑮ Click the file.

Note: You can apply the GPO to a file on any of the servers in your domain; Windows prevents a user, attempting to alter the Access Control List (ACL) for this file via Windows Explorer, from doing so.

⑯ Click OK.

The Database Security dialog box appears for the file you selected.

⑰ Click a group.

⑱ Click Allow or Deny (☐ changes to ☑).

⑲ Click OK.

Your access permissions are configured.

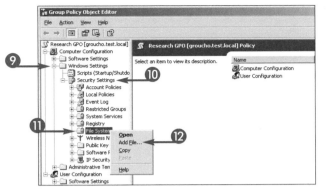

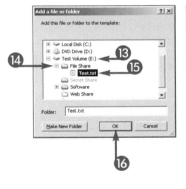

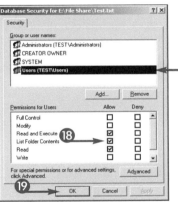

How can I tell if my security configuration for a file or folder was successful?

▼ Under Security Settings, you can select File System to view the file object in the main display pane. If you double-click the object, the file security Properties dialog box appears. You can click one of four options (☐ changes to ☑) to configure the file or folder, propagate inheritable permissions to subfiles and folders, replace existing permissions with inheritable permissions, or prevent permissions from being replaced. This last selection is important because it lets you maintain the integrity of protected files and folders, by ensuring that other users cannot change the permission settings. You can click Edit Security to reset the Access Control List.

How can I use the option settings in the Security Policy Setting tab in the file or folder Properties dialog box?

▼ You can configure two options. The first option, "Configure this file or folder then" (☐ changes to ☑), offers you two mutually exclusive choices: either Propagate inheritable permissions to all subfolders, or Replace existing permissions on all subfolders with inheritable permissions. The second option, "Do not allow permissions on this file or folder to be replaced" (☐ changes to ☑), causes the two choices above to be greyed out, so that whatever setting you have selected there becomes permanent.

PART V

Configure Wireless Network Security

You can configure Wireless Local Area Network (WLAN) security with Group Policy to create specific settings for all of the wireless traffic in your domain. This allows you to provide consistent WLAN security application and improved WLAN security administration over a large network. You can also enable 802.1x wireless authentication protocols to specify preferred methods of allowing domain users to securely log on to a wireless network.

The basic characteristics of a WLAN are defined by the IEEE 802.11 protocol. This standard defines the medium access and physical network layer specifications for 1- and 2-Mbps connectivity between a mobile and fixed network node or

between two wireless network nodes. 802.1x is the WLAN specification that is designed to increase security by user authentication using RADIUS, Extensible Authentication Protocol (EAP), and Lightweight Access Directory Protocol (LDAP).

Currently, most WLANs operate under either the 802.11b or 802.11g standards. Both standards specify a radio frequency bandwidth of 2.5 GHz. The 802.11b standard supports a maximum data transfer rate of 11 Mbps, while the 802.11g standard supports transfer rates up to 54 Mbps. Both standards use direct sequence wireless technology and are unlicensed.

Configure Wireless Network Security

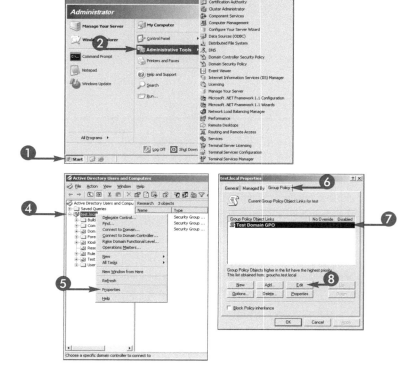

① Click Start.

② Click Administrative Tools.

③ Click Active Directory Users and Computers.

The Active Directory Users and Computers snap-in window appears.

④ Right-click the domain.

⑤ Click Properties.

The Properties dialog box appears for the domain you selected.

⑥ Click the Group Policy tab.

⑦ Click the GPO.

⑧ Click Edit.

The Group Policy Object Editor appears.

9 Under Computer Configuration, expand Windows Settings.

10 Expand Security Settings.

11 Right-click Wireless Network Policies.

12 Click Create Wireless Network Policy.

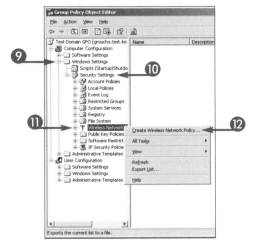

The Wireless Network Policy Wizard appears.

13 Click Next.

The Wireless Network Policy Name page appears.

14 Type a name for the Wireless Network Policy.

15 Click Next.

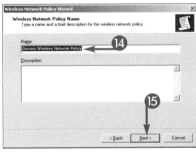

Can I set a Wireless Network Security Policy at other levels besides the domain level?

▼ Yes. You can configure a GPO for Wireless Security and link it to any of the three Active Directory container objects. This security policy then applies to the wireless network devices that are operating within the confines of that container. For example, if you configure wireless network security in a GPO and link it to an OU, then all of the wireless network devices in that OU must comply with that particular security configuration. You can create different wireless security scenarios and attach them to different container objects, depending on your needs.

What is the IEEE and what are 802 standards?

▼ The IEEE is the Institute of Electrical and Electronic Engineers. It is an organization that establishes the standards for participating in, and the development of, protocols for all manner of data transmission systems in the United States. The IEEE 802 project is the working group that establishes the standards for all local area, metropolitan area, and wide area computer networks. This includes all of the standards that pertain to computer communication over the radio frequency medium as well as copper wire and fiber optic media. The 802.11 standard describes radio frequency computer communications standards.

continued

Configure Wireless Network Security *(Continued)*

Y ou can use the Wireless Network Policy Wizard to configure the name of your wireless network, the type of data encryption that you use, and how a wireless computer in your domain connects and authenticates to the network. Configuring all of these features in one GPO makes it easier for you to administer wireless security on your network and reduces the risk that unauthorized users will access your wired network from the wireless network.

One of the greatest dangers to your Windows Server 2003 network is a wireless network with insufficient security. This can occur when one or more users in your network bring

in an unauthorized access point and plug it into the network to allow them to work wirelessly. Although you can take every precaution to prevent intrusion from the Internet or from other wired parts of the network, an unauthorized access point plugged into your wired network offers immediate, unrestricted access to the LAN. You can defend your network from vulnerabilities in both authorized and unauthorized equipment with a well-configured wireless network security policy.

Configure Wireless Network Security *(continued)*

The Completing the Wireless Network Policy Wizard page appears.

16 Click Edit properties (☐ changes to ☑).

17 Click Finish.

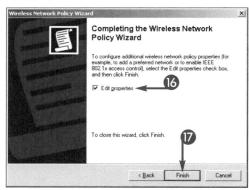

The Wireless Network Policy Properties dialog box appears.

18 Type the frequency in minutes with which you want it to check for policy changes.

19 Click here and select "Any available network (access point preferred)."

20 Click "Use Windows to configure wireless network settings for clients" (☐ changes to ☑).

21 Click the Preferred Networks tab.

22 Click Add.

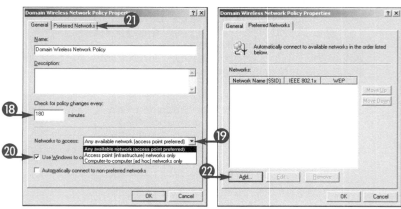

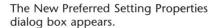
The New Preferred Setting Properties dialog box appears.

㉓ Type a name for the SSID.

㉔ Click "Data encryption (WEP enabled)" (☐ changes to ☑).

㉕ Click "The key is provided automatically" (☐ changes to ☑).

㉖ Click the IEEE 802.1x tab.

The IEEE 802.1x options appear.

㉗ Click "Enable network access control using IEEE 802.1x" (☐ changes to ☑).

㉘ Click here and select "Protected EAP (PEAP)".

㉙ Click "Authenticate as computer when computer information is available" (☐ changes to ☑).

㉚ Click OK.

㉛ Click OK in the Domain Wireless Network Policy Properties dialog box

Your wireless security settings are applied.

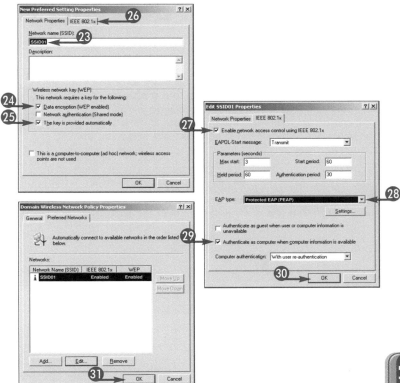

PART V

What is RADIUS and how does it enable a user or computer to authenticate onto the network?

▼ RADIUS stands for Remote Authentication Dial-In User Service. It is a protocol that allows for security authentication in server/client network infrastructures. Internet Service Providers commonly use RADIUS as the authentication method for dial-up networks. RADIUS authentication is also often used with tunneling networks, such as Virtual Private Networks (VPN). VPN allows mobile users to connect to their work LAN over the Internet as if they were connecting through a dedicated "tunnel" using special encryption protocols, such as IP Security.

What is an SSID and why does a wireless network have to use it for the wireless network name?

▼ SSID stands for Service Set Identifier. It is defined as an alphanumeric, case-sensitive identifier value that provides a unique name for a WLAN. The SSID can be from 2 to 32 characters long. SSIDs provide a very basic level of security because no wireless device can associate with a WLAN unless it is using the same SSID value as the wireless network to which it wants to connect. Wireless computers commonly connect to a WLAN through an access point, which operates like a wired switch.

Set Software Restriction Policies

Y ou can set Software Restriction Policies to only allow certain types of software to run on your network and to restrict the users who are allowed to run certain software applications on your network. Doing this prevents harmful types of programs from executing in your domain.

You can also prevent software from running on your network if the software is not supported by the IT department of your organization. Users sometimes do not understand that it is inefficient to expect the support

techs to support all kinds of software. When these users download or install software that your IT department does not support, for work or recreational purposes, and the software malfunctions, they may call company technicians to resolve the issue. This can prevent your technicians from performing other computer and network maintenance tasks.

You can use Group Policy to restrict the types of software that users can run, thus avoiding this problem. You can prevent unsupported software from running at all or you can allow software to run, based on the access rights of the user who is trying to use the application.

Set Software Restriction Policies

① Click Start.

② Click Administrative Tools.

③ Click Active Directory Users and Computers.

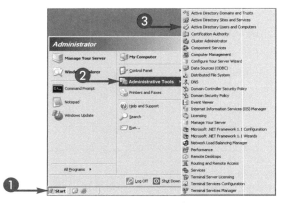

The Active Directory Users and Computers snap-in window appears.

④ Right-click the OU.

⑤ Click Properties.

The Properties dialog box appears for the OU you selected.

⑥ Click the Group Policy tab.

⑦ Click the GPO.

⑧ Click Edit.

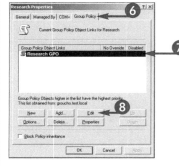

The Group Policy Object Editor appears.

⑨ Under Computer Configuration, expand Windows Settings.

⑩ Expand Security Settings.

⑪ Click Software Restriction Policies.

⑫ Double-click Designated File Types.

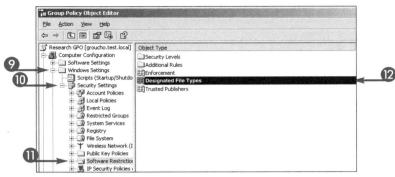

The Designated File Types Properties dialog box appears.

⑬ Type the file extension you want to use.

⑭ Click Add.

● The file type is added.

⑮ Click OK.

Software Restriction Policies applied.

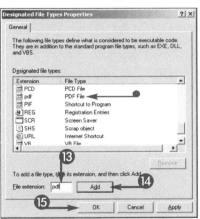

What happens if I select a file type and click Remove in the Designated File Types Properties dialog box?

▼ If you select one of the file types in the list and click Remove, the Software Restriction Policies dialog box appears and states that if you delete this file type, then programs of this type will run with unrestricted privileges. You can click Yes to continue the removal process or No to cancel it. If you click Yes, then the file extension is removed from the list. Only those file extensions listed in the Properties dialog box are restricted on the network and in the domain.

How do I enforce which users are affected by Software Restrictions Policies on my network?

▼ You can double-click the Enforcement item in the Software Restrictions Policies folder. You can apply the Software Restrictions Policies to either all users, or to all users except local administrators. In the same dialog box, you can let the policy restrictions apply to all software in the list, or you can exempt library files, such as DLL files. You can also open the Trusted Publishers item to select which users are considered trusted publishers of software; you can select End Users, Local computer administrators, or Enterprise administrators.

Set IP Security Policies

You can set Internet Protocol (IP) Security Policies to control how IP Security (IPSec) is implemented on computers in your network. This improves how encryption security further protects the domain. It also allows you to set the IPSec configuration for every computer that is affected by the GPO, rather than require you to set the policy on each computer manually.

The IPSec Protocol Suite is an encryption policy that adds security to the network at the IP in the Network Layer or Layer 3 of the OSI Reference Model. IP is responsible for

forwarding packets of information and routing them between different networks or subnets. This allows you to set network security policies on information that can travel from one subnetwork to the next in your domain or between your domain and others.

IPSec provides for secure communication between network nodes, even over the Internet, and it is commonly used in concert with Virtual Private Network (VPN) technology. You can also use IPSec within the domain and the local network to provide improved security for transmission of sensitive data.

Set IP Security Policies

① Click Start.

② Click Administrative Tools.

③ Click Active Directory Users and Computers.

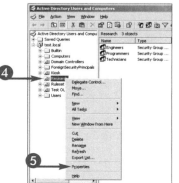

Active Directory Users and Computers snap-in window appears.

④ Right-click the OU.

⑤ Click Properties.

The Properties dialog box appears for the OU you selected.

⑥ Click the Group Policy tab.

⑦ Click the GPO.

⑧ Click Edit.

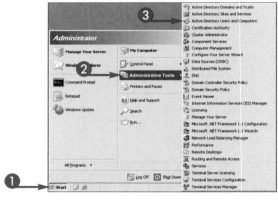

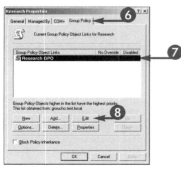

The Group Policy Object Editor appears.

9 Under Computer Configuration, expand Windows Settings.

10 Expand Security Settings.

11 Right-click IP Security Policies.

12 Click Create IP Security Policy.

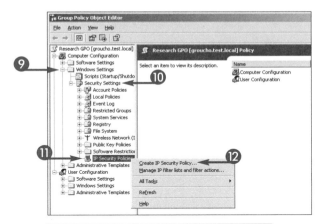

The IP Security Policy Wizard appears.

13 Click Next.

Once I set up an IPSec Security Policy, how can I monitor the IPSec activity on my network?

▼ You have several options. For example, you can add an IP Security Monitor snap-in on your server. To add the snap-in, click Start, and then click Run. In the Run dialog box, type **mmc** and then click OK. When the mmm console appears, click File and then click Add/Remove Snap-in. Click IP Security Monitor and then click Add. After that, click the Close button (☒) and then click OK. The IP Security Monitor monitors the main policy by name, description, last modified, and other attributes. You can also monitor activity by using Generic and Specific Filters, Internet Key Exchange Policies, Statistics, and Security Associations.

If the IPSec Service stops on my server, how can I restart it?

▼ You can restart the IPSec Service either through the Graphical User Interface (GUI) in Windows or through the command line commands `net stop policyagent` and `net start policyagent`. In the GUI, click Start, click Administrative Tools, and then click Services. The Services window appears. Scroll down the list of services until you locate IPSEC Services. Select it to view options to stop and restart the service. Regardless of the method that you use, when you stop and restart the service, you disconnect all computers on the network that are accessing network resources using IPSec.

continued

Set IP Security Policies *(Continued)*

Y ou can use the IP Security Policy Wizard to create or add more security rules to a Security Policy, to name a security policy, to determine how authentication is managed using IPSec, and to edit the properties of the rule that you are creating or adding. This allows you to manage your IPSec Policies on your domain in an easy, step-by-step fashion and to change your configuration as easily as when you created it.

Because you can access the properties of any rule that you create or modify, you can configure how often the rule checks for changes in policy. This means that a security rule does not continue to operate after you change settings in Group Policy. You do not have to manually re-configure each individual rule after Group Policy settings change. You can also configure the Internet Key Exchange (IKE) that is applied to Windows XP and Windows Server 2003 computers. IKE is a standard protocol that IPSec uses to describe an automatic method of negotiation and authentication. You can use both IKE and Public Key Encryption to identify a third party on a network when they are using public and private keys to sign packets and decrypt data.

Set IP Security Policies *(continued)*

The IP Security Policy Name page of the Wizard appears.

⑭ Type the name of the policy.

⑮ Click Next.

The Requests for Secure Communication page of the Wizard appears.

⑯ Click "Activate the default response rule" (☐ changes to ☑).

⑰ Click Next.

The Default Response Rule Authentication Method page of the Wizard appears.

⑱ Click "Active Directory default (Kerberos V5 protocol)" (◯ changes to ◉).

⑲ Click Next.

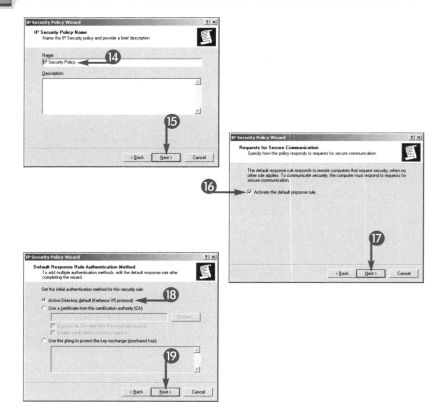

The Completing the IP Security Policy Wizard
page appears.

⑳ Click Edit properties (☐ changes to ☑).

㉑ Click Finish.

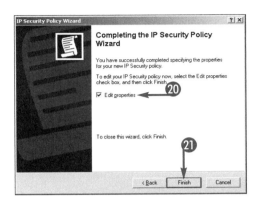

The IP Security Policy Properties dialog box
appears.

㉒ Click the General tab.

㉓ Type a name for the policy.

㉔ Type the frequency in minutes with which
you want it to check for policy changes.

㉕ Click OK.

Windows applies your IP Security Policies.

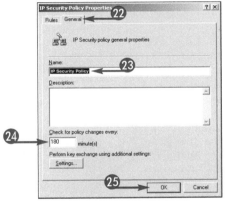

**After I create an IP Security Policy, can I change
the security rules for the policy or change
authentication methods?**

▼ Yes. Open the new IP Security Policy that you
created by double-clicking it. The IP Security Policy
Properties dialog box appears. Click the Rules tab
to view the security rule that you want to change.
To modify the IP filter list rule, select it and click
Edit. The Edit Rule Properties dialog box appears.
The dialog box has two tabs, Security Methods
and Authentication Methods. You can add, edit,
and remove any of the security methods, as well
as change the order in which they are applied. You
can also add or edit the authentication methods
for this policy.

**Do I have to create a new IP Security Policy
before IPSec is configured in my network?**

▼ No. There are three default IP Security Policies
already created for the Active Directory: Server
(Request Security), Client (Respond Only), and
Secure Server (Require Security). The default rules
require any Windows Server 2003 server on your
network to request security using a Kerberos trust.
Client computers have a respond-only rule that
permits them to communicate on the network
through an unsecure channel by using the default
rule to exchange data with the local server. Secure
servers also use Kerberos trusts but do not allow
unsecure exchange of data with other computers
on the network.

Understanding Server Security Configurations

You can create a more secure Active Directory Domain infrastructure by using a wide variety of methods and tools. Chapter 15 discusses how to make your Active Directory network more secure by using Group Policies and linking them to the different Active Directory container objects, such as sites, domains, and Organizational Units (OU). This chapter discusses other methods besides Group Policies that you can use to create and improve security in your computing environment.

Physical Security

Regardless of the types of security technologies that you use to protect your network, it is also important to keep your servers, routers, switches, and other network devices physically safe. Otherwise, an intruder may gain physical access to your data, thus making it as vulnerable as when an intruder accesses your servers from the Internet.

Although it seems like common sense, locking the server room is sometimes overlooked. You should locate all of your sensitive network devices in a room that you can lock, and limit the number of people who have physical access to the room. You should also place ancillary hubs, switches, and routers that are not located with the main group in locked rooms or containers. If an intruder gains access to a connectivity device such as a hub or switch, they can plug an unauthorized laptop into the device and access network traffic.

Risk Management

You can use Risk Management to determine which methods of protection enable a company network to defend itself in a cost-effective way. You should consider the methods of self-defense that efficiently shield the network from threats, remembering that the method should not cost more to implement than what your data is worth. To do this, you must first determine how much it may cost your company if you lose all of your data, or if your data falls into the hands of a competitor. You can then create a Risk Management plan in accordance with your evaluation.

Administrative Access

You do not have to log onto the network with your Administrative account to do all of your network tasks. Best Practice states that you should use the account with the least amount of privileges that still allows you to perform these tasks. Therefore, you should read e-mail or conduct research on the Web with your domain user account, and reserve the use of your Administrative account for tasks requiring higher permission levels.

Authentication and Authorization

You should ensure that you have adequate authentication and authorization methods in place. Authentication is the means by which a user gains access to the network and the domain. A user may authenticate to the domain through a username and password, along with other methods, such as smart cards. Authorization is the means by which a user gains access to specific resources in the Active Directory.

After users authenticate to the domain, they are issued Security IDs, or SIDs, based on their user rights and the rights of the groups to which they belong. The system uses SIDs to determine which resources users can access and assigns a level of access, such as Read Only, Modify, or Full Control. You usually assign levels of access to a resource using the Access Control Lists that are associated with different groups.

Domain Controller Deployment

Depending on the circumstances in the domain, the deployment or placement of your Domain Controllers can greatly affect your domain security. For example, deployment of Domain Controllers is different, depending on whether you place them in the Main Office, an Intranet Datacenter, an Extranet Datacenter, or a Branch Office.

Intranet Datacenters are generally the most accessible to you because they are located on the main business site and are routinely monitored by IT staff. *Extranet Datacenters* are similar to their intranet counterparts because they are also placed in a central location and technicians frequently monitor them; however, they also have an "outward-facing" function in that users are more likely to access them from the Internet.

Domain Controllers located in a *Branch Office* are considered the most vulnerable because the branch office almost never has a dedicated IT staff or dedicated, secure physical facilities. These Domain Controllers are more likely to share the same subnet with user computers and other devices in the office. They are also likely to run several different systems on the same Domain Controller, including file and print services, which makes it difficult for you to "harden" them in the same way that you can a dedicated Domain Controller because a dedicated DC is not accessed for other services and can have those service access ports closed. For more about Domain Controllers, see Chapters 1 to 4.

Threats

You must be aware of the different types of security threats that can compromise your server system and network. One of the more common threats is *Spoofing*, which involves an intruder accessing your network with authentic network credentials. *Data Tampering* attacks allow the intruder to change sensitive server data without you or the domain users being aware of it. *Information Disclosure* results when an intruder accesses your data and either publicly reveals it on the Internet or another forum, or provides the data to a competitor. A *Denial of Service* attack makes your services unavailable to customers. For example, an intruder may shut down your Web servers and prevent eCommerce from taking place.

PART V

Create a REG File

Y ou can create a REG file to store specific Registry settings from one server. Doing so allows you to write a scripting solution to export those Registry settings to other servers in your domain. This enables you to securely modify the configuration of multiple servers and Domain Controllers.

You can use Registration Entities, or REG files, to add, modify, or delete Registry subkeys and values on your Windows Server 2003 servers. When you run the REG file, the stored values are distributed remotely over the network, and the contents of the file merge with the local Registry keys in each designated server.

Although you can use REG files with the Regedit Registry editor, you cannot use them with the Regedit32 Registry editor. Keep in mind that if you use either editor incorrectly, then you may cause serious problems on the server, and this may require you to reinstall the Operating System. You can use Regedit to modify the Registry database for 16-bit Windows systems. You generally use Regedit32 to edit the Registry in Windows NT systems. Regedit is the preferred Registry database editor for Windows XP and Windows Server 2003. Although you can use Regedit32 on Windows Server 2003 systems, it only launches and runs Regedit.

Create a REG File

① Click Start.

② Click Run.

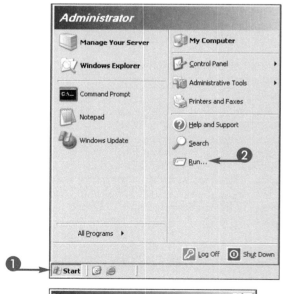

The Run dialog box appears.

③ Type **regedit** in Run dialog box.

④ Click OK.

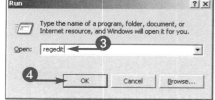

The Registry Editor appears.

⑤ Navigate to the key you want.

⑥ Click the key.

⑦ Click File.

⑧ Click Export.

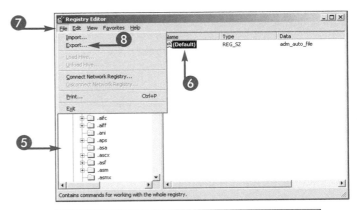

The Export Registry File dialog box appears.

⑧ Type a name for the file.

⑨ Click Save.

Regedit creates the REG file.

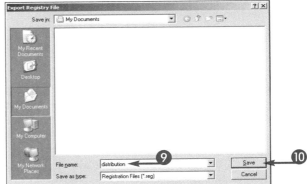

Can I use REG files to delete Registry keys and values?

▼ Yes. To delete a Registry key and value, you must place a hyphen (-) in front of the RegistryPath sequence in the REG file. For example, to delete a subkey called exit, from the Registry key, HKEY_LOCAL_MACHINE\Software\Exit, type **[-HKEY_LOCAL_MACHINE\Software\Exit]**. To delete a Registry value, place a hyphen after the DataItemName sequence in the REG file after "ExitValue." For example, type **[HKEY_LOCAL_ MACHINE\Software\Exit"ExitValue"=-]**. You can use Regedit to export the key that you want to delete to a REG file, and then use Notepad to edit the file and insert the hyphen.

How can I distribute REG files across the network?

▼ You can send a REG file as an e-mail attachment to selected users. You can also place the REG file on a network server share, notifying the users how to access it, and giving them appropriate permissions. You can also add a command to the user logon scripts to automatically import the REG file to user computers when the users log on to the network. When users run a REG file, interactive messages ask them whether they want to accept the file. You can prevent these messages from appearing using the command line utility and switch regedit.exe/s. Because the Registry has access control lists that affect who can access it, the user performing this task must possess sufficient permissions.

Create a Reserve File

You can create a Reserve File for sensitive data files on your Windows Server 2003 Domain Controllers. This protects your information from disk-space attacks and improves the security of your network. A *disk-space attack* is one where an intruder attempts to load a large number of files to a directory, thus exhausting the resources of one or more Domain Controllers in your network infrastructure and making it impossible for the Domain Controllers to provide domain services. This type of attack is similar to a Denial of Service (DoS) attack, where a malicious user floods a server with numerous service requests, thus overwhelming it and causing it to lock up or otherwise stop providing services.

The Reserve File occupies space in the Active Directory database (ntds.dit files). On a Domain Controller, besides deleting the reserve file, you must also delete any unauthorized objects that fill your disk space. Additionally, to help prevent your Domain Controllers from such an attack, you can place them in the most secure location available in your business, keep your DCs up current with the most up to data security updates, and disable all unnecessary services on your DCs.

Create a Reserve File

① Click Start.

② Click Command Prompt.

Command Prompt appears.

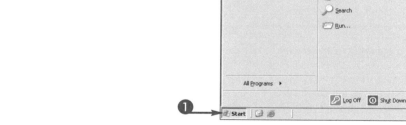

③ Type **fsutil file createnew %systemroot%\ ntds\reservefile 256000000**.

This creates a reserve file 250 Mb in size.

④ Press Enter.

● A message appears verifying that Windows has created the reserve file.

⑤ Click the Close button (☒).

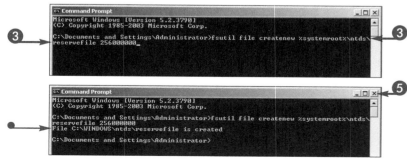

6 Click Start.

7 Click Run.

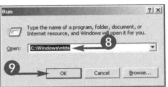

The Run dialog box opens.

8 Type **C:\Windows\ntds**.

9 Click OK.

The Ntds folder opens.

10 Verify that the reserve file is 250000 kb or 250 mb in size.

11 Click the Close button (⊠).

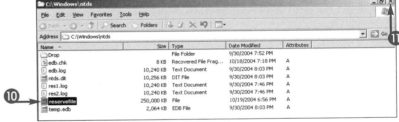

Is creating a Reserve File the only defense against a disk-space attack on a Domain Controller?

▼ No. If you are an administrator, you can also assign Object Ownership Quotas on your Windows Server 2003 Domain Controller. This limits the number of objects that users can create in a particular directory, thus preventing them from adding too many objects. However, this defense is limited because it does not specify the size of each particular object that a user may add. For example, even if users only add a few objects, if these objects are very large in size, then they can still consume all of the available space in a directory.

If an intruder adds objects to a directory, and the objects consume all of the disk space in the directory, then how does occupying space with a Reserve File save space?

▼ You may not be able to immediately delete all of the objects from the Active Directory that an intruder adds due to tombstoning. However, once you are the victim of a disk-space attack, you can delete the Reserve File and free the amount of space that the unauthorized files consume in your directoy. This also buys you time because you cannot immediately identify which file objects are unauthorized objects in order to delete them.

Enable Monitoring for Anonymous Active Directory Access

You can enable monitoring for Anonymous Active Directory access. This protects your domain from the threat posed by having the decreased security boundaries required to allow pre-Windows 2000 devices and services to access domain resources. By default, your Windows Server 2003 system does not allow explicit access to domain resources to devices or users who have logged on anonymously. However, special pre-Windows 2000-compliant groups require an Anonymous Logon identity for the Read access rights needed to view some Active Directory objects.

Although you must allow Anonymous Active Directory access under these circumstances, you can still monitor which users and devices are using Anonymous access to determine whether they are legitimate. An example of a legitimate client requiring an Anonymous Logon is a Local System on a server running Windows NT in a forest. Another example is a Local System running Windows NT, Windows 2000, or Windows Server 2003 in a domain in a different forest, where the local system has an external trust with your domain. Although you may think of the logon process as one that your users exclusively access on your domain, services and devices must also logon to perform their functions.

Enable Monitoring for Anonymous Active Directory Access

① Click Start.

② Click Run.

   The Run dialog box appears.

③ Type **adsiedit.msc**.

④ Click OK.

   The ADSI Edit window appears.

⑤ Navigate to the domain folder.

⑥ Navigate to the DC=test,DC=local folder.

⑦ Click the CN=System folder.

⑧ Right-click CN=Server.

⑨ Click Properties.

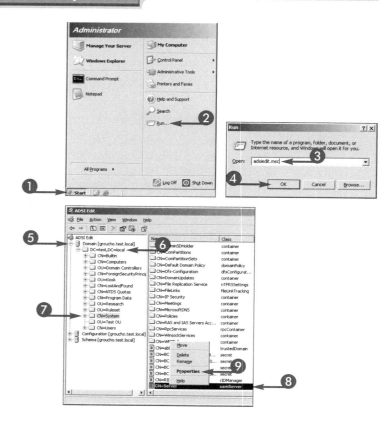

The CN=Server Properties dialog box appears.

⑩ Click the Security tab.

⑪ Click Advanced.

The Advanced Security Settings for the Server dialog box appears.

⑫ Click the Auditing tab.

⑬ Click Add.

The Select User, Computer, or Group dialog box appears.

⑭ Type **anonymous**.

⑮ Click OK.

The Auditing Entry for Server dialog box appears.

⑯ Under the Successful column, click the Read All Properties option (☐ changes to ☑).

⑰ Under the Successful column, click the Enumerate Entire SAM Domain option (☐ changes to ☑).

⑱ Click OK.

Successful Entries are added to Anonymous Logon.

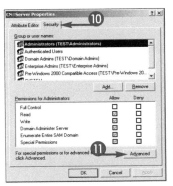

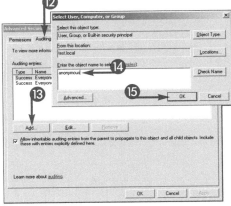

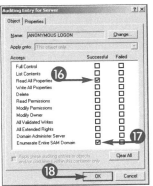

Is the adsiedit.msc utility a standard part of my Windows Server 2003 support tools?

▼ No. To add this utility, insert your Windows Server 2003 installation CD-ROM into your server CD-ROM or DVD drive. If the Welcome to Microsoft Windows Server 2003 splash page appears, click Exit. Click Start and then click My Computer. Right-click CD Drive, and then click Explore. Open the Support folder, and then open the Tools folder. When you double-click SUPTOOLS.MSI, the Windows Support Tools Setup Wizard appears. Click Next and follow the instructions to install the Windows Support Tools package. You can then use the Adsi editor.

Now that I have enabled Anonymous Active Directory access monitoring, how do I collect monitoring data?

▼ You must first collect data for a minimum of 30 days. Afterwards you can aggregate all of the relevant event logs from all of your Domain Controllers into a single database, such as Access or SQL. You can then query the database to locate and identify any log entries marked Event ID=565 (directory service access events), with the text "anonymous" included in the log entry. You can access the logon and logoff events associated with these entries by querying the database to locate Event ID=528 (logon events) or Event ID=540 (logoff events).

PART V

Rename the Default Administrator Account

You can rename the default Administrator account to protect the account from attack and compromise. This prevents an intruder from gaining administrative access to a standalone server or Domain Controller on your network. The most frequently attacked type of account on your network is the Administrator account. If an intruder gains access to this account, then your network becomes extremely vulnerable to attacks. In fact, an intruder with administrative privileges can monitor network activities, copy data out of the system, and insert false information while remaining undetected for weeks or months.

You must also change the default description of the account so that an intruder cannot discover the inconsistency between the account name and how it is described. You can give the Administrator account any name, including Guest or a fictional username. When you do this, the intruder believes that the account has no special privileges worth attacking. Renaming the Administrator account is one of the easiest methods you can use to protect your domain, and it is also one of the most frequently overlooked methods. For this method to work, you should limit the number of people who know the true name of the Administrator account.

Rename the Default Administrator Account

① Click Start.

② Click Administrative Tools.

③ Click Active Directory Users and Computers.

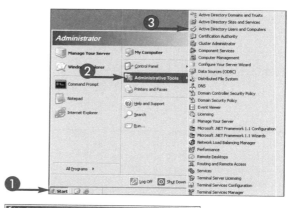

The Active Directory Users and Computers snap-in window appears.

④ Expand the domain.

⑤ Click Users.

⑥ Right-click Administrator.

⑦ Click Rename.

⑧ Type a fake name.

⑨ Double-click the newly renamed administrative account.

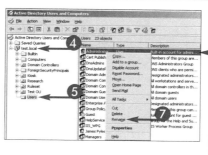

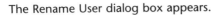
The Rename User dialog box appears.

🔟 Type a fake full name.

⓫ Type a fake first name.

⓬ Type a fake last name.

⓭ Type a user logon name.

The domain name autofills.

⓮ Click OK.

⓯ Right-click the account.

⓰ Click Properties.

The Properties dialog box appears for the user you selected.

⓱ Remove any text from the Description field.

⓲ Click OK.

Default Administrator account is now renamed.

PART V

Does anything else change on the Administrator account when I change the name?

▼ No. You only change the default name and description of the Administrator account with this procedure. No other characteristics, rights, or privileges are changed when you change the name. For example, you do not affect your ability to use this account to boot into Directory Services Restore mode on the local server. This action changes only the local Administrator account name on this particular server or Domain Controller. It does not change all of the Administrator account names for domain administrators on any other Domain Controller. If you change the account name back to Administrator, the account description automatically changes back, as well.

Is there any way that I can rename the Domain Administrator account on my Domain Controllers?

▼ Yes. You can rename the Domain Administrator account using the GPO Editor. In the Active Directory Users and Computers snap-in, open the GPO that links to the domain. Under Computer Configuration, navigate to the Local Policies folder, which is under the Windows Settings and the Security Settings folders. Click Security Options folder and then double-click Accounts: Rename administrator account. The Accounts: Rename administrator account Properties dialog box appears. Click the "Define this policy setting" option (☐ changes to ☑), type the name that you want to give the Domain Administrator account, and then click OK to apply.

Create a Decoy Administrator Account

I f you change your local Administrator account name to one that does not attract the attention of an intruder, that intruder may likely suspect what you have done when they cannot find an account named "administrator". To avoid this problem, you can divert suspicion by creating a decoy account named administrator, which has only domain user rights. This decoy account can also serve to lure intruders into attacking an "administrator" account that does not actually have special privileges. You can then detect and prevent malicious users from invading your domain infrastructure.

You can monitor the decoy account for attack events and, if you detect one, you may be able to locate the source of the attack and take steps to identify and have law enforcement arrest the attacker. Once you rename the true administrator account and create a decoy administrator account, you must reveal these changes only to staff that must access the true administrator account in order to preserve the secrecy of these account name changes. When you create such account name changes, you fulfill your obligation to protect your system and prevent malicious hacking of your network.

Create a Decoy Administrator Account

① Click Start.

② Click Administrative Tools.

③ Click Active Directory Users and Computers.

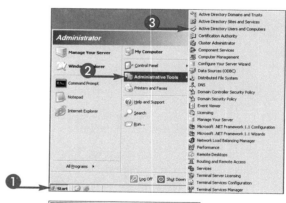

The Active Directory Users and Computers snap-in window appears.

④ Right-click the Users folder.

⑤ Click New.

⑥ Click User.

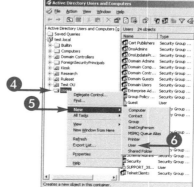

The New Object – User dialog box appears.

⑦ Type **administrator** in the First name field.

⑧ Type **administrator** in the User logon name field.

⑨ Click Next.

The Password page appears.

⑩ Type a password.

⑪ Retype the password.

⑫ Click Password never expires (☐ changes to ☑).

⑬ Click Next.

The User Account summary page appears.

⑭ Click Finish.

The decoy account is created.

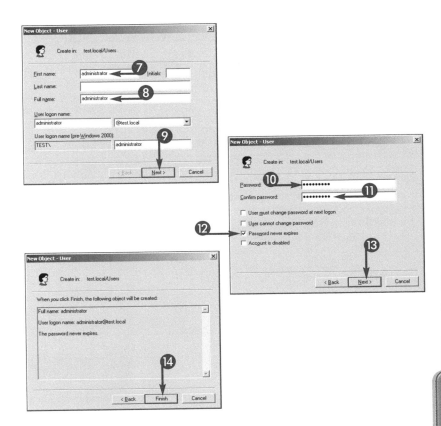

If I name an account the Administrator account, why does Windows not recognize it as the Administrator account?

▼ When you create a decoy Administrator account, you are actually adding an ordinary user account to the Users folder of your server. Although the account has the name "administrator", in this case, the name has no more meaning than "John Smith." The server treats the name "administrator" as if it were just another first name. The attributes that give the true Administrator account special privileges are not associated with that name. The privileges and access rights are actually associated with the type of group to which the account belongs, and not the actual account.

How does creating a decoy Administrator account for the express purpose of luring intruders violate ethical principles?

▼ If you attempt to deliberately lure a person into attacking some part of your network, and that action results in the person's arrest and conviction, one interpretation of your action is that you entraped the intruder. *Entrapment* is an attempt on the part of one party to attract another party to commit a crime that they may not otherwise commit. However many system administrators agree that they are actually under a ethical obligation to protect their systems by whatever means necessary. Also, a private citizen or private company is less likely to be accused of entrapment than a government or law enforcement agency.

Deny Logon Access to the Domain

You can configure Deny Logon Access to the domain for the various administrative accounts. This limits the number of computers and servers from which users with administrative privileges can logon to the domain, and thus the likelihood that they would logon at a remote location for unauthorized purposes. By default, anyone with sufficient administrative privileges can log on to the domain from any computer or server that is located in the domain. If someone with admin rights wants to commit unethical or illegal acts in the network, he or she is more likely to log on to the domain from a remote location

where detection is limited. To prevent illegal acts, you can restrict the ability of admins to log on to the domain from only highly visible places.

When you configure this option, you affect several built-in accounts, including the Enterprise Admins, the Domain Admins, Server Operators, Backup Operators, and Account Operators groups at the domain level. To do this, you create a list that includes the particular IDs you want to add. When you enable this method, you may also prevent any Administrative group from logging on to local workstations and servers, as well as the rest of the domain.

Deny Logon Access to the Domain

1 Click Start.

2 Click Administrative Tools.

3 Click Active Directory Users and Computers.

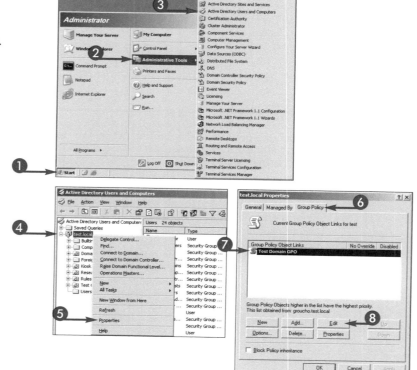

The Active Directory Users and Computers snap-in window appears.

4 Right-click the domain.

5 Click Properties.

The Properties dialog box appears for the domain you selected.

6 Click the Group Policy tab.

7 Click the GPO.

8 Click Edit.

The Group Policy Object Editor appears.

9 Under Computer Configuration, expand Windows Settings.

10 Expand Security Settings.

11 Expand Local Policies.

12 Click User Rights Assignment.

13 Double-click Deny log on locally.

The Deny log on locally Properties dialog box appears.

14 Click Define these policy settings (☐ changes to ☑).

15 Click Add User or Group.

The Add User or Group dialog box appears.

16 Type **administrator**.

17 Click OK.

● The Administrator account is added.

18 Click OK.

Administrator account is now denied the ability to logon from anywhere in the domain.

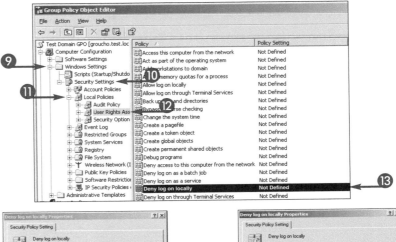
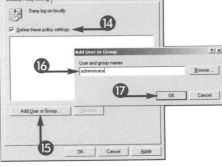
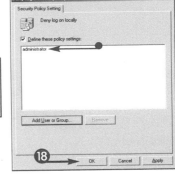

When would I want administrators to be able to log on to local servers?

▼ You want to prevent Administrative accounts to log onto the domain at a workstation, but let them log onto the same machine locally. To do this, you must open the Active Directory Users and Computers snap-in and access the Admin Workstations OU. If the OU does not exist, you can create it by right-clicking the domain, clicking New, and then clicking Organizational Unit. Create an OU named Admin Workstations. Make sure to move the admin workstations to the OU. Right-click this OU and then click Properties. In the OU Properties box, click the Group Policy tab, and then click New. Under the Computer Configuration folder in the Local Policies folder, open "Allow Logon Locally" and apply the Group Policy.

What if the Deny Log on Locally Group Policy item is already configured, and domain users and groups are in the list?

▼ You may inherit from a previous administrator, a set of configurations on your domain and your Domain Controllers and Servers. If you encounter this situation, examine which user and group names are in the list in the Deny log on locally Properties dialog box to determine whether these users and groups are currently in use on the network. The list may include names of accounts that are no longer valid in the domain because they were not removed by the previous administrator. If this is the case, immediately remove the names from that list and deselect the "Define these policy settings" option (☐ changes to ☑).

Install Certificate Services

You can install Certificate Services onto your Domain Controller to allow users to authenticate onto the domain with smart cards. This improves security by providing a method of authentication other than a username and password. For example, a malicious individual may compromise a username and password to gain access to the domain and thus to whatever privileges the compromised user account possesses. Smart card authentication requires the use of both an electronic smart card and a PIN number. If the user loses the card, then others cannot use it if they do not have the appropriate PIN number.

You can use the Certificate Services snap-in to generate and issue certificates on the domain. This allows a smart card enrollment station to issue certificates to smart card users. The certificates verify the smart card users' identity when they use the card to logon to the domain.

Besides a Certificate Services snap-in, you need the required hardware, cards, readers, and an enabled Public Key Infrastructure (PKI) in order to implement smart card authentication on your network.

Install Certificate Services

① Click Start.

② Click Control Panel.

③ Click Add or Remove Programs.

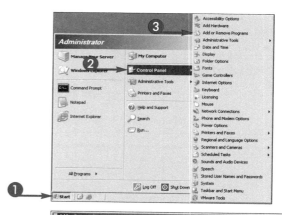

The Add or Remove Programs window appears.

④ Click Add/Remove Windows Components.

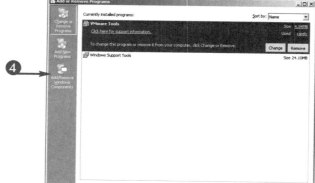

The Windows Components Wizard appears and displays the Windows Components page.

⑤ Click Certificate Services.

The Microsoft Certificate Services warning dialog box appears.

⑥ Click Yes.

The Microsoft Certificate Services warning dialog box closes.

⑦ Click Next.

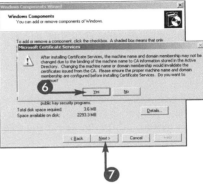

The CA Type page appears.

⑧ Click the type of CA you want (☐ changes to ⦿).

⑨ Click Next.

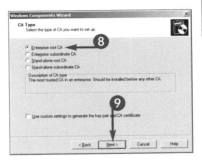

Why can I not change the name of my Windows Server 2003 server or the domain membership of the server after I install Certificate Services?

▼ When you make your server a Certificate Authority (CA), it issues certificates that act as a guarantee between the public key and that identify information of the subject requesting the certificate. You must make the identity of the Certificate Authority Server absolutely clear. This ensures that the certificates that it issues are considered a valid proof of the certificate holder's identity. If the credentials of the server change, for example, the name or domain to which it belongs, then the certificates provided after the change are not considered acceptable.

What are the differences between Enterprise Root and Enterprise Subordinate CA, and Standalone Root and Subordinate CA?

▼ A Root Certificate Authority server is authoritative for the realm in which it operates. If the server is an Enterprise Root CA, then the server is the primary CA server for a domain. An Enterprise Subordinate CA server requests certificates from the Root CA server and operates in different segments of the company infrastructure. A Standalone Root CA server is similar to an Enterprise Root except that it has authority over a different realm or area of authority, for example, a workgroup but not a domain. A Standalone Subordinate CA server requests certificates from the Standalone Root and operates in different areas of the workgroup network.

continued

Install Certificate
Services *(Continued)*

Y ou can use certificates as digital signatures on
documents and other objects that require a
guarantee as to the identity of the sender. This
ensures secure authentication between client and server
computers in your domain. You can also use certificates
issued by commercial Certificate Authorities (CAs), such as
VeriSign. However, Microsoft has certificate services that
allow you to control the CA process within your
infrastructure, thus allowing for greater security and more
control over certificate issuance.

You can use only CA services for authentication on the
network. However, if you want to use an SSL connection to
send encrypted information over the Internet, you must

also install IIS services for only on servers. An SSL-
enabled Web server can process two different types of
authentication: users sending secure information, such
as a credit card number; and users requesting secure
information, such as a bank statement.

You can associate a certificate with the domain on which it
is issued. This means that every time a user logs on with
this type of certificate, the username and user domain are
both authenticated on the Web Server at the same time.
This allows you to avoid using other forms of
authentication.

Install Certificate Services *(continued)*

The CA Identifying Information page appears.

(10) Type a common name for the CA.

(11) Click Next.

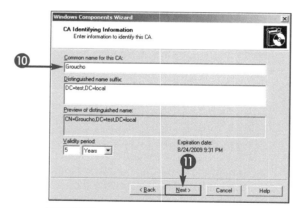

The Certificate Database Settings page
appears.

(12) Click Next.

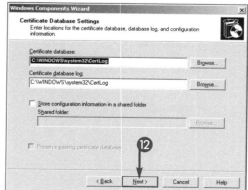

The Configuring Components page appears.

The Insert Disk dialog box appears.

⑬ Insert the Windows Server 2003 installation CD-ROM into your CD-ROM drive.

⑭ Click OK.

The Internet Information Services (IIS) warning dialog box appears.

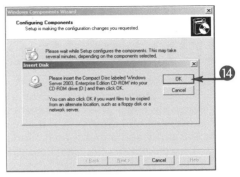

⑮ Click OK.

The Completing the Windows Components page appears.

⑯ Click Finish.

The Certificate Services are installed.

When I type the Common Name for the CA, do I always have to use the name of the server?

▼ No. You typically use whatever name identifies the CA and the role that it plays on the domain. Although you commonly use the server name, you can use any name that you want; the CA is able to perform regardless. You may want to use a common name, such as "SmartCard," so that the CA is identified by function. Keep in mind that once you select a name for the CA, you can never change it. In the steps in this section, the Common Name (CN) is linked to the Distinguished Name of the domain, in this case DC=test,DC=local.

Once I install Certificate Services, can I immediately begin issuing certificates?

▼ No. After you make your domain controller a CA, you must go into Certificate Services and configure requesting certificates from the server. Click Start, then click Administrative Tools, and then click Certificate Authority. When the CA snap-in appears, navigate to the CA name and right-click Certificate Templates. Choose New Certificate Template to Issue, select Enrollment Agent, and scroll down to select either Smartcard Logon or Smartcard User in the list. Click OK. There are also a number of certificate templates that are installed by default.

Lock Down Your Server with Trust-No-Exe

Y ou can install the Trust-No-Exe utility to prevent users on your domain from opening potentially hazardous e-mail attachments that could release harmful viruses and other malicious software into your network. This utility also prevents users from running port scanners or executing software from floppy diskette drives and CD-ROM or DVD drives on their work computers. This reduces the risk of virus contamination or the introduction of software onto the network that conflicts with applications that you support.

Although you can set NTFS permissions on your hard drive volumes to prevent executable software from running, you

cannot prevent users from running applications on drives that you cannot format with NTFS, such as CD-ROM and DVD drives. You can configure the Trust-No-Exe tool to prevent the use of some or all ancillary drives on user computers.

Trust-No-Exe is an executable file filter that you can attach to the operating system and that filters executable files that have extensions such as .exe, .com, .dll, .drv, and .sys. Although Microsoft does not provide this type of tool, you can download it for free from Beyond Logic at: www.beyondlogic.org/solutions/trust-no-exe/trust-no-exe.htm. You can save it to any location on your server including the desktop.

Lock Down Your Server with Trust-No-Exe

① Double-click the trustnoexev304 shortcut.

The Trustnoexev304 folder appears.

② Double-click Install.exe.

The Trust-No-Exe Install wizard appears.

③ Click Next.

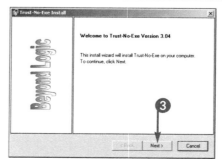

A License Agreement page appears.

④ Click Yes.

The Trust-No-Exe Installation Complete page appears.

⑤ Click Finish.

Trust-No-Exe is installed.

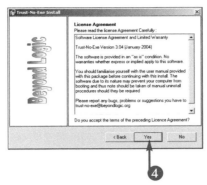

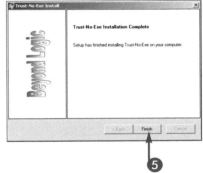

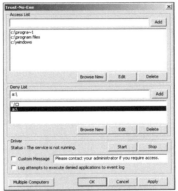

How can I use Trust-No-Exe to control which drives can and cannot be used on my domain?

▼ Open the Trust-No-Exe applet in the Control Panel by clicking Start, and then clicking Control Panel. Double-click the Trust-No-Exe applet to open the utility. You can use two lists in the utility, the Access and the Deny Lists. Programs on the C:\ drive, such as Windows, Progra~1, and Program Files, are automatically added to the Access List. You must add any drives to either the Access or Deny List by clicking the Browse New button. Then browse to the location of the drive or other object and double-click the object to select it. Click the Add button in the Trust-No-Exe utility to add the objects to the Access or Deny List.

How can I install Trust-no-Exe on multiple workstations at the same time?

▼ You can either install the utility on one workstation and use a utility like Norton Ghost to create an image to install on other workstations, or you can use the Trust-No-Exe multiple workstation feature. Open the Trust-No-Exe applet in Control Panel and click Multiple Computers. Browse the network and select the computers on which you want to install Trust-No-Exe. Click Apply Settings. Trust-No-Exe connects to each selected computer, and installs the utility automatically. You must configure the utility for the exact Accept and Deny lists that you want distributed before you install the utility on the workstations. You can also use GPO software distribution to distribute this tool. See Chapter 14 for more on deploying a software package.

Understanding Internet Connections 330

Set Up an Internet Connection..................332

Set Up a Demand-Dial Internet
    Connection 334

Set Up Routing and Remote Services
    for NAT..338

Understanding Remote Connections..........342

Set Up VPN Services 344

Set Up VPN Client...................................348

Enable Terminal Services for
    Remote Desktop 352

Enable Remote Assistance 354

Install Terminal Services with
    Configure Your Server Wizard 356

Install Terminal Services License Server......358

Manage Terminal Services Users 360

Install IPv6 Protocol 362

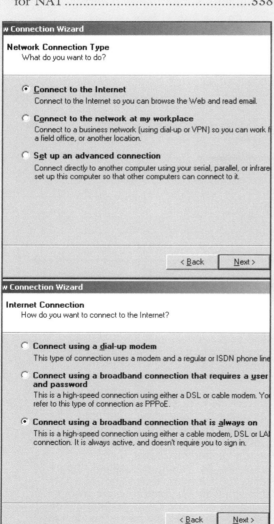

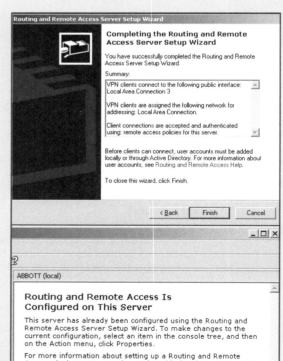

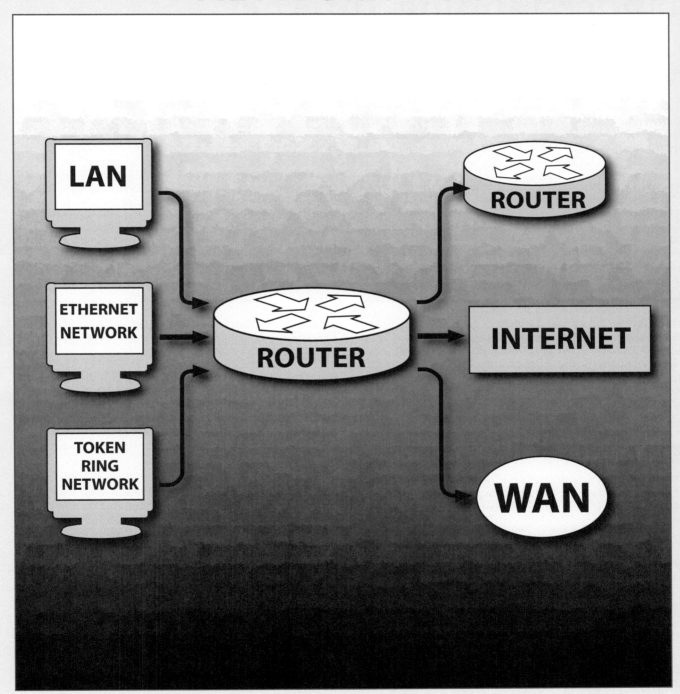

Understanding Internet Connections

You can configure your Windows Server 2003 servers and your network to connect to the Internet. This allows users to conduct eCommerce for your company, to send and receive e-mails, to download security patches for your computer systems, to do research, and to conduct a wide variety of other business-related activities.

However, you must consider many other factors when you connect a business LAN to the Internet. Connecting a server system, a network, and a domain to the Internet is far more complicated than configuring an Internet connection for a home computer or a small office network. Besides the much larger scale that you are managing, you must consider the other types of network devices that participate in connecting your network to the Internet, such as routers, switches, and hubs. You must also consider the greater security needs of a business domain, such as firewalls and intrusion detection devices.

Another concept to understand is Virtual Private Network (VPN). This a method of creating a virtual point-to-point connection over a public communication systems, such as the Internet, using encryption protocols to create a "tunnel." This tunnel allows remote users to connect to their home network as if they were connected on the LAN. Point-to-Point Protocol over Ethernet (PPPoE) is a protocol that allows a user on a LAN to simulate a dial-up session and connect to the Internet using a broadband connection. Point-to-Point Tunneling Protocol (PPTP) is similar to VPN, developed by Microsoft, which supports a wider variety of encryption protocols.

Security

One of the critical security factors that you must consider is how to configure a firewall or router that provides network traffic filtering to protect your LAN. You can configure Application Filtering to determine which type of application traffic you want to allow on and off the network. Datagram or Packet Filtering allows only packet traffic onto the network from reliable sources. Protocol Filtering can allow only certain types of network protocols to access the network, based on which ports you keep open and which you close.

You can prevent network users from sending certain types of traffic to the Internet, thus protecting valuable data. You can also configure your Internet connection so that it is only active during certain hours. Additionally, you can install certain commercial software packages to filter Web sites, allowing users to access some Web sites while blocking others.

Reliability

You can provide reliability for your network and Internet connection by using additional or redundant devices and connection links to your business network. One critical connection to which you can add redundancy is your network gateway to the Internet. However, you may find reliability and security at odds here.

To ensure that your network can still connect to the Internet even when your primary gateway goes down, you can add a secondary gateway to ensure that there is no interruption of service. However, this redundant gateway may also be a security threat if both gateways are active at the same time. This is because an intruder may use the backup gateway to access the LAN.

You can configure your redundant gateway connection to remain down until you are notified that the primary gateway connection is not active. Then you can bring the secondary connection up, but only as long as the primary gateway is inactive. Once the primary Internet connection comes up again, you can take down the secondary link, to ensure that there is only one way in and out of your network at any point in time.

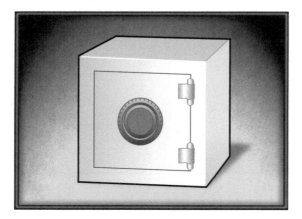

Domain Name Service

You can configure several Domain Name Service, or DNS, servers on your network to add fault tolerance to name resolution services on your network. You can allow the DNS servers that belong to your ISP to provide all name resolution services for your traffic that is destined for the Internet. However, you can also provide more reliability to your resolution services by configuring your in-domain DNS server to communicate with the DNS servers of your ISP and the Internet root DNS servers.

You can also provide redundant DNS servers in a single site or domain to take over, should your primary DNS server fail. Additionally, you can install DNS servers at each physical location within your domain so that a local office does not have to request name resolution services across a slow WAN link to an off-site DNS server.

Network Address Translation

You can configure Network Address Translation, or NAT, services to provide additional security for your internal network. NAT prevents anyone on the Internet from "seeing" the namespace of your internal LAN and allows them only to see one public interface. NAT is used both on Routing and Remote Access Services (RRAS) servers and when you configure Internet connections using Internet Connection Sharing (ICS). *RRAS* is a service that lets users make network connections over a modem, ISDN connection, or null-modem.

When a user on your network requests a connection with a particular node on the Internet, the network traffic containing the user hostname is translated to a public name by a device at your network gateway, such as a RRAS server, an ISA server, or even a router. An *Internet Security and Acceleration* (ISA) server provides application-layer firewall, VPN and web caching. The traffic on the Internet using the public name reaches the destination and is processed, and any response is returned to the public name and IP address. Once the traffic reaches the network gateway and the NAT device, the IP and hostname converts to the IP address possessed by the internal user who made the request, and traffic is forwarded to that user.

Internet Connection Sharing

You can set up a single server to connect to the Internet and then share that one connection to many different nodes on your network; this provides a single point of entry and exit, and thus protects your internal LAN. You can configure Internet Connection Sharing, or ICS, mainly for smaller business networks using Windows Server 2003. Larger, enterprise-level networks use a primary gateway router and firewall device to manage their greater traffic needs. ICS only allows the Internet to view the IP address of the server WAN interface, and protects the address space of all the other nodes inside the LAN.

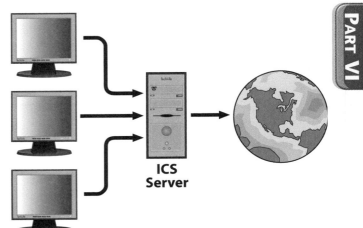

ICS Server

192.168.0.2 NAT 65.37.2.200

Set Up an Internet Connection

Y ou can configure your Windows Server 2003 server to connect to the Internet. This allows the server to download critical security patches for its protection, to receive Virtual Private Network (VPN) connections from users traveling on business or working from home, and to provide eCommerce services, such as connecting to customer and supplier networks. You can use a connection wizard to set up the Internet connection for your server as easily as if you were setting up an Internet connection for a small business or even a home computer.

You can activate your Windows Server 2003 with Microsoft using an Internet connection. Once activated, you can

receive support services from Microsoft. You may also register your server with Microsoft over the Internet at the same time that you activate it.

Windows Server 2003 services can fully integrate with the Internet. Your server system no longer needs to use NetBIOS or NetBEUI for network functioning, and all network services are TCP/IP compliant. Windows Server 2003 also uses .NET services to provide authentication to Web sites and allows your network to interact seamlessly with Web-based services and applications on the Internet.

Set Up an Internet Connection

① Click Start.

② Click Control Panel.

③ Click Network Connections.

④ Click New Connection Wizard.

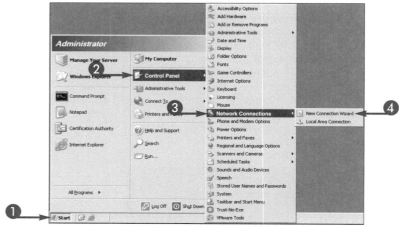

The New Connection Wizard appears.

⑤ Click Next.

The Network Connection Type page appears.

6 Click Connect to the Internet (☐ changes to ☑).

7 Click Next.

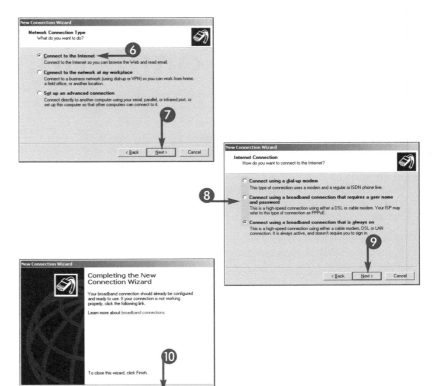

The Internet Connection page appears.

8 Click the type of connection you want to use (☐ changes to ☑).

9 Click Next.

The Completing the New Connection page appears.

10 Click Finish.

Your Internet Connection activates.

What are the different types of Internet connections that I can configure on my server?

▼ The most common type of connection is an always-on broadband connection, which provides Internet access on a continual basis to the network. A broadband connection requires you to authenticate with your ISP each time you want to establish a connection. Although a broadband connection is not common, you can use it for added security. A dial-up modem connection also connects your server to the Internet, and can act as a fallback connection in case your main, high-speed DSL or cable connection fails.

What if I cannot connect to the Internet after I configure a high-speed Internet connection?

▼ You can troubleshoot your Internet connection problem by first checking the status light on your DSL or cable modem to ensure that the connection provided by your ISP is actually working. Then cycle the power to the broadband modem by powering down then powering up the device. If your connection is still not active, then call your ISP to verify that there is no interruption of service at their end. Next, in the Network Connections page, right-click the LAN or High-Speed Internet icon and select Repair from the pop-up menu to allow Windows Help and Support services to attempt to repair the problem.

Set Up a Demand-Dial Internet Connection

You can create and configure a Demand-dial connection on your Windows Server 2003 device to ensure a continued Internet connection for your network in the event that your primary Internet connection fails. You can even configure your server to act as a router on your network and connect to other routers on the Internet or on a dedicated WAN connection. This enables your business site to communicate with other offices and to continue business transactions in the event of a connection failure.

You can also ensure that the Domain Controllers on your Web site receive replication data from other locations in

your domain when your primary WAN connection is down. A slow dial-up link is not the preferred replication conduit, but it is only meant as a backup until you can bring up your main link.

You can configure one of two types of Demand-dial connections, on-demand connections and persistent connections. An on-demand connection only comes up when it is needed and is the preferred connection for both financial and security reasons. You can also configure a persistent or always-up link over a dial-up connection. In addition, you can configure dial-up links as either one-way or two-way.

Set Up a Demand-Dial Internet Connection

① Click Start.

② Click Administrative Tools.

③ Click Routing and Remote Access.

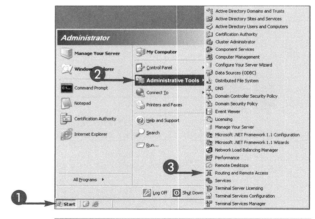

The Routing and Remote Access snap-in window appears.

④ Expand the local server.

⑤ Right-click Network Interfaces.

⑥ Click New Demand-dial Interface.

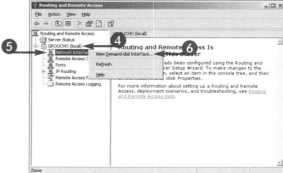

The Demand-Dial Interface Wizard appears.

7 Click Next.

The Interface Name page appears.

8 Type a name for the interface.

9 Click Next.

The Protocols and Security page appears.

10 Click the desired options for the connection (☐ changes to ☑).

11 Click Next.

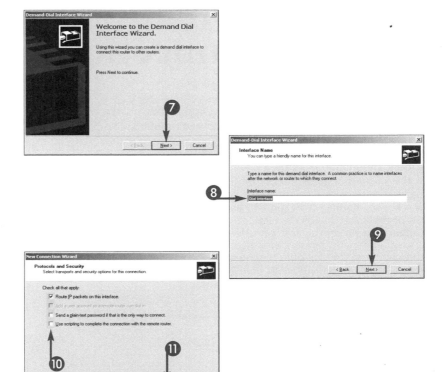

Do I need to configure any special services before setting up a Demand-dial interface?

▼ Yes. You must ensure that Routing and Remote Access Services (RRAS) are started on your server. You configure RRAS via the Routing and Remote Access snap-in, by right-clicking the server, and then clicking "Configure and Enable Routing and Remote Access" on the menu. The Routing and Remote Access Server Setup Wizard guides you through the necessary steps to start RRAS services. Once services are running, right-click the server and click Properties. In the Properties dialog box, click the Router option (☐ changes to ☑) and then click the LAN and demand-dial routing option (☐ changes to ☑). You can now enable a Demand-dial interface on your server.

What else can I configure in the server Properties dialog box?

▼ You can configure Security, IP, PPP, and Logging for your RRAS server. In the General tab of the Properties dialog box, select the role of Router, Remote Access Server, or both by clicking the appropriate option (☐ changes to ☑). You can also choose between the LAN routing only, and the LAN and Demand-dial routing option (☐ changes to ☑). In the Security tab, you can select both the Authentication provider and the Accounting provider, and choose between Windows and RADIUS in the appropriate menus. In the IP tab, you can enable IP routing and enable IP-based remote access (☐ changes to ☑). You can also choose between DHCP and a static IP address pool (☐ changes to ☑). In the PPP tab, you can configure the PPP options, including Multilink and Software compression (☐ changes to ☑).

PART VI

continued

Set Up a Demand-Dial Internet Connection *(Continued)*

You can continue to configure a Demand-dial Internet connection by configuring a static IP address for the destination router to ensure that the network interface only accesses the destination-routing device needed to make the desired connection. Demand-dial connections are most often used to connect to a specific destination through a WAN link, rather than to access the Internet in general. Because the bandwidth is limited, you can create a link that only connects to another location in your domain. You can also configure the metric, or cost, of the link. Usually, the higher the cost of the connection, the slower the link is to the destination.

You can configure the dial-out credentials of the link so that the RRAS server has sufficient permissions to initiate a dial-up connection when it is notified that the primary connection is down. You can only configure a Demand-dial connection if you have Administrator permissions, thus preventing an unscrupulous person from creating a link in order to access your network from the outside. Once you create the new link, it is added to the default links that are already present on your server.

To perform the steps in this section, you need a *metric*, which is a numerical value that defines the reliability of a remote link. The lower the value, the more reliable the link. You also must acquire the destination IP address and Network Mask from the administrator at the destination location.

Set Up a Demand-Dial Internet Connection *(continued)*

The Static Routes for Remote Networks page appears.

⑫ Click Add.

The Static Route dialog box appears.

⑬ Type a destination for your IP address.

⑭ Type a value for a Network Mask of destination.

⑮ Type a metric.

⑯ Click OK.

⑰ Click Next.

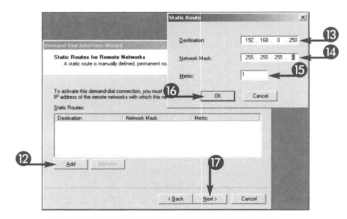

The Dial Out Credentials page appears.

⑱ Type your username.

⑲ Type a domain.

⑳ Type a password.

㉑ Retype the password.

㉒ Click Next.

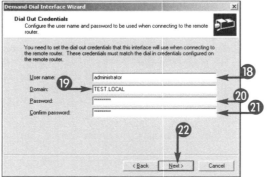

The Completing the Demand-Dial Interface page appears.

㉓ Click Finish.

The Demand-dial interface is applied.

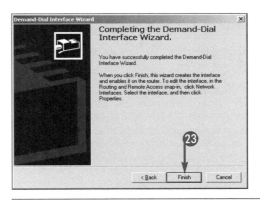

The new interface appears in the Routing and Remote Access snap-in window.

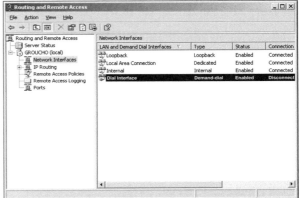

Once I create the Demand-dial interface, how can I access it and configure it?

▼ You can open the Routing and Remote Access snap-in in the Administrative Tools menu, navigate to the server, and select Network Interfaces. Right-click the interface in the main display pane and select Properties. The Dial Interface Properties dialog box appears. In the General tab, you can only add an optional service name. In the Options tab, you can configure the connection as either a Demand-dial connection or a persistent connection. In the Security tab, you can select Typical security options to require a secured password or to allow an unsecured password, and to require data encryption. The Networking tab controls IP addressing.

What other configuration options are available for the Demand-dial interface?

▼ You can right-click the new Interface in the Routing and Remote Access snap-in and select Set IP Demand-dial Filters in the menu list. When the Set Demand-dial Filters dialog box appears, click Add. When the Add IP Filter dialog box appears, you can select a Source IP address and Subnet mask, a Destination IP address and Subnet Mask, and either TCP, TCP (established), UDP, ICMP, Any, or Other protocols to filter. This enables you to choose which networks and particular protocols you allow onto your network through the interface. You can also right-click the interface and select Dial-out hours to specify the hours that you want the interface to be active.

Set Up Routing and Remote Services for NAT

You can designate a server on your network as a dedicated Internet Connection server. You can then configure Network Address Translation (NAT) services on that server to protect your internal LAN by presenting only a single IP address and one network name to the Internet, thus improving network security.

You can install the specific hardware in or on your server, depending on the type of connection you set up. You can install either a dial-up modem or an ISDN adapter in your computer. Alternatively, you can ensure that you have a Network Interface Card and patch cable, which connects to a broadband modem to establish an Internet connection.

Your Windows Server 2003 Internet Connection server works as a gateway for the rest of your network, and you can configure all of the user computers to point to this server as the default gateway. You can either set up each computer manually, or configure DHCP services to hand out an IP address, subnet mask, and gateway assignment automatically. You can set up your LAN IP addressing scheme to use non-routable addresses that cannot be sent out onto the Internet. Only the external interface of your server or broadband modem needs a routable address.

Set Up Routing and Remote Services for NAT

① Click Start.

② Click Administrative Tools.

③ Click Routing and Remote Access.

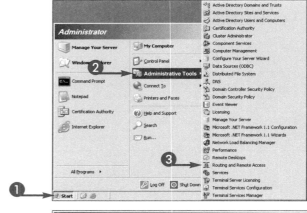

The Routing and Remote Access snap-in window appears.

④ Right-click the server.

⑤ Click Configure and Enable Routing and Remote Access.

The Routing and Remote Access Server Setup Wizard appears.

6 Click Next.

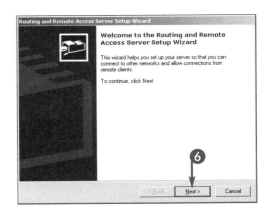

The Configuration page appears.

7 Click Network address translation (NAT) (□ changes to ⊙).

8 Click Next.

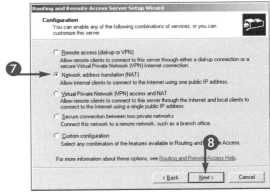

What other options can I configure in the Routing and Remote Access Server Setup Wizard?

▼ In addition to NAT services, you can set up remote access by either dial-up or Virtual Private Network (VPN). You can set up VPN access using NAT, create a secure connection between two networks, or do a custom configuration. You can choose the Custom Configuration option to select multiple services to configure on the RRAS server. You can choose any combination of VPN access, dial-up access, Demand-dial connections used for branch office routing, NAT and basic firewall, and LAN routing. If you use any of the other standard options (□ changes to ⊙) in the wizard, you can only configure RRAS for one type of connection.

What are the differences between some of the different types of connections that I can configure in RRAS?

▼ You can configure remote access for either dial-up or VPN. If you access your network remotely using a dial-up, then your user computers use a modem to dial into your RRAS server inside the business network. Data is sent in plain text, and security is managed by authentication with a RADIUS server. You can configure your RRAS server to act as a router, establishing a secure connection between two private networks inside your domain. When you choose the "Secure connection between two private networks" option (□ changes to ⊙) in the Configuration page of the wizard and click Next, a small wizard runs, and your server takes on the router role directly, connecting the two networks.

PART VI

continued

Set Up Routing and Remote Services for NAT *(Continued)*

Y ou can continue to enable Routing and Remote Services and configure Network Address Translation (NAT) to ensure that the correct network addressing scheme is used, so that the computers inside your LAN are assigned IP addresses. These addresses let them connect to the default gateway so that they can communicate off of their network segment. You can also use the RRAS Server Setup Wizard to set up other security features on your connection, such as Basic Firewall.

The wizard detects the type of interface that your server uses and automatically provides the appropriate options to configure that interface. For example, if your router uses a

dial-up modem, the option to use your LAN card is grayed out on the NAT Internet Connection page of the wizard. You can also choose to configure name and address services in the wizard, or to wait until after the wizard is completed. You can configure the specific subnet or network-segment addressing scheme in the wizard and have addresses assigned to your network nodes from that address pool. In addition, you can end the wizard and configure a static address mapping that is different from the default setting.

Set Up Routing and Remote Services for NAT *(continued)*

The NAT Internet Connection page appears.

9 Ensure that the "Create a new demand-dial interface to the Internet" option is selected (☐ changes to ⦿).

10 Click the "Enable security on the selected interface by setting up Basic Firewall" option (☐ changes to ☑).

11 Click Next.

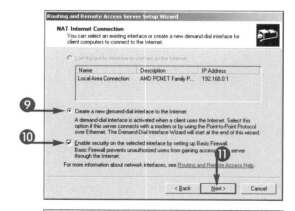

The Name and Address Translation Services page appears.

12 Click Enable basic name and address services (☐ changes to ⦿).

13 Click Next.

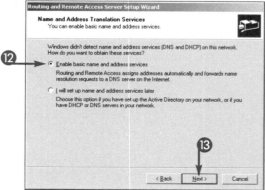

The Address Assignment Range page appears.

⑭ Click Next.

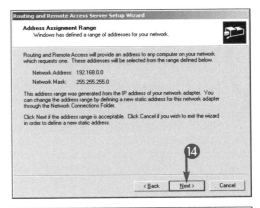

The Ready to Apply Selections page appears.

⑮ Click Next.

The Demand-Dial Wizard starts.

Note: *For more information on this Wizard, see the section "Set Up a Demand-dial Internet Connection."*

The Routing and Remote Services start.

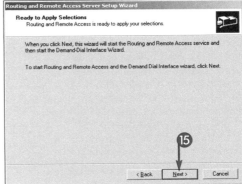

What types of connections does the Demand-dial Wizard configure once RRAS and NAT are configured?

▼ You can choose from a hardware connection, VPN, or PPP over Ethernet (PPPoE). Hardware solutions for creating a Demand-dial connection using NAT include a modem, ISDN adapter, or other physical connection device. VPN involves a logical connection that encrypts data traveling over a public network, such as the Internet or a WAN link. PPPoE is Point-to-Point Protocol over an Ethernet connection that allows you to create a virtual dedicated connection between two routing devices in a LAN environment.

Do I have to configure an interface after I set up RRAS and NAT, or are the services enabled beforehand?

▼ You must continue to set up an interface for the connection; otherwise, both NAT and RRAS services will fail. If you abort the wizard by clicking Cancel, the Cannot Complete page appears, and your only option is to click Finish. At this point, you can proceed only by relaunching the wizard to enable RRAS services and configure NAT. If you choose another option besides NAT, you can activate the service without specifically configuring an interface. In Custom Configuration, choose Dial-up access and click Next; RRAS starts without a specific interface configuration.

Understanding Remote Connections

You can configure and enable Routing and Remote Access Services (RRAS) on your Windows Server 2003 domain. This enables remote network services on all different connection types and media, and allows you to maintain control of all remote communication. Connection types and media include Wide Area Networks (WAN), Local Area Networks (LAN), and Virtual Private Networks (VPN).

When you configure remote connections, you can control the security of those connections so that malicious users cannot capture sensitive data while the data transmits over various networking media. Remote connections consist of LAN-to-LAN links, LAN-to-WAN links, and VPN and Network Address Translation (NAT) routing services.

Routing

You can configure your Windows Server 2003 system to function as a router, rather than having to use a separate, dedicated routing device on your network. A *router* allows traffic from dissimilar networks to transverse boundaries, such as traffic from one subnet to another on a LAN, or traffic from an Ethernet network to a Token Ring network.

All network data traffic is broken up into segments called *packets*, or datagrams. Each packet is tagged with information that identifies its source, destination, and the order in which it needs to be reassembled at the destination. As packets are routed, they may not take the same path to the destination from the source, instead traveling by the best available path at the time the packet traverses a router. Each time a packet goes from one router to the next, this action is called a *hop*.

Routers contain a list of routes called a *routing table* that determines where to send traffic that is tagged for various destinations. A router is designed with various interfaces,

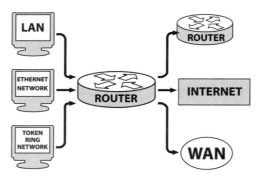

and each interface leads from and to a different next hop router, also referred to as a destination router.

You can equip a Windows Server 2003 routing device with multiple Network Interface Cards (NIC) to serve a similar purpose. A server with multiple NICs is called a *multihomed server*. You can install the number of NIC cards in your server that correspond with the number of different routes that you need to next hop routers. One interface or gateway generally leads to the Internet, while others may lead to dedicated WAN links between different offices of your organization or between different routers that are designated for different network segments in a building or campus.

In addition to source, destination, and segment data, metric information is also necessary. You can assign a metric to a particular route or destination, based on the speed of the link and how many hops are required to send packets from source to destination. A slower link with many hops has a higher metric than a fast link with fewer hops.

Static and Dynamic Routes

You can configure either static or dynamic routes for your network traffic on an interface-by-interface basis, depending on your needs. If there is only one route from a source to a destination, or you need to ensure that all traffic from the source reaches the destination securely, then you can configure a static route.

When you create a *static route*, you are defining a single IP address and subnet mask as the destination, and only one physical connection, such as through a dedicated WAN or LAN link. When you configure a *dynamic route*, you are allowing source data to be sent to multiple destinations using whatever route has the least metric at any given point in time.

Because metrics can change very quickly, a data transmission that is broken up into multiple packets can take many different routes and even arrive out of order. Once the data is at its destination, it is up to the receiving device to reassemble the message in the proper order so that it can be correctly read.

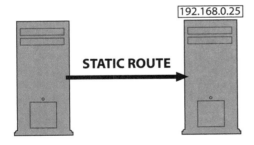

192.168.0.25

STATIC ROUTE

Windows Server 2003 RRAS Features

Both Windows NT and Windows 2000 are equipped with Remote Connection and Routing Services (RRAS) features, including RIPv2 and OSPF routing protocols, PPTP support, Internet Group Management Protocol (IGMP), and L2TP. However, Windows Server 2003 RRAS contains the following important additions; Point-to-Point over Ethernet (PPPoE), Background Intelligent Transfer Service (BITS) version 1.5, and Network Address Translation (NAT) Transversal Using Universal Plug and Play.

Point-to-Point Protocol over Ethernet (PPPoE)

PPPoE is a dial-on-demand feature that you can configure to allow all LAN users on an Ethernet connection to share a link to the Internet using a broadband connection. This feature can use a Demand-dial link and NAT to shield the LAN from Internet scrutiny.

Background Intelligent Transfer Service Version 1.5

Background Intelligent Transfer Service, or BITS, is a file transfer and queue manager that runs as a background service on your Windows Server 2003 device. You can use it to control the speed at which large amounts of data are introduced to the network in order to preserve bandwidth resources. Otherwise, if a large amount of data hits the LAN without regard to either the traffic that is already on the network, or the data transfer capacity of the LAN, then the sudden infusion may bring network throughput to a standstill.

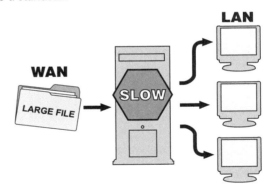

LAN

WAN

LARGE FILE

SLOW

NAT Traversal Using Universal Plug and Play

You can use this technology to allow network applications to detect the use of NAT on your network and to enable them to create a mapped port. This allows network applications to move across, or traverse, the "barrier" between two network layers separated by NAT.

Set Up VPN Services

You can configure Virtual Private Network (VPN) services on your Windows Server 2003 remote server. This allows users traveling on business or working from home to securely connect to the private business LAN over a public Wide Area link, such as the Internet. VPN is an extension of the private business LAN because you can connect from a remote location, such as your home or even from a different city, over the Internet and interact with the LAN as if you were sitting in your office or cubicle.

When you configure your Windows Server 2003 remote server as a VPN server, you are creating a server that

accepts VPN connections from the computers of recognized clients over the Internet. You can also set up your VPN server to accept client-to-server connections and server-to-server connections. You can use VPN tunnels to provide a secure connection over wireless media as well as wired connections.

VPN connections must allow a link across your network security devices and protocols. You can set up VPN so that VPN tunnels can traverse your enterprise-level firewall, as well as NAT services.

Set Up VPN Services

① Click Start.

② Click Administrative Tools.

③ Click Routing and Remote Access.

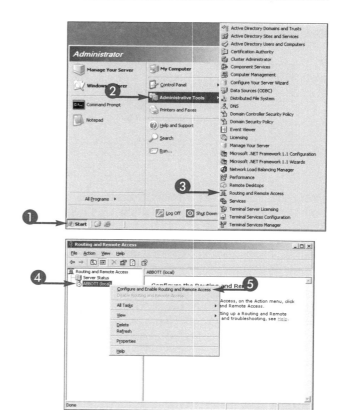

The Routing and Remote Access snap-in window appears.

④ Right-click the server.

⑤ Click Configure and Enable Routing and Remote Access.

The Routing and Remote Access Server Setup Wizard appears.

6 Click Next.

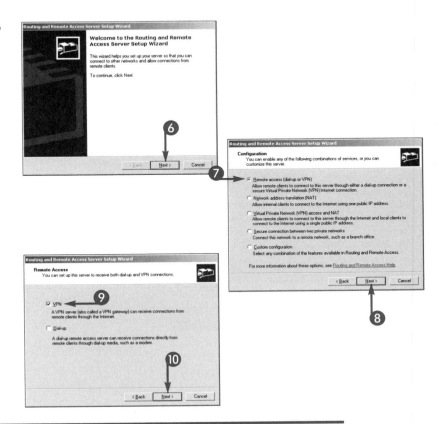

The Configuration page appears.

7 Click Remote access (dial-up or VPN)
(◯ changes to ⦿).

8 Click Next.

The Remote Access page appears.

9 Click the VPN option (☐ changes to ☑).

10 Click Next.

How many VPN connections can my RRAS server accept at one time?

▼ With your Windows Server 2003 Server Web Edition and Standard Edition, you can create up to 1000 Point-to-Point Tunneling (PPTP) or Layer Two Tunneling Protocol (L2TP) connections at one time. Although Web Edition can create 1000 PPTP or L2TP tunnels, it can only support one VPN connection at a time using tunneling. Standard Edition can support 1000 VPN connections using either tunneling protocol. If you use over the maximum number of connections, then you cannot connect to the RRAS server with a new connection. Once the current number of connections is below 1000, your connection attempt is accepted.

What is the difference between PPTP and L2TP tunneling protocols?

▼ Point-to-Point Tunneling Protocol is an extension of Point-to-Point Protocol (PPP) and uses the authentication, compression, and encryption mechanisms first used by PPP. By default, PPTP is installed in your Windows Server 2003 device with TCP/IP. PPTP uses Microsoft Point-to-Point Encryption (MPPE) for encryption. Windows XP has built-in client support for PPTP. Layer Two Tunneling Protocol is based on industry standards and was first used with Windows 2000 clients and servers. L2TP uses IPSec for encryption. Windows XP has built-in support for L2TP, which is also installed with TCP/IP by default.

PART VI

continued

Set Up VPN Services *(Continued)*

Yₒu can continue to configure your RRAS server to act as a VPN server by configuring one network interface to connect to the Internet and another to connect to the business LAN; this allows VPN clients access from the public to the private network through the server. Unlike a dedicated physical router, your server uses one Network Interface Card (NIC) by default. To configure the server as a VPN server, you can install at least one additional NIC so that the server can act as a conduit between the public and private networks. If you want your server to connect to more than one private network, then you must install an additional NIC.

Your VPN clients require IP addresses that use the same network as the private VPN interface of the server. You can dynamically assign IP addresses to VPN clients either by using DHCP services or by configuring a preset range of IP addresses in the RRAS Setup Wizard. Once you configure encryption and authentication, you can enable your VPN server and RRAS services, so that clients can connect to the LAN.

Set Up VPN Services *(continued)*

The VPN Connection page appears.

⑪ Click the interface that is connected to the Internet.

⑫ Click Next.

The IP Address Assignment page appears.

⑬ Click an IP address assignment option (○ changes to ◉).

⑭ Click Next.

The Managing Multiple Remote Access Servers page appears.

⑮ Click an authentication option (○ changes to ◉).

⑯ Click Next.

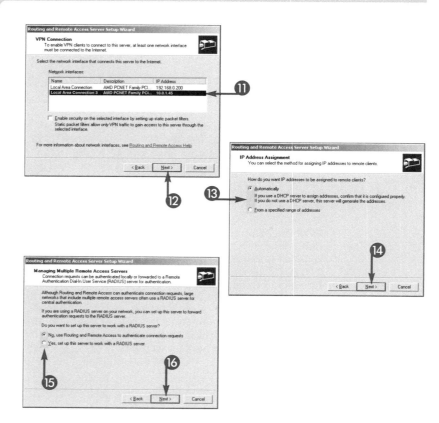

The Completing the Routing and Remote Access Server Setup Wizard page appears.

(17) Click Finish.

The RRAS and VPN services are activated.

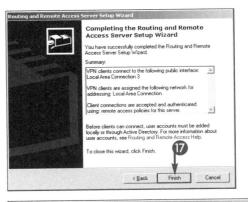

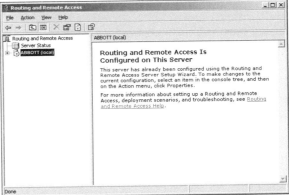

When a VPN client connects over the Internet to the LAN through RRAS, what can they do?

▼ You can allow a remote VPN client to work on the business LAN just as if they were sitting at their desk in the office. The VPN client can access network shares on your file-sharing servers, print documents, access databases such as SQL, and even check their e-mail. The only difference that the clients may experience is a slower network response. The slower response is due to WAN links running at slower data rates than high-speed Ethernet networks.

What protects a VPN server from being broken into by someone who guesses the username and password?

▼ You can configure Remote Access Account Lockout in much the same way that you configure a domain user account to lock out an on-site user account. Intruders often use a *dictionary attack* to "guess" a user password. This involves trying hundreds of possible passwords very quickly with a remotely attached computer. When you enable Remote Access Account Lockout, the user account locks after only a few attempts. Any further authentication attempts are not accepted. You can set the lockout to release after a certain period of time, or require that an Administrator manually unlock the account so that users can use it again.

PART VI

Set Up
VPN Client

You can configure user client computers to have VPN client software enabled so that they can establish a connection with the company VPN server. Doing this allows a client to connect to and work on their business LAN over the Internet.

Any computer that you want to connect to a private network using VPN must have VPN client software installed. You can either use third-party VPN client software or the VPN client software that is native to your Windows user computer. VPN is supported by any of the Windows operating systems from Windows 95 and on.

A client computer must be able to connect to the Internet and to use TCP/IP as its communication protocol. The client can use any type of connection to the Internet, including a dial-up modem or a broadband solution. Computers with Windows NT 4.0, Windows ME, and Windows 98 do not support the use of L2TP unless you install IPSec VPN client software. All of the Windows operating systems after and including Windows 95 support PPTP.

Set Up VPN Client

① Click Start.

② Click Connect To.

③ Click Show all connections.

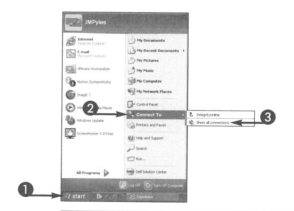

The Network Connections window appears.

④ Click Create a new connection.

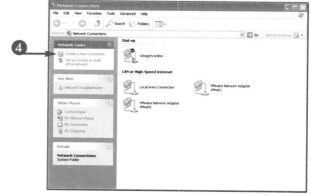

The New Connection Wizard appears.

⑤ Click Next.

The Network Connection Type page appears.

⑥ Click "Connect to the network at my workplace" (⬜ changes to ⦿).

⑦ Click Next.

The Network Connection page appears.

⑧ Click Virtual Private Network connection (⬜ changes to ⦿).

⑨ Click Next.

When I create a VPN connection from my Windows VPN client computer, can I directly connect to my company VPN server?

▼ Yes. You can directly connect to the company VPN server if your VPN client is already connected to the Internet and can directly dial into the VPN server. This requires that you use an always-on Internet connection such as cable or DSL, which allows your computer to connect to the Internet as soon as you power it up. However, if you use a dial-up service, then you must first connect to the Internet Service Provider (ISP) PPP server. Once you have authenticated to the ISP server, you can make a second call to the VPN server over the Internet.

What are some of the advantages of using a VPN client to remotely connect to my business LAN?

▼ You can avoid expensive long-distance connections by using a VPN tunnel through the Internet, whether you connect through your ISP or through a broadband solution. VPN allows you to communicate with added security, both by encrypting any data that traverses the Internet and by using authentication protocols to connect to the RRAS server. VPN supports TCP/IP communication, which is the only protocol of the Internet. It also supports other protocols, such as IPX/SPX, if you use it on your local network. In addition, your IP addresses are encrypted so that internal addressing schemes cannot be detected from the Internet.

PART VI

continued

Set Up VPN Client *(Continued)*

You can continue to configure your user computer as a VPN client by configuring the host name or IP address of the VPN server. This allows the client computer to locate the VPN gateway to the business network, and to establish a tunneling connection.

All computers that are connected to the Internet access their destinations by locating their unique IP address on the Internet. For example, when a user who is surfing on the World Wide Web types a domain name in a Web browser, the computer requests the domain name be resolved to the

IP address of the destination using DNS services on the Internet. By configuring the VPN server IP address, you can ensure that your VPN client uses only one static address to locate the correct destination.

You can configure your VPN clients to use Certificate Services to verify their identity when they connect to the business network. The Certificate Authority (CA) on the network can issue a certificate to the user's or client's computer to verify the server identity. The server can then use the certificate to authenticate the client before data is exchanged across the VPN link.

Set Up VPN Client *(continued)*

The Connection Name page appears.

⑩ Type the company name.

⑪ Click Next.

The Public Network page appears.

⑫ Click the type of connection you want (○ changes to ◉).

⑬ Click Next.

The VPN Server Selection page appears.

⑭ Type the host name or IP address of the VPN server.

⑮ Click Next.

The Completing the New Connection Wizard
page appears.

⑯ Click Finish.

● The Virtual Private Network connection is
added.

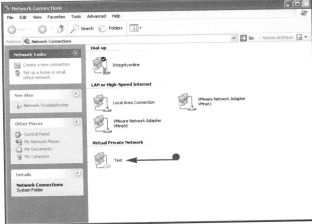

How can I change the identity authentication information on my VPN client computer?

▼ To change the identity authentication
information, click Start, click Connect To, and
then click Show all connections. In the Network
Connections dialog box, right-click the VPN
connection and then click Properties. In the
VPN connection Properties dialog box, click
the Security tab. In the Security tab, you
can click Typical (recommended settings)
(changes to ⦿), and under the "Validate my
identity as follows" menu, you can select different
methods of identity authentication. For example,
you can select "Automatically use my Windows
logon name and password (and domain if any)",
or you can select the "Require data encryption
(disconnect if none)" option (changes to ⦿).
If the latter is not enabled, then encryption is
optional in your VPN connection.

What types of authentication protocols can I use when I create a VPN link to my company RRAS server?

▼ You can use a variety of protocols, including
CHAP, MS-CHAP, MS-CHAPv2, and EAP/TLS.
CHAP, or Challenge Handshake Authentication
Protocol, is a very popular authentication method
that sends a challenge string to the user and
returns the string plus the password for
authentication. MS-CHAP and MS-CHAPv2 are
Microsoft proprietary implementations of the
original CHAP Protocol. Extensible Authentication
Protocol (EAP) is an extension of Point-to-Point
Protocol (PPP) that allows a variety of
authentication methods, and that supports
certificate and smart card authentication. For
more information, see the section "Set Up VPN
Services."

Enable Terminal Services for Remote Desktop

You can enable Remote Desktop on your Windows Server 2003 server to allow client computers to remotely run applications on the Terminal server. This helps you save resources on individual workstations and personal computers.

Your business workstations or personal computers often do not have the hard drive space, RAM, and processing speed necessary to run many high-end software applications. By letting your user computers access these applications on a Terminal server, you can avoid buying expensive

workstations for users and save money for the company. You then only have to install the application software on a few servers, rather than on many client computers.

Your users can run a terminal session as a virtual machine session. This means that although they use a keyboard and mouse to manipulate the program on the server and then view output on their monitor, they actually use all of the resources on the Terminal server, just as if they were sitting directly in front of the server keyboard. Your high-speed LAN connection allows users to access the server without any noticeable delay in performance.

Enable Terminal Services for Remote Desktop

① Click Start.

② Right-click My Computer.

③ Click Properties.

The System Properties dialog box appears.

④ Click the Remote tab.

⑤ Click "Allow users to connect remotely to this computer" (☐ changes to ☑).

The Remote Sessions dialog box appears.

⑥ Click OK.

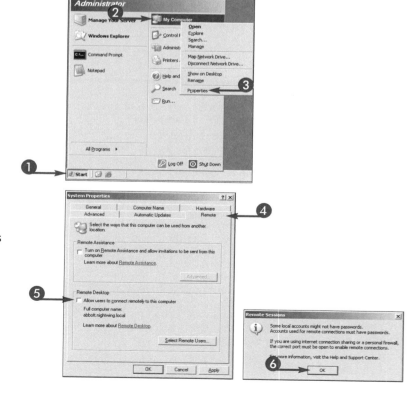

⑦ Click Select Remote Users.

The Remote Desktop Users dialog box appears.

⑧ Click Add.

The Select Users or Groups dialog box appears.

⑨ Type the remote username.

⑩ Click OK.

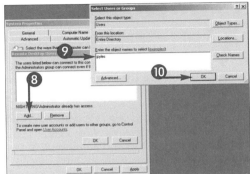
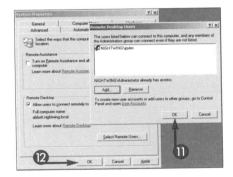

The Remote user is added to the system.

⑪ Click OK.

⑫ Click OK.

Your changes are applied.

Can I use a Remote Desktop connection to access a Terminal server using any Windows operating system?

▼ No. Remote Desktop services run natively only on Windows Server 2003 computers and Windows XP Professional computers. If you want to remotely connect to a Terminal server with Remote Desktop from any other Windows operating system, then you can connect to the Remote Desktop Connection Software Download page at www.microsoft.com. Once you download the software from Microsoft and install it, you can click Start, and then click All Programs, or Programs, depending on the operating system. Click Accessories, then click Communications, and then click Remote Desktop Connection. Type the host name or IP address of the server, and click Connect.

What type of security can I use to protect Terminal Services on my network?

▼ The GPO Editor limits user access to computer features that require a connection to a Terminal server. You can require that network clients use a 128-bit high-encryption mode to connect to the Terminal server. You can also configure your Terminal server to run in either Full Security mode or in Relaxed Security mode. When you use Full Security mode, you can prevent network users from accidentally installing, uninstalling, or damaging software applications on the Terminal Services server. You can also prevent users from moving data directories. You can use Relaxed Security mode to support legeacy applications.

Enable Remote Assistance

When you enable Remote Assistance on your Windows Server 2003 server, you can connect to your server from a remote location and operate the server as if you were at the server keyboard. You can easily administer servers that are located in a wide variety of settings from a single location and avoid traveling to these sites. Also, if you are at a branch office and need to access a server at your main site, you can use any workstation to connect to and administer to that server. Remote Assistance allows a workstation user to request help from an administrator or help desk technician. The user initiates Remote Assistance at his or her workstation. This is

in contrast to Remote Desktop that an administrator uses to access a remote machine directly. For more on Remote Desktop, see the section "Enable Remote Desktop."

Just as a user can access a server with a Terminal Services session to run applications remotely, you can access a server to perform administrative tasks in the same way. You can install applications, hotfixes, and security updates, or perform any other task that you would normally perform at the server keyboard. However, you must not install any applications that involve Windows components because you may accidentally lock yourself out of the Terminal Services session.

Enable Remote Assistance

① Click Start.

② Right-click My Computer.

③ Click Properties.

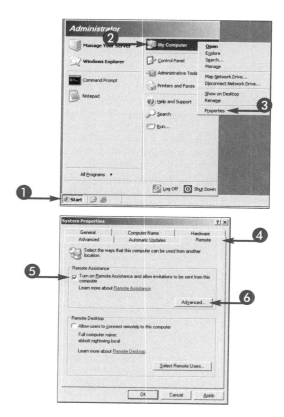

The System Properties dialog box appears.

④ Click the Remote tab.

⑤ Click "Turn on Remote Assistance and allow invitations to be sent from this computer" (☐ changes to ☑).

⑥ Click Advanced.

The Remote Assistance Settings dialog box appears.

7 Click "Allow this computer to be controlled remotely" (☐ changes to ☑).

8 Click here and select the maximum units of time that you want invitations to remain open.

9 Click here and select Minutes, Hours, or Days.

10 Click OK.

11 Click OK.

Your Remote Assistance is enabled.

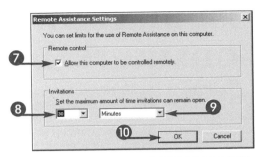

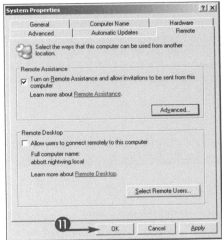

Can I only use Remote Assistance over the LAN?

▼ No. There are actually three connection types through which you can remotely administer a server using Remote Assistance. You can use Remote Assistance over a LAN connection, over the Internet, or between a public and private network through a firewall. To traverse the corporate firewall from the Internet using Terminal Services, you must open Port 3389. Best Practice states that you should keep Port 3389 closed until you need to request assistance from someone outside the network. You can then advise them by phone that the port is open and ready for them to make the terminal connection. You can often allow a consultant to access your server in this way.

How can I secure or stop a Remote Assistances connection to my servers?

▼ You can stop a current Remote Assistance connection to your server by pressing the Escape (Esc) key on your server keyboard. You can also close the connection, but leave the Remote Assistance window open, by clicking Disconnect. If you want to close the window, then click the Close button (☒). If you want to prevent any Terminal Services connections to your server, then open the System Properties dialog box, click the Remote tab, then click Advanced, and deselect the "Allow this computer to be controlled remotely" option (☑ changes to ☐).

Install Terminal Services with Configure Your Server Wizard

You can use a wizard to configure your Windows Server 2003 server to act as a Terminal server. Not only does this ease your administrative duties, but it also allows both remote administration of the server system and local and remote user access to applications through Terminal Services.

Although you can allow a user to connect to any server through a Remote Desktop, or allow an Administrator to manage a remote server with Remote Assistance, these are not examples of a true Terminal server. A Terminal server actually offers a wider range of features than remote connectivity.

You can use local disk drive redirection to Terminal Services so that a network drive on the Terminal server appears to be a local drive with a drive letter on a client computer. With disk drive redirection, you must redirect all of the drives on the user's computer to the Terminal server. This means that when users believe that they are accessing the C:\ drive on their local workstation, they are actually reading and writing data to a drive partition on the Terminal server, and using almost no local resources. You can also configure Terminal Services for Printer Redirection and Local Time Zone Redirection.

Install Terminal Services with Configure Your Server Wizard

① Click Start.

② Click Administrative Tools.

③ Click Configure Your Server Wizard.

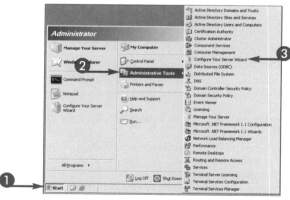

The Configure Your Server Wizard appears.

④ Click Next.

The Preliminary Steps page appears.

⑤ Click Next.

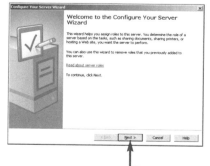

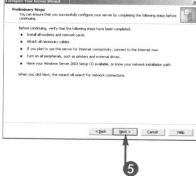

The Server Role page appears.

6 Click Terminal server.

7 Click Next.

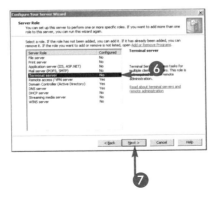

The Summary of Selections page appears.

8 Click Next.

A confirmation page appears.

The Windows Components are installed, and your server restarts.

The This Server is Now a Terminal Server page appears.

9 Click Finish.

The server is now a Terminal Server.

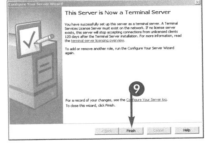

How does a Terminal server manage Printer Redirection on my network?

▼ You can redirect all print job requests from user computers to the Terminal server. You can redirect print jobs from users for both network shared printers and any printers that connect directly to a user's computer. This means that instead of a print job being spooled on the user's local computer for a printer that is directly connected by a parallel or USB cable, the job is sent to the Terminal server for spooling and then sent back to the local print device for printing. You can save resources on all local user computers by using Terminal services to redirect and manage all print job requests.

Can I manage Terminal services and Resource Redirection from the command line?

▼ Yes. You can reference a redirected drive using the Universal Naming Convention (UNC) format, \\tsclient\drive_letter. You can then create a directory listing that uses this UNC path. Browse the drive and conduct file transfers on the command line by opening a command shell and typing **net use * \\tsclient\c:** where c: is the drive that you want to access. You can automatically map the local drive to the next available drive letter, starting from Z: and working back through the alphabet. At the command prompt, type **Z:** and press Enter. When you are finished conducting operations on the drive and want to disconnect, type **net use Z: /delete** and press Enter.

Install Terminal Services License Server

Y ou can install a Terminal Services License server to allow Terminal Services clients to connect to and access resources on a Terminal server. You must also buy Client Access Licenses (CALs) for each Terminal Services client computer that you intend to connect to your Windows Server 2003 Terminal server.

Because the Terminal Services License server is a separate server role from the Terminal server, you can configure it to run on a separate server. The License server is responsible for issuing the CALs to any client that requests a Terminal

Services server connection. The Terminal Services server also contacts the License server when a connection is requested to verify that a license has been issued to that client.

You can install and use a Terminal Services server on your network for 120 days before you are required to have a License server available. You are not required to install a License server if you run Remote Desktop because no CALs are required. After you install the Terminal Services License server, you must activate the server with Microsoft either over the Internet or by phone.

Install Terminal Services License Server

1 Insert the Windows Server 2003 installation CD-ROM.

2 Click Start.

3 Click Control Panel.

4 Double-click Add or Remove Programs.

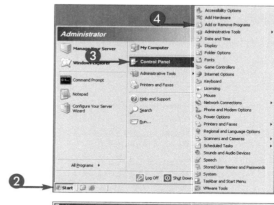

The Add or Remove Programs window appears.

5 Click Add/Remove Windows Components.

The Windows Components Wizard appears.

6 Click Terminal Server Licensing (☐ changes to ☑).

7 Click Next.

The Terminal Server Licensing Setup page appears.

8 Click to select the scope of licensing for your server (☐ changes to ☉).

9 Click Next.

The components are installed from the CD-ROM.

The Completing the Windows Components Wizard page appears.

10 Click Finish.

The Terminal Services License server is installed.

What do I have to do to activate my Terminal Services License server?

▼ You can open Terminal Services Licensing by clicking Start, then clicking Administrative Tools, and then double-clicking Terminal Server Licensing. The Terminal Server Licensing dialog box appears. Right-click the Terminal Server and select Activate Server. The Terminal Server License Server Activation Wizard appears. Click Next to advance through the wizard. You can select your connection type from a menu, and choose either Automatic connection, Web Browser, or Telephone. The wizard also asks you to identify your company information. Once you complete the form, your Licensing server activates over the connection, and you can issue Terminal Services licenses.

How do I install Client Access Licenses (CALs) on my Terminal Services License server?

▼ Once you activate your License server, open the Terminal Services License server from the Administrative Tools menu. Right-click the Terminal Server and click Install Licenses. This option is not available until you activate the License server. The Install Terminal Server Licenses Wizard appears, and The Licensing server connects to the Microsoft activation server over the Internet. You can choose the type of license program that your company wants to use and then enter the license or agreement number for your licensing pack in the available field. You can choose the type of license, such as per user or per device, and select either the 2000 or 2003 systems options (☐ changes to ☉).

Manage Terminal Services Users

You can manage Terminal Services users so that only those users who require access to a Terminal Services server are able to connect to it. This enables you to conserve the number of Terminal Service Client Access Licenses (CALs) that you can issue with your Licensing server.

You can create a Terminal Services user account for each user who needs to connect to a Terminal Services server. The Terminal Services user account is separate from the domain user account and contains more information about the conditions under which the Terminal Services user can connect to the Terminal Services server. Windows Server

2003 has a built-in group called Remote Desktop Users that is designed to manage Terminal Services users.

You can also set up a domain user account for a Terminal Services user in the Active Directory Users and Computers snap-in under the Users folder. In the User Properties dialog box, you can configure a Terminal Services profile for that user so that you can restrict user access to applications on the Terminal Services server. You can create and save network connections, printer access, and connections to other resources in the Terminal Services profile. You can also use a GPO to control and manage user access to Terminal Services.

Manage Terminal Services Users

① Click Start.

② Click Administrative Tools.

③ Click Active Directory Users and Computers.

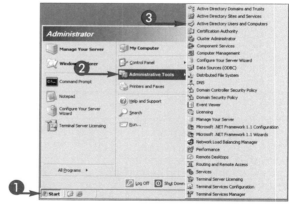

The Active Directory Users and Computers snap-in window appears.

④ Right-click the domain.

⑤ Click Properties.

The Properties dialog box appears for the domain you selected.

⑥ Click the Group Policy tab.

⑦ Click the GPO.

⑧ Click Edit.

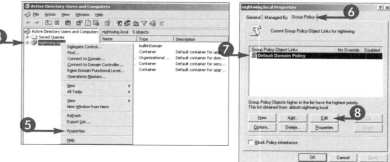

The Group Policy Object Editor appears.

9 Under Computer Configuration, expand Administrative Templates.

10 Expand Windows Components.

11 Expand Terminal Services.

12 Click the Client/Server data redirection folder.

13 Double-click Do not allow clipboard redirection.

The GPO Properties dialog box appears for the items you selected.

14 Click Enabled (○ changes to ⦿).

15 Click OK.

The GPO settings are applied.

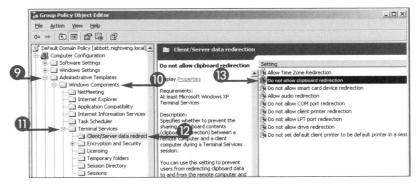

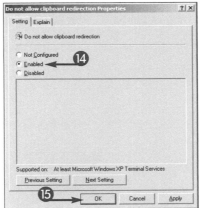

What does it mean when I set a GPO to disallow redirection under Terminal Services?

▼ You can allow or disallow data or services to redirect between the Terminal Services server and the Terminal Services client. When you do not configure Terminal Services redirection in Group Policy, Terminal Services redirection is allowed by default. You can disallow Terminal Services redirection by opening the Properties dialog box for the GPO item and selecting the Enabled option (○ changes to ⦿). This prevents any sharing of this type of data or service. To specifically allow Terminal Services redirection, click the Disabled option (○ changes to ⦿) in the Properties dialog box for the GPO item. Even if you do not configure Terminal Services redirection, you can still disable redirection by using the Terminal Services Configuration tool.

What other aspects of Terminal Services can I configure in the GPO Editor?

▼ In addition to Client/Server data redirection, you can configure Encryption and Security, Licensing, Temporary folders, Session Directory, and Sessions in the GPO Editor. Under the Security and Encryption folder, you can configure your Terminal server to require secure RPC communication with all clients. Under the Licensing folder, you can control which of your servers are issued Terminal Services licenses, as well as what kinds of licenses are issued. Under Temporary Folders folder, you can prevent users from using temporary folders or from deleting them upon exit. Under Session Directory folder, you can have Terminal services track user sessions, and under Sessions folder, you can place time limits on sessions.

PART VI

Install IPv6 Protocol

You can install Internet Protocol version 6 (IPv6) on your Windows Server 2003 server to allow your server to communicate on the Internet using the next generation of Internet communication protocols. This allows you to access a virtually unlimited supply of routable IP addresses.

Most computers currently use the Internet Protocol version 4 (IPv4) addressing scheme to communicate on both LANs and on the Internet. IPv4 uses 32-bit addressing as the basis for computer network addressing. This addressing scheme provides approximately 4.2 billion IP addresses. However, current technology has created a wide variety of devices, each of which needs a routable IP address, and so IPv4 does not provide sufficient addresses to meet present-day needs.

IPv6 uses 128-bit addressing, which provides a maximum of 2 to the 128th power number of addresses, or 667 billion IP addresses for every square meter of the Earth's surface. Countries such as China and Japan already make extensive use of IPv6, which is considered the IP communications protocol of the twenty-first century. IPv4 addresses are commonly expressed as a set of four decimal values separated by periods (.), while IPv6 addresses are expressed as a hexadecimal value.

Install IPv6 Protocol

① Click Start.

② Click Control Panel.

③ Click Network Connections.

④ Right-click Local Area Connection.

⑤ Click Properties.

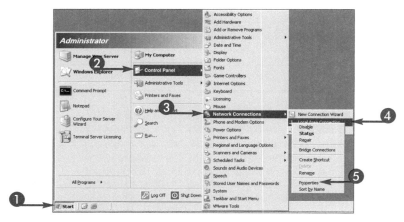

The Local Area Connection Properties dialog box appears.

⑥ Click Install.

The Select Network Component Type dialog box appears.

⑦ Click Protocol.

⑧ Click Add.

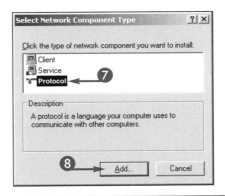

The Select Network Protocol dialog box appears.

⑨ Click Microsoft TCP/IP version 6.

⑩ Click OK.

The IPv6 Protocol installs.

You do not have to restart your server for the installation to take effect.

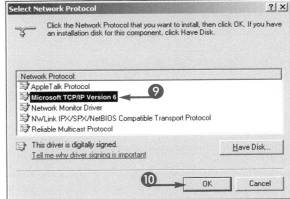

How can I tell if IPv6 has been installed on my Windows Server 2003 server?

▼ You can open the Local Area Connections Properties dialog box. Microsoft TCP/IP version 6 should appear in the list, along with the other standard items such as File and Printer Sharing and Internet Protocol (TCP/IP). You can also open a command line window by clicking Start, and double-clicking Command Prompt, and then type **ipconfig/all** at the prompt. Along with the usual IP addressing information, you can also view DNS server addresses and Gateway addresses, which display as hexadecimal values. If you type **ping localhost** and press Enter, the on-board NIC responds with an address in hexadecimal format rather than the standard decimal value.

Can my IPv6-enabled computer still communicate with IPv4 computers and networks?

▼ Yes. You can communicate with an IPv4 computer on your network and with other IPv4 networks from a Windows Server 2003 server that is enabled for IPv6. The IPv6 protocol is backwards compatible with IPv4. This is because it is unlikely that all worldwide network nodes that are connected to the Internet will simultaneously install and upgrade to IPv6. When you ping an IPv4 node by name from an IPv6 computer, the echo response displays the standard IPv4 addressing scheme. When you ping an IPv6 computer from an IPv4 computer, the echo returns the IPv6 computer address in an IPv4 format.

PART VI

Understanding SharePoint Installation 366

Install IIS v6 and ASP.NET.........................368

Install SharePoint Services...........................370

Understanding the Intranet
 as a Work Area..372

Configure a Virtual Server 374

Extend a Virtual Server 378

Create a Top-level Web Site 380

Configure Self-Service Site Creation 382

Access Default Site from IIS
 and Create New Site 384

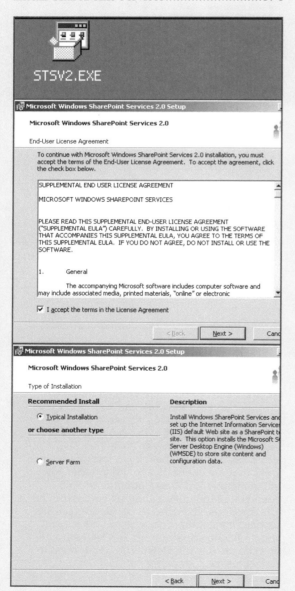

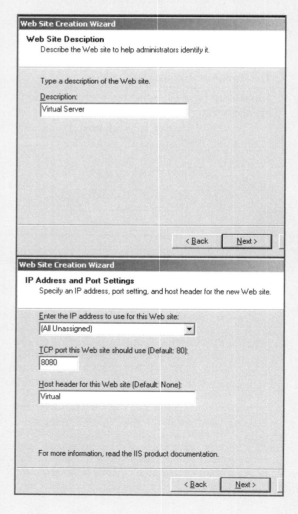

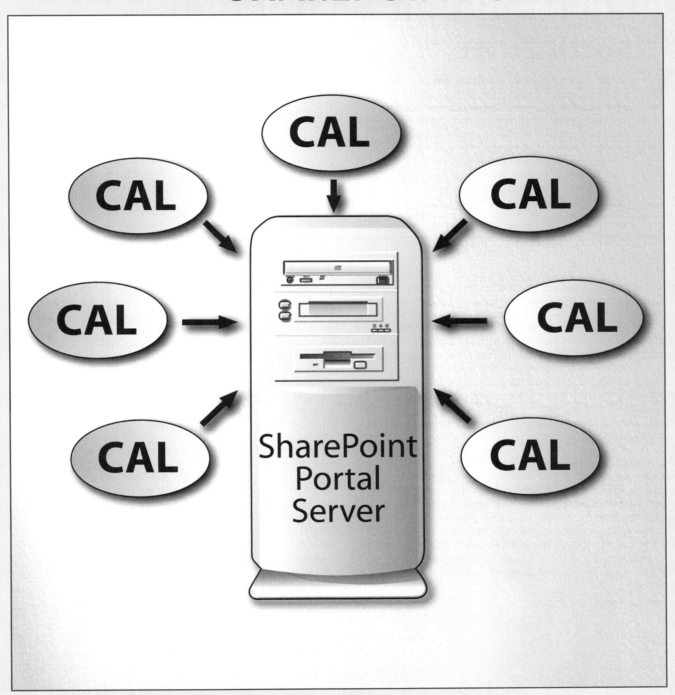

Understanding SharePoint Installation

You can install and use SharePoint services to provide a forum on your company intranet for users to share data, collaborate on common projects, manage project documents, and search for content using custom Web sites and portals on your business network. SharePoint extends the functionality of Microsoft Office and Windows products, allowing you to construct and configure shared work projects that users can access through a Web interface. It enables you to manage the team collaboration needs of individuals, groups, Organizational Units, and divisions in your enterprise.

Before you can install SharePoint Services, you must install IIS v6 (version 6) and ASP.NET in order to create Web content on your Windows Server 2003 server. If you try to install SharePoint Services without first installing IIS v6 and ASP.NET, then you will receive an error message and cannot proceed.

For more on installing SharePoint, see the section "Install SharePoint Servers." For more on installing IIS v6 and ASP.NET, see the section "Install IIS v6 and ASP.NET."

Web Site Portals

SharePoint services use Web site portals to allow business partners, outside consultants, and customers to access information about how your company conducts business and what goods and services you offer. A Web site portal is a Web interface, similar to an eCommerce Web site. Examples of common Web site portals include MSN and Yahoo! You can use SharePoint to provide a container for a shared pool of information that is provided by workgroups within your company. You can then share this information through a Web server with your target audience over the Internet. When you expose the server to the Internet in this manner, you must purchase an Internet Connector License.

Intranet

You can use an intranet to provide a Web interface for company employees in order to share important internal information and announcements to your company workforce. A user can only access the intranet Web site from inside the company LAN, and not from the Internet. You can use an intranet site to consolidate information from different offices into one site that any company user can access with a Web browser such as Internet Explorer.

Extranets

An extranet is a specific type of Web interface that allows your customers to access your inventory and to purchase goods from you over the Internet. Only customers who can authenticate to the extranet site are allowed access to your inventory, and these customers are usually large enterprises that purchase substantial quantities of goods and services, rather than smaller, retail customers. You can also use extranet sites to allow remote employees to connect to your network through a RRAS server or to allow *thin clients* — client computers with limited on-board resources — to connect to and use the resources on network servers through an authentication process.

Internet Information Services

You can use Internet Information Services (IIS) to host and manage your own secure Web site, rather than using an Internet Service Provider's (ISP) Web-hosting services. IIS enables you to use common Web protocols such as Hypertext Transfer Protocol (HTTP) and File Transfer Protocol (FTP) to create Web pages and present and transfer data over the Internet. You can often use IIS in conjunction with Microsoft FrontPage, which is a software application that allows you to construct Web pages and content that you can then publish to your company Web server for Internet access.

SharePoint

The core function of SharePoint is to create and maintain top-level Web sites on your network, create sub-level Web sites from each of the top-level sites, and provide the core components and engine. This enables you to control all of your company Web sites without using outside consultants, Web design specialists, and Web-hosting services.

SharePoint is supported by Windows Server 2003 Standard, Enterprise, Data Center, or Web editions, and can operate in a Windows NT 4.0, Windows 2000, or Windows Server 2003 Active Directory domain. SharePoint typically uses SQL Server 2000 for the database and integrates Microsoft Office and Web services as part of the Web site components. Windows SharePoint Services installs Windows Microsoft SQL Server 2000 Desktop Engine (WMSDE) by default. SharePoint Web sites can be accessed by Web browsers such as Internet Explorer 5.01 or higher and Netscape Navigator 6.2 or higher.

Windows SharePoint Services 2003

You can use SharePoint Services 2.0 (also called WSS) as an integrated part of your Windows Server 2003 operating system. SharePoint Services uses various Windows components to provide the tools that allow you to create Web sites, and enables document and data management. It also provides a platform for company employee collaboration through a Web interface. You do not need to purchase any additional Microsoft products to enable Windows SharePoint Services on your Windows Server 2003 system. You only need to download the SharePoint application from Microsoft. For more on information on this, go to www.microsoft.com/windowsserver2003/techinfo/sharepoint/wss.mspx.

SharePoint Portal Server 2003

You can purchase SharePoint Portal Server 2003 (SPS) as an individual server operating system product. You must also purchase a Client Access License (CAL) for each user who will access your SharePoint Server 2003 system. You can configure SharePoint Portal Server to allow an unlimited number of connections from customers and other contacts outside of the company network. SharePoint Portal Server offers the same types of services and options as SharePoint Services, as well as the use of other components such as enterprise search engine, user profile management, audience targeting, single logon, diagnostic tools, and additional configuration settings. Although SharePoint is integrated with Office 2003, you can also integrate it with Office 2000 and Office XP. This is true of both WSS and SPS.

Install IIS v6 and ASP.NET

Before you can install SharePoint Services, you must install IIS v6 (version 6) and ASP.net in order to create Web content on your Windows Server 2003 server. If you try to install SharePoint Services without first installing IIS v6 and ASP.net, then you will receive an error message and cannot proceed.

IIS v6 provides a collection of applications that build and administer Web sites for both public networks, such as the Internet and extranet, and private networks, such as an intranet. IIS v6 also allows support for search engines and

Web applications that can access databases, such as SQL and Access. IIS v6 is integrated into Windows Server 2003, to allow for quicker Web site construction and more rapid serving of Web sites from your Windows Web server.

Active Server Pages, or ASP.NET, allows you to build Web pages dynamically, rather than as part of a predefined development process for static HTML pages. You can develop Web content with ASP.NET, based on inserting queries into a relational database, such as SQL, in a Web page. ASP.NET also supports the use of languages such as Visual Basic, C++, and Perl.

Install IIS v6 and ASP.NET

① Insert the Windows Server 2003 installation CD-ROM.

② Click Start.

③ Click Control Panel.

④ In the Control Panel window, click Add or Remove Programs.

The Add or Remove Programs window appears.

⑤ Click the Add/Remove Windows Components option.

The Windows Components Wizard appears.

⑥ Click Application Server (□ changes to ☑).

⑦ Click Details.

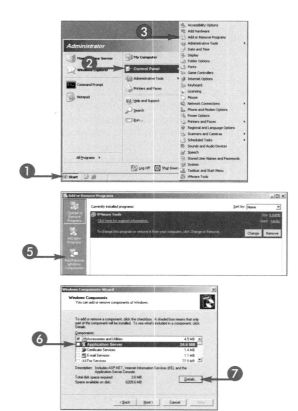

The Application Server page appears.

⑧ Click ASP.NET (☐ changes to ☑).

- The Enable network COM+ access and Internet Information Services (IIS) options are automatically selected (☐ changes to ☑).

⑨ Click OK.

The Windows Components page of the Wizard reappears.

⑩ Click Next.

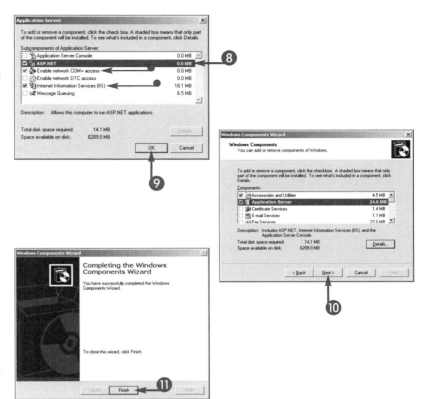

The components are installed.

The Completing the Windows Components Wizard page appears.

⑪ Click Finish.

The Wizard closes.

Is ASP.NET a completely separate component from IIS, or are they related?

▼ ASP.NET is installed with IIS, and appears as a Web Service Extension when you open the Internet Information Services (IIS) Manager from the Administrative Tools menu. You can only use IIS to serve static Web content for your Web sites. IIS depends on dynamic extensions such as ASP, ASP.NET, or FrontPage server to deliver dynamic Web content. When serving only static Web content (HTML files, images, etc.), it is not necessary to enable any of these dynamic extensions, and they should be left disabled for security reasons. To enable or configure Web service extensions, you must log on to the server as an Administrator to the local computer.

Does it matter if I insert the Windows Server 2003 installation CD-ROM before I begin to install a Windows component?

▼ If you do not want to have your installation of Windows components interrupted while the Windows Components Wizard is running, then you can put the CD-ROM in the CD-ROM drive before you run the wizard. If you insert the CD-ROM at the beginning of the process, the installation CD splash screen may appear. To close the splash screen, click Exit in the lower left-hand corner of the screen. You can wait until after the wizard launches and displays the prompt before you insert the CD-ROM into the server CD-ROM drive.

Install SharePoint Services

Y ou can install SharePoint Services on your Windows Server 2003 server to access a wide range of SharePoint Services. This enables you to share documents, manage team meetings using a Web site, and search for documents within a workgroup without the expense and commitment required to purchase SharePoint Portal Server as a separate product. Although SharePoint Portal Server has more features, SharePoint Services on Windows Server 2003 can provide a significant set of team management features for mid- and enterprise-level network business environments.

You can install SharePoint Services either by using the Microsoft Windows Update Web site or by downloading the

SharePoint Services executable file. If you choose to download SharePoint as an executable file, then you can decide on which server you want to host SharePoint Services and when you want to install SharePoint. If you use the Windows Update Web site, you must download and install SharePoint onto the server from which you are accessing the Windows Update.

When you install SharePoint Services, you also install the Microsoft SQL Server Desktop Engine, which allows you to use SQL database functionality without purchasing SQL server software and Client Access Licenses. You can also choose not to install the SQL Server Desktop Engine and have SharePoint connect to an existing SQL database on your network.

Install SharePoint Services

① Double-click STSV2.EXE.

Windows extracts the installation files from the executable file.

The Microsoft Windows SharePoint Services 2.0 Setup window appears.

② Click the "I accept the terms in the License Agreement" option (☐ changes to ☑).

③ Click Next.

The Type of Installation page of the Wizard appears.

④ Click the type of installation you want (☐ changes to ⊙).

⑤ Click Next.

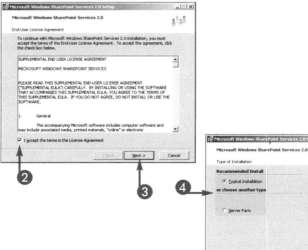

The Summary page appears.

6 Click Install.

Windows installs the SharePoint Services components.

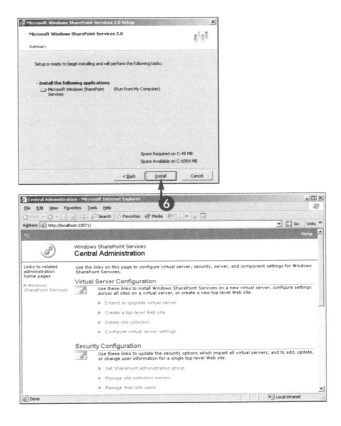

The Windows SharePoint Services Central Administration Web page appears, stating that the installation is complete.

Note: *At this point you are free to configure the Central Administration Web page to provide whatever content is appropriate for your purpose.*

How do I download the SharePoint Services executable file from Microsoft?

▼ You can locate the SharePoint Services STSV2.EXE download file at www.microsoft.com/windowsserver2003/techinfo/sharepoint/wss.mspx. Download the file and then install SharePoint Services on the server you want. You can also burn the file to a CD-ROM or save the file to a folder in your directory so that you can install SharePoint Services at a later time. You can also download and install the STSTPK.EXE file, which is a service pack for SharePoint that provides support in languages other than English. To read more information regarding WSS, you can go to www.microsoft.com/windowsserver2003/technologies/sharepoint/default.mspx.

On the Type of Installation page of the SharePoint Services 2.0 Setup Wizard, what is the difference between choosing Typical Installation and Server Farm?

▼ If you select the Typical Installation option (◻ changes to ◉), the SharePoint Services Installation Wizard automatically installs the Microsoft SQL Server Desktop Engine (WMSDE) as the database component. This enables you to store any Web-site content and configuration data as part of SharePoint Services. If you select the Server Farm option (◻ changes to ◉), then WMSDE is not installed, and you must have a SQL Server 2000 server already operational on your network. You are prompted to provide a path to the SQL Server so that SharePoint Services can access it.

PART VII

Understanding the Intranet as a Work Area

Y ou can use SharePoint technology on your company intranet site to manage storage and indexing of data, manage workspaces, document libraries, create on-line discussion boards, manage meetings and events, and publish photos to the intranet. SharePoint can perform all the tasks that are necessary to organize small team projects and company-wide events that are accessible only by your employees through a Web browser. You can avoid having to send multiple, broadcast e-mails or voice mails, as well as schedule meetings with staff who are located at different physical locations. SharePoint can create a virtual work area for all of your company's collaborative needs.

Storing and Indexing Data

Unlike SharePoint Services, which is limited in its ability to search for organizational data, SharePoint Portal Server 2003 can index and search for data both within your SharePoint infrastructure and outside of your company content structure. You can use both SharePoint Services and SharePoint Portal Server 2003 to replace your shared data storage system on your file and print servers.

You can create SharePoint document libraries that can access content directly from Microsoft Office 2003 applications, thus decreasing access time. A document library is a repository for files from applications such as Word, Excel, and PowerPoint.

When you create document libraries, you can create keywords and profiles that you can use to categorize and store data; you can then use the keywords and profiles to search for documents. Users can also continue to access documents directly using Microsoft Office rather than SharePoint, and still use the other SharePoint features, such as group discussions.

Discussion Boards

You can use SharePoint to create Discussion Boards, which allow users to discuss shared projects and tasks in a Web format, rather than through e-mail, telephone calls, or live meetings. A Discussion Board is a list in SharePoint that is similar to an on-line message board. Any team member can create a topic or "post" with a particular title. Other team members can respond, and the series of transactions on this

specific topic becomes a "thread," with the most recent responses being added to the bottom of the "list." Discussion Board lists are not embedded into a particular document or Web page, but rather exist as an independent SharePoint application.

In addition to Discussion Boards, you can use SharePoint to create another type of electronic discussion forum, called Web Discussions, which allows users to focus on the content of a particular document or Web page. Any member of a project can insert comments directly into the document or Web page, and any other project member can respond to these comments. This allows team members to provide feedback and interactive commentary directly within the content of the document, rather than having to reference the document as a separate item.

Sites and Workspaces

You can use sites and workspaces to access or search your document libraries. A SharePoint site is not the same as a regular site, as described in Chapter 4. A SharePoint site is actually a collection of Web Part pages. A Web Part Page is a page that includes Web Part Zones as well as other HTML content. A Web Part Zone is a flexible container that manages and displays Web Parts. A Web Part is a type of ASP.NET control designed to manage SharePoint and is used at the user interface element in SharePoint. You can also think of a Web Part as a single, custom-made Web page that you create for a specific purpose or topic on your intranet.

A SharePoint site is similar to an Internet Web site, which is a collection of Web pages that is designed for a specific purpose and is accessible on the World Wide Web. A workspace is a type of site that you can create for use as a working area for a particular project. A workspace is not designed to be a permanent part of your intranet. You create a workspace for a project and delete it once the project is completed. Although you can store document libraries in both sites and workspaces, if you want to store the document libraries in your workspace, then you must move them to a more permanent location before you delete the workspace.

Manage Events

You can use a SharePoint workspace to manage project-related events, enter data about upcoming meetings, and link them to your Outlook 2003 calendar. You can use Outlook 2003 to create a workspace site in SharePoint for one-time or regular meetings. You can also specify who is allowed to access a meeting by assigning users rights to the meeting workplace site. You can create and manage single or multiple meeting workspaces to manage several projects that are running simultaneously.

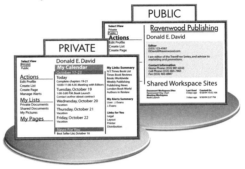

Custom SharePoint Sites

SharePoint allows you to create customized or personalized sites using a standardized SharePoint site template. You can use two separate views of a custom SharePoint site: a personal view and a public view. When you use the personal view, only a particular user can access it. That user can, but does not have to be the site owner. Each page has one shared view and can have a private view for each user who has a personalized page. The personal view contains a left-hand sidebar menu that offers controls such as Actions, My Lists, and My Pages, and allows you to configure the content and features of the site. The public view is what all of the users see when they access the site with a Web browser.

Configure a Virtual Server

You must create a virtual server before you can use SharePoint Services to create any Web sites on your Windows Server 2003 server. You can create a virtual server on your physical server and configure it as a separate Web server with a separate domain name and IP address. You can create a new virtual server in the Internet Information Services (IIS) snap-in, instead of in SharePoint Services. You can then extend or upgrade the virtual server from the Windows SharePoint Services Central Administration page after you create the virtual server in IIS.

You can use a virtual server to access network applications. All network clients that attempt to access the virtual server must have access to the physical server that acts as the host computer. Although the virtual server resides on the host, it requires its own network identity, including a unique name, IP address, or separate port.

You can create virtual servers in server clusters using Windows Server 2003 Enterprise and Datacenter Editions. When you use server clustering, your virtual server is not hosted by any single server. Therefore, if one physical server fails, you can still access the virtual server, as long as other devices in the server cluster support it.

Configure a Virtual Server

① Click Start.

② Click Administrative Tools.

③ Click Internet Information Services (IIS) Manager.

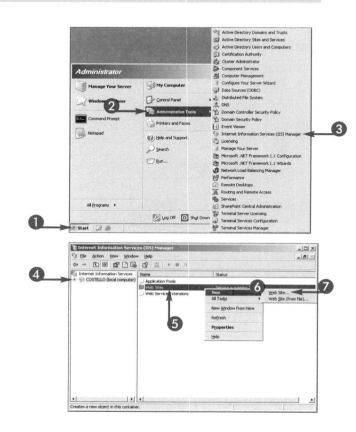

The Internet Information Services (IIS) Manager snap-in window appears.

④ Click the local computer.

⑤ Right-click Web Sites.

⑥ Click New.

⑦ Click Web Site.

The Web Site Creation Wizard appears.

8 Click Next.

The Web Site Description of the Wizard page appears.

9 Type **Virtual Server**.

10 Click Next.

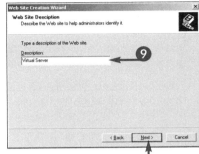

The IP Address and Port Settings page of the Wizard appears.

11 Type **8080** here.

12 Type a unique name here.

13 Click Next.

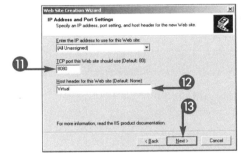

When I create a virtual server, why is the IP address left unassigned?

▼ When you create a virtual server on a physical server, you must differentiate it from all other virtual and physical servers on the network. You can single out a virtual server using one of three methods. You can give the virtual server a unique IP address in the "Enter the IP address to use for this Web site" menu. You can also create a separate TCP port, rather than a unique IP address, using a port such as port 8080 in the "TCP port this Web site should use" field. The key concept is that the combination of the address, port, and header must be unique.

When I type a description of the virtual server in the Web Site Description page, is that the same as giving the virtual server a unique name?

▼ No. When you type a name in the Description field in the Web Site Description page, you are creating a description that helps other Administrators to identify the virtual server on the network. The network only identifies the virtual server by a unique IP address, unique TCP port number, or unique header name that you create in the IP Address and Port Settings page of the Web Site Creation Wizard on your server.

Configure a
Virtual Server *(Continued)*

You can continue to configure a virtual server by creating a path to the Home directory of the Web site that you are creating. A Home directory, or Home folder, is a folder that is located in your Windows Server 2003 directory structure that you can assign to users, groups, computers, or Web sites to contain all necessary files.

When you create a Home directory for a Web site, the directory holds all of the files necessary for that Web site to function. The Home directory for your virtual server is the

default location to which you save any changes that you make to this Web site. Each Web site that you create must have a different Home directory.

You can also configure the type of access permissions that you want users to have to your Web site. Access permissions enable you to allow or deny visitors the privileges to perform certain tasks when they access your virtual server on the Web site. This is similar to permissions that you configure to allow or deny users access to a file, folder, or service on your Windows Server 2003 network.

Configure a Virtual Server *(continued)*

The Web Site Home Directory page of the Wizard appears.

⑭ Type the path to the Home directory for the Web site.

⑮ Click the "Allow anonymous access to this Web site" option (☐ changes to ☑).

⑯ Click Next.

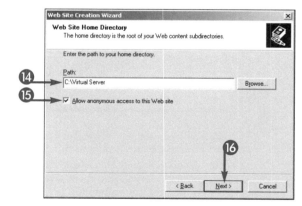

The Web Site Access Permissions page of the Wizard appears.

⑰ Click the access permissions you want (☐ changes to ☑).

⑱ Click Next.

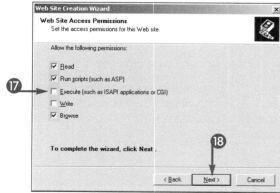

A page appears stating that you have successfully completed the Web site creation.

⑲ Click Finish.

● The Virtual Server appears under the Web Sites folder.

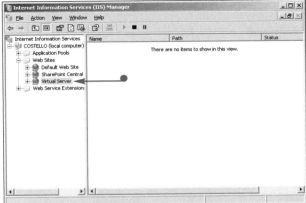

How do I create a Home directory for my virtual server Web site?

▼ You can create a Home directory for your Web site in several different ways. You can create a folder somewhere in your directory structure ahead of time, and on the Web Site Home Directory page of the Web Site Creation Wizard, you can type the path to that directory. You can also click Browse on the same page and browse the directory structure to the location of your folder. If you have not created a folder ahead of time, then you can browse the directory to a place where you want to create a folder and click New Folder to create the Home directory folder.

How and why would I allow anonymous access to my Web site?

▼ You can allow anonymous access to your Web site on the Web Site Home Directory page of the Web Site Creation Wizard. Click the "Allow anonymous access to this Web site" option (☐ changes to ☑). You allow anonymous access to your Web site when you want users on your network to access your Web site without needing to authenticate to the site through a username and password. You can still protect your site from access outside the corporate LAN by not publishing the site to the Internet on your Web server.

PART VII

Extend a Virtual Server

You can use SharePoint Services to extend a virtual server that you create in Internet Information Services (IIS). This allows you to create a blank Web site and to use the new site to manufacture a collaborative workspace. If you do not extend the virtual server, then it is impossible to create a new Web site using SharePoint Services with your new virtual server.

When you create a virtual server in IIS, the server is not initially associated with Windows SharePoint Services. However, when you extend the virtual server, you are applying SharePoint Services to the server, and therefore allowing SharePoint to integrate with the virtual server.

Once you extend your virtual servers, these servers act as Web servers, hosting the Web sites that you create with SharePoint Services. This allows you to host multiple Web sites on multiple virtual Web servers, even though you are actually only using a single, physical server. You must associate each virtual server with a database and an application pool. An *application pool* is a collection of one or more URLs served by a particular process. SharePoint Services does not require a full SQL database like SharePoint Portal Server but by default uses Microsoft SQL Server Desktop Engine.

Extend a Virtual Server

① Click Start.

② Click Administrative Tools.

③ Click SharePoint Central Administration.

The Windows SharePoint Services Central Administration page appears.

④ Click the "Extend or upgrade virtual server" link.

The Virtual Server List page appears.

⑤ Select a virtual server.

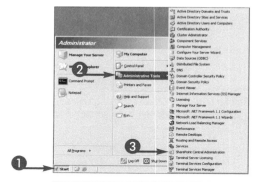

The Extend Virtual Server page appears.

6 Click the "Extend and create a content database" link.

The Extend and Map to Another Virtual Server page appears.

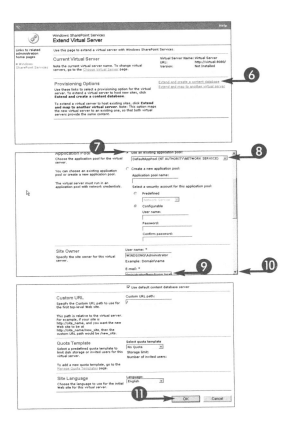

7 Click the "Use an existing application pool" option (○ changes to ⊙).

8 Click here and select DefaultAppPool (NT AUTHORITY\NETWORK SERVICE).

9 Type the e-mail address for the site owner.

10 Click here to scroll down.

You can use the default settings for Custom URL, Quota Template and Site Language.

11 Click OK.

Your virtual server is extended.

What happens after I extend a virtual server?

▼ After you extend your virtual server, you can create a blank Web site that is ready for you to insert content. You can open a Web browser to view the new Web site by typing **http://virtualservername/** in the address bar, and then pressing Enter. In addition to the new virtual server that you have created, a default Web site appears that was created when you installed IIS v6. The path to the default Web site is http://*servername* where *servername* is the name of your Windows Server 2003 device. If you have created a virtual server with a unique TCP port, then the name syntax is http://virtualservername:8080/ with the port number appended at the end.

On the Virtual Server List page, why is my virtual server referred to as Not Installed under the version number?

▼ Your virtual server has not yet been extended through SharePoint Services. Once the process of extending the virtual server is complete, the Not Installed indicator is replaced by a version number that is similar to or the same as the one for the default Web site. In addition, the Extend notation disappears. If you do not extend a virtual server, then you cannot create a Web site. Also, instead of extending the virtual server by creating a content database, you can map it to another virtual server machine on the Extend Virtual Server page.

Create a Top-level Web Site

Y ou can create a Top-level Web site on a virtual server in SharePoint Services that you can use as the basis for a series of subordinate Web sites; you can then use these Web sites for project collaboration, document sharing, and a variety of other shared tasks in your organization. When you use SharePoint Site Administration to create a Web site, you can create it under an existing Web site and integrate them with SharePoint-compliant application packages such as Microsoft Office 2003. You can then use Microsoft Office applications such as Word and Outlook to create the content for this Web site.

You can also use Self-service Site Creation to create top-level sites. Self-service Site Creation allows users to create a large number of top-level sites because it is easy to operate, and you do not have to be a member of the Administrators group to use this utility.

Sites that are located under top-level sites are called subsites. You can use subsites to divide site content into sites that are separately administered from each other or from the top-level site. An entire team can share the top-level site, and can use subsites for sub-projects.

Create a Top-Level Web Site

1 Click Start.

2 Click Administrative Tools.

3 Click SharePoint Central Administration.

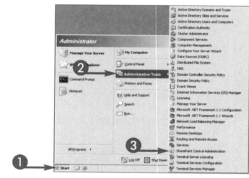

The Windows SharePoint Services Central Administration page appears.

4 Click the "Create a top-level Web site" link.

The Virtual Server List page appears.

5 Click a virtual server.

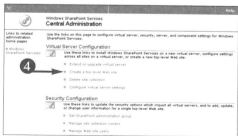

The Create Top-level Web Site page appears.

⑥ Click the Create site at this URL option
(☐ changes to ◉).

⑦ Click here and select (root).

⑧ Type the domain name and the name of the
site owner.

⑨ Click here to scroll down.

⑩ Type the e-mail address of the site owner.

⑪ Click OK.

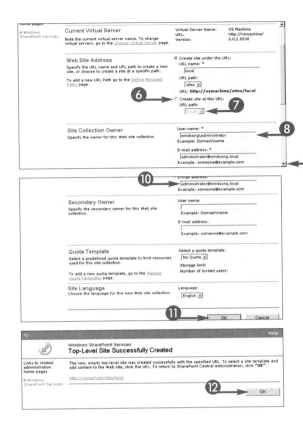

⑫ Click OK.

The top-level site is successfully created.

When I create a top-level site, why do I create a URL that is appended to the URL of a virtual server?

▼ You can use a virtual server as the host for one or more top-level Web sites in SharePoint Services. In the Web Site Address section of the Create Top-level Web Site page, the address for the virtual server is already referenced. When you type the additional URL information in the URL name field, the full address appears under the URL path menu. If you select "sites" in the menu, then "sites" is included in the URL path as you type.

What is a Quota template and what effect does it have on how I create a top-level Web site?

▼ You can use SharePoint Services to specify quotas for sites so that you can manage site and service resources. You can set a quota to limit the amount of data that can be stored on your virtual server. You can also configure a Quota template to send you an e-mail when the site storage reaches a particular size. You can limit the number of users who can connect to the site at any given point in time. After you configure the template, you can go into SharePoint Central Administration and modify the template to adapt to your changing needs.

Configure Self-Service Site Creation

You can configure Self-Service Site Creation to allow any user with access to SharePoint Services to create a SharePoint intranet Web site without needing administrative permissions to the server, thus easing your administrative burden. You must grant any user that you want to create a Web site permissions to the Web site where the Self-Service Site Creation is to be hosted.

After Self-Service Site Creation is enabled, any designated user can fill in various basic questions regarding site configuration to create their own Web site for team collaboration. When Self-Service Site Creation is not

enabled, only members of the Administrators group and the Web Designer group can create a Web site.

When you allow users to control the construction of their own SharePoint Web sites, you can place them in charge of making collaborative, intranet workspaces for their own projects and providing the on-going management for those Web sites. This allows users to control their own work environment so that they can create a set of Web sites that best fits their needs. However, this can also create an administrative burden if too many sites are created in your network environment.

Configure Self-Service Site Creation

① Click Start.

② Click Administrative Tools.

③ Click SharePoint Central Administration.

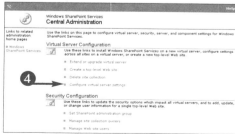

The Windows SharePoint Services Central Administration page appears.

④ Click the "Configure virtual server settings" link.

The Virtual Server List page appears.

⑤ Click a virtual server.

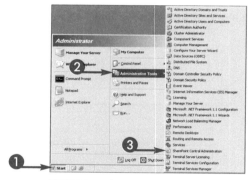

The Virtual Server Settings page appears.

6 Click the "Configure Self-Service Site Creation" link.

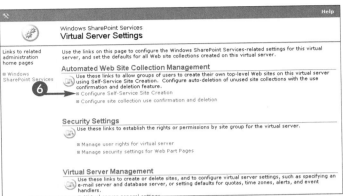

The Configure Self-Service Site Creation page appears.

7 Click the On option for Self-Service Site Creation (○ changes to ●).

8 Click OK.

Self-Service Site Creation is now active.

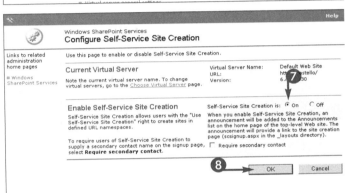

Besides from the SharePoint Central Administration can I configure Self-Service Site Creation (SSC) any other way?

▼ Yes. You can configure Self-Service Site Creation from the command line. To do this, click Start and then click Command Prompt to open a command line shell. You must know the URL parameter for the SSC you are enabling. Type the following syntax, which includes the URL to enable Self-Service Site Creation: **stsadm –o enablessc –url http://***My_Server*, where *My_Server* is the name of the virtual server that you have created and extended in SharePoint Services. You can add the optional syntax—**requiresecondarycontact**—if you need to have two contact names associated with the site.

When I turn on Self-Service Site Creation, is it turned on for all virtual servers on my physical server?

▼ No. You can only turn on Self-Service Site Creation for one virtual server at a time. To enable Self-Service Site Creation on additional virtual servers, you must access each one in SharePoint Central Administration and turn on Self-Service Site Creation for that server. You can turn off Self-Service Site Creation by clicking the Off option (○ changes to ●) next to Self-Service Site Creation is:. You can also require a second contact name by clicking Require secondary contact (☐ changes to ☑) before you click OK.

Access Default Site from IIS and Create New Site

You can use the default Web site in the Internet Information Services (IIS) Manager snap-in to create a new, managed intranet site for Windows SharePoint Services. You can allow any of your users to access the default site and to create as many sites as they want, using templates that are specific to their needs. This gives your users control of the construction, development, and management of their own intranet Web sites when they use Windows SharePoint Services tools.

Once a user has created a team site Home page, they can configure the Web Part pages on the team site to meet the specific requirements of the team project. A Web Part page

is a special set of Web page components that allow you to organize data such as lists, charts, and Web content into a single, dynamic Web portal. Users can adapt the information and design of the Web Part page to any project or task that a team needs to work on. A Web Part page is analogous to the control panel of a machine, as it contains all of the components needed to conduct the smooth operation of a particular task.

Access Default Site from IIS and Create New Site

① Click Start.

② Click Administrative Tools.

③ Click Internet Information Services (IIS) Manager.

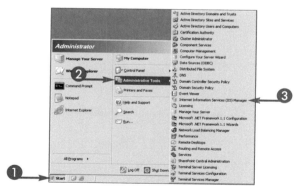

The Internet Information Services (IIS) Manager snap-in window appears.

④ Expand the local computer.

⑤ Expand Web Sites.

⑥ Right-click a virtual server.

⑦ Click Browse.

The Team Web Site Home page appears.

⑧ Click the "Self-Service Site Creation" link.

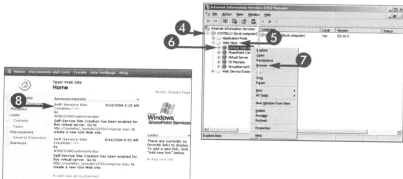

The Announcements: Self-Service Site Creation page appears.

⑨ Click the "http://costello/layouts/1033/scsignup.aspx" link.

The New SharePoint Site page appears.

⑩ Type a title.

⑪ Type a description.

⑫ Type a URL.

⑬ Type your e-mail address.

⑭ Click Create.

The My Site Template Selection page appears.

⑮ Click a template.

⑯ Click OK.

Windows creates a new site.

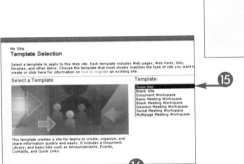

Once I create a new team Web site with Self-service Site Creation, how do I access and modify the site?

▼ You can open up any Web browser, such as Internet Explorer, and type the specific URL to the Web site that you created. In this example, in the Web browser address field, you type **http://costello/sites/mysite/default.aspx** and press Enter. The Home page appears for your new site. An authentication dialog box may appear, asking for a username and password. Type the username and password of the creator/owner of the site. Once you are authenticated, you can perform a wide variety of configuration tasks, such as adding shared documents, pictures, lists, announcements, and links.

Besides a team site, what other sorts of sites can I create using the My Site Template Selection page?

▼ You can create a wide variety of sites from templates, including a document workspace, a meeting workspace, a social meeting workspace, and a blank site or workspace. When you use the template for a blank site, the site contains only the most basic formatting. You can use a basic site when none of the available templates completely suits your needs or when you want to have more creative control over site construction than a template allows. You can also use a blank meeting workspace rather than any of the more specific meeting workspace templates when you want to have more control over your meeting environment.

PART VII

Understanding Server Disasters 388

Understanding Backup and
   Recovery 389

Back Up the System State with
   Backup Utility 390

Back Up the Registry with ASR and
   Create System Recovery Disk..................394

Schedule Data Backups 398

Understanding Active Directory
   Maintenance 404

Move the Active Directory Database 408

Perform Offline Defragmentation
   of Active Directory 410

Using replmon 416

Using repadmin 418

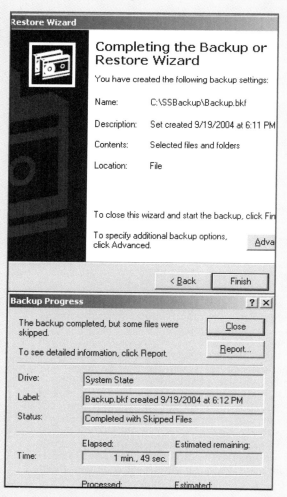

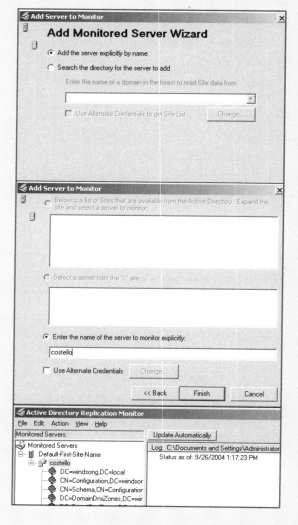

23 | Monitoring the Server

Tools to Monitor your Server 420

Using chkdsk and chkntfs 422

Customize the Event Viewer......................424

Configure Detail Level in Event Viewer 426

Filter Event Viewer Logs...........................428

Add a Counter to the System Monitor 430

Create Counter Logs.................................432

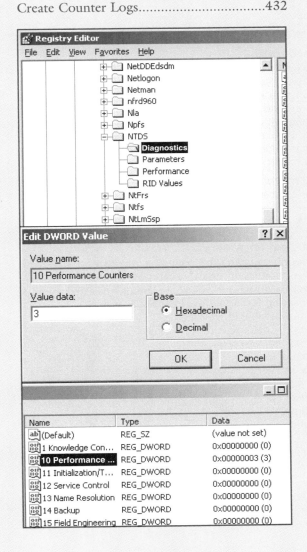

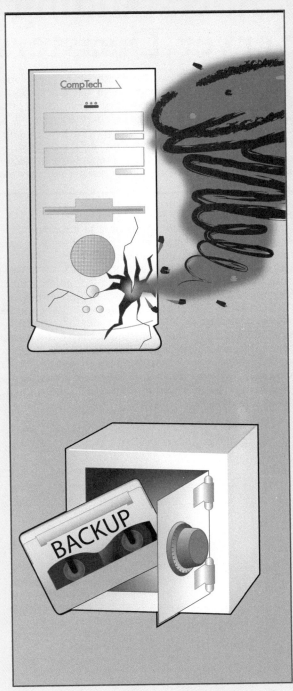

Understanding Server Disasters

Although Windows Server 2003 is a very reliable and robust operating system, like any computer operating system, it is vulnerable to threats that may damage or destroy your data. There are a variety of events that can jeopardize your servers. By being aware of the different threats that you must defend against, presented in this section, you can prepare and protect your servers and your data by creating a disaster recovery plan.

To avoid loss of data due to the types of disasters listed in this section, you must backup your data. For more on the types of back up you can perform, see the section "Understanding Backup and Recovery." Please note that if a server disaster occurs, any data that you created after a backup is unrecoverable.

Power Failure

You can lose data on your servers due to a sudden loss of electrical power in your server room. However, you can protect your system against power failures by using Uninterruptible Power Supplies (UPS). A UPS is a device that stands in between the power conduit that enters your server room and the servers to which it supplies power. The UPS filters the electrical power through a battery and passes it along to your servers. When the power fails, the UPS battery immediately takes over. The battery is not meant to operate the servers indefinitely, but you can use the time that your servers are on battery power to save your data and gracefully power down your servers. If you do not use a UPS system or there is a failure to the UPS system, then you can still lose data.

Hardware Failure

A hard drive failure is generally the single greatest cause of server hardware failure and data loss. This is why you should ensure that your servers use hot-swappable hard disk drives, and that you configure your servers to use a RAID 5 configuration. You can use a hardware solution for RAID 5 with basic disks, and a software solution for RAID 5 with dynamic disks. You can learn more about RAID 5 solutions in Chapter 9. You can also use RAID 1 and RAID 10 solutions.

You may also experience other types of hardware failure that can cause data loss. These include problems with a server motherboard, the Central Processing Unit (CPU), RAM, disk controllers, and other hardware components.

Physical Disasters

Although you can take many precautions to protect your server equipment, disasters can pose a threat to your server hardware and your data. Natural disasters such as hurricanes, tornadoes, and earthquakes may be unavoidable in your area. Your only defense is to ensure that you regularly back up your data and keep the storage media in a separate location.

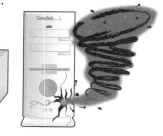

Understanding Backup and Recovery

You can implement backup and recovery procedures on your Windows Server 2003 servers to protect valuable data in the event of a disaster. For more on the various disasters that threaten your data, see the section "Understanding Server Disasters." If you lose data, a backup tape can restore any lost data. A *backup* is a copy of your data that you transfer to an independent storage device or medium, such as tape or CD-ROM. You can only restore data that you have backed up; any data that you lose after the last backup is unrecoverable.

If you have a great amount of data to back up, backing up all of your data on a daily basis is impractical. For example, within a corporate environment a backup may take a great deal of time; restoring data after a disaster may take equally long. For this reason, familiarize yourself with the different types of backup, discussed in this section, to keep all of your data safe while minimizing backup and recovery times.

Normal Backup

Also called a *full backup*, this is the foundation of your backup strategy. You can use a normal backup to save all of the data that you have selected to protect. When you use a normal backup, you can back up your data and remove the archive marker or bit in the files that indicates that the files have been backed up. An archive marker is a special attribute of a file that marks a file that has been modified since the last backup.

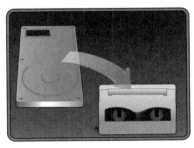

Incremental Backup

You must use an incremental backup in conjunction with a normal backup. An *incremental backup* saves only the information that changed in your server since the last back up. This way, you do not have to back up all of your data every day. When you do an incremental backup, the data archive bits are removed. To restore your data, you must first restore your normal backup as well as all of the daily incremental backups made since the last normal backup.

Copy Backup

A *copy backup* takes a *snapshot* of the exact state of your server and stores that snapshot offsite. Although a copy backup saves all of the data that you select, it does not remove the archive bit. As a result, there is no indication that your data files have been backed up.

Differential Backup

A *differential backup* saves all of the data changed since the last backup, but it does not remove the archive bit. Each time you use a differential backup, you record all of the changed data since the last Normal backup, so that each subsequent backup records increasing amounts of data. To restore your data, you must first restore from your normal backup tape, and then only the most recent differential backup.

Daily Backup

You can use a daily backup to save only the data that changed on a particular day; this does not change the archive bit for the saved data. You use daily backups to perform a quick backup of a limited amount of data.

Back Up the System State with Backup Utility

You can back up your server System State so that, if your Registry configuration or other settings become corrupt, you can restore your server to operation. You can also install a fresh copy of Windows Server 2003 on a new server and restore the System State that was backed up from a dead server to recreate the configuration of the old server on the new one. Any damage that is done to any of the System State components can result in a completely unusable server. The System State includes the Registry, which is the hierarchical configuration database for your Windows Server 2003

server. It also includes COM+ class registration database files, and the system boot files.

You can use a built-in backup utility called ntbackup.exe to back up the System State of your server. The ntbackup.exe application is the standard utility for backing up any or all of the data and configuration settings on a Windows Server 2003, Windows XP, or Windows 2000 computer. By default, ntbackup.exe backs up all of the data on the server and makes a system recovery disk that you can use to restore your server in the event of a disaster.

Back Up the System State with Backup Utility

① Click Start.

② Click Run.

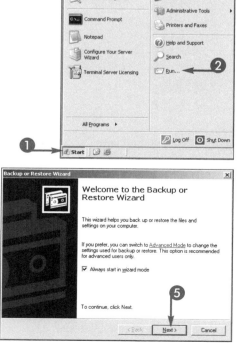

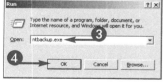

The Run dialog box appears.

③ Type **ntbackup.exe**.

④ Click OK.

The Backup or Restore Wizard appears.

⑤ Click Next.

The Backup or Restore page of the Wizard appears.

6 Click the "Back up files and settings" option (○ changes to ◉).

7 Click Next.

The What to Back Up page of the Wizard appears.

8 Click the "Let me choose what to back up" option (○ changes to ◉).

9 Click Next.

The Items to Back Up page of the Wizard appears.

10 Expand My Computer.

11 Click the System State option (□ changes to ☑).

12 Click Next.

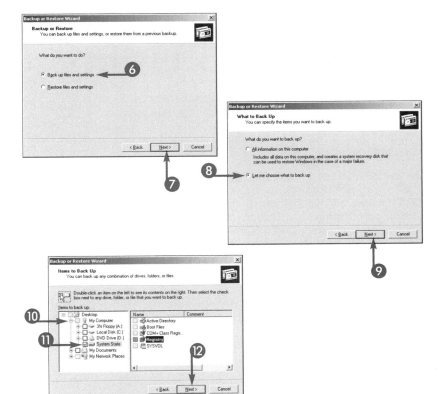

What is the COM+ Class registration database, and why is it important to the System State?

▼ COM+ is the next step in the evolution of the Microsoft Component Object Model and Microsoft Transaction Server (MTS). You can use COM+ to handle many of the resource management tasks that you previously had to program yourself. These tasks include thread allocation and security. COM+ can automatically make your applications more scalable by providing thread pooling, object pooling, and just-in-time object activation. You can also use COM+ to help protect the integrity of your data by providing transaction support, even if a transaction spans multiple databases over a network.

Is there any other way to run ntbackup.exe other than from the Run dialog box?

▼ Yes. You can also run ntbackup.exe from a command prompt. Click Start, then double-click Command Prompt. A command shell appears. To back up a file or folder, type **ntbackup backup@bks file name**. When you add @bks file name, you can indicate the name of the backup selection file, also known as the BKS file. You must use the @ character in this string when you want to specify the name of a backup selection file. You can also indicate a backup job name by adding the /J switch to the end of the string.

continued

Back Up the System State with Backup Utility *(Continued)*

Because of the dependencies between the various System State components, you can only back up the entire System State using ntbackup.exe. Saving your System State is the key to restoring a damaged server to its original condition after a failure.

When you back up the System State of a Domain Controller, you can also back up the Active Directory and the SYSVOL Directory so that you do not have to search for the individual components manually. When you back up the System State of other special role servers on your network, you can automatically back up any dependent

databases at the same time. This includes backing up the Certificate Services database on a Certificate server.

Although you cannot choose the specific components that you want to back up or restore in the System State, when you restore back to the original source, you can make alternative choices when you restore to an alternate location. When you choose to restore to an alternate location, you can restore only the Registry database, the SYSVOL Directory files, Cluster database information, and system boot files. You cannot restore the Active Directory services database, Certificate Services database, and COM+ Class registration database.

Back Up the System State with Backup Utility *(continued)*

The Backup Type, Destination, and Name page of the Wizard appears.

⑬ Click Browse.

The Save As dialog box appears.

⑭ Browse to a folder or device where you want to back up the System State.

⑮ Click Save.

The Backup Type, Destination, and Name page of the Wizard reappears.

● The path to the backup location for the System State appears here.

⑯ Type the backup name.

⑰ Click Next.

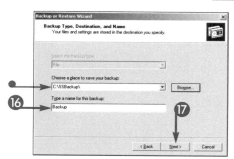

The Completing the Backup or Restore Wizard page of the Wizard appears.

⑱ Click Finish.

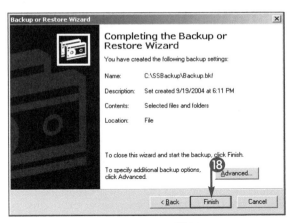

The backup process begins.

● The Backup Progress dialog box appears with information about the backup.

● For more information on the backup details, you can click Report.

Note: *The backup process may skip some files if a user or system process is currently using them.*

⑲ Click Close.

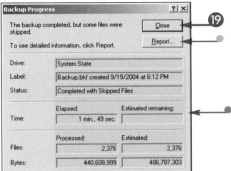

When I back up my System State, what backup locations can I browse to in the Backup Type, Destination, and Name page?

▼ You can back up your System State to any location that is connected to your Windows Server 2003 server. This includes any devices, either internal or external, that can store your data, such as a CD-ROM or DVD drive, or an external tape drive. You can also back up your System State to any location to which you are connected over the corporate network. This can include a particular server that is backed up regularly so that the System State data for all connected servers is saved to a single tape or other medium.

In the Backup Progress dialog box, what happens when I click Report?

▼ You can click Report in the Backup Progress dialog box to receive a detailed listing of the backup results. This listing is similar to that which appears in the dialog box. The report appears in a Notepad file, which is usually called *backup_name*01. log, where *backup_name* is actually the name you assigned to the backup job. The report includes more detail than what appears in the Backup Progress dialog box, and you can save it to an alternate location and print it out if necessary. The default location for these logs is in Documents and Settings, in the Administrator folder.

Back Up the Registry with ASR and Create System Recovery Disk

You can use the built-in backup utility ntbackup.exe to back up the Registry of your Windows Server 2003 server. This protects your server configuration files and enables you to restore the original configuration if the Registry database becomes corrupt. The Registry is the hierarchical database that contains all of the configuration information for your Windows server. If this database is damaged or corrupt, you cannot depend on the reliable service of the computer, and your server may refuse to boot. You can also install a fresh copy of the Windows Server 2003 operating system onto new server hardware and then restore the exact configuration of a dead server onto the new one. Once you reinstall all of the original

application software and then restore the data, your new server behaves just as if it were the original server. See the section "Understanding Backup and Recovery" for more information.

When you back up the Registry on a Windows 2000 Server computer, you can use ntbackup.exe to make an Emergency Repair Disk (ERD). Keep in mind that your Windows Server 2003 computer needs more information for a repair than you can place on a floppy. You can also use Automated System Recovery (ASR) to specifically back up the Registry but not all of the System State data in both 2000 and 2003 systems. ERD is not available in Windows Server 2003.

Back Up the Registry with ASR and Create System Recovery Disk

① Click Start.

② Click Run.

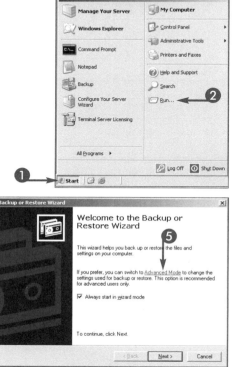

The Run dialog box appears.

③ Type **ntbackup.exe**.

④ Click OK.

The Backup or Restore Wizard appears.

⑤ Click the Advanced Mode link.

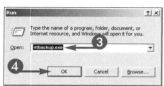

The Welcome page appears.

6 Click the Automated System Recovery Wizard icon.

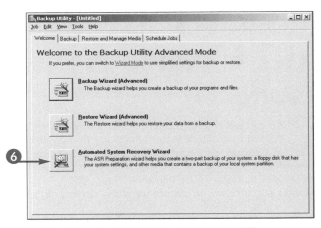

The Welcome to the Automated System Recovery Preparation Wizard page appears.

7 Click Next.

Are ASR and the System Recovery Disk the only ways that I can recover from a disaster?

▼ No. There are other methods that you can use to recover from a catastrophic server disaster. For example, you can try to recover from a server incident using the Last Known Good configuration startup option. You can use this configuration when your server has become unstable after a recent change, such as updating device drivers. You can also use the Recovery Console if the Last Known Good configuration does not work. You can use the Windows Server 2003 installation disk if the method in this section is unsuccessful. You should only use ASR as a last resort.

How do I conduct an Automated System Recovery Restore?

▼ You first need the ASR floppy diskette that you created during the backup process, the media on which you stored the backup, and the Windows Server 2003 installation CD-ROM. Insert the installation CD-ROM into the server CD-ROM drive and restart the server. Then press F2 at the beginning of the text-only mode of setup. You must follow the instructions that appear until the system has been recovered. If you have a mass storage controller and the manufacturer requires a separate driver file, then you must obtain that file before starting the recovery.

continued

Back Up the Registry with ASR and Create System Recovery Disk

(Continued)

You can use the Automated System Recovery (ASR) Wizard to create a System Recovery Disk as well as to back up the Registry. This means that if your server suffers a catastrophic disaster, then you can use the recovery disk to restart your Windows Server 2003 computer and attempt to restore all of the configuration files.

When you create the System Recovery Disk on a floppy diskette, you should ensure that it contains all of the disk configuration data. This includes information on both basic and dynamic volumes as well as about how to restore your

server. The diskette also contains log files with details about what information was actually backed up and what information is contained on the disk.

You can use the ASR Wizard to accomplish two separate but related tasks: backing up the Registry and other related files, and creating the System Recovery Disk. When you use ASR to attempt a recovery, you use the System Recovery Disk to reboot the server and to work with the backed-up data that is saved on a different storage medium to recover from your disaster. You cannot restore actual data files with ASR, and you must back up your file and folder data in a separate operation.

Back Up the Registry with ASR and Create System Recovery Disk *(continued)*

The Backup Destination page of the Wizard appears.

8 Type the path to the backup destination in the Backup media or file name field.

9 Click Next.

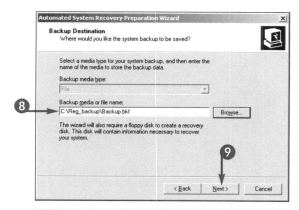

The Completing the Automated System Recovery Preparation Wizard page appears.

10 Click Finish.

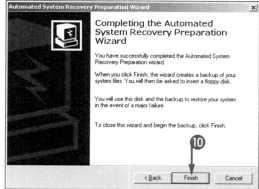

Windows runs the System Recovery and Backup processes.

The Backup Utility dialog box appears.

⓫ Insert a blank floppy diskette into the A:\ drive.

⓬ Click OK.

The files are copied to the ASR diskette.

The Backup Utility dialog box appears.

⓭ Remove the floppy diskette from the A:\ drive.

⓮ Label the diskette "Windows Automated System Recovery Disk for Backup.bkf" and insert the date and time.

⓯ Click OK.

Your backup is complete.

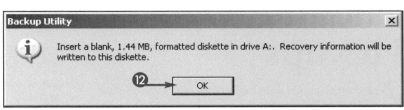

Backup Utility

Insert a blank, 1.44 MB, formatted diskette in drive A:. Recovery information will be written to this diskette.

⓬ → OK

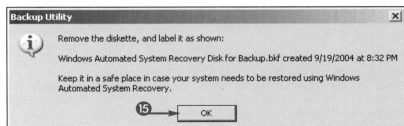

Backup Utility

Remove the diskette, and label it as shown:

Windows Automated System Recovery Disk for Backup.bkf created 9/19/2004 at 8:32 PM

Keep it in a safe place in case your system needs to be restored using Windows Automated System Recovery.

⓯ → OK

What if I want to create an ASR backup on a server that does not have a floppy drive?

▼ You can manually locate and copy the asr.sif and asrpnp.sif files from the server on which you want to perform the ASR backup, and transfer those files to a computer that does have a floppy drive. You can transfer those files over the network or copy them to another portable medium such as a USB thumb drive, then load them onto a computer with an A:\ drive and create the ASR backup disk. You can locate the asr.sif and asrpnp.sif files in the %systemroot %\repair directory.

What if I do not have the original floppy disk that I made with ASR and I need to do an ASR restore on this server?

▼ When you do an ASR restore, you are prompted to insert the floppy diskette containing the asr.sif and asrpnp.sif files that were created at the time of the original ASR backup. If you do not have the original floppy diskette, then you can obtain the same files from the ASR backup set that you made at the same time the floppy backup was made. You can access the media on which you backed up your server and locate the two .sif files that you need. Copy the two .sif files to a floppy diskette and then begin the ASR restore process.

Schedule Data
Backups

Y ou can schedule data backups so that your valuable corporate data is automatically backed up to a storage medium on a regular basis. This ensures that your data is safe and that you can restore it in the event of a server disaster.

Without regular server data backups, your company is vulnerable; business can drastically slow or completely stop if a server accident results in partial or total loss of corporate data. You can schedule automatic backups and specify the type of backup that you want to occur so that the process occurs automatically and with little administrative effort.

You then only need to manually remove and replace the tape media without having to manually trigger each backup event.

You can also control the frequency with which data is backed up from your company servers. The more often you schedule data backups, the safer your company data becomes. The trade off is that more backups require more tapes and more down-time for the servers because you can generally only back up data when the server is not being used. To solve this problem, you may want to schedule automatic backups to occur in the evenings and on weekends, when no one is working on your servers.

Schedule Data Backups

1 Click Start.

2 Click Run.

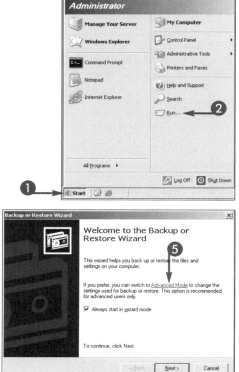

The Run dialog box appears.

3 Type **ntbackup.exe**.

4 Click OK.

The Backup or Restore Wizard appears.

5 Click the Advanced Mode link.

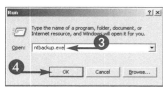

The Welcome page of the Wizard appears.

6 Click the Backup Wizard (Advanced) icon.

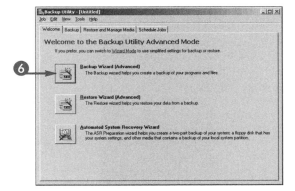

The Backup Wizard appears.

7 Click Next.

The What to Back Up page of the Wizard appears.

8 Select Back up selected files, drives, or network data (changes to).

9 Click Next.

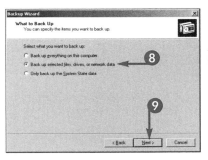

In the What to Back Up page of the Backup Wizard, what happen when I select the "Back up everything on this computer" option?

▼ If you select the "Back up everything on this computer" option (changes to), then you schedule a backup to include all data on your Windows Server 2003 computer, including data files, folders, Operating System, System Stateprogram files, and everything in the My Computer, My Documents, and My Network Places folders. Because this requires a lot of storage space, you can instead select the specific files and folders that you want to back up, to save backup time as well as server and network resources.

When I select Back up selected files, drives or network data in the Backup Wizard, how specifically can I select data that I want to back up?

▼ You can either back up the entire contents of the My Computer, My Documents, or My Network Places folders, or select only specific subfolders and files in each one of these folders. You can browse your server using Windows Explorer, expand specific folders and files in the file structure, and select only those files and folders that you want to back up, including files and folders at remote locations over the network.

Schedule Data Backups *(Continued)*

When you schedule automatic backups of your data, you can specify the types of data and data locations that you want to back up. This ensures that only the data that you need to preserve is stored on your backup media. You can also choose the frequency with which you back up data to conserve server and network resources, and schedule backups when they do not interfere with normal business operations.

To back up server data, you can log onto the server or the domain as a member of the Administrator group, the

Backup Operator group, or the Server Operator group. This gives you the appropriate permissions to set up an automatic backup schedule.

In addition to scheduling automatic backups, you can schedule special backups before conducting hardware upgrades, such as adding RAM or installing a hard disk drive. This protects your data from any potential accident that may occur during an upgrade procedure. You should also conduct a special backup prior to any major upgrade in application software.

Schedule Data Backups *(continued)*

The Items to Back Up page of the Wizard appears.

⑩ Select the files and folders that you want to back up.

⑪ Click Next.

The Backup Type, Destination, and Name page of the Wizard appears.

⑫ Type a destination path.

⑬ Click Next.

The Completing the Backup Wizard page appears.

⑭ Click Advanced.

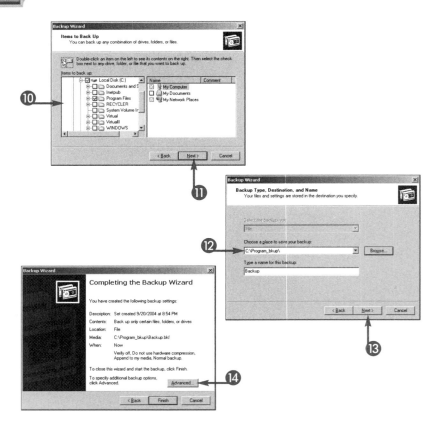

The Type of Backup page of the Wizard appears.

⑮ Click here and select the type of backup you want.

⑯ Click Next.

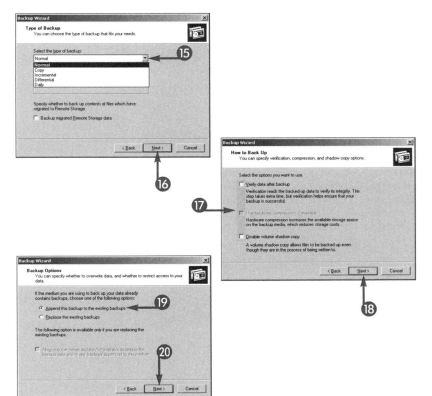

The How to Back Up page of the Wizard appears.

⑰ Click the options you want to use (☐ changes to ☑).

⑱ Click Next.

The Backup Options page of the Wizard appears.

⑲ Click the type of option you want (◯ changes to ◉).

⑳ Click Next.

In the Completing the Backup Wizard page, what happens if I click the Finish button instead of the Advanced button?

▼ If you choose to finish the Backup Wizard at this point without clicking Advanced, then you can still back up data to a specific location, from one or many locations on your server and your network. However, you cannot select the type of backup—such as normal, copy, differential, or incremental—and you cannot select a specific schedule for your backup, either as a single or a regularly repeating event.

In the Backup Wizard under Backup Options, what is the difference between appending versus replacing data?

▼ You can choose either of these options (◯ changes to ◉) when you are using a backup medium that already contains data. You can choose to append the data when you want to add the new data while leaving the current data on the medium intact. This occurs when you conduct differential backups that require the data from one day to be added to the previous data that you have recorded. You can choose to replace data on a medium when you no longer need the older data and are recycling your media. For more on the various kinds of backups available to you, see the section "Understanding Backup and Recovery."

continued

Schedule Data Backups *(Continued)*

You can schedule the specific dates and times that your backup utility automatically saves selected data files and folders to your backup medium. This saves administrative effort and ensures that all of your important data is backed up. Differential and incremental data backups are the most common types of backups for preserving corporate data. You can use advanced features in the Backup Wizard to not only schedule a backup but also to select which backup scheme you want to use. Therefore, you do not have to manually select a scheme each time you back up your data; instead, you can specify an initial

scheduling configuration and then leave it in place as long as it serves your needs. For more on differential and incremental data backups, see the section "Understanding Backup and Recovery."

Although you can delegate responsibility to configure and conduct backup procedures to another user, you must also ensure that you have not set any NTFS disk quotas for that user. This is because NTFS disk quotas can make it difficult for a user to conduct backup operations by restricting user access to a drive volume.

The When to Back Up page of the Wizard appears.

㉑ Click Later (changes to).

㉒ Click Set Schedule.

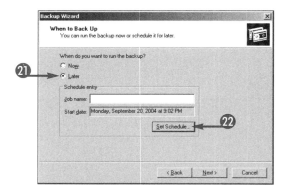

The Schedule Job dialog box appears.

㉓ Click here and select a backup frequency.

㉔ Click here and select a backup start time.

㉕ Click here and select the date of the backup.

㉖ Click OK.

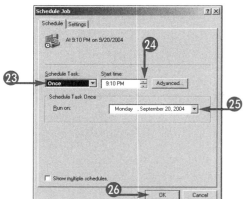

The Set Account Information dialog box
appears.

27 Type your administrative password.

28 Retype your administrative password.

29 Click OK.

The When to Back Up page of the Wizard
reappears.

30 Type a job name.

31 Click Next.

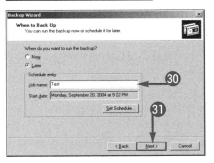

The Completing the Backup Wizard page
appears.

32 Click Finish.

Your backup is scheduled for the settings that
you have selected.

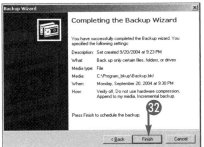

When I schedule a backup in the Backup Wizard, do I have to specify a name for the backup job?

▼ Yes. When you schedule a backup job and return to the When to back up page of the Backup Wizard, you must give the backup job a name. If you do not type a name in the Job name field before you click Next, then an error message appears, stating that you must give the job a name. You can only schedule named jobs because the backup utility uses the name to keep track of the backup job and to create a log for the job.

What happens if I schedule a backup job for a date and time that has already passed?

▼ When you schedule a job for a date and time that has already passed, and you click Next in the When to back up page, an error message appears, stating that the date and time has passed and that the backup will not take place. You can now accept the option to reschedule the date and time. You can return to the Schedule Job dialog box and adjust the date and time settings to a future date and time so that your backup will occur.

Understanding Active Directory Maintenance

Y ou can conduct maintenance activities on your Active Directory database in your Windows Server 2003 domain. This allows you to optimize Active Directory Services on your network and to prevent or correct issues in the Active Directory that may impair or stop Active Directory replication.

You can diagnose issues related to Active Directory replication, and repair these issues so that domain database information can be shared among all of your Domain Controllers. This also allows resources to remain available to your domain users, regardless of physical location. If the Active Directory is impaired, then your domain users may not be able to log on to the domain or access shared resources such as network printers or shared disk volumes that store their working files. There are a number of issues related to Active Directory problems, listed in this section, and troubleshooting that you can address.

Slow Resource Access

You may receive reports of domain users that have intermittent difficulty, such as long waiting times, when they authenticate to the domain. You may also receive reports of domain users experiencing slow response times when they attempt to search for or access domain resources.

One of the causes that you can investigate is the possibility that users are attempting to access the nearest domain controller over a low-bandwidth network link. This can occur when a physical site does not have a Domain Controller present and your domain users must use a slow, Wide Area Network (WAN) connection to access a Domain Controller at the remote location. These domain users may also be located in a place that is not associated with a site, or that is associated with an incorrect site. You can read more about Active Directory sites and services in Chapter 4.

Slow Active Directory Replication

You may receive information that Active Directory replication is unusually slow in the domain. Slow replication can be due to insufficient links between different Active Directory sites or because no site link bridges exist in your Active Directory infrastructure. Without sufficient links between different Active Directory site locations, you can experience unusually long replication times between intersite locations within your domain or between domains. You may also discover that replication intervals are not frequent enough to allow timely replication between Domain Controllers at different sites.

No Active Directory Replication

You may determine that Active Directory replication has completely stopped within a site or between sites. If you see that replication activities are not occurring within a site, then you can check your physical network connections, network configuration elements, and the availability of individual Domain Controllers within the site. You may also discover that there are errors in DNS services that prevent Domain Controllers from resolving domain names to IP addresses, and that prevent Domain Controllers from being located within the site.

If Active Directory replication between sites has stopped, then you can also investigate DNS issues as well as connection issues, along with the possible absence of site links between sites. You must have at least one site link to allow Active Directory replication between all sites in your domain.

RPC Server is Unavailable Error

You may receive an RPC Server is Unavailable error message in the Active Directory Replication Monitor (replmon) for a number of reasons, including the fact that a replication partner has gone offline, and is not available on the network. You can confirm this by attempting to force replication; if the replication partner is offline, then your attempt will not be successful. You may also receive an RPC Server is Unavailable error message if your DNS service is not correctly configured on the network. You can investigate a number of different DNS elements that cause this error, including issues with the registered CNAME record, the registered A resource record, and the DNS zone having a correct delegation to any available child zones. See the section "Using replmon" later in this chapter.

Active Directory Sites and Services Access Errors

You may receive an Access Denied error between replication partners in your Active Directory sites and services, and you may not be able to replicate the Active Directory database. The Access Denied error may be caused by not having the Replication Synchronization permission when you try to force a manual Active Directory database replication between your replication partners.

Domain Naming Master Error

You may only discover a failure in the Domain Naming Master when you attempt to create a new domain or to rename or delete a domain that you administer. When a Domain Naming Master server fails, you must seize the role from another Domain Controller. You must never allow the failed Domain Naming Master to be reactivated without reformatting the hard disk drive, reinstalling the Windows Server 2003 operating system, and assigning it a different role on the network.

Infrastructure Master Error

You may only discover a failure in the Infrastructure Master when you attempt to move or rename a large number of user or other accounts in your domain. When the Infrastructure Master fails, you must seize the role of this Operations Master while verifying that it is not on the same server as the Global Catalog Server role. When you seize the Infrastructure Master role, you must use a server that is on the same site as the Global Catalog Server.

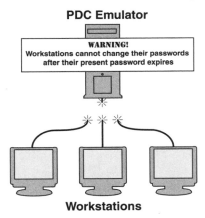

Workstations

PDC Emulator Error

You may discover a PDC Emulator failure if your domain contains Windows Domain Controllers that are pre-Windows 2000 computers, such as Windows NT Backup Domain Controllers (BDCs). When you discover a PDC Emulator error, you may receive reports that Windows NT workstations that connect to Windows NT BDCs cannot change their passwords after their prior passwords expire.

Move the Active Directory Database

Y ou can move the Active Directory Database on your Windows Server 2003 Domain Controller to a different hard disk partition. This allows you to provide more disk space as the Active Directory database grows, and to place it on a different partition from the Active Directory log files.

Active Directory log files are constantly written to on your Domain Controller, and you can make the Active Directory database more immediately responsive to users by placing it on a partition that is not overly active due to log file writes. When the Active Directory database is on the same

hard drive as your log files and a user or process queries the database, the disk heads must move to read the ntds.dit files, thus reducing hard disk performance on your Domain Controller.

As your domain or domains continue to grow, the Active Directory database also grows, and can eventually fill up the default location that you provided when you created it. You can move the database to a larger physical hard disk or to a larger disk partition on the same drive to allow the database to expand without filling up the allowed disk space.

Move the Active Directory Database

① Click Start.

② Click Shut Down.

   The Shut Down Windows dialog box appears.

③ Click here and select Restart.

④ Click Planned (☐ changes to ☑).

⑤ Click here and select Other (Planned).

⑥ Type a comment.

⑦ Click OK.

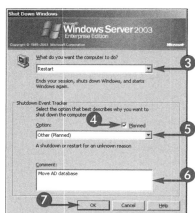

The computer restarts.

⑧ Press F8 when the computer begins to restart.

   The Windows Advanced Options Menu appears.

⑨ Select Directory Services Restore Mode (Windows domain controllers only).

⑩ Press Enter.

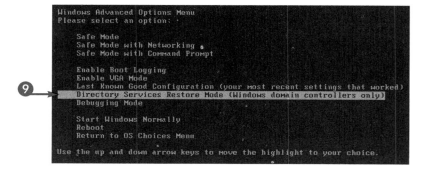

The computer boots into Safe Mode without loading the Active Directory.

⑪ Press Ctrl+Alt+Del.

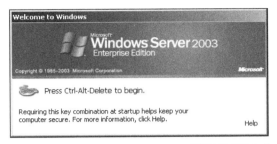

The Log On to Windows dialog box appears.

⑫ Type **Administrator**.

⑬ Type the password for the local server.

⑭ Click OK.

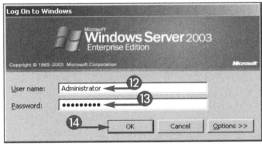

The Desktop warning dialog box appears.

⑮ Click OK.

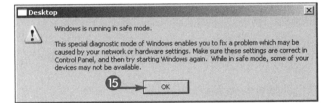

When I restart my computer in order to boot into Safe Mode, why do I have to choose a reason for doing this?

▼ This feature is new with Windows Server 2003. If you do not select a reason for your server restart or shutdown in the Shutdown Event Tracker menu, you cannot complete this action. You can select from a series of planned shutdown options, including Hardware Maintenance or Installation, Operating System Reconfiguration, and Application Maintenance or Installation. Windows records this information in log files that you can review as part of your overall server maintenance logs. You can also choose the Other (Planned) option when none of the other selections apply.

When I restart my Domain Controller in Safe Mode, why is my administrator password different from the one that I use to log onto the domain?

▼ When you installed and configured Windows Server 2003 on your domain controller, you were prompted to create a password on the server that is different from the one that you use to authenticate onto the domain. You can use this password to authenticate onto the local server without being connected to the network. You log on to the local server and are given rights to administer different maintenance functions on the server, rather than performing Active Directory management functions at the domain level.

continued

Move the Active Directory Database *(Continued)*

Y ou can use the ntdsutil.exe command line utility to move the Active Directory transactional database in Safe Mode to prevent the Active Directory database from being damaged in the move to the new location. This also enables you to preserve the integrity of the database and to ensure that the Domain Controller continues to function effectively.

The ntdsutil.exe application is an Active Directory maintenance tool that you can use to perform multiple Active Directory management tasks. You can use ntdsutil.exe to manage single master operations, to remove

metadata left behind by Domain Controllers that you have removed from service on the network due to a malfunction, and to perform authoritative restores of the database.

Safe Mode is a method of booting up your Windows Server 2003 Domain Controller, and loading only the most basic files and drivers. When you boot your server into Safe Mode, the Active Directory database is not loaded. Because it is inactive, you can safely move the Active Directory database without damaging it. In Safe Mode, the Active Directory is not connected to the network or the domain, and cannot receive or transmit replication information.

Move the Active Directory Database *(continued)*

The desktop appears in Safe Mode.

⑯ Click Start.

⑰ Click Command Prompt.

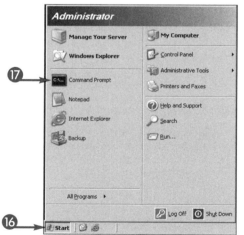

The command shell appears.

⑱ Type **ntdsutil**.

⑲ Press Enter.

The ntdsutil prompt appears.

⑳ Type **files**.

㉑ Press Enter.

The file maintenance prompt appears.

㉒ Type **move db to E:\database**.

㉓ Press Enter.

Windows moves the database.

㉔ Type **quit**.

Windows exits the command shell.

㉕ Click Start.

㉖ Click Shut Down.

The computer restarts.

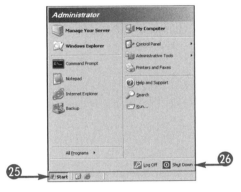

What happens when I open a command shell and access ntdsutil.exe while the server is operating in normal mode?

▼ You can open a command shell while your Windows Server 2003 Domain Controller is operating in normal mode and type **ntdsutil** at the prompt to access this utility. You cannot safely manage NTDS database files when you are not in Safe Mode because the Active Directory database is loaded and operational in the domain. If you type **files** at the ntdsutil command prompt, the following message appears: Error: Operation only allowed when booted in DS restore mode "set SAFEBOOT_OPTION=DSREPAIR" to override – NOT RECOMMENDED!

When I try to move the Active Directory database to a new location, do I have to create the destination folder in advance or can I create it when I move the database?

▼ When you type the specific path to the location where you want to move the Active Directory database, the drive partition and folder must already exist. At the file maintenance prompt in the command shell, you do not have the option to create the path to the destination for your Active Directory database before you move it. You must either create the folder on your server in the GUI while in normal mode, or create it from the command line in an action previous to your Restore Mode operation.

Perform Offline Defragmentation of Active Directory

You can perform an offline defragmentation of your Active Directory database on a Domain Controller. This ensures that your Active Directory database files are organized in a contiguous structure and allows you to recover any space on the Domain Controller hard disk drive is lost due to data fragmentation. As a result, your system performance improves and available space is maximized.

All data and database files on any computer hard drive become fragmented with normal use. *Fragmentation* occurs when files are written to a hard drive in discontiguous locations so that your hard drive heads must move over

many different parts of the disk platters to access a single file or directory. This slows down data retrieval and overall disk performance of the server.

Although you can defragment your Active Directory database while the server is in normal mode, the process is slow because the database is in use during the defragmentation process. Also, although you can do online defragmentation, you cannot reduce the overall size of the Active Directory database; the space that now-deleted database files once occupied remains unavailable for reuse, even though the specific files are reorganized so that they are contiguous as possible given the space left behind by deleted files.

Perform Offline Defragmentation of Active Directory

① Power up your server.

② Press F8 during startup.

The Windows Advanced Options Menu appears.

③ Select Directory Services Restore Mode (Windows domain controllers only).

④ Press Enter.

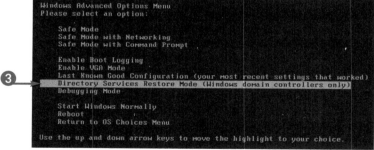

The computer boots in Safe Mode, without loading the Active Directory.

⑤ Press Ctrl+Alt+Del.

The Log On to Windows dialog box appears.

⑥ Type **Administrator**.

⑦ Type your password.

⑧ Click OK.

The Desktop warning dialog box appears.

9 Click OK.

The desktop appears in Safe Mode.

10 Click Start.

11 Click Command Prompt.

The command shell appears.

12 Type **ntdsutil**.

13 Press Enter.

When I want to boot into Directory Services Restore Mode, do I have to reboot my server from normal mode, or can I boot it when it is powered down?

▼ You can only enter into Directory Services Restore Mode after you reboot the Domain Controller. You can do this while it is active by rebooting the device and pressing the F8 key as the server restarts, or you can power up a completely inactive server and then press F8 as the device is powering up. You are most likely to perform the former operation because you rarely have a Domain Controller that is completely offline, unless you are installing new hardware.

What is the difference between Safe Mode and Directory Services Restore Mode?

▼ *Safe Mode* is a method of accessing your computer or server and performing maintenance tasks on it while only minimal files and drivers are installed. You can boot any Windows computer into Safe Mode or Safe Mode with Networking to determine the cause of a malfunction. *Directory Services Restore Mode* is a form of Safe Mode operations that is only available on Domain Controllers. Directory Services Restore Mode enables you to boot your Domain Controller without loading the Active Directory database. This way, you can perform maintenance tasks on the Active Directory database more safely and not have an impact on the domain.

continued

PART VIII

411

Perform Offline Defragmentation of Active Directory *(Continued)*

You can only recover lost space on your Domain Controller hard disk drives when you defragment the Active Directory database while it is offline. Offline defragmentation allows you to not only reorganize your Active Directory database files so that they are now contiguous with each other, but also to recover any lost space that deleted objects once occupied. As a result, you can recover all of your lost space on the drives and reuse it for new data, thus maximizing disk use efficiency.

Consider performing an offline defragmentation on a copy of the Active Directory database, and not the original database files. This enables you to protect your Active

Directory database files from damage or the corruption that can occur during the defragmentation process. You are most likely to use offline defragmentation after you delete large amounts of objects from the Active Directory database, which leaves a large amount of unused space.

Once you complete defragmentation, you can archive your original Active Directory database and replace it with the defragmented database. For normal operations on your Domain Controller, online defragmentation is sufficient to maintain data in a contiguous form. Online defragmentation occurs automatically every 12 hours on your Domain Controller.

Perform Offline Defragmentation of Active Directory *(continued)*

The ntdsutil prompt appears.

14 Type **files**.

15 Press Enter.

The File maintenance prompt appears.

16 Type **info**.

17 Press Enter.

The drive information and DS Path information data appears.

18 Type **compact to C:\offline**.

19 Press Enter.

Operation completed successfully message appears.

⑳ Type **quit**.

㉑ Press Enter

Returns to the ntdsutil prompt.

㉒ Type **quit**

㉓ Press Enter.

When I use the ntdsutil utility in the command shell, why do I type "info" at the file maintenance prompt, before performing offline defragmentation?

▼ When you type **info** at the file maintenace prompt in the command shell, you can verify the current size of the Active Directory database and the Active Directory database log files, as well as verify the current path of the database and log files. You can then determine whether the location that you have selected to move the Active Directory database for defragmentation is large enough to accommodate the database. If the destination folder is too small, then the move and defragmentation operation will fail.

When I move my database files for defragmentation, does it matter what drive I use or how I name the destination folder?

▼ You can move your Active Directory database to any drive or folder on your Domain Controller that is large enough to receive the database. You can use the C:\ drive and create a new folder there for the purpose of defragmenting the database, or you can use another drive partition on the server. You can specify any name for the destination folder, although you should use a name that you can later recognize as the location of the defragmented Active Directory database. If you use a folder name that contains spaces, you must type the entire path in quotes, for example, **"C:\New Folder"**.

continued

Perform Offline Defragmentation of Active Directory *(Continued)*

You can continue to perform an offline Defragmentation of the Active Directory database file by compacting the file to the directory you previously created for it so that you can successfully defragment the directory and recover any "lost" space on your hard disk drives. Because you can only completely defragment the AD database while Active Directory is not running, you must replace the defragmented AD database with the AD database located in the NTDS folder in the Windows folder on the C: drive. This is the default location of the domain controller AD database. Once the

defragmented AD database replaces the current database, you can restart your server and any previously occupied HDD space is returned for future use.

Offline Defragmentation of the Active Directory database is only recommended after you have deleted a large number of AD objects from AD. You can encounter this situation, for example, when your company downsizes and removes a branch office. This office likely contained a large number of AD objects including users, computers, printers and so on. Under normal operational use, you perform offline defragmention infrequently.

Perform Offline Defragmentation of Active Directory *(continued)*

㉕ Return to command prompt.

㉖ Type **copy c:\offline\ntds.dit c:\windows\ntds\ntds.dit**

㉗ Press Enter.

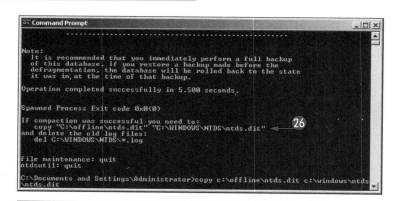

● A message appears asking to overwrite c:\windows\ntds\ntds.dit

㉘ Type **all**.

㉙ Press Enter.

● The copied files message appears.

30 Type **del C:\windows\ntds*.log**

31 Press Enter.

The old ntds log files are deleted.

32 Type **exit** to close command window.

The Command window closes.

33 Click Start.

34 Click Shutdown.

The server restarts and any previously occupied HDD space previously is returned for future use.

After copying the defragmented AD database to the default location for the ntds.dit files, why do I delete the ntds log files.

▼ The AD database or ntds log files contain information regarding the condition of the Active Directory database up to the time you took the DC offline to perform the offline defragmentation process. Once you defragment and replace the AD database, the previous log files are no longer relevant and can provide misleading information regarding the state of the current AD database. Once you delete the old AD database log files, new log files are written reflecting the current state of the database.

If the location of the current Active Directory Database files are not in their default location, how will I know where they are so I can copy the defragmented database to that location?

▼ After you reboot the domain controller to safe mode, open a command window and type **ntdsutil**, you can type **files**, and then type **info** to receive to a successive set of prompts. After you type **info** and press Enter, a set of information appears that includes the current location of the AD database and the size of the database. At that point, you can make note of the location of the database so that you can later copy the defragmented AD database to the location you noted.

Using replmon

You can use the Active Directory Replication Monitor, or replmon, tool to conduct Active Directory monitoring and troubleshooting tasks so that when you suspect a problem with Active Directory replication, you can quickly determine the source and correct it. Quick and accurate diagnosis of replication problems is the key to maintaining a continually functioning Active Directory infrastructure, and you can minimize any potential downtime resulting from Active Directory problems by using replmon to find the source of the problem.

The Active Directory Replication Monitor is a Graphical User Interface (GUI) tool that you can use as an Administrator to view Active Directory replication and to force Active

Directory synchronization between Domain Controllers. You can use the replmon context-sensitive File, Edit, Action, and View menus to access different replmon functions. You can also create a list of servers that are monitored by replmon.

The replmon tool does not install by default on your Windows Server 2003 computer, and is not installed when you promote a server to a Domain Controller with dcpromo. Dcpromo is a utility that you can use to promote a Windows Server 2003 server to a domain controller or demote a DC to a member server. You must load replmon from the Support Tools folder located on the Windows Server 2003 installation CD-ROM.

Using replmon

① Click Start.

② Click Run.

The Run dialog box appears.

③ Type **replmon**.

④ Click OK.

The Active Directory Replication Monitor snap-in window appears.

⑤ Click Edit.

⑥ Click Add Monitored Server.

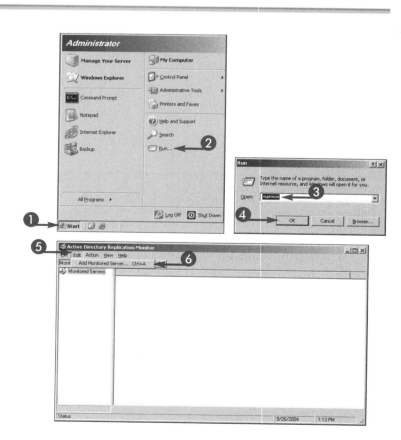

The Add Monitored Server Wizard appears.

7 Click the "Add the server explicitly by name" option (○ changes to ◉).

8 Click Next.

The Add Server to Monitor dialog box appears.

9 Type a server name.

10 Click Finish.

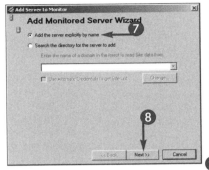
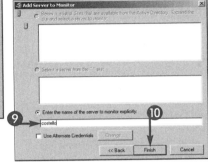

● Windows adds the server to the Active Directory Replication Monitor.

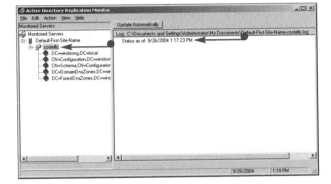

Once I add a server to the Active Directory Replication Monitor, how can I monitor the server?

▼ You can monitor the server in a variety of ways. First, click Action in the Active Directory Replication Monitor toolbar. A list of functions appears. You can choose to update the status of the server, check replication topology, and synchronize the directory partition with all of the connected servers. You can use this list to display data from a number of different categories. For example, you can display all domain controllers in the domain, replication topologies, and group policy status.

What are some of the other functions of the Active Directory Replication Monitor?

▼ You can click Action in the toolbar, then click Domain, and then click Search Domain Controllers for Replication Errors. You can also click View in the toolbar, and then click Options to open the Active Directory Replication Monitor Options dialog box. In the General tab, you can select the "Show Retired Replication Partners," "Show Transitive Replication Partners and Extended Data," or "Notify when replication fails after this number of attempts" options (☐ changes to ☑). In the last option, you must type the number of attempts that you want to set.

Using repadmin

You can use the Replication Diagnostics, or repadmin, command-line tool to conduct a wide variety of Active Directory monitoring and management tasks. This allows you to diagnose and locate problems with Active Directory replication, and to repair these problems and restore Active Directory Domain Controller replication functions. If you are unable to locate an Active Directory problem, then you cannot access resources and keep the domain database consistent. You must also load Rapadmin from support tools.

You can use repadmin to perform most of the tasks that you can do with the replmon GUI utility. You can also use a comprehensive collection of switches or parameters with

repadmin at the command prompt to exercise more specific administrative control over how you can manage the Active Directory on your Windows Server 2003 Domain Controllers. The list of repadmin.exe switches is lengthy, and you can access it by opening a command window and typing **repadmin /?**

You can also use repadmin to monitor the replication topology of your domain from the point of view of each Domain Controller in the domain. This allows you to determine whether a particular Domain Controller is experiencing an issue that interferes with replication to the other Domain Controllers in the domain.

Using repadmin

① Click Start.

② Click Command Prompt.

The command shell appears.

③ Type **repadmin /showsig** *servername.domain* replacing *servername* with the name of your server, and *domain* with your domain name.

④ Press Enter.

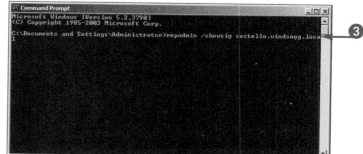

The command shell displays any retired signatures.

5 Type **repadmin /showctx** *servername.domain* replacing *servername* with the name of your server, and *domain* with your domain name.

6 Press Enter.

```
Command Prompt                                              _ □ ×
Microsoft Windows [Version 5.2.3790]
(C) Copyright 1985-2003 Microsoft Corp.

C:\Documents and Settings\Administrator>repadmin /showsig costello.windsong.loca
l
Default-First-Site-Name\COSTELLO

Current DC invocationID: 4725956f-a35e-4380-becf-81a6dae0a310

No retired signatures.

C:\Documents and Settings\Administrator>repadmin /showctx costello.windsong.loca
l_
```
5

The command shell displays the open context handles.

7 Type **exit**.

8 Press Enter.

The command shell closes after having performed the diagnostics task.

```
Command Prompt                                              _ □ ×
l
Default-First-Site-Name\COSTELLO

Current DC invocationID: 4725956f-a35e-4380-becf-81a6dae0a310

No retired signatures.

C:\Documents and Settings\Administrator>repadmin /showctx costello.windsong.loca
l
Caching GUIDs.
.
3 open context handles.

NTDSAPI client @ 10.0.1.2 (PID 1524) (Handle 0x2849bd0)
        bound, refs=1, last used 2004-09-26 10:49:12

Default-First-Site-Name\COSTELLO @ 10.0.1.2 (PID 508) (Handle 0x267ba8)
        bound, refs=1, last used 2004-09-26 14:03:42

NTDSAPI client @ 10.0.1.2 (PID 3864) (Handle 0x2801848)
        bound, refs=2, last used 2004-09-26 14:06:37

C:\Documents and Settings\Administrator>exit_
```
7

What other types of commands can I use with the repadmin.exe command line utility?

▼ You have a long list of command-line parameters. The showrepl command displays the replication partners for any Domain Controller in your domain. At the command prompt, type **repadmin / showrepl** *servername.domain* — replacing *servername* with the name of your server, and *domain* with your domain name — and press Enter. The command shell displays all of the Inbound Neighbors by name objectGuid, last replication attempt, and whether it was successful or unsuccessful. ObjectGuid is an attribute that applies only to Active Directory objects. You can also force replication between two partners by typing **repadmin /replicate** *servername1.domain servername2.domain name* dc=domain,dc.com. Substitute the terms *servername1* and *servername2* with the actual names of the Domain Controllers between which you want to create a connection.

Can I only view replication partners and issues using repadmin, or can I also add and subtract partners?

▼ You can manually add a partner using the /add switch with the repadmin command. This allows you to create a replication connection between two Domain Controllers in your Active Directory domain. You must use either the server Global Unique Identifier (GUID) or DNS Fully Qualified Domain Names (FQDNs) when you create the link. For example, you can type **repadmin /add cn=configuration,dc=domain name,dc=com** *servername1.domain.com servername2.domain. com* and then press Enter. Substitute the terms *servername1* and *servername2* with the actual names of the Domain Controllers between which you want to create a connection.

Tools to Monitor Your Server

Y ou can use a number of different tools to monitor the health and performance of your Windows Server 2003 computer to ensure that it is functioning normally and to know when it is not. You can then diagnose and repair any problem that the monitoring process detects. If you do not monitor your server activity, you cannot identify issues that arise with your server. As a result, you cannot manage your servers, and this may endanger your business network and data.

You can also use logging and monitoring tools to establish a baseline for normal server operations and to compare subsequent server behavior with the baseline to identify any changes that indicate either a problem or the need to expand server resources to maintain adequate operations.

Task Manager

You can use Task Manager to quickly access and review a variety of operations on your Windows Server 2003 server. Task Manager is available on most Windows operating systems, including Windows 9x, Windows ME, Windows 2000, Windows XP, and Windows Server 2003.

You can open the Task Manager by using the Ctrl+Alt+Del key combination and then clicking the Task Manager button. You can review five basic functions using the Task Manager: Applications, Processes, Performance, Networking, and Users. Applications show which software packages are running on your server as well as their operational status. Processes show all of the active processes that are running on the server, including Image Name, User Name, CPU and Memory Usage. Performance displays CPU and Page File Usage on the server in graph format, as well as information on Physical and Kernel Memory, and other data. Networking shows graphed data of activity on the different network interfaces on the server, including load and link speed. Users show the names of the users currently connected to the server. You can log off, disconnect, or send a message to any connected user from this window.

Event Viewer

You can use the Event Viewer to monitor various logs that record common activities on your server. The default logs are Application, Security, and System, although other logs are added to the Event Viewer as other roles are added to the server.

Each log file provides three types of data: Information, Warning, and Error. Information logs provide data such as when a service stops or starts under normal operation. Warning log data provides information such as a potential problem with the server that does not immediately result in an impairment of service but may develop into a greater problem. An Error message log usually provides data that a service or necessary operation on the server or network has failed and requires that you take some action to repair or restore the service or function.

System Monitor

You can use the System Monitor to get a picture of the overall functioning of your server. While Task Manager can provide a graphical snapshot of how your server is functioning, Performance Monitor can

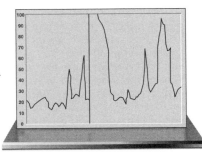

provide a much wider range of graphical tools, as it monitors a much larger number of operations and tasks on your server.

You can use Performance Logs and Alerts to receive and record detailed information of how different processes are being used in relation to operating system resources. Not only can you monitor active processes in real time through the graphical interface, you can also create and view log data and create alerts for Performance Monitor using the Administrative Tools menu. As a result, you can receive data through logs and alerts on a periodic basis.

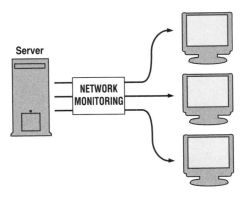

You can even run System Monitor from another server if the server you want to monitor has stopped or is not responding. You can add as many or as few features as you want to monitor to the System Monitor as long as you realize that the more functions you monitor, the more processing and memory overhead you require.

Network Monitoring

You can use Network Monitoring, or Netmon, to analyze the performance of your network communications traffic from your server. This allows you to determine whether there are any network problems that are inhibiting computer communication, access to services, and Active Directory replication, and that require your attention.

Netmon can provide statistics on network utilization loads and can capture packets going through the network so that you can analyze their structure and contents. All network traffic is divided into numerous packets or frames, with each frame containing header information about the source and destination in addition to the data that is being sent. You can analyze these packets for abnormalities that may affect your network. You can also determine whether there are any bottlenecks occurring on the network and locate their sources.

Netmon works as both a network troubleshooting utility and a packet analysis tool or "sniffer" on your network. Windows Server 2003 ships with a version of Netmon that can only capture network packets sent to and from your local server. However, you can purchase a full-featured version that you can use to monitor an enterprise-level network. You can use this version of Netmon to monitor your network from any computer connected to the system. Although a smaller version of Netmon is available on Windows Server 2003, it is not enabled by default and must be installed before you can use it. You can install this version of Netmon using Add/Remove Programs and the Windows Server 2003 CD. For more about network monitoring visit: go.microsoft.com/fwlink/?LinkId=299.

Using chkdsk
and chkntfs

You can use the chkdsk.exe command line utility to run various diagnostic tests on the file system of any disk volume running on your server system. This can alert you to any possible hardware or file system issues on your hard disk drive system. You can also run the chkntfs.exe command line utility in the same command window to determine whether the NTFS file system on any disk volume on your server is experiencing a problem, and then receive a report on the problem so that you can initiate repairs.

You can use chkdsk to not only receive status reports and data regarding a file system on a server disk, but you can also use it to repair any file system errors that it encounters on the disk. For example, chkdsk can report when a volume is *dirty*, which is an indicator that the file system is corrupted. When a Windows file system is corrupted, the system marks the modified or corrupted data with a bit called a *dirty bit*, which is then detected by the chkdsk program. Chkntfs is a program that displays when automatic system checking is set to run on a disk volume.

Using chkdsk and chkntfs

① Click Start.

② Click Command Prompt.

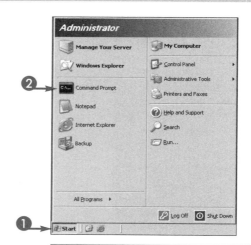

The command shell appears.

③ Type **chkdsk E: /f**

Note: Although you can run this command without the "f" option, using the "f" option allows chkdsk to automatically fix any errors it finds.

④ Press Enter.

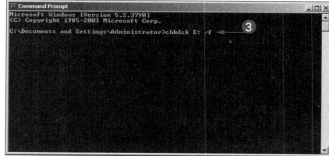

- Chkdsk analyzes the disk volume, and displays information about the volume.

⑤ Type **chkntfs E:**

⑥ Press Enter.

```
Command Prompt                                                    _|□|×

C:\Documents and Settings\Administrator>chkdsk E: /f
The type of the file system is NTFS.
Volume label is New Volume.

CHKDSK is verifying files (stage 1 of 3)...
File verification completed.
CHKDSK is verifying indexes (stage 2 of 3)...
Index verification completed.
CHKDSK is verifying security descriptors (stage 3 of 3)...
Security descriptor verification completed.

   2096450 KB total disk space.
     12328 KB in 3 files.
        12 KB in 11 indexes.
         0 KB in bad sectors.
     13130 KB in use by the system.
     12544 KB occupied by the log file.
   2070980 KB available on disk.

      2048 bytes in each allocation unit.
   1048225 total allocation units on disk.
   1035490 allocation units available on disk.

C:\Documents and Settings\Administrator>chkntfs E:_          ⑤
```

- Chkntfs analyzes the NTFS volume and displays information about whether it has found any sign of corrupted data on the disk.

⑦ Type **exit**.

⑧ Press Enter.

Windows exits the command shell.

```
Command Prompt                                                    _|□|×

CHKDSK is verifying files (stage 1 of 3)...
File verification completed.
CHKDSK is verifying indexes (stage 2 of 3)...
Index verification completed.
CHKDSK is verifying security descriptors (stage 3 of 3)...
Security descriptor verification completed.

   2096450 KB total disk space.
     12328 KB in 3 files.
        12 KB in 11 indexes.
         0 KB in bad sectors.
     13130 KB in use by the system.
     12544 KB occupied by the log file.
   2070980 KB available on disk.

      2048 bytes in each allocation unit.
   1048225 total allocation units on disk.
   1035490 allocation units available on disk.

C:\Documents and Settings\Administrator>chkntfs E:
The type of the file system is NTFS.
E: is not dirty.

C:\Documents and Settings\Administrator>exit      ⑦
```

Can I use chkdsk or chkntfs on any of my drive volumes and receive immediate results?

▼ Not always. When you run chkdsk or chkntfs on your server and specify a disk volume that is currently in use, you receive a message stating that the utility cannot lock the current drive because the drive is in use by another process. You must either close all processes currently running on that volume or schedule the utility to run the next time the server is rebooted. The utility allows you to indicate "yes" or "no" as to whether you want to schedule the run at reboot. You also receive a report on the type of file system that is running on the volume.

What options do I have when I run chkntfs?

▼ You have a number of parameters or switches that you can use with the chkntfs.exe utility, including not using a switch at all. When you type **chkntfs** with no switch, you receive a report on whether the file system is dirty and whether it is scheduled to be checked on reboot. If you type the drive letter with a colon, then you can choose which volume you want to check. You can use the /D switch to restore a computer to the default setting, which is to schedule a check at reboot and run chkdsk on any volumes that are dirty.

Customize the Event Viewer

You can customize the Event Viewer Microsoft Management Console (MMC) so that the Event Viewer logs only display the features and data that you need to monitor and manage your Windows Server 2003 computer. Event Viewer is the utility you can use to view and manage event logs on your Windows computer or server. Event logs gather information about hardware and software issues as well as security events on your computer. Depending on your administrative needs, you may require more or less features than are offered in the default settings of the Event Viewer. When you alter the view options in the Event Viewer, you can expand or limit the available options with which you can view logged information.

You can use the View feature on the toolbar to customize the Event Viewer interface. When you select or deselect features in the MMC, these features appear or disappear immediately, allowing you to view the differences before you save the changes. If you are unsure what a particular feature does, then you can use the question mark symbol in the upper right-hand corner of the Customize View dialog box to view an explanation in a pop-up window.

Customize the Event Viewer

① Click Start.

② Click Administrative Tools.

③ Click Event Viewer.

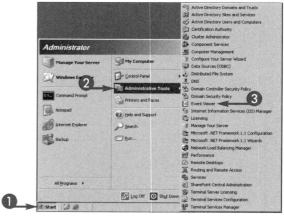

The Event Viewer snap-in window appears.

④ Click View.

⑤ Click Customize.

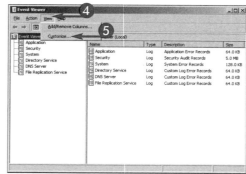

The Customize View dialog box appears.

6 Click the features you want
(☐ changes to ☑).

If you want to know what a feature does, you
can click the question mark symbol (?) and
position your cursor over the option to view a
description.

7 Click OK.

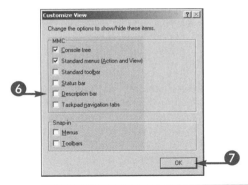

The Event Viewer is customized to show the
items you selected.

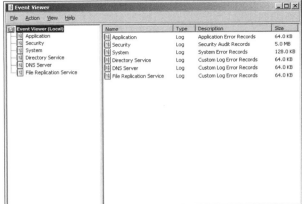

What other options do I have when I click View in the toolbar of the Event Viewer MMC?

▼ When you click View in the toolbar, the menu
displaysAdd/Remove Columns and Customize
options. If you select the Add/Remove Columns
option, the Add/Remove Columns dialog box
appears, allowing you to select which columns you
want to display in the Event Viewer MMC. You can
select combinations of four different types of
columns, including Name, Type, Description, and
Size, and you can add or remove any combination
of columns. You can also move the columns up or
down, depending on the priority you want to assign
them, or restore the default settings for the Event
Viewer columns. Selecting or unselecting check
boxes in the customize box lets you show or hide
different features in Event Viewer such as Console
Tree, Standard Menus, and Standard Toolbar
among others.

How can I use the Event Viewer to view the log files on another computer?

▼ When you click Action in the toolbar, a menu
displays several options, including Connect to
another computer. When you click Connect to
another computer, the Select Computer dialog box
appears. You can select the Event Viewer to manage
logs on the local computer or select a remote
computer for the Event Viewer MMC snap-in to
manage. If you select the Another Computer option,
you can either type the name of the computer or
browse the network for that computer. You can
then use the snap-in on your computer to view logs
on the remote device.

Configure Detail Level in Event Viewer

You can increase the level of detail in the logs that display in the Event Viewer MMC so that you can view more details about critical tasks and processes that are running on your server. This enables you to detect potential problems earlier and take steps to correct them.

The default settings for the logs in the Event Viewer are configured to present a minimum of information when you open a particular event log. Depending on your administrative needs, you can increase the amount of data that appears for some or all events. To do this, you must adjust settings in Registry keys using the regedit Registry Editor utility.

The Registry is the configuration database of your Windows Server 2003 computer and contains all of the information about every configurable aspect of your computer. You must use regedit with caution because any misconfiguration of the Registry may result in severe damage to your server. You may even cause your server to be unusable if your Registry settings are corrupted. You can read more about Registry security in Chapter 15, and about backing up the Registry in Chapter 21.

Configure Detail Level in Event Viewer

1 Click Start.

2 Click Run.

The Run dialog box appears.

3 Type **regedit**.

4 Click OK.

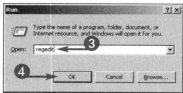

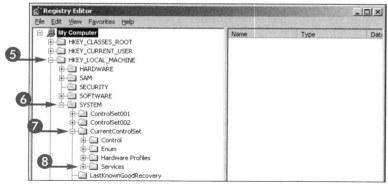

The Registry Editor snap-in window appears.

5 Expand HKEY_LOCAL_MACHINE.

6 Expand SYSTEM.

7 Expand Current ControlSet.

8 Expand Services.

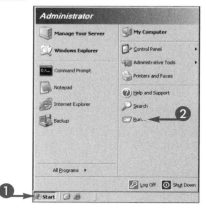

9 Expand NTDS.

10 Click Diagnostics.

11 Double-click the Registry key you want to edit.

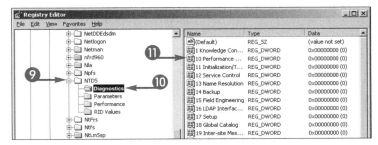

The Edit DWORD Value dialog box appears.

12 Type a value from 1 to 5 to increase the information detail level.

13 Click OK.

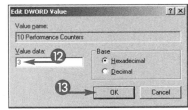

14 Click File.

15 Click Exit.

The Registry Editor closes.

Detail level of Event View is configured.

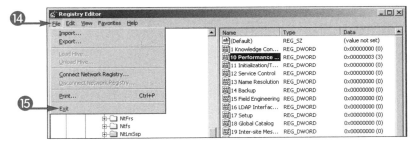

In the Diagnostics folder under NTDS in the Registry Editor, how many different features can I configure to produce more detailed log reports?

▼ You can configure the detail values of over 20 different reports in the Diagnostics folder under NTDS. You can open each item either by double-clicking it or by right-clicking it and then clicking Modify in the menu that appears. The Edit DWORD Value dialog box appears for each item, and you can alter the level of detail by typing values from 1 to 5. The default level is 0, and the higher the value you input, the more detail appears in the log file in the Event Viewer.

Besides modifying the value in the Edit DWORD Value dialog box, is there any other way to alter the level of detail in the data that appears in the Event Viewer?

▼ Yes. In the Registry Editor, you can right-click any item in the Diagnostics subfolder of the NTDS folder and select Modify Binary Data in the menu that appears. The Edit Binary Value dialog box appears and enables you to alter the Value data as a binary value rather than as a hexadecimal or decimal value, which you can do in the DWORD Value dialog box. You must be comfortable with the binary system if you intend to use this method because it would be easy to misconfigure the values resulting in an erroneous configuration.

Filter Event Viewer Logs

You can filter the output of the logs that you want to view in the Event Viewer so that it only displays those details that you want to keep track of when you are managing your server. By default, all event types are selected in the System Properties dialog box for any log type in the Event Viewer. You can filter out the event types that do not interest you so that only the ones that you want to monitor display regularly.

You can filter five event types: Information, Warning, Error, Success audit, and Failure audit. You can filter out any event type by deselecting the option for that event. For example,

if you deselect the Information check box, then that particular type of event data does not display when you open the event log in the Event Viewer. The Information, Warning, and Error event types are more commonly encountered in Application and System logs, and Information, Warning and Error notices also appear in categories such as Directory Service, DNS Server, and File Replication Service. The Success audit and Failure audit event types are most commonly found in the Security log in the Event Viewer.

Filter Event Viewer Logs

① Click Start.

② Click Administrative Tools.

③ Click Event Viewer.

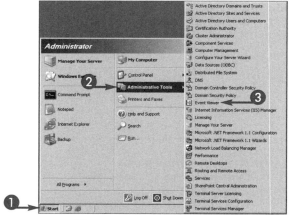

The Event Viewer snap-in window appears.

④ Click a log.

⑤ Click View.

⑥ Click Filter.

The System Properties dialog box appears, displaying the Filter tab.

⑦ Click the Event types that you want to filter out (☐ changes to ☑).

⑧ Click here and select All.

⑨ Click here and select All.

⑩ Click OK.

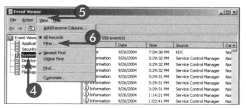

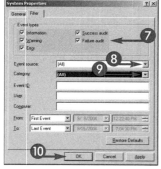

⑪ Double-click a log.

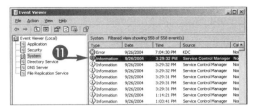

The Event Properties dialog box appears.

You can verify that details are filtered properly by making sure that the appropriate event types are visible in the dialog box.

⑫ Click Cancel.

⑬ Click File.

⑭ Click Exit.

The Event Viewer closes.

Event logs are now filtered.

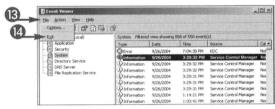

What happens if I click the General tab in the Properties dialog box for an event type in the Event Viewer MMC?

▼ When you click the General tab in the Properties dialog box for any of the event types in the Event Viewer, several types of information appear about the event type. They include the display name, such as Application or Security, and the path to the location of the log file. The General tab also displays the size of the file, when it was created, when it was last modified, and when it was last accessed. The log size field displays the maximum size of the log in kilobytes (KB).

Can I apply filtering to all of the different types of events in the Event Viewer MMC in a single action?

▼ No. You cannot create a central interface that applies uniform filtering to all of the event types at the same time. To filter out the types of information you do not want to see in the Event Viewer Event Logs, you must select each event type individually and filter it out by selecting or clearing the accompanying check boxes. If you want to filter each event type the same way, you can select each type individually and apply the identical filtering configuration to all event types.

Add a Counter to the System Monitor

Y ou can add one or more counters to the System Monitor on your Windows Server 2003 server to selectively monitor server functions in real time on a graphical display. This enables you to monitor only those activities that are critical to server operations.

You can monitor an almost endless list of server performance objects and the various counters that are available for each of those objects. If you monitor them all, then you can end up spending many hours trying to track all of the functions on your server while accomplishing little else. In addition,

by monitoring too many object types, you can increase processing and memory overhead and inhibit the optimal performance of your server.

You can select only those objects whose performance you want to monitor and choose only the counters for those object types that provide the data that you need. This allows you to optimize server performance and to conserve both server resources and administrative effort on your part. Keep in mind that if you add monitors on a temporary basis, you must remember to remove them when you no longer need them.

Add a Counter to the System Monitor

① Click Start.

② Click Administrative Tools.

③ Click Performance.

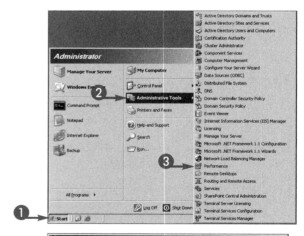

The System Monitor appears.

④ Click the Plus icon (⊞).

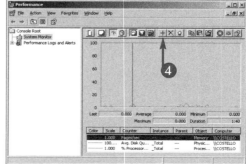

The Add Counter dialog box appears.

5 Click here and select a performance object type.

6 Click a counter.

7 Click Add.

Note: You can also select instances including a CPU object on a multiprocessor machine or disk drives on a server with more than one hard disk drive.

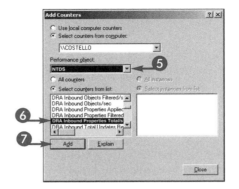

The System Monitor adds the counter.

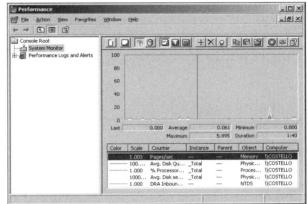

How many Performance object types can I select to monitor in the System Monitor snap-in window?

▼ You can select all of the objects that are available in the Performance Object menu in the Add Counters dialog box. Although you can select them all, to do so creates a system resources slowdown on your server and displays more data than you probably need. The actual number of performance objects varies, depending on the role or roles that the server plays. For example, if the server uses SQL Server software as part of SharePoint Services, then you can monitor a number of objects related to SQL Server. However, these objects are not available on a server that is not configured to use SharePoint services.

What if I do not understand all of the available types of counters that are related to a particular performance object?

▼ The number and type of available counters can be confusing and difficult to understand. If you need an explanation of what a particular counter does, in the Add Counters dialog box, click the counter you want and then click Explain. The Explain dialog box appears beneath the Add Counters dialog box, with a paragraph of information about the selected counter. After reading the explanation, you can close the dialog box and decide whether to add the counter based on the explanation or to choose another counter.

Create Counter Logs

When you receive data from System Monitor counters, you can create counter logs in the System Monitor to store that data in log files for later review. This allows you to create baseline information for your server, to create maintenance records, and to use counter log files for troubleshooting. The System Monitor displays counter data graphically in a real-time display, enabling you to study the performance of various objects on your server and to determine their operational status. For example, you can create a counter log that records live counter data for a particular period of time and then ceases. Before you create a counter log, you must create a counter. To do so, see the section "Add a Counter to the System Monitor."

You can reduce monitoring overhead on your server by recording or sampling data for very brief periods of time and entering that data into a counter log. Otherwise, if you record data to your log for substantially longer time periods, you increase your server's processing requirements, and will probably not get an accurate sampling of the actual server performance that you are trying to measure. Another method that you can use to reduce your System Monitor overhead is to run the System Monitor in graph view and then select the fewest possible objects and performance counters that you need to log and still gather the data you need.

Create Counter Logs

① Click Start.

② Click Administrative Tools.

③ Click Performance.

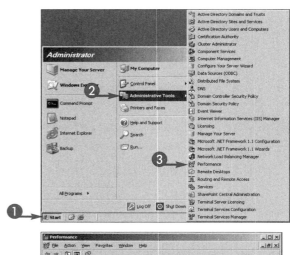

The System Monitor snap-in window appears.

④ Expand Performance Logs and Alerts.

⑤ Right-click Counter Logs.

⑥ Click New Log Settings.

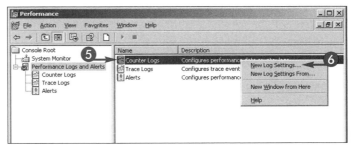

The New Log Settings dialog box appears.

⑦ Type a name for the new log.

⑧ Click OK.

The dialog box appears for the new log.

⑨ Click Add Objects.

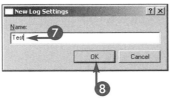

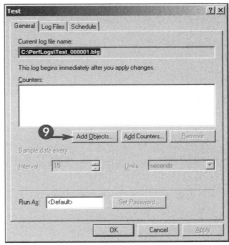

Is there any other way that I can create a counter log outside of the System Monitor MMC snap-in?

▼ Yes. You can also create a counter log on the command line. To create a counter log on the command line, click Start, then click Command Prompt. When the command shell appears, at the prompt, type **logman create counter** then type the name of the collection **–c path_to_log –cf filename**. To complete this action, you must know the path to the performance counter log. For example, to specify a remote computer that you want to monitor, you must know the name or IP address of the device.

Can I use the System Monitor MMC snap-in to configure my counter log to record data either from my local computer or from a remote device?

▼ Yes. You can record a counter log with data that is either from you local server or from a remote server on your network. To do this, in the Performance Console, double-click Performance Logs and Alerts and then click Counter Logs. In the details pane, double-click the log where you want to add a counter. The log dialog box open. For the local machine, click the Use Local computer counters option (changes to). To log counters from a remote machine, click the Select counters from computer option (changes to), then specify the UNC name, such as \\Remote Computer.

Create Counter Logs *(Continued)*

By adding objects and counters to the counter log, you can gather data that helps you to diagnose and treat server problems. You can select only those objects that you want to add to the counter log and then determine which counters you want to add. Although you can add as many or as few objects and counters as you want to your counter log, keep in mind that more objects and counters increase your server performance overhead.

You can configure counter logs to use comma- or tab-delimited text files that you can then import into a spreadsheet or database program such as Microsoft Excel

or Access. You can also configure the recording format to be a binary log file format (.blg) that you can then view with either the System Monitor snap-in or with a SQL database file. You can use the Performance Logs and Alerts feature in the Performance console to configure recording start and stop times, as well as set filenames and the sizes of log files. You can also set the snap-in to send you alerts and messages when counters record data that is beyond a particular performance threshold.

Create Counter Logs *(continued)*

The Add Objects dialog box appears.

10 Click an object.

11 Click Add.

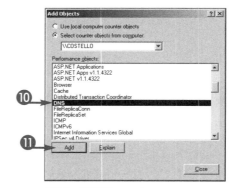

The dialog box appears for the object you selected.

12 Click Add Counters.

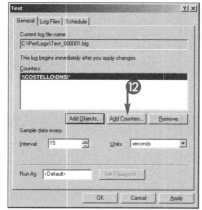

The Add Counters dialog box appears.

13 Click here and select a performance object.

14 Click a counter.

15 Click Add.

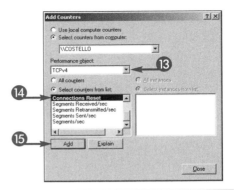

16 Click OK.

The counter log starts recording data.

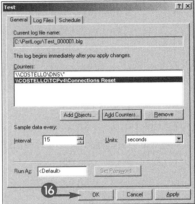

Can I add a counter from the command line as well as from the System Monitor MMC snap-in?

▼ Yes. To add a counter from the command line, click Start, then click Command Prompt. When the command shell appears, type **logman update** followed by the collection name *–c* **path to log,** *-cf* **filename**. You use *–c* to specify the path from the performance counter to log, and *–cf* for the filename. An example of this is **logman update perf_log** *–c* **\\COSTELLO\Processor(*)\ %Interrupt Time**. The asterisk (*) is used as a wildcard symbol when specifying a counter path if you want to specify all instances of % Processor Time.

When I add an object by clicking Add Objects in the dialog box for a new log, and then click Add Counters, do the counters always associate with the object?

▼ No. When you add an object such as DNS services to the dialog box for the new log, and you click Add Counters, you are given the option to add a different performance object, such as TCPv4. When you add the performance object in the Add Counters dialog box, you can then choose the specific counter that you want to use in the "Select counters from list" menu. As a result, you can either add an object by clicking Add Object or choose a performance object and counter by clicking Add Counters.

A

Access Control Entities (ACEs), 204
Access Control Lists (ACLs), 19, 204
account operators, Active Directory, 71
Account Policies
    Group Policy, 276
    organizational units, 276
Active Directory
    about, 4
    command-line tools
        automate tasks with scripts, 87
        Command Shell, 86
        dsadd command, 88–89
        dsget command, 90–91
        dsmod.exe command-line utility, 94–95
        dsquery command, 91–93
        nesting command shell, 87
        power, 87
        remote administration, 87
        scalability, 87
        syntax, 86
    database, move to new location, 409
    Domains and Trusts, 4–19
        creating forest trusts, 6–11
        domain controllers, 4
        domain forest trusts, 5
        domain forests, 5
        domain tree trusts, 5
        domain trees, 5
        domains, 4
        shortcut trusts, 12–15
        validating trusts, 16–17
    maintenance
        about, 404
        Active Directory sites, 405
        Domain Naming Master error, 405
        Infrastructure Master, 405

        move Active Directory database, 406–409
        no replication, 404
        offline defragmentation, 410–413
        PDC Emulator error, 405
        RPC Server is Unavailable error, 405
        services Access errors, 405
        slow replication, 404
        slow resource access, 404
        using repadmin, 418–419
        using replmon, 416–417
    shortcut trust password, 15
Active Directory authentication dialog box, 17
Active Directory Computers
    add group to groups, 78–79
    add groups, 80–81
    add users, 74–77
    create groups, 74–77
    create organizational units, 80–81
    create users, 72–73
    delegate control of organizational unit, 82–85
Active Directory Replication Monitor, 416–417
Active Directory services
    add domain controller to new site, 56–57
    assign subnet to site, 60–61
    choose licensing server for site, 58–59
    configure intersite replication, 68–69
    configure site link bridge, 64–65
    configure site links, 62–63
    create new site, 54–55
    designate preferred bridgehead server, 66–67
    intersite replication cost, 53
    multiple sites and multiple domains, 53
    multiple sites and single domain, 52
    physical networking of sites, 52
    replication and network bandwidth, 53
    single sites and single domains, 52
Active Directory sites
    about, 52–53
    Active Directory maintenance, 405

add domain controller to new site, 56–57

assign subnet to site, 60–61

choose licensing server for site, 58–59

configure intersite replication, 68–69

configure site link bridge, 64–65

configure site links, 62–63

create new site, 54–55

designate preferred bridgehead server, 66–67

intersite replication cost, 53

moving computers from, 55

multiple sites and multiple domains, 53

multiple sites and single domain, 52

physical networking of sites, 52

replication and network bandwidth, 53

single sites and single domains, 52

Active Directory Sites and Services snap-in, 54

Active Directory Users

add group to groups, 78–79

add groups, 80–81

add users, 74–77

create groups, 74–77

create organizational units, 80–81

create users, 72–73

delegate control of organizational unit, 82–85

Active Directory Users and Computers snap-in

account operators, 71

administrators, 70

backup operators, 71

built-in groups, 71

built-in users, 70

guest, 70

incoming forest trust builders, 71

network configuration operators, 71

organizational units, 70–71, 71

print operators, 71

support, 70

Active Server Pages (ASP.NET), 126–127, 368–369

ActiveX, 127

Add Counters dialog box, 431, 435

Add Hardware Wizard, 215, 218–219

Add Objects dialog box, 434

Add/Remove Columns dialog box, 425

add switch, 419

adding

Administrative Templates in Global Policy Object Editor, 258–259

counter to System Monitor, 430–431

domain controller to new site, 56–57

group to groups, 78–79

groups, 80–81

new hard drive, 156–157

users, Active Directory, 74–77

administration privileges, trusts, 17

administrative access, server security, 308

Administrative Templates

add in Global Policy Object Editor, 258–259

User and Computer Configuration, 251

administrators, 70, 210–213

Advanced button, 83

advanced Performance, 145

anonymous access, Web sites, 377

Anonymous Active Directory access, 314–315

anti-virus software, 251

Application Handlers/Worker Processes, 127

application pool, 378

Assign Drive Letter or Path page, 150

assigning

permissions to users and groups, 204–205

subnet to site, 60–61

authentication

forests, 19

level, trusts, 9

scope of trust, 18–19

server security configurations, 309

authorization, server security configurations, 309

automate tasks with scripts, 87

Automated System Recovery (ASR) backup registry, 394–397

Automated System Recovery Wizard, 395

automatic updates, configuring, 222–223

B

Background Intelligent Transfer Service (BITS), 343
backup
    about, 389
    copy, 389
    create system recovery disk, 394–397
    daily, 389
    differential, 389
    floppy disks, 396–397
    full, 389
    incremental, 389
    normal, 389
    ntbackup.exe, 391–393
    registry with ASR, 394–397
    scheduling, 398–403
    System State, 390–391
Backup Destination page, 396
backup operators, Active Directory, 71
Backup or Restore Wizard, 390–391, 401
Backup Progress dialog box, 393
Backup Utility dialog box, 397
Backup Wizard (Advanced), 399
Basic Input Output System (BIOS), 214
Basic Share Permissions, NTFS, 194–195
bat file extension, 87
batch files, 87
BIOS, 214
bridge, site link, 64–65
broadband connection, 333
built-in groups, Active Directory, 71
built-in users, Active Directory, 70

C

C++, 87
cable modem connections, 333
changing
    description, organizational units, 95
    location of Print spooler folder, 128–131

child domains, 5, 15
chkdsk.exe command, 422–423
chkntfs, 422–423
clusters, NTFS Share Permissions, 192
cmd file extension, 87
COM+ Class registration database, 391
com file extensions, 326
COM objects, 127
command line, convert disk to dynamic disk, 142–143
command line management, NTFS Share Permissions, 193
Command Shell, Active Directory, 86
Common Name, 35
Compatible-level Security Templates, Group Policy, 277
Completing the Backup Wizard, 401
Completing the New Trust Wizard page, 11
Computer Configuration, organizational units, 250
Computer Management snap-in, 140–141
computers, moving from Active Directory Sites to another, 55
Configure DHCP server, 106–109
configuring
    automatic updates, 222–223
    Block Policy Inheritance, 262–263
    detail level in Event Viewer, 426–427
    file server, 110–111
    File System Security, 296–297
    filtering on Global Policy Object, 268–269
    intersite replication, 68–69
    Loopback policy mode, 260–261
    mail server, 116–117
    No Override option, 264–265
    Point and Print services, 122–123
    print server, 112–115
    Registry Security, 294–295
    Restricted Groups, 290–291
    site link bridge, 64–65
    site links, 62–63
    system services, 292–293
    virtual server, 374–377

Web browser proxy settings, 254–255
Windows Automatic Updates with Administrative Templates, 256–257
Wireless Local Area Network (WLAN), 298–301
Confirm Incoming Trust page, 11
Confirm Outgoing Trust page, 10
Connect to Domain Controller dialog box, 41
Control Panel Applets, 237
Convert Disk Wizard, 157
converting
    disk to dynamic disk manually, 140–141
    disk to dynamic disk on command line, 142–143
copy backup, 389
copying defragmented database, 415
counter logs, creating, 432–435
counter to System Monitor, adding, 430–431
Create a New Trust Wizard, 13
custom forest trusts, 8
custom SharePoint sites, 373
Customize View dialog box, 425
customizing Event Viewer, 424–425

D

daily backups, 389
data backups, 398–403
data compression, 138
data encryption
    disk storage systems, 139
    NTFS Share Permissions, 200–201
data storage disk systems
    create spanned volume, 158–161
    create striped volume, 164–167
    extend simple and spanned volumes, 162–163
    mirrored volumes, 168–171
    RAID 5 array, 172–175
Data Tampering, 309
dates, backups, 402

dcpromo command, 39
deactivate schema object, 38–39
decoy Administrator account, 318–319
Default-First-Site-Name, 57
default Web site access from IIS, 384–385
DEFAULTSITELINK, 55
defragmentation, Active Directory, 410–413
defragmented database, copying, 415
delegate control of organizational unit, 82–85
Delegation of Control Wizard, 83–85
demand-dial connection, Internet, 334–337
Denial of Service, 309
Deny Logon Access to domain, 320–321
deploy software packages, 252–253
designating
    global catalog server, 28–29
    preferred bridgehead server, 66–67
device drivers
    identify unsigned device drivers with sigverif.exe, 226–227
    manually update, 224–225
    roll back device drivers, 226–227
Device Manager, troubleshooting with, 220–221, 225
DHCP Server, 106–109
Diagnostics folder, 427
dial-up connections, 333
dialog boxes
    Active Directory authentication dialog box, 17
    Add Counters dialog box, 431, 435
    Add Objects dialog box, 434
    Add/Remove Columns dialog box, 425
    Backup Progress dialog box, 393
    Backup Utility dialog box, 397
    Connect to Domain Controller dialog box, 41
    Customize View dialog box, 425
    Disks to Convert dialog box, 141
    Domain Properties dialog box, 7
    Driver Signing Options dialog box, 230–231

continued

dialog boxes *(continued)*

    File Signature Verification dialog box, 229

    Group Properties dialog box, 77

    Local Area Connection Properties dialog box, 362

    Log On to Windows dialog box, 407

    Members dialog box, 76

    Move Server dialog box, 57

    New Object - Organizational Unit dialog box, 80

    New Object - User dialog box, 72

    Raise Forest Functional Level dialog box, 25

    Role Transfer Confirmation Dialog box, 51

    Run dialog box, 426

    Schedule job dialog box, 402

    Select Groups dialog box, 79

    Select Network Component Type dialog box, 363

    Set Account Information dialog box, 403

    Shut Down Windows dialog box, 406

    System Properties dialog box, 217, 230–231

    USB Root Hub Properties dialog box, 232–233

differential backup, 389

Direction of Trust page, 8

directories, NTFS Share Permissions, 193

directory based security, 139

Directory Services Restore Mode, 411

dirty bits, 422

dirty volumes, 422

disabling Global Policy Object, 270–273

disasters, redundant array of independent disks (RAID), 388

Discussion Boards, intranet, 372

disk management, shared and redirected folders, 176

Disk Quotas, NTFS Share Permissions, 196–197

disk size, NTFS Share Permissions, 192

disk storage systems

    add new hard drive, 156–157

    convert disk to dynamic disk manually, 140–141

    convert disk to dynamic disk on command line, 142–143

    create partition or logical drive, 148–151

    create spanned volume, 158–161

    creating simple volume, 152–155

    data compression, 138

    data encryption, 139

    fault tolerance, 138

    file and directory based security, 139

    file management systems, 138

    increase disk performance on dynamic disk, 144–145

    initialize hard drive, 156–157

    reactivate missing or off-line disks, 146–147

    redundant array of independent disks (RAID), 139, 142, 152, 159, 162

`diskpart` command, 142–143

diskpart.exe command, 155

Disks to Convert dialog box, 141

distribution group, 74

dll file extensions, 326

DMA resource type, 220

DNS Server, configuring, 102–105

domain controller deployment, 309

Domain Controller in Safe Mode, restarting, 407

domain controller to new site, adding, 56–57

domain controllers, 4

domain forest trusts, 5

domain forests, 5

domain functional levels

    about, 20–21

    raising, 22–23

domain local group, 74

Domain Name Service (DNS), 13, 331

Domain Naming Master

    error, 405

    Flexible Operations Masters, 27

    transfer, 40–41

Domain Properties dialog box, 7

domain tree trusts, 5

domain trees, 5

domain-wide operations masters, 26

domains, 4, 19

Driver Signing Options dialog box, 230–231

drivers

    Add Hardware Wizard, 215

    configure automatic updates, 222–223

    device drivers, 214

    electrostatic discharge (ESD), 215

    Hardware Compatibility List (HCL), 214

    identify unsigned device drivers with sigverif.exe, 226–227

    install PnP devices, 216–217

    installation management, 215

    manually update device drivers, 224–225

    Plug and Play functionality, 214–215

    roll back device drivers, 226–227

    set driver signing with System Properties dialog box, 230–231

    troubleshoot installed devices, 218–219

    troubleshoot with Device Manager, 220–221

    view USB hub power allocations, 232–233

drivers, print, 121

drv file extensions, 326

dsadd command, 88–89

dsget command, 90–91

DSL connection, 333

dsmod.exe command-line utility, 94–95

dsquery command, 91–93

dynamic disks

    convert disk to dynamic disk on command line, 142–143

    manually convert, 140–141

    redundant array of independent disks (RAID), 159

dynamic routes, remote connections, 343

E

edit Global Policy Object in Organizational Unit, 248–249

electrostatic discharge (ESD), 215

Emergency Repair Disk (ERD), 394–397

enabling

    computer to use offline files, 190–191

    monitoring Anonymous Active Directory access, 314–315

    remote assistance, 354–355

    terminal services for remote desktop, 352–353

Encrypting File System (EFS), 200

encrypting offline files, 189

errors, maintenance, 405

Ethernet (PPPoE) connections, 341

Event Viewer

    configure detail level, 426–427

    customizing, 424–425

    server monitoring, 420

exe file extensions, 326

exporting Security Templates, 277

extend

    simple and spanned volumes, 162–163

    virtual server, 378–379

Extend Virtual Server List page, 379

Extend Virtual Server page, 379

Extensible Authentication Protocol (EAP), 298

External trusts, 9

Extranet Datacenters, 309

extranets, 366

F

FAT file system, 143, 192

FAT32 file system, 143

fault tolerance, 138

fdisk, 156

file and directory based security, 139

file compression, 198–199

file management systems, 138

file servers, configuring, 110–111

File Signature Verification dialog box, 229

file size, NTFS Share Permissions, 192

File System Security, configuring, 296–297
filter Event View logs, 428–429
filters, 326–327
find FSMO roles, 44–47
first domain controller, 27
Flexible Operations Masters
 domain naming masters, 27
 domain-wide operations masters, 26
 first domain controller, 27
 forest-wide operations masters, 26
 infrastructure master, 27
 PDC emulator, 27
 relative master (RID) master, 27
 schema, 27
 transfer infrastructure master using ntdsutil, 48–51
 Windows 2000, 26
 Windows NT, 26
 Windows Server 2003, 26
floppy disks, backup and restore, 396–397
folders
 Print spooler, 128–131
 redirection, 177
 shared, 176–191
 SYSVOL, 4
forest functional levels, 21, 24–25
forest trusts, 6–11, 8
forest-wide operations masters, 26
forests, authenticating, 19
format, 156
Format Volume page, 154
format.exe command, 155
fragmentation, 410–413
FSMO roles, 44–47
FTP, 127
full backup, 389

G

Generic Hardware Device Troubleshooter, 221
global catalog server, 28–29

Global Catalog Server role, 405
Global Group Membership, 208
global groups, 74
Global Policy Object Editor, 258–259
Global Policy Object Policy Application Sequence, 266–267
Graphical User Interface (GUI), 200
Group Name, 75
Group Policy
 Account Policies, 276
 Compatible-level Security Templates, 277
 configure File System Security, 296–297
 configure Registry Security, 294–295
 configure Restricted Groups, 290–291
 configure system services, 292–293
 configure Wireless Local Area Network (WLAN), 298–301
 edit Global Policy Object in Organizational Unit, 248–249
 environment, 237
 Group Policy Containers (GPCs), 237
 Group Policy environment, 237
 Group Policy Object (GPO), 236
 Group Policy Object Inheritance, 236
 Group Policy Templates (GPTs), 237
 High Security Templates, 277
 importing and exporting Security Templates, 277
 link Group Policy Object to Organizational Unit (OU), 244–245
 Local Policies, 276
 new Global Policy Object in Organizational Unit, 246–247
 open Group Policy Object Editor, 242–243
 organizational units, 236, 245
 password policies, 278–279
 Security Settings, 276–277
 Security Templates, 277
 set Account Lockout policies, 280–281
 set Audit Policy for Event Viewer, 282–283
 set Event Log Security, 288–289
 set Internet Protocol (IP) Security Policies, 304–307

set Security Options, 286–287
set Software Restriction Policies, 302–303
set User Rights Assignment, 284–285
shared and redirected folders, 177
Standalone Group Policy Object, 238–239
unlinked Group Policy Object, 240–241
windows file protection, 186–187
Windows Settings, 276–277
Group Policy Containers (GPCs), 237
Group Policy Object Editor, 188–189, 242–243
Group Policy Object Inheritance, 236
Group Policy Objects (GPOs), 4, 236, 240–241
Group Policy Templates (GPTs), 237
Group Properties dialog box, 77
groups
    Active Directory Users and Computers, 74–77
    add, 80–81
    add to groups, 78–79
    domain, 19
guests, Active Directory Users and Computers snap-in, 70

H

hard drives
    adding new, 156–157
    initialize hard drive, 156–157
Hardware Compatibility List (HCL), 214
High Security Templates, Group Policy, 277
Home directory
    shared and redirected folders, 177
    virtual server Web site, 377
HTTP, 127

I

identify unsigned device drivers with sigverif.exe, 226–227
IEEE 802.11 protocol, 298–299
importing Security Templates, 277
incoming forest trust builders, 71
increase disk performance on dynamic disk, 144–145

incremental backups, 389
indexing data, intranet, 372
Information Disclosure, 309
Infrastructure Master, 27, 405
initialize hard drive, 156–157
installation CD-ROM, Windows Server 2003, 218
installation management, 215
installing
    Certificate Services, 322–325
    IPv6 Protocol, 362–363
    I IIS v6 and ASP.NET, 368–369
    PnP devices, 216–217
    Schema snap-in, 30–33
    SharePoint Services, 370–371
    Terminal Services License Server, 358–359
    terminal services with Configure Your Server Wizard, 356–357
installing SharePoint
    extranets, 366
    install IIS v6 and ASP.NET, 368–369
    Internet Information Services (IIS), 366
    intranet, 366
    SharePoint, 367
    SharePoint Portal Server 2003, 367
    Web site portals, 366
    Windows SharePoint Services 2003, 367
Internet Connection Sharing (ICS), 331
Internet connections
    Demand-dial connection, 334–337
    Domain Name Service (DNS), 331
    Internet Connection Sharing (ICS), 331
    Network Address Translation (NAT), 331
    reliability, 330
    Routing and Remote Access for NAT, 338–341
    security, 330
    set up, 332–333
Internet Information Services (IIS), 366
Internet Information Services (IIS) Manager, 127
intersite replication cost, 53

Intranet Datacenters, 309
intranets
    about, 366
    access default Web site from IIS, 384–385
    configure Self-Service Site Creation, 382–383
    configure virtual server, 374–377
    create new Web site, 384–385
    create Top-level Web site, 380–381
    custom SharePoint sites, 373
    Discussion Boards, 372
    extend virtual server, 378–379
    manage events, 373
    SharePoint sites and workspaces, 373
    storing and indexing data, 372
IO resource type, 220
IP address, virtual server, 375
IP Security Policy Wizard, 306–307
ipconfig, 363
IPSec Protocol Suite, 304
IRQ resource type, 220

J

JavaScript, 87

K

Knowledge Consistency Checker (KCC), 66

L

Layer Two Tunneling Protocol (L2TP), 345
legacy devices, 218
letters for volume on drives, 155
licensing server for site, 58–59
Licensing Settings tab, 59
Lightweight Access Directory Protocol (LADP), 298
link Group Policy Object to Organizational Unit (OU), 244–245
Local Area Connection Properties dialog box, 362

local area networks, 52
Local Forest page, 9
Local Group Membership, 208
Local Permissions, 208
Local Policies, 276
local print device, 121
Local Privileges, 208
local user profiles, folders, 177
Location buttons, 83
Log On to Windows dialog box, 407
logical drives
    creating, 148–151
    disk storage systems, 148–151
login information, 4
lowest common denominator, domain controllers, 20

M

mail servers, configuring, 116–117
Manage Your Server Wizard, 100–101
Managed By tab, 77
managing
    events, intranet, 373
    Terminal Services users, 360–361
managing devices and device drivers
    Add Hardware Wizard, 215
    configure automatic updates, 222–223
    device drivers, 214
    electrostatic discharge (ESD), 215
    Hardware Compatibility List (HCL), 214
    identify unsigned device drivers with sigverif.exe, 226–227
    install PnP devices, 216–217
    installation management, 215
    manually update device drivers, 224–225
    Plug and Play functionality, 214–215
    roll back device drivers, 226–227
    set driver signing with System Properties dialog box, 230–231

troubleshoot installed devices, 218–219

troubleshoot with Device Manager, 220–221

view USB hub power allocations, 232–233

manually convert disk to dynamic disk, 140–141

manually update device drivers, 224–225

Master File Table, NTFS Share Permissions, 192

Members dialog box, 76

Memory resource type, 220

metafiles, NTFS Share Permissions, 192–193

Microsoft Component Object Model, 391

Microsoft Management Console (MMC), 31, 32

Microsoft Transaction Server (MTS), 391

mirrored volumes

data storage disk systems, 168–171

redundant array of independent disks (RAID), 169

mixed mode, 20

modify Global Policy Object Policy Application Sequence, 266–267

mounted drives, 151

Move Server dialog box, 57

moving

Active Directory database, 406–409

computers from Active Directory Sites to another, 55

multihomed server, 342

multiple sites and multiple domains, 53

multiple sites and single domain, 52

My Site Template Selection page, 385

N

NAT. See Network Address Translation (NAT)

native mode, 20

nesting command shell, 87

NetBIOS name, 13, 75

Netmon server monitoring, 421

Network Address Translation (NAT)

about, 331

Routing and Remote Access, 338–341

Traversal Using Universal Plug and Play, 343

network configuration operators, Active Directory, 71

network interface device (NIC), 121

Network Monitoring, 421

network print device, 121

networks, 52

New Connection Wizard, 332–332

New Global Policy Object in Organizational Unit, 246–247

new hard drive, adding, 156–157

New Object - Organizational Unit dialog box, 80

New Object - User dialog box, 72

New Partition Wizard, 149, 151

new sites, Active Directory sites and services, 54–55

New Technology File System (NTFS). See NTFS (New Technology File System)

New Trust Wizard, 7–11

New Volume Wizard, 153

new Web site, intranets, 384–385

NIC (network interface device), 121

NNTP, 127

no replication, Active Directory, 404

normal backup, 389

ntbackup.exe, 391–393

NTDS partition, 4

ntdsutil command-line tool, 44–47

ntdsutil.exe command line utility, 408

NTFS (New Technology File System)

about, 143

Effective Permissions

Global Group Membership, 208

Local Group Membership, 208

Local Permissions, 208

Local Privileges, 208

Share Permissions

about, 206–209

assign permissions to users and groups, 204–205

Basic Share Permissions, 194–195

clusters, 192

continued

NTFS (New Technology File System) *(continued)*

    Share Permissions *(continued)*

        command line management, 193

        data encryption, 200–201

        directories, 193

        Disk Quotas, 196–197

        disk size, 192

        FAT, 192

        file compression, 198–199

        file size, 192

        Master File Table, 192

        metafiles, 192–193

        operating systems, 193

        ownership of files and folders, 210–213

        Shadow Copies, 202–203

O

object information, retrieving, 91

Object Types button, 83

offline defragmentation, Active Directory, 410–413

offline files

    enabling use, 190–191

    encrypting, 189

Ongoing Trust Authentication Level, 9

open Group Policy Object Editor, 242–243

operating systems, NTFS Share Permissions, 193

Organizational Units (OUs)

    Account Policies, 276

    Active Directory Users and Computers, 80–81

    Active Directory Users and Computers snap-in, 70–71

    change description, 95

    Computer Configuration, 250

    creating, 80–81

    delegate control, 84

    dsadd command, 88

    dsget command, 90

    link Group Policy Object to, 236, 244–245

    schema, 30

    server security, 308

    SharePoint services, 366

ownership of files and folders, NTFS Share Permissions, 210–213

P

packets, 342

parent domains, 5

partitions

    creating, 148–151

    disk storage systems, 148–151

passwords

    Group Policy, 278–279

    shortcut trusts, 14

    users, 73

PDC Emulator

    error, 405

    Flexible Operations Masters, 27

    transfer, 42–43

Perl, 87

permissions

    assign to users and groups, 204–205

    Basic Share Permissions, NTFS, 194–195

    NTFS Effective Permissions, 208

    NTFS Share Permissions, 206–209

    Web Site Access Permissions page, 376

physical networking of sites, Active Directory, 52

physical security, server security configurations, 308

Plug and Play functionality, 214–215

Point and Print services, configure, 122–123

Point-to-Point Protocol Ethernet, 343

Point-to-Point Tunneling protocol (PPTP), 345

power, Active Directory command-line tools, 87

Primary Domain Controller (PDC), 4

print devices, 120

print drivers, 121

print operators, 71
Print Queue window, 135
print queues, 134–135
print servers
    about, 120
    configure, 112–115
Print spooler folder, 128–131
printers
    about, 120
    pooling, 121
    setting priority and availability levels, 132–133
printing
    about, 120–121
    change location of Print spooler folder, 128–131
    configure Point and Print services, 122–123
    local print device, 121
    network print device, 121
    print device, 120
    print driver, 121
    print queues, 134–135
    print server, 120
    printer pooling, 121
    printers, 120
    set printer priority and availability levels, 132–133
    TCP/IP port print device, 121
    Web-based printer management, 124–127

Q

Quota template, 381
quotation marks, 91

R

RADIUS (Remote Authentication Dial-in User Service), 298, 301, 335, 339
RAID 1 array, 175, 388
RAID 5 array, 172–175
RAID 10 array, 388

RAID (redundant array of independent disks). *See* redundant array of independent disks (RAID)
Raise Forest Functional Level dialog box, 25
raising
    domain functional levels, 22–23
    forest functional levels, 24–25
reactivate missing or off-line disks, 146–147
Reactive Volume option, 147
Realm trusts, 9
redirected folders
    disk management, 176
    enable computer to use offline files, 190–191
    folder redirection, 177
    group policy, 177
    home directory, 177
    local user profiles, 177
    restrict offline file usage with Group Policy, 188–189
    share types, 176
    shared folder with Windows Explorer, 178–179
    Shared Folders snap-in, 182–185
    shared Web folders, 180–181
    special path, 177
    Universal Naming Convention (UNC), 177
    windows file protection with Group Policy, 186–187
    workgroups and domains, 176
redundant array of independent disks (RAID)
    disasters, 388
    disk storage systems, 139, 142, 152, 159, 162
    dynamic disks, 159
    mirrored volumes, 169
    RAID 1 array, 175, 388
    RAID 5 array, 172–175
    RAID 10 array, 388
    striped volumes, 164
REG file, server security configurations, 310–311
Regedit Registry, 310–311
register schema snap-in, 30–33
Registry Editor, 427

Registry Security configure, 294–295
registry with ASR backup, 394–397
regsvr32, 31
relative identifier (RID) master, 27
reliability, Internet connections, 330
remote administration, Active Directory command-line tools, 87
Remote Authentication Dial-in User Service (RADIUS), 298, 301, 335, 339
Remote Connection and Routing Services (RRAS), 343
remote connections
    Background Intelligent Transfer Service (BITS), 343
    dynamic routes, 343
    enable remote assistance, 354–355
    enable terminal services for remote desktop, 352–353
    install IPv6 Protocol, 362–363
    install Terminal Services License Server, 358–359
    install terminal services with Configure Your Server Wizard, 356–357
    manage Terminal Services users, 360–361
    NAT Traversal Using Universal Plug and Play, 343
    Point-to-Point Protocol Ethernet, 343
    Remote Connection and Routing Services (RRAS), 343
    routing, 342
    static routes, 343
    Virtual Private Network (VPN) services, 344–347
Remote Desktop Users, 360
remote procedure call (RPC), 126
remote services, VPN client, 348–351
rename default Administrator account, 316–317
repadmin, 418–419
replication
    and network bandwidth, 53
    schedules, 63, 69
Replication Diagnostics, 418–419
replmon, 416–417
Reserve File, server security, 312–313

restarting
    computer in Safe Mode, 407
    Domain Controller in Safe Mode, 407
    Windows Server, 141
restore floppy disks, 396–397
restrict offline file usage with Group Policy, 188–189
retrieving object information, 91
risk management, server security, 308
Role Transfer Confirmation Dialog box, 51
roll back device drivers, 226–227
routers, 342
Routing and Remote Access, 334
Routing and Remote Access for NAT, 338–341
Routing and Remote Access Server Setup Wizard, 339, 345
routing table, 342
RPC Server is Unavailable error, 405
RRAS (Remote Connection and Routing Services), 343
Run dialog box, 426

S

Safe Mode
    restarting computer, 407
    restarting Domain Controller, 407
scalability, Active Directory command-line tools, 87
schedule
    data backups, 398–403
    replication, 69
Schedule job dialog box, 402
schema
    attribute create, 34–35
    class, 36–37
    Flexible Operations Masters, 27
    object deactivate, 38–39
    organizational units, 30
Schema snap-in
    install, 30–33
    register, 30–33

INDEX

secedit.exe command line utility, 289
security, Internet connections, 330
security group, 74
Security Settings, Group Policy, 276–277
Security Templates, Group Policy, 277
Select Groups dialog box, 79
Select Network Component Type dialog box, 363
Select Partition Type page, 149
Select Volume Type, 153
Self-Service Site Creation (SSC)
    about, 380
    configure, 382–383
server management
    Configure a DNS Server Wizard, 102–105
    Configure DHCP server, 106–109
    configure file server, 110–111
    configure mail server, 116–117
    configure print server, 112–115
    configure WINS Server, 118–119
    Manage Your Server Wizard, 100–101
    server roles, 98–99
server monitoring
    about, 420
    add counter to System Monitor, 430–431
    chkdsk.exe command, 422–423
    chkntfs, 422–423
    configure detail level in Event Viewer, 426–427
    create counter logs, 432–435
    customize Event Viewer, 424–425
    Event Viewer, 420
    filter Event View logs, 428–429
    Netmon, 421
    Network Monitoring, 421
    System Monitor, 421
    Task Manager, 420
server roles, 98–99
server security
    administrative access, 308
    authentication and authorization, 309

decoy Administrator account, 318–319
Deny Logon Access to domain, 320–321
domain controller deployment, 309
enable monitoring Anonymous Active Directory access, 314–315
Install Certificate Services, 322–325
organizational units, 308
physical security, 308
REG file, 310–311
rename default Administrator account, 316–317
Reserve File, 312–313
risk management, 308
threats, 309
Trust-No-Exe utility, 326–327
Service Set Identifier (SSID), 301
Services Access errors, 405
Set Account Information dialog box, 403
setting
    Account Lockout policies, 280–281
    Audit Policy for Event Viewer, 282–283
    driver signing with System Properties dialog box, 230–231
    Event Log Security, 288–289
    Internet connections, 332–333
    Internet Protocol (IP) Security Policies, 304–307
    Security Options, 286–287
    Software Restriction Policies, 302–303
    User Rights Assignment, 284–285
Shadow Copies, NTFS Share Permissions, 202–203
share types, folders, 176
shared folders
    disk management, 176
    enable computer to use offline files, 190–191
    folder redirection, 177
    group policy, 177
    home directory, 177
    local user profiles, 177
    restrict offline file usage with Group Policy, 188–189
    share types, 176

shared folder with Windows Explorer, 178–179
Shared Folders snap-in, 182–185
shared Web folders, 180–181
special path, 177
Universal Naming Convention (UNC), 177
with Windows Explorer, 178–179
windows file protection with Group Policy, 186–187
workgroups and domains, 176
Shared Folders snap-in, 182–185
SharePoint
about, 367
installing, 370–371
intranet sites, 373
intranet workspaces, 373
organizational units, 366
Services 2003, 367
Web Service Extensions, 369
SharePoint Portal Server 2003, 367
SharePoint Services 2.0 Setup Wizard, 371
shortcut trusts
creating, 12–15
passwords, 14, 15
verifying selections, 14
showrep1 command, 419
Shut Down Windows dialog box, 406
sides of trust, verify, 11
Sides of Trust page, 8
sides of trust relationship, verify, 17
Simple Mail Transport Protocol (SMTP), 62
simple volume, create, 152–155
single domains, 52
single sites, Active Directory, 52
site names, 55
sites, 52
slow replication, Active Directory, 404
slow resource access, Active Directory, 404
SMTP, 127

snap-ins
Active Directory Sites and Services, 54
Active Directory Users and Computers, 71
Computer Management snap-in, 140–141
Shared Folders, 182–185
snapshots, 202
software settings, User and Computer Configuration, 251
spanned volume, create, 158–161
spanned volumes, 158–161
special path, folders, 177
Specified Forest page, 9
Spoofing, 309
SQL, 368
Standalone Group Policy Object, 238–239
static routes, remote connections, 343
storing data, intranet, 372
striped volumes, data storage disk systems, 164–167
subnet to site, assign, 60–61
support, Active Directory Users and Computers snap-in, 70
switches, 93
syntax, Active Directory command-line tools, 86
sys file extensions, 326
System Monitor, 421
System Properties dialog box
about, 217
set driver signing with, 230–231
System Recovery Disk, 394–397
system services, configure, 292–293
System State with backup utility, 390–391
SYSVOL folder, 4

T

Task Manager, server monitoring, 420
tasks with scripts, automate, 87
TCP/IP port print device, 121
Team Web Site Home page, 384
Terminal Service Client Access Licenses (CALs), 360

This domain only option, 7

threats, server security, 309

Top-level Web sites, 380–381

transfering

    domain naming master, 40–41

    infrastructure master using `ntdsutil`, 48–51

    PDC emulator, 42–43

troubleshooting

    with Device Manager, 220–221

    installed devices, 218–219

Trust Creation Complete page, 14

Trust Name page, 13

Trust-No-Exe utility, 326–327

Trust Selection Complete page, 10

Trust tab, 7

Trust Type page, 7

trusts

    administration privileges, 17

    authentication level, 9

    relationships, 5

    validating, 16–17

Two-way option, 8

U

universal groups, 74, 79

Universal Naming Convention (UNC), folders, 177

unlinked Group Policy Object, 240–241

USB hub power allocations, 232–233

USB Root Hub Properties dialog box, 232–233

User and Computer Configuration

    add Administrative Templates in Global Policy Object Editor, 258–259

    Administrative Templates, 251

    configure Block Policy Inheritance, 262–263

    configure filtering on Global Policy Object, 268–269

    configure Loopback policy mode, 260–261

    configure No Override option, 264–265

    configure Web browser proxy settings, 254–255

    configure Windows Automatic Updates with Administrative Templates, 256–257

    deploy software packages, 252–253

    disable Global Policy Object, 272–273

    disable Global Policy Object node, 270–271

    modify Global Policy Object Policy Application Sequence, 266–267

    software settings, 251

    User Configuration nodes, 251

    Windows settings, 250

User Configuration nodes, 251

users

    Active Directory Users and Computers, 72–73

    add, Active Directory Users and Computers, 74–77

Users folder, 73

V

validating trusts, 16–17

verifying

    both sides of trust relationship, 17

    selections, shortcut trusts, 14

    sides of trust, 11

view USB hub power allocations, 232–233

Virtual Disk service, 154

Virtual Private Network (VPN), 304, 344–347

Virtual Server List page, 378

virtual servers

    configure, 374–377

    IP address, 375

    Web sites, 377

Visual Basic, 87

Volume Shadow Copy Service (VSS), 202

VPN client, remote services, 348–351

W

Web-based printer management, 124–127

Web Part pages, 384

Web Service Extensions
    about, 127
    SharePoint, 369
Web Site Access Permissions page, 376
Web Site Creation Wizard, 375
Web Site Home Directory page, 376
Web sites
    access default from IIS, intranets, 384–385
    anonymous access, 377
    creating, 384–385
    portals, SharePoint, 366
    Top-level, 380–381
    virtual server, 377
wide area networks (WAN), 52
Windows 2000
    domain functional levels, 20
    Flexible Operations Masters, 26
    native level, 20
Windows 2003 interim level, 20
Windows 2000 Server domains, 4
Windows Components Wizard, 124–125
Windows file protection with Group Policy, 186–187
Windows NT
    domains, 4
    Flexible Operations Masters, 26
Windows Server, restarting, 141
Windows Server 2003
    domain functional levels, 20
    Enterprise and Datacenter Editions, 374
    Flexible Operations Masters, 26
    installation CD-ROM, 218
Windows Settings
    Group Policy, 276–277
    User and Computer Configuration, 250

Windows SharePoint Services 2003. *See* SharePoint
Windows SharePoint Services Central Administration, 374
WINS Server, 118–119
Wireless Local Area Network (WLAN), 298–301
Wireless Network Security Policy, 298–299
wizards
    Add Hardware Wizard, 215, 218–219
    Automated System Recovery Wizard, 395
    Backup or Restore Wizard, 390–391
    Backup Wizard (Advanced), 399
    Completing the Backup Wizard, 401
    Convert Disk Wizard, 157
    Create a New Trust Wizard, 13
    Delegation of Control Wizard, 83–85
    IP Security Policy Wizard, 306–307
    Manage Your Server Wizard, 100–101
    New Connection Wizard, 332–332
    New Partition Wizard, 149, 151
    New Trust Wizard, 7–11
    New Volume Wizard, 153
    Routing and Remote Access Server Setup Wizard, 339, 345
    SharePoint Services 2.0 Setup Wizard, 371
    Web Site Creation Wizard, 375
    Windows Components Wizard, 124–125
workgroups and domains, folders, 176

X

X500 Object ID (OID), 35

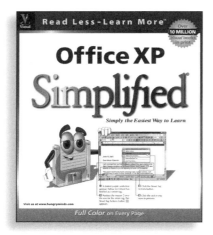

. . . all designed for visual learners-just like you!

Top 100 Simplified® Tips & Tricks

Tips and techniques to take your skills beyond the basics. Full color.

Visual Blueprint™

Where to go for professional level programming instruction. Two-color.

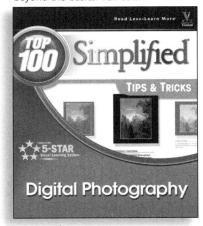

 Read Less-Learn More®

For a complete listing of Visual books, go to wiley.com/go/visualtech

Also available:

- **Windows XP: Top 100 Simplified Tips & Tricks, 2nd Edition**
- **Photoshop Elements 3: Top 100 Simplified Tips & Tricks**
- **Mac OS X v.10.3 Panther: Top 100 Simplified Tips & Tricks**
- **eBay: Top 100 Simplified Tips & Tricks**
- **HTML: Top 100 Simplified Tips & Tricks**
- **Office 2003: Top 100 Simplified Tips & Tricks**
- **Excel 2003: Top 100 Simplified Tips & Tricks**
- **Photoshop CS: Top 100 Simplified Tips & Tricks**
- **Internet: Top 100 Simplified Tips & Tricks**

Also available:

- **HTML: Your visual blueprint for designing effective Web pages**
- **Excel Programming: Your visual blueprint for creating interactive spreadsheets**
- **Unix for Mac: Your visual blueprint to maximizing the foundation of Mac OS X**
- **MySQL: Your visual blueprint for creating open-source databases**
- **Active Server Pages 3.0: Your visual blueprint for developing interactive Web sites**

- **Visual Basic .NET: Your visual blueprint for building versatile programs on the .NET Framework**
- **Adobe Scripting: Your visual blueprint for scripting in Photoshop and Illustrator**
- **JavaServer Pages: Your visual blueprint for designing dynamic content with JSP**
- **Access 2003: Your visual blueprint for creating and maintaining real-world databases**

You can master all kinds of topics visually, including these

All designed for visual learners-just like you!

Read Less—Learn More®

eBay Business Kit
0-7645-6816-7

iPod and iTunes
0-7645-7702-6

Creating Web Pages
0-7645-7726-3

Visual
An Imprint of ⊕WILEY
Now you know.